THIRD EDITION

RUNNING MS-DOS®

THIRD EDITION

RUNNING MS-DOS®

By VAN WOLVERTON

The classic, definitive work on DOS — now *completely* revised and expanded to include all versions of PC/MS-DOS — including hard-disk management tips and techniques

PUBLISHED BY
Microsoft Press
A Division of Microsoft Corporation
16011 NE 36th Way, Box 97017, Redmond, Washington 98073-9717

Library of Congress Cataloging in Publication Data
Wolverton, Van, 1939–
Running MS-DOS / Van Wolverton.—3rd ed.
Includes index.
1. MS-DOS (Computer operating system) 2. PC DOS (Computer operating system) 3. IBM Personal Computer—Programming.
4. Microcomputers—Programming. I. Title.
QA76.76.063W65 1988 87-31520
005.4'469—dc19 CIP

Printed and bound in the United States of America.

1 2 3 4 5 6 7 8 9 FGFG 8 9 0 9 8

Distributed to the book trade in the United States by Harper & Row.

Distributed to the book trade in Canada by General Publishing Company, Ltd.

Distributed to the book trade outside the United States and Canada by Penguin Books Ltd.

Penguin Books Ltd., Harmondsworth, Middlesex, England
Penguin Books Australia Ltd., Ringwood, Victoria, Australia
Penguin Books N.Z. Ltd., 182–190 Wairau Road, Auckland 10, New Zealand

British Cataloging in Publication Data available

Project Editor: JoAnne Woodcock Technical Editor: Michael Halvorson

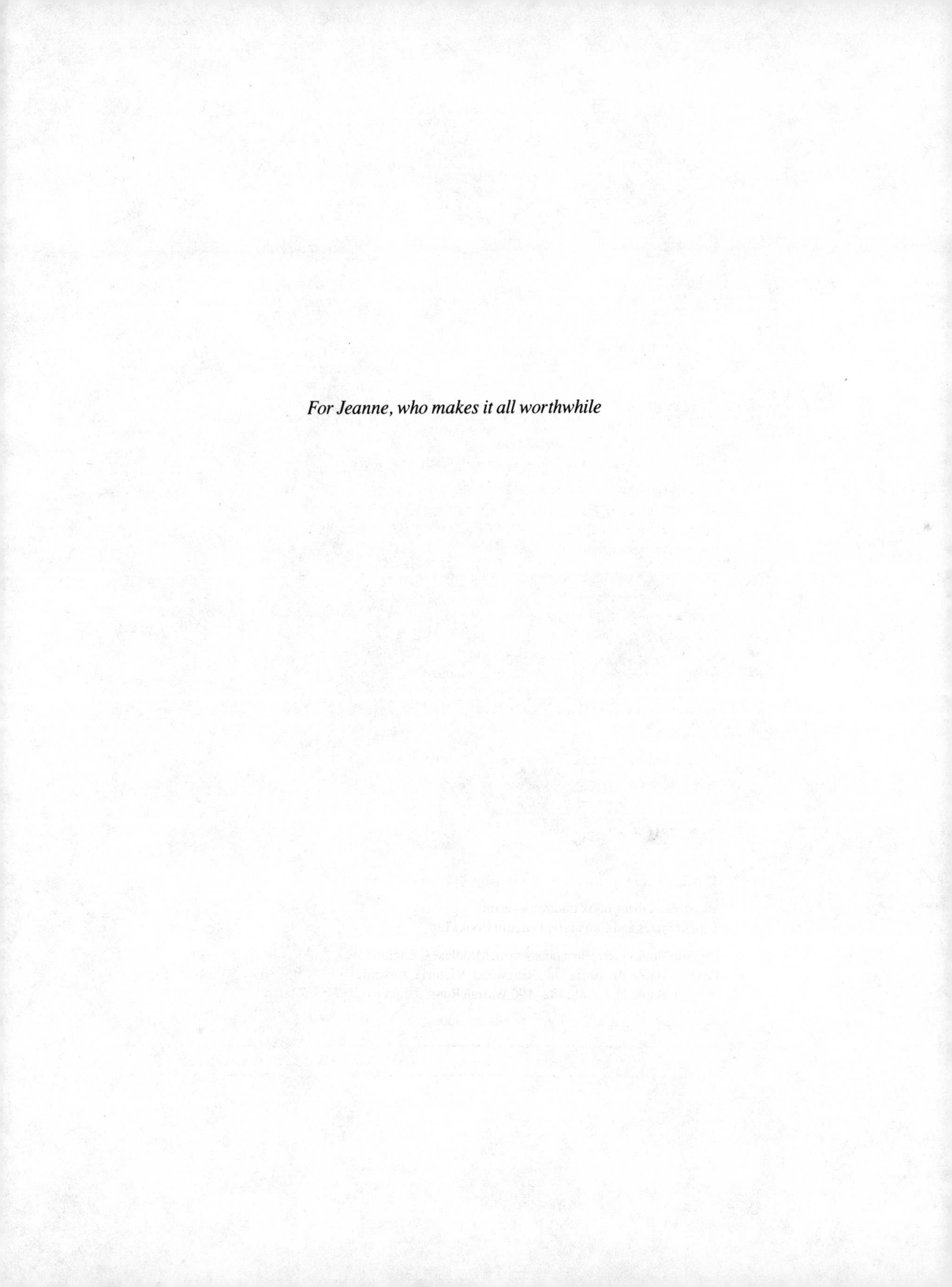

For Jeanne, who makes it all worthwhile

CONTENTS

PART 3: APPENDIXES

ACKNOWLEDGMENTS

It's been three years since the first edition of this book hit the shelves, and the world of computers has changed mightily. The person who bought the first edition of this book most likely had a 64 K IBM PC with two diskette drives. Those of you who buy this edition probably have an IBM PC/AT with a megabyte or more of memory—or, even more likely, a machine that is made by some other company but whose behavior is nonetheless indistinguishable from the IBM version.

They all use MS-DOS, so I'd like to thank all those folks who have labored to put an MS-DOS computer on everyone's desk. Thanks, too, to IBM, for making the whole thing possible in the first place.

And special thanks to the people of Montana who have made Jeanne and me feel so welcome. It's good to be back.

Van Wolverton
Rubicon
Sawmill Gulch Road
Alberton, MT
December 1987

INTRODUCTION

It may be tempting to skip these opening words and "get to the meat of it," but please read this introduction anyway. The information included here is both useful and brief.

You may want to know whether this book applies to you. It does, if your computer uses MS-DOS. The book itself was written with an IBM Personal Computer but, with the exception of a few commands, the contents of the book apply equally to any machine that uses MS-DOS.

You bought this book—or at least took the time to pick it up and glance through it—despite the hefty manual you got with your copy of DOS. Why? What else can a book like this offer? It can offer simplicity. The DOS manual is thorough and complete. It is your official, comprehensive reference guide to DOS, but it also includes a good deal of technical information you don't really need in order to *use* DOS.

This book does not show you how to set up your computer, nor does it describe in detail the pieces of the system, such as the keyboard or the display. These matters should be covered thoroughly in the manuals that came with your computer.

The book assumes neither that you are, nor that you aspire to become, a programmer. It doesn't try to explain how DOS works, and it leaves to the DOS manual the task of explaining some of the more technical features. The book does assume that you have access to an IBM Personal Computer or one of the many other machines that run MS-DOS, and that you want to put the machine to work. It includes dozens of examples, and is organized by what you want the computer to do, not by how DOS itself is structured. The examples reflect real-life situations.

You don't have to be a mechanical engineer to drive a car well, but you do need experience. You don't have to be a computer scientist to use DOS well, either, and this book starts you on your way.

WHAT'S IN THE BOOK, AND WHERE

This book covers all versions of DOS, through 3.30, used with machines that have a fixed disk drive and one or two diskette drives or that have two diskette drives.

Part 1, Chapters 1 through 4, describes the pieces of the computer system, defines some terms and concepts, and provides hands-on examples that show you the major capabilities of DOS.

Part 2, the bulk of the book, includes Chapters 5 through 17. These chapters show you how to operate your computer system and manage all its parts with the DOS commands.

Chapters 5, 6, and 7 show you how to manage your files, diskettes, and computer devices. Chapter 8 describes the DOS multilevel filing system that allows you to set up a personalized computer file system that matches the way you work. Chapter 9 shows you how to manage the files and directories on a fixed disk.

Chapters 10 and 11 make up an extended example that shows you how to create and modify files of text with Edlin, the DOS text editor. Chapter 12 shows you how to create your own commands to automate tasks you perform frequently.

Chapter 13 shows you how to use a special set of commands called filter commands to control where the other DOS commands get their input and where they send their output. Chapters 14 and 15 show you how to create more advanced commands of your own. Chapter 16 shows you how to tailor your system to suit your needs. It includes several useful techniques that can make DOS immediately useful in its own right. And Chapter 17 introduces you to the capabilities and commands of Microsoft Networks, which works with version 3 of DOS.

Appendix A shows you how to prepare and format a fixed disk. Appendix B shows you how to control the way DOS displays the date, and how to type, display, and print characters from international alphabets. Appendix C briefly describes version 4 of MS-DOS, which is based on version 3.2 and is available only in Europe. Appendix D, the Glossary, defines the terms used in the book, plus a few others you may have seen or heard. Finally, Appendix E is the DOS Command Reference, which describes the DOS commands and includes page references to the detailed discussions and examples in the preceding chapters.

If you plan to use your computer for word processing, spreadsheets, database management, or perhaps a household accounting package and some games, this book is probably all you'll need. Not only does it show you how to use DOS so you can run your programs, it shows you how DOS can make your computer a more valuable tool without additional software.

ABOUT THE EXAMPLES

The best way to learn how to put DOS to work is to use it. This book, therefore, is devoted primarily to examples. Terms and concepts are defined as you need them to follow the examples. Because the book covers several versions of DOS and several types of machines, there are variations in some examples; these alternatives are identified. Unless an example specifically states it is for an earlier version, the DOS displays shown in this book are the IBM version 3.3 responses. If you are using a different version, the responses you see may vary somewhat. Do not be concerned.

What to Type and When

There's an awkward mismatch between a computer and a book that shows you how to use it. The computer is dynamic: It displays messages, moves data back and forth between disks and memory, prints words and pictures, chirps now and then to announce completion of another task. When you use the computer, you enter into a dialogue: You type something, the computer responds, you type something else, and so on, back and forth, until your work is done.

A book, however, is static. It can only show snapshots of your dialogue with the system, yet it must describe that dialogue well enough so that you can take part in it. In this book, we have to show what you type and how the computer responds. We have to distinguish parts of this dialogue, such as the names of files and messages displayed on the screen, from the surrounding prose. Here are the conventions we've adopted to cover those situations:

- Hands-on examples are shown in different type, on separate lines, just as you would see them on your display. The characters you type are printed in lowercase colored type; DOS doesn't care whether you type in uppercase or lowercase, but lowercase seems to be easier. Here is an example showing these conventions:

```
C>format b:
Insert new diskette for drive b:
and strike any key when ready
```

- Occasionally, similar information occurs in text. In these instances, the interaction between you and DOS is printed in italics to distinguish it from the surrounding text. For example, you may see: "Type *n* when DOS displays *Format another (Y/N)?*"

- Many DOS commands include options, or parameters, that allow you to specify a particular disk drive, file, or piece of equipment, or to use a particular form of the command. Options are shown in angle brackets <> when they represent a variable entry, such as the name of a file. When they must be entered exactly, they are shown in the form you must use. For example, here are some options of the Format command used in the preceding examples (don't worry about understanding the command at this point):

format <drive> /V /1 /4 /8

Now it's time to meet DOS. This book was written to be used at the system, so put it beside your keyboard, turn to Chapter 1, and get ready to put DOS to work.

PART 1

GETTING TO KNOW DOS

Part 1 describes the terms and the basic operating principles of DOS. The chapters show you how to start DOS and how to control the system with DOS commands. The information is primarily tutorial, and many examples are included. Later parts of the book contain all detailed reference information that describes the DOS commands and their capabilities.

Part 1 introduces you to the concept of an operating system: What it is, what it does, and why you need it. Together, these chapters give you the foundation for using DOS effectively in your daily work with the computer.

CHAPTER 1

WHAT IS DOS?

You've got your computer and you've probably got one or two programs, such as a word processor or a spreadsheet, to use with it. But what is this thing called DOS? Why do you hear so much about it, and why have hundreds of pages of instructions been written for it?

DOS IS A PROGRAM

DOS is a program, but it's not just any program. Chances are none of your other programs would work without it, because DOS controls every part of the computer system. DOS not only makes it possible for your other programs to work, it also gives you complete control over what your computer does, and how. DOS is the link between you and your computer.

To appreciate the role DOS plays, take a quick look at the pieces of your computer system and what they do.

HARDWARE MAKES IT POSSIBLE

Your computer equipment, called *hardware,* probably includes a keyboard, display, printer, and one or more disk drives. The purposes of the first three are straightforward: You type instructions at the keyboard, and the system responds by displaying or printing messages and results.

The purpose of a disk drive isn't quite so obvious, but it quickly becomes apparent as you use the system: A disk drive records and plays back information, much as a tape deck records and plays back music. The computer's information is recorded in files on disks; you'll find that disk files are as central to your computer work as paper files are to more traditional office work.

SOFTWARE MAKES IT HAPPEN

No matter how powerful the hardware, a computer can't do anything without programs, called *software.* There are two major types of software: *system programs,* which control the operation of the computer system, and *application programs,* which perform more obviously useful tasks, such as word processing.

Each program uses the hardware. It must be able to receive instructions from the keyboard, display and print results, read and write files from and to a disk, send and receive data through the computer's communications connection, change the colors on a color display, and so on through all the capabilities of the hardware.

So that each program doesn't have to perform all these functions for itself, a system program called the *operating system* manages the hardware. The operating system allows an application program to concentrate on what it does best, whether it's moving paragraphs about, tracking accounts receivable, or calculating stress in a bridge beam. DOS is an operating system.

DOS IS A DISK OPERATING SYSTEM

The operating system for many computers, including the IBM personal computers, is the Disk Operating System from Microsoft. It is called a disk operating system because much of its work involves managing disks and disk files.

What Does an Operating System Do?

An operating system plays a role something like a symphony conductor. When the score calls for the violins to play, the conductor cues the violins; when the score says the cellos should play more softly, the tympani should stop, or the entire orchestra should pick up the tempo, the conductor so instructs the musicians.

The players in the orchestra and their instruments represent the hardware. The experience and skill of the conductor represent the operating system. The score represents an application program.

When one score is replaced by another—Vivaldi's *Mandolin* Concerto is put aside and replaced by Haydn's *Surprise* Symphony, for example—the same musicians use the same instruments, and the same conductor uses the same experience and skills. A different sound, a different mood, perhaps, but the elements are the same.

When one application program is replaced by another—for example, an accounting program is put aside and replaced with a word processor—the same hardware carries out the instructions of the same operating system. A different program, a different purpose, perhaps, but the elements are the same.

DOS coordinates the computer system, just as the conductor coordinates the orchestra. Your application programs run in concert with DOS, trusting it to keep the system humming.

Much of what DOS does, such as how it stores a file on a disk or prints on the printer, is invisible to you. But DOS lets you control the things you care about, such as which program to run, what report to print, or what files to erase. These functions share an important characteristic: They need disks and disk drives.

Disk Drives

Personal computers use two types of disk: a flexible disk in a protective plastic jacket, called a *diskette,* which you can remove from the drive, and a permanently mounted platter called a *fixed disk.* There are two types of diskette: 5.25 inches square in a flexible plastic jacket, and 3.5 inches square in a rigid plastic shell.

A fixed disk holds much more information than a diskette—from 15 to 100 times as much, or even more—and is much faster. Most personal computers have either one fixed disk and one diskette drive, or two diskette drives.

To distinguish among the types of disk, this book uses *diskette* to mean either type of flexible disk, *fixed disk* to mean only a fixed disk, and *disk* to refer to both types.

Disk Files

Just as you organize and store your written records in paper files, you organize and store computer information in disk files.

A disk file—usually just called a file—is a collection of related information stored on a disk. It could be a letter, an income tax return, or a list of customers. It could also be a program, because the programs you use are stored in files.

Virtually all your computer work revolves around files. Because one of the major functions of DOS is to take care of files, much of this book is devoted to showing you how to create, print, copy, and otherwise manage files. As you go through the practice sessions in the following chapters, you'll notice references to some versions of DOS that have more file-handling abilities than other versions.

Different Versions of DOS

DOS has been revised a number of times since its release in 1981; the first version was numbered 1.00. DOS is revised to add more capability, to take advantage of more sophisticated hardware, and to correct errors. Each time you start up your system, DOS displays the version number that you are using.

When a new version of DOS appears, a change in the number following the decimal point—3.20 to 3.30, for example—marks a minor change that leaves DOS substantially the same as the previous version. A change in the number preceding the decimal point marks a major change. Version 2.00, for example, offered almost three times as many commands as version 1.10.

This book covers all versions of DOS. Even though newer versions have much more capability, they remain compatible with earlier versions. Thus, if you start with version 2.1, you can still use all your knowledge and experience, plus all your files and diskettes, when you move to a newer version.

For simplicity, this book refers to all 1.xx versions of DOS as version 1, all 2.xx versions of DOS as version 2, and all 3.xx versions as version 3.

What Is Compatibility?

You may have seen the terms DOS-compatible or IBM-compatible used in an article or advertisement. What does compatible mean? Although some technical issues are involved, the most meaningful measure of compatibility is the extent to which you can use the diskettes from one system in another:

- If two systems are totally compatible, you can freely exchange diskettes. This situation is common among IBM-compatible computers.
- If two systems are incompatible, you cannot exchange diskettes because neither system can read files stored by the other. That's why you can't use a diskette from an Apple computer in an IBM Personal Computer.

- If two systems are partially compatible, you can interchange some diskettes, particularly those that contain files of information rather than programs.

This last level of partial compatibility is what is usually meant by the term MS-DOS–compatible and is one of the advantages of using an operating system that runs on so many different machines.

To maintain consistency, this book describes how DOS works on the IBM PS/2 (all models), IBM PC/AT, IBM PC/XT, and IBM PC. If your computer is a compatible machine, however, the descriptions apply equally to your system.

WHAT CAN YOU DO WITH DOS?

DOS coordinates the operation of the computer for your application programs. That's valuable—essential, really—but DOS has much more to offer. You can use DOS, controlling it with instructions called *commands,* to manage your files, control the work flow, and perform useful tasks that might otherwise require additional software.

For example, DOS includes a program called Edlin that lets you create and revise files of text. Although it's not a word processor, Edlin is fine for short memos and lists. Using Edlin, you can write short documents in less time than it might take to start your word-processing program and store the file.

You can tailor DOS to your specific needs by creating powerful commands made up of other DOS commands, and you can even create your own small applications. For example, this book shows you how to create a simple file manager—a program that lets you search a file for specific information—using nothing but DOS commands.

Your knowledge of DOS can range from just enough to use a single application program to mastery of the full range of capabilities in the later versions. But no matter how far you go, you needn't learn to program. It's all DOS, and it's all in this book.

CHAPTER SUMMARY

This quick tour of DOS may have introduced several new terms and concepts. Here are the key points to remember:

- A computer system needs both hardware (equipment) and software (programs).
- DOS (the Microsoft Disk Operating System) coordinates the operation of all parts of the computer system.
- A file is a collection of related information stored on a disk. Most of your computer work will involve files.
- Besides running your application programs, DOS is valuable in its own right.

The next chapter starts you off at the keyboard.

CHAPTER

2

STARTING DOS

Now that you have been introduced to some of the things DOS does for you, it's time to start your system and do something. Whenever you start your computer, whether it is to use a word processor, an accounting program, or DOS itself, you begin by *loading* DOS into the computer's memory, its workplace. Loading the DOS program and starting it running is sometimes called "booting the system" or "booting the disk." This term is borrowed from the phrase "pulling yourself up by your bootstraps," because DOS essentially pulls itself up by its own bootstraps, loading itself from disk into memory, where it then waits for a command from you.

The examples in this chapter assume you have set up your system and are familiar with its control switches. If you're using a fixed disk, the examples also assume you have prepared the fixed disk so DOS can use it. If your computer system is new, you haven't yet prepared the fixed disk, and you need some assistance, turn to Appendix A. Follow the instructions there—including those for copying the DOS programs from diskette onto the fixed disk—before continuing with the examples in this chapter.

ENTERING DOS COMMANDS

The instructions you give DOS are called *commands.* For the first few commands you enter in this session, you need only the standard typewriter keys on the keyboard. Two of those keys, Enter and Backspace, are shown on the keyboards in Figures 2-1 and 2-2 and are worth separate mention.

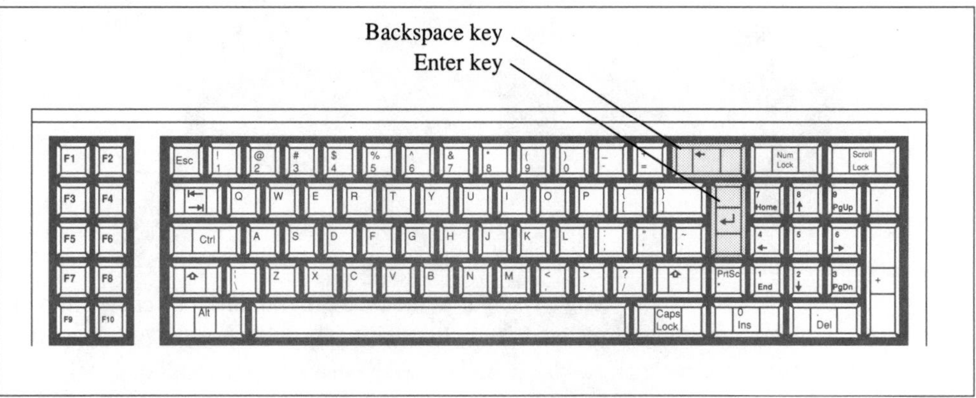

Figure 2-1. The Backspace and Enter keys on the IBM PC and PC/XT keyboards

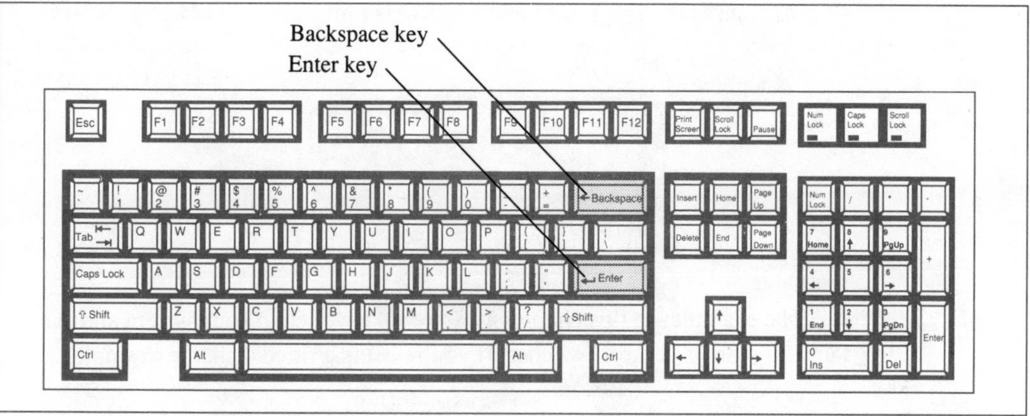

Figure 2-2. The Backspace and Enter keys on the enhanced IBM PC/AT keyboard

The Enter Key

The Enter key is labeled with a bent left arrow (↵) or the word *Enter*. Like the return key on a typewriter, it marks the end of a line. In general, DOS doesn't know what you have typed until you press Enter, so remember: End a command by pressing Enter.

The Backspace Key

The Backspace key is labeled with a long left arrow (⟵) or the word *Backspace*. It erases the last character you typed; use it to correct typing errors.

STARTING THE SYSTEM

If you're using a fixed disk with DOS on it, the DOS program must be copied into the computer's memory from the fixed disk (usually known to DOS as drive C). All you need to do before starting the system is make sure the latch on drive A (the diskette drive) isn't closed; otherwise, the system will try to load the DOS program into the computer's memory from the diskette in drive A.

If you're not using a fixed disk, the DOS program must be copied into the computer's memory from the diskette in drive A. Open the latch of drive A (either the left-hand or upper diskette drive) and put in the diskette you use to start DOS—called the *system disk* in this book—with the label up and away from the machine, as in Figure 2-3 on the following page. If you're using 5.25-inch diskettes, close the latch.

Turn on the system. The computer seems to do nothing for several seconds, but this is normal. Each time you turn on the power switch, the computer checks its memory and all attached devices to be sure everything is working properly. The system beeps once after it has made sure that all is well, the drive lights flash, and the computer begins loading DOS into memory.

As soon as the program is loaded, DOS is running and ready to go to work.

Figure 2-3. Inserting the DOS system disk

Date

The first thing you usually see after DOS starts is a message like the following:

```
Current date is Tue  1-01-1980
Enter new date (mm-dd-yy): _
```

If you don't see such a message, type:

```
C>date
```

and press Enter.

The blinking underline that follows the colon is the *cursor*. It shows where DOS will display whatever you type next. It also tells you that DOS is waiting for you to type something—in this case, a date in response to its *Enter new date* request. Such a request is called a *prompt*; DOS frequently prompts you to enter information so that you don't have to memorize operating procedures.

To enter the date, you type the numbers that represent the month, day, and year, separated by hyphens, and then you press the Enter key. You do not type the day of the week; as you will see later in this chapter, DOS figures out the day for you and displays both the day and date whenever you ask for them.

For this example, set the date to October 16, 1987, by typing the following (be sure to press Enter after the last number):

```
Current date is Tue  1-01-1980
Enter new date (mm-dd-yy): 10-16-87
```

Note: You can also use a slash (/) or a period to separate the numbers. Whichever you use, if you don't do it exactly right (in other words, in a way that DOS recognizes), DOS displays Invalid date *and waits for you to try again. If you make a mistake or enter the wrong date, don't be alarmed. As you'll see in the next example, it's easy to fix such errors.*

After it accepts the date, DOS displays a message asking you to enter the time and again waits for you to respond. The screen should look something like this:

```
Current date is Tue  1-01-1980
Enter new date (mm-dd-yy): 10-16-87
Current time is  0:01:30.00
Enter new time: _
```

If you don't see the preceding time message, type *time* and press Enter.

Before you enter the correct time, try the following exercise to see how easily you can fix typing errors.

Backspacing to Correct Typing Errors

Try out the Backspace key. Type some characters, such as the following, at random, but don't press Enter:

```
Current date is Tue  1-01-1980
Enter new date (mm-dd-yy): 10-16-87
Current time is  0:01:30.00
Enter new time: w710273_
```

This isn't a valid time; if you were to press Enter now, DOS would display the message *Invalid time* and wait for your next attempt. Correct your typing "error" by pressing the Backspace key until all the characters are erased and the cursor is back to its original position, just to the right of the colon. The screen looks like it did before:

```
Current date is Tue  1-01-1980
Enter new date (mm-dd-yy): 10-16-87
Current time is  0:01:30.00
Enter new time: _
```

Time

You enter the time by typing the numbers that represent the current hour and minute, separated by a colon or a period. Don't worry about seconds and hundredths of seconds. For this example, set the time to 8:15 A.M. by typing the following (don't forget to press Enter):

```
Current date is Tue  1-01-1980
Enter new date (mm-dd-yy): 10-16-87
Current time is  0:01:30.00
Enter new time: 8:15
```

Note: DOS works on the basis of a 24-hour clock, so you type 1:15 P.M. as 13:15 or 10:00 P.M. as 22:00.

If your system doesn't keep the date and time current, and you just press Enter in response to the date and time prompts when you start the system, DOS starts from its baseline date and time of midnight on January 1, 1980. This is a quick way to start the system, but DOS marks all the disk files you create or change with the time and date. Such information is useful, so it's a good idea to set the correct date and time each time you start the system.

Startup

After you have entered the date and time, DOS normally displays a startup message to identify itself and the version you are using and waits for further instructions. The exact wording of the lines that give the name of the operating system and the version number depend on which computer and version of DOS you're using.

The following message (truncated here), which shows the date and time you just entered, is the opening display for the IBM version of DOS 3.3:

```
Current date is Tue  1-01-1980
Enter new date (mm-dd-yy): 10-16-87
Current time is  0:01:30.00
Enter new time: 8:15

The IBM Personal Computer DOS
Version 3.30 (C)Copyright International Business Machines...
             (C)Copyright Microsoft Corp 1981, 1986

C>_
```

If you're not using a fixed disk, the last line is A>, instead of C>, because A is the letter DOS uses to identify the diskette drive from which you started the system.

The System Prompt

The C> (or A> if you're not using a fixed disk) is called the *system prompt,* because the system program (DOS) is prompting you to type a command. At this point, DOS is at what is often called *command level,* because it's ready and waiting for a command.

The system prompt also identifies the *current drive,* the drive where DOS looks for a file. DOS identifies your drives by letter. On a system with two diskette drives, the left-hand or upper drive is drive A, the right-hand or lower drive is drive B; on a system with one diskette drive and one fixed disk, the diskette drive is identified as both A and B, the fixed-disk drive as drive C.

If you are using a fixed disk with the DOS programs on it and DOS is loaded from the fixed disk (drive C), DOS assumes drive C is the current drive, and the initial system prompt is C>. If you're not using a fixed disk, DOS is loaded from drive A; DOS assumes that drive A is the current drive, and the initial system prompt is A>.

This book contains many examples for you to try. With a few exceptions, the examples show the system prompt as C>. If you're not using a fixed disk, you're told specifically when and how to prepare for an example; if there are no instructions, simply proceed with the example, but bear in mind that where you see C> in the book, you will see A> on your screen.

A WORD ABOUT DOS AND YOUR COMPUTER

Both DOS and the computers it runs on have evolved in the years since the introduction of version 1 and the IBM PC (the machine for which DOS was originally created). Changes are especially evident in the number and variety of computers that have become available.

The examples in this book are designed to work correctly with your computer and any release of DOS that supports the commands described. There are, however, some variations in computer setups and in the way the DOS command files are organized in different versions and computer manufacturers' releases of DOS. Here are some examples:

- Your computer might have two diskette drives, one diskette drive and one fixed disk, or two diskette drives and one fixed disk.
- If you have a fixed disk, the files on it, including your DOS files, might be organized in any of a number of different ways, just as different people might organize and label paper folders in a file drawer according to their own preferences. (The reasons for this will become clear in chapters 8 and 9, when you encounter the terms *directory* and *path.*)

- The organization of your DOS diskettes varies, depending on the version of DOS you use and the original equipment manufacturer that produced it. For example, the IBM release of version 3.3 on 5.25-inch diskettes comes with most of the commands on a supplemental diskette labeled *Operating*; other manufacturers' releases of this same version of DOS might include these commands on the diskette you normally use to start your system.

None of these variations affect either your use of DOS or your use of the commands described in this book.

As mentioned earlier, the examples in this book are based on version 3.3 of DOS, as it is released by IBM and as it runs on an IBM PC/AT or compatible computer with one fixed disk and one diskette drive. Although your display might differ from what is shown, especially in the chapters dealing with the DOS diskettes themselves, don't be concerned. Where necessary, the examples give specific instructions for other systems and other versions of DOS.

If you're using IBM's release of version 3.3 on a system with 5.25-inch disk drives and no fixed disk, you're asked throughout this book to start the system with the Startup diskette, then to replace the Startup diskette with the Operating diskette before using the system. That's probably how you'll routinely use your system, too, because most of the files you need in day-to-day operation are on the Operating diskette.

COPYING THE DOS DISKETTES

You've probably heard or read about the importance of copying valuable diskettes to protect yourself from loss in case of damage. If you have not made copies of your DOS diskettes, follow the step-by-step procedure given here, under the heading that describes your system. Don't worry if you don't yet understand everything that is happening. It's important that you do this copying as soon as possible, so that you don't chance damaging the originals.

If you have already made copies of your DOS diskettes, go on to the heading "Changing the Current Drive."

If You Have One Diskette Drive

During the procedure, DOS might prompt you to exchange the *source* and *target* diskettes in the drive several times. Follow the prompts, and remember that the DOS diskette is the *source* and the blank diskette is the *target.*

1. If you're using IBM's version 3.3 with a 5.25-inch diskette drive, place the diskette labeled *Operating* in your diskette drive. Otherwise, place your DOS system diskette (usually labeled *DOS* or *DOS Programs*) in the diskette drive. Make sure the latch is closed.

2. If you have a fixed disk, type:

```
C>a:
```

to tell DOS to use your diskette drive.

3. Type the following (but not the A>, and don't forget to press Enter):

```
A>diskcopy
```

This command tells DOS to copy everything on the source diskette to the target diskette. DOS responds:

```
Insert SOURCE diskette in drive A:

Press any key when ready . . .
_
```

The correct diskette is already in drive A, so press the spacebar or any other key. DOS responds:

```
Copying 40 tracks
9 Sectors/Track, 2 Side(s)
```

This message may vary, depending on the version of DOS you're using and the type of diskette drive you have. Regardless, DOS reads as much of the diskette as it can, then asks you to exchange diskettes:

```
Insert TARGET diskette in drive A:

Press any key when ready . . .
_
```

4. Remove the DOS diskette, put in a blank new diskette, and press the spacebar or any other key. DOS writes the data it read from the system diskette onto the blank diskette. It might then request that you put the DOS diskette back in the drive:

```
Insert SOURCE diskette in drive A:

Press any key when ready . . .
_
```

5. Continue exchanging diskettes as DOS prompts you. After the last exchange, DOS tells you it has finished:

```
Copy another diskette (Y/N)?_
```

6. Remove the diskette to which you copied DOS and label it with the name on the original DOS diskette—OPERATING, for example, or DOS. Use a felt-tip pen, not a ballpoint pen, to avoid damaging the surface of the diskette.
7. Remove the original DOS diskette and put it in its plastic sleeve in the manual binder (or some other safe place).

8. Unless you're using 3.5-inch diskettes, you have another diskette to copy, so type *y* in answer to the *Copy another diskette* question. DOS replies with the message to put the source diskette in drive A, as in step 3. If you are using 3.5-inch diskettes, there is only one DOS diskette, so go on to the heading "Changing the Current Drive."
9. If you're using IBM's version 3.3 of DOS, insert the diskette labeled *Startup* in the diskette drive. Otherwise, put your second DOS diskette (usually labeled *Supplemental* or *Supplemental Programs*) in the diskette drive.
10. Press the spacebar or any other key. DOS responds as in step 3. When DOS prompts you to exchange diskettes, remove the original DOS diskette, put in a blank new diskette, and press the spacebar or any other key.
11. If necessary, continue to exchange the diskettes as you did before. When the copy is complete and DOS asks if you want to make another copy, remove the diskette to which you copied the DOS programs, label it with the name on the original DOS diskette, and put it with your other working diskettes.
12. Remove the original DOS diskette and put it in its plastic sleeve in the manual binder (or some other safe place).
13. If you don't have a fixed disk, put your new copy of the DOS system diskette in your diskette drive (Operating diskette if you're using IBM's version 3.3).
14. Type *n* to answer the *Copy another diskette* question. DOS responds by displaying the system prompt.
15. If you have a fixed disk, change the system prompt back to C> by typing:

    ```
    A>c:
    ```

    Go on to the heading "Changing the Current Drive."

If You Have Two Diskette Drives

These instructions assume that your DOS system diskette is in drive A, that you have performed the startup steps of entering the date and time, and that you have the DOS system prompt, A>, on the screen. During the procedure, DOS prompts for the *source* and *target* diskettes. Remember that the DOS diskette is the *source* and the blank diskette is the *target*.

1. If you're using IBM's version 3.3 of DOS with 5.25-inch diskette drives, place the diskette labeled *Operating* in drive A.
2. Put a blank new diskette in drive B.
3. Type the following (but not the A>, and don't forget to press Enter):

    ```
    A>diskcopy a: b:
    ```

This command tells DOS to copy everything on the diskette in drive A to the diskette in drive B. DOS responds:

```
Insert SOURCE diskette in drive A:

Insert TARGET diskette in drive B:

Press any key when ready...
_
```

4. Your source (DOS) and target (blank) diskettes are in the correct drives, so press the spacebar or any other key. DOS responds:

   ```
   Copying 40 tracks
   9 Sectors/Track, 2 Side(s)
   ```

   A short while later, DOS displays:

   ```
   Formatting while copying
   ```

   The message may vary, depending on the version of DOS you're using and the type of diskette drives you have. It takes about a minute to copy the diskette. When the diskette is copied, DOS responds:

   ```
   Copy another diskette (Y/N)?_
   ```

5. Remove the diskette from drive B and label it with the name on the original DOS diskette—OPERATING, for example, or DOS. Use a felt-tip pen, not a ballpoint pen, to avoid damaging the surface of the diskette.

6. Remove the original DOS diskette from drive A and put it in its plastic sleeve in the manual binder (or some other safe place).

7. Unless you're using 3.5-inch diskettes, you have another diskette to copy, so type *y* to answer the *Copy another diskette* question. DOS replies with the messages to put the source and target diskettes in drives A and B as in step 3. If you're using 3.5-inch diskettes, there is only one DOS diskette, so go on to the heading "Changing the Current Drive."

8. If you're using IBM's version 3.3 of DOS, put the diskette labeled *Startup* in drive A. Otherwise, put your second DOS diskette (usually labeled *Supplemental* or *Supplemental Programs*) in drive A.

9. Put a blank new diskette in drive B.

10. Press the spacebar, or any other key. DOS responds as in step 4.

11. When the copy is complete and DOS asks if you want to make another copy, remove the copy from drive B, label it with the name on the original DOS diskette, and put it with your other working diskettes.

12. Remove the original DOS diskette from drive A and put it in its plastic sleeve in the manual binder (or some other safe place).
13. If you don't have a fixed disk, put your copy of the system diskette in drive A.
14. Type *n* to answer the *Copy another diskette* question. DOS responds by displaying the system prompt.

CHANGING THE CURRENT DRIVE

You can change the current drive by typing the letter of the new drive, followed by a colon. To change the current drive to drive B, for example, type:

```
C>b:

B>_
```

Now the system prompt is B>, confirming that DOS will look in drive B unless told otherwise. (If you have one diskette drive, you may have a message on your screen telling you to insert a diskette in drive B; don't worry about it.)

If you're using a fixed disk, change the current drive back to drive C by typing the following:

```
B>c:

C>_
```

The system prompt returns to C>.

If you're not using a fixed disk, change the current drive back to drive A by typing the following:

```
B>a:

A>_
```

The system prompt returns to A>.

CHANGING THE DATE

The computer has an electronic clock that keeps time to the hundredth of a second. DOS uses this clock to keep track of both the time of day and the date. If you're using the system when midnight arrives, the date advances to the next day (and, if necessary, the next month and year).

In some models of computers, the clock doesn't run when the system is shut off, so each time you start the system DOS sets the date to January 1, 1980 (1-01-1980) and sets the time to midnight (0:00:00.00). That's why DOS might prompt you for the correct date and time whenever you start the system.

The clock in the IBM PS/2 series, the PC/AT, and compatible computers—plus the clock in some IBM PC and PC/XT compatibles—runs all the time, powered by its own battery. If you're using version 3.3 of DOS, or if you have a clock-calendar card and timekeeping software in your system, the date and time in this system clock remain correct without your having to do anything, even when the system is turned off.

You can change the date whenever you want with the Date command. To tell DOS you want to change the date, type:

```
C>date
```

DOS displays the current date (here, it is the date you set earlier) and prompts you to type a new date:

```
Current date is Fri 10-16-1987
Enter new date (mm-dd-yy): _
```

Type the correct date and press the Enter key. DOS sets its calendar to the new date and displays the system prompt. If you had just pressed Enter, DOS would have left the date unchanged. You can check and change the time the same way, with the Time command. To set the clock to the correct time, type:

```
C>time
```

DOS displays the time (based on what you set earlier) and prompts for the new time:

```
Current time is  8:22:33:55
Enter new time: _
```

Type the correct time (such as 13:30 for 1:30 P.M.) and press Enter.

PRINTING WHAT IS ON THE SCREEN

The screen shows you a record of your commands and the responses from DOS; it can show a maximum of 25 lines. When all the lines are filled, each additional line causes the entire screen to shift up, or *scroll,* to make room for the new line at the bottom; the top line disappears from view.

Because a copy of what is on the display is often useful, DOS makes it easy to print what's on the screen. Locate the key labeled PrtSc (for *Print Screen,* spelled out on some keyboards). Make sure your printer is turned on, hold down the Shift key, and press PrtSc (this combination is referred to in text as Shift-PrtSc).

Each line of the screen is printed. Another way to print what is on the screen is described in the next chapter.

Note: If Shift-PrtSc does not produce a printed copy of what's on the screen, you might need to help your printer understand the instruction. With the Hewlett-Packard LaserJet Plus, for example, you press the button labeled ON LINE, *press the* FORM FEED *button to print the page, then press* ON LINE *again to return the printer to its earlier status. If necessary, check the documentation that came with your printer.*

CLEARING THE SCREEN

Sometimes, when the screen is filled with commands and responses, you might want to clear it before continuing with your work. You can erase everything on the screen with the Clear Screen (cls) command. Try it by typing:

```
C>cls
```

The screen is cleared, except for the system prompt in the upper left-hand corner.

TURNING THE SYSTEM OFF

If DOS is displaying the system prompt, all you have to do to shut the system down is turn off the power switch. You can do it anytime, except when the light on a disk drive is on; turning the power off while a drive is in use can cause you to lose the data on the disk. (If you're using an application program and decide to shut the system down, first follow the program's instructions for saving your work and quitting. When the program returns you to the DOS prompt, you can shut down without risking loss of data.)

Some devices attached to your system may have special requirements for shutting down, such as a specific sequence in which they should be turned off. Be sure you know any special instructions for the devices attached to your system.

After you shut the system down, be sure to remove any diskettes you are using and store them where they will be safe. Remove your diskettes before you turn off the power, as long as the disk drive is not in use.

CHAPTER SUMMARY

You have completed your first session with DOS. It wasn't very long, but you started the system, entered a few DOS commands, and printed what was on the screen. These are the key points:

- You control DOS by typing commands.
- DOS doesn't know what you have typed until you press the Enter key.
- The Backspace key erases the last character you typed.
- The system prompt tells you that DOS is at the command level, ready to accept a command from you.
- The letter in the system prompt identifies the current drive; you can change the current drive by typing the new drive letter, followed by a colon.
- The computer keeps track of the time and date. You can also set them with the Date and Time commands.
- Pressing Shift-PrtSc prints the contents of the screen.
- Typing *cls* clears the screen.

CHAPTER 3

TAKING A TEST DRIVE

When you test drive a car, you already know how to start it. The test drive helps you become familiar with the controls, the steering, the brakes, the overall feel of the car. You learned how to start DOS in the last chapter. Now it's time for a test drive—time to begin learning to control DOS, how to steer it in the direction of one task or another, and how to call a halt if you want or need to.

That's what this chapter is all about. It introduces you to the directory of files that DOS keeps on each disk and shows you how to use the special keys on your keyboard. You use these keys to tell DOS to cancel lines or commands, to freeze the display, and to restart DOS itself.

Note: Part of this chapter deals with keys that have special meaning for DOS. If your keyboard does not have the key used in an example, check your system's documentation for equivalent keys.

The examples in this chapter use the DOS system diskette. To try the examples given here, start the computer with your copy of the system diskette in drive A, even if you have a fixed disk from which you normally use DOS. If necessary, enter the appropriate date and time, so that DOS responds with the system prompt. If you're using IBM's version 3.3 on 5.25-inch diskettes, take the Startup diskette from drive A and put in the Operating diskette.

Don't worry about leaving your computer on while you read the text between examples; DOS is patient.

THE DIRECTORY

Recall from Chapter 1 that information stored on a disk is stored as a file. DOS automatically keeps and updates a list of every file you save on every disk you use. This list is called the *directory*.

If you create and save a new file, DOS adds it to the list. If you revise an old file, DOS keeps track of that, too. The directory eliminates the need for you to keep a separate record of everything you save on each disk. You can tell DOS you want to see the directory whenever DOS is displaying the system prompt.

The example in the next section serves the double purpose of showing you a directory and showing you around your DOS disk itself. As you use the system more, you will come to recognize many of the DOS files as DOS commands. Before you look at a directory, though, you should know a little about how DOS saves your files.

Whenever you create a file, you give it a descriptive name, called the *file name,* of up to eight characters. If you want, you can add a suffix, called the *extension,* of up to three more letters. (Chapters 4 and 5 present more on files.)

Whenever you ask DOS to show you the directory of a disk, DOS lists your files by file name (and extension, if there is one). It also shows you the size of each file, in units called *bytes,* and gives you the date and the time the file was either created or last changed; that's why DOS might prompt you for the date and time.

Note: A byte is the amount of storage required to hold one character in computer memory or on disk. Here are a few familiar items and their sizes, in bytes: the letters abcd, *4 bytes (1 byte per letter); the words* United States, *13 bytes (blanks count); a double-spaced, typewritten page, 1500 bytes; this book, 900,000 bytes (approximately).*

Depending on the version of DOS you're using and the type of drives you have (diskette, fixed disk, or both), your diskettes can hold anywhere from 163,840 to 1,474,560 bytes. Your fixed disk, if you have one, can hold 10,240,000 or 20,480,000— even 40,960,000 bytes or more. For convenience, large quantities are usually given in kilobytes (K) or megabytes (MB). One kilobyte equals 1024 bytes, and one megabyte equals 1000 kilobytes, so disk capacity can range from 160 K to 40 MB or more.

DISPLAYING THE DIRECTORY OF A DISK

To display the directory of the disk in the current drive, you simply type *dir,* the name of the Directory command. Type the command and press Enter:

```
A>dir
```

DOS displays the directory of the current disk. In this example, you see a list of the files on your DOS diskette. The directory is longer than the 25 lines the screen can show at one time, so some of the directory scrolls off the top; you'll see how to handle this in a moment.

Figure 3-1 on the next page shows the Directory command display.

Note: The Directory command is used in examples throughout the book. Unless stated otherwise, the IBM version 3.3 display is shown. If you are using a different version of DOS, your directory listing differs from the listing illustrated. For comparison purposes, Figure 3-2 on page 27 shows the directory of the system diskette for Microsoft's version of DOS 3.3. As you can see, the names of the files, their sizes, and the dates vary from one version of DOS to another. Don't be concerned. Such variations have no effect on the way you use DOS or the way DOS responds to commands.

```
 Volume in drive A has no label
 Directory of  A:\
APPEND    EXE      5825   3-17-87  12:00p
ASSIGN    COM      1561   3-17-87  12:00p
ATTRIB    EXE      9529   3-17-87  12:00p
BACKUP    COM     31913   3-18-87  12:00p
BASIC     COM      1063   3-17-87  12:00p
BASICA    COM     36403   3-17-87  12:00p
CHKDSK    COM      9850   3-18-87  12:00p
COMMAND   COM     25307   3-17-87  12:00p
COMP      COM      4214   3-17-87  12:00p
DEBUG     COM     15897   3-17-87  12:00p
DISKCOMP  COM      5879   3-17-87  12:00p
DISKCOPY  COM      6295   3-17-87  12:00p
EDLIN     COM      7526   3-17-87  12:00p
FIND      EXE      6434   3-17-87  12:00p
FORMAT    COM     11616   3-18-87  12:00p
GRAFTABL  COM      6128   3-17-87  12:00p
GRAPHICS  COM      3300   3-17-87  12:00p
JOIN      EXE      8969   3-17-87  12:00p
LABEL     COM      2377   3-17-87  12:00p
MORE      COM       313   3-17-87  12:00p
PRINT     COM      9026   3-17-87  12:00p
RECOVER   COM      4299   3-18-87  12:00p
RESTORE   COM     34643   3-17-87  12:00p
SHARE     EXE      8608   3-17-87  12:00p
SORT      EXE      1977   3-17-87  12:00p
SUBST     EXE      9909   3-17-87  12:00p
TREE      COM      3571   3-17-87  12:00p
XCOPY     EXE     11247   3-17-87  12:00p
BASIC     PIF       369   3-17-87  12:00p
BASICA    PIF       369   3-17-87  12:00p
MORTGAGE  BAS      6251   3-17-87  12:00p
       31 File(s)     55296 bytes free
```

Figure 3-1. A directory display of IBM's version 3.3 Operating diskette

The two lines at the top of the directory give information about the disk itself and are explained in detail in Chapter 6, "Managing Your Diskettes." The last line shows the number of files on the disk and the number of bytes that are still unused.

Figure 3-3 shows a breakdown of one entry from a directory. The file name is DISKCOPY; note it is eight letters long, the maximum length of a DOS file name. The next item, COM, is the file's extension. The next item tells you the file is 6295 bytes long—about the number of characters you see on three double-spaced, typed pages. The final two entries give the date and time the file was either created or last changed.

```
 Volume in drive A has no label
 Directory of  A:\
4201      CPI     17089   7-24-87  12:00a
5202      CPI       459   7-24-87  12:00a
ANSI      SYS      1647   7-24-87  12:00a
APPEND    EXE      5794   7-24-87  12:00a
ASSIGN    COM      1530   7-24-87  12:00a
ATTRIB    EXE     10656   7-24-87  12:00a
CHKDSK    COM      9819   7-24-87  12:00a
COMMAND   COM     25276   7-24-87  12:00a
COMP      COM      4183   7-24-87  12:00a
COUNTRY   SYS     11254   7-24-87  12:00a
DISKCOMP  COM      5848   7-24-87  12:00a
DISKCOPY  COM      6264   7-24-87  12:00a
DISPLAY   SYS     11259   7-24-87  12:00a
DRIVER    SYS      1165   7-24-87  12:00a
EDLIN     COM      7495   7-24-87  12:00a
EXE2BIN   EXE      3050   7-24-87  12:00a
FASTOPEN  EXE      3888   7-24-87  12:00a
FDISK     COM     48919   7-24-87  12:00a
FIND      EXE      6403   7-24-87  12:00a
FORMAT    COM     11671   7-24-87  12:00a
GRAFTABL  COM      6136   7-24-87  12:00a
GRAPHICS  COM     13943   7-24-87  12:00a
JOIN      EXE      9612   7-24-87  12:00a
KEYB      COM      9041   7-24-87  12:00a
LABEL     COM      2346   7-24-87  12:00a
MODE      COM     15440   7-24-87  12:00a
MORE      COM       282   7-24-87  12:00a
NLSFUNC   EXE      3029   7-24-87  12:00a
PRINT     COM      8995   7-24-87  12:00a
RECOVER   COM      4268   7-24-87  12:00a
SELECT    COM      4132   7-24-87  12:00a
SORT      EXE      1946   7-24-87  12:00a
SUBST     EXE     10552   7-24-87  12:00a
SYS       COM      4725   7-24-87  12:00a
       34 File(s)     58368 bytes free
```

Figure 3-2. A directory display of Microsoft's version 3.3 system diskette

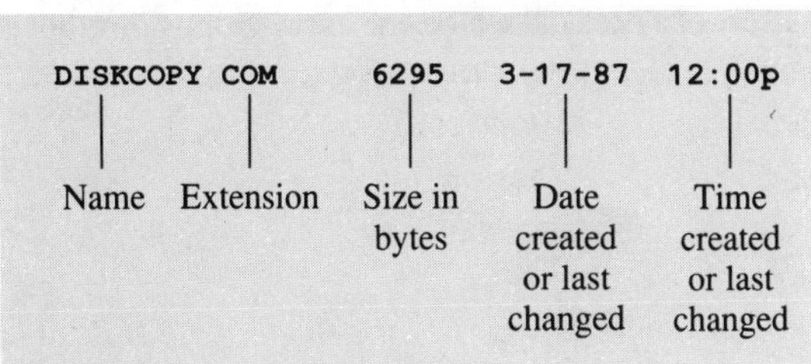

Figure 3-3. A directory entry

SOME IMPORTANT KEYS

In the examples in the previous chapter, you used the standard typewriter portion of the keyboard—including the Backspace and Enter keys—to enter commands. Several other keys have important meanings to DOS; you'll find yourself using them frequently while you're using DOS. Figures 3-4 and 3-5 show where these keys are located on two common versions of the IBM keyboard.

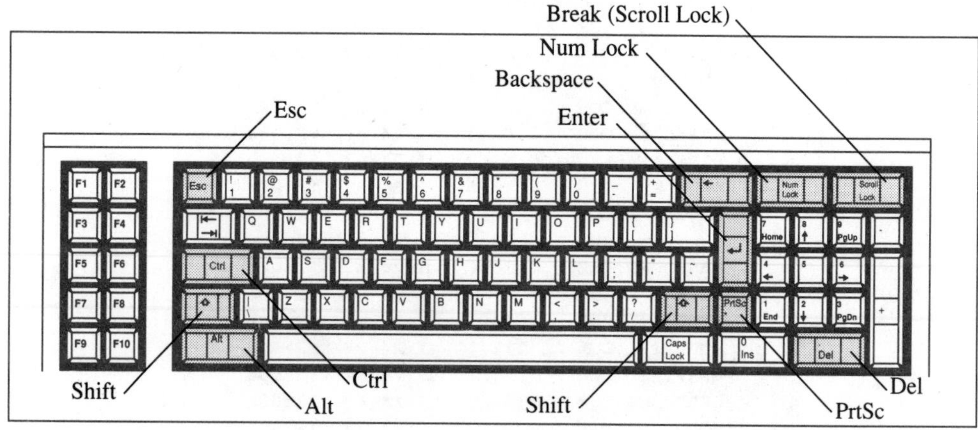

Figure 3-4. Some important keys on the IBM PC and PC/XT keyboards

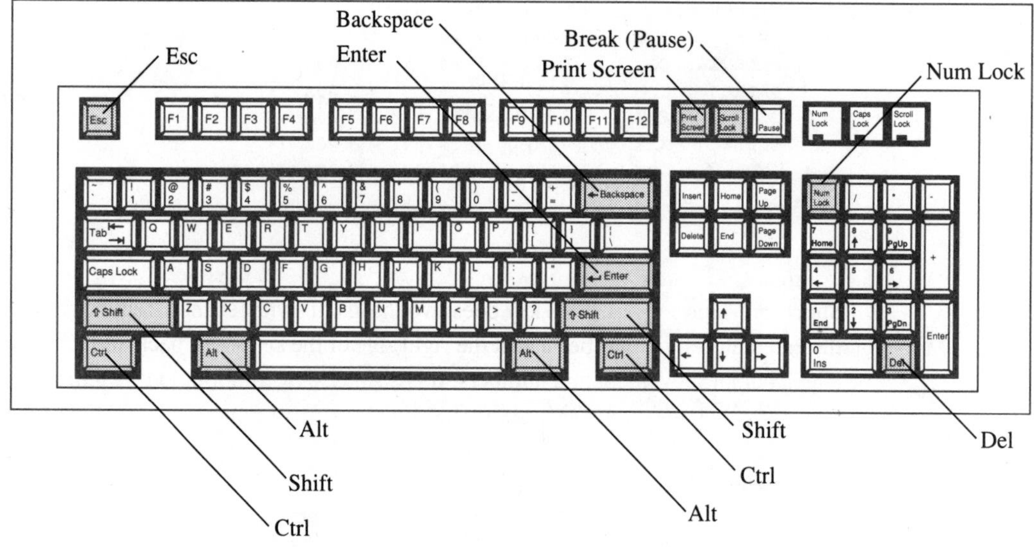

Figure 3-5. Some important keys on the enhanced IBM PC/AT keyboard

Shift

The Shift keys are labeled with an open arrow or the word *Shift.* Like the Shift keys on a typewriter, they have no effect by themselves; they shift the keyboard to uppercase letters and special characters.

Esc

Short for *Escape.* This key cancels a line you have typed. To see how it works, type several characters (but don't press Enter):

```
A>Now is the time
```

To erase this line, you could repeatedly press the Backspace key; press the Escape key instead:

```
A>Now is the time\
```

DOS displays a reverse slash (\) to indicate that the line was canceled, and moves the cursor to the beginning of the next line. DOS doesn't repeat the system prompt, but the cursor indicates it is still ready for you to type a command. Press the Enter key, and DOS displays the system prompt and the cursor on the next line:

```
A>_
```

Pressing the Escape key is the quickest way to cancel a line you have typed.

Ctrl

Short for *Control.* This key has no effect by itself, but it is used like the Shift keys to change the effect of pressing another key. The combination of the Control key and some other key is represented in this book by Ctrl- followed by the other key. Ctrl-Break, for example, means "hold down the Control key and press the Break key." The Control key combinations and what they do are described in a moment.

Num Lock

Short for *Numeric Lock.* This key does two things. It switches the effect of the keys in the calculator-style number pad at the right side of the keyboard back and forth between cursor movement and numbers. It is also used in combination with the Control key to freeze the display. To test the first function, press Num Lock and then press the 4 key in the numeric pad several times:

```
A>444_
```

The keys produce numbers on the screen. Now press Num Lock again and press the same 4 key you pressed before:

```
A>44_
```

Pressing Num Lock a second time switched the keys to their cursor-movement functions. The 4 key is labeled with a left arrow in addition to the number 4; pressing it moves the cursor left, in the direction of the arrow, and erases a character just as the Backspace key does. Press Num Lock and the same 4 key again:

```
A>444_
```

You switched back to numbers. Press Num Lock one more time to switch back to cursor movement, press Esc to cancel the line, and press the Enter key to return to the system prompt:

```
A>444\

A>_
```

You won't often use the arrow-marked direction keys for cursor movement with DOS, but many application programs, such as word processors, require frequent cursor movements.

Break

This key is usually labeled *Scroll Lock* or *Pause* on the top surface and *Break* on the front. It has no effect on DOS by itself, but it is used with the Control key to cancel a command you have entered.

Alt and Del

Short for *Alternate* and *Delete*. These keys have no effect on DOS by themselves, but are used with the Control key to restart DOS.

PrtSc or Print Scrn

Short for *Print Screen*. This key is used with the Shift and Control keys to print the contents of the screen. You used Shift-PrtSc in the previous chapter; you'll use Ctrl-PrtSc, and see the difference, in a short while.

CONTROL-KEY FUNCTIONS

Figure 3-6 shows the effects produced by holding down the Control key and pressing another key. You'll probably use these combinations fairly often with DOS, so the next few topics show you examples of each combination. When you are being shown exactly what to type, the names of the keys are separated by hyphens and enclosed in angle brackets to represent pressing a Control key combination. Thus, when you see <Ctrl-Break> in a command, it means "press Ctrl-Break."

Ctrl-Num Lock	Halts whatever the system is doing until you press another key. Typically used to freeze the display when information is scrolling by too fast or scrolling off the top of the screen. Can also be entered as Ctrl-S (Ctrl, plus the letter S).
Ctrl-Break	Cancels whatever the system is doing. Use this when you really don't want the computer to continue what it's doing. Can also be entered as Ctrl-C (Ctrl, plus the letter C).
Ctrl-PrtSc	Pressing this key combination once causes DOS to start printing every line as it is displayed; pressing Ctrl-PrtSc a second time stops simultaneous displaying and printing. Can also be entered as Ctrl-P (Ctrl, plus the letter P).
Ctrl-Alt-Del	Restarts DOS. This combination is unique; no other keys can be used to do the same thing.

Figure 3-6. Control key combinations

Before trying the examples, you should also note that DOS displays the Control key as the symbol ^. DOS does not acknowledge all Control key commands on the screen, but when it does, it uses the symbol ^ in combination with a letter. Control-Break, for example, shows on the screen as ^C and can also be typed by holding down the Control key and typing the letter C.

Freezing the Display

When you displayed the directory earlier, the first few lines scrolled off the screen. To let you read such long displays, DOS lets you temporarily halt the display by pressing Ctrl-Num Lock. When you do this, the display remains frozen, giving you time to read it. To start the display moving again, you simply press any key.

To test this function, type the following to display the directory. When the entries start appearing on the screen, press Ctrl-Num Lock to freeze the display:

```
A>dir
```

Press any key, and the display resumes. You can press Ctrl-Num Lock to stop and start the display as many times as you like, so you can view displays that are many screens long.

Pressing Ctrl-S has the same effect as pressing Ctrl-Num Lock.

Canceling a Command

If you enter a command and then change your mind or realize that you meant to enter some other command, you can cancel the command you entered by pressing Ctrl-Break. To test this function, type the Directory command again. This time, press Ctrl-Break when DOS begins to display the directory entries:

```
A>dir

 Volume in drive A has no label
 Directory of  A:\

APPEND   EXE      5825   3-17-87  12:00p
ASSIGN   COM      1561   3-17-87  12:00p
ATTRIB   EXE      9529   3-17-87  12:00p
BACKUP   COM     31913   3-18-87  12:00p
BASIC    COM      1063   3-17-87  12:00p
BASICA   COM     36403   3-17-87  12:00p
CHKDSK   COM      9850   3-18-87  12:00p
COMMAND  COM     25^C

A>_
```

Your display probably stopped somewhere else in the directory, but when you press Ctrl-Break, DOS stops what it is doing, displays ^C at the stopping point, and returns to the command level.

Pressing Ctrl-C has the same effect as pressing Ctrl-Break.

Printing and Displaying Simultaneously

In the previous chapter you printed the contents of the screen by pressing Shift-PrtSc. There's another way to print from the screen: Pressing Ctrl-PrtSc tells DOS to start printing everything it displays. DOS continues to print and display simultaneously until you press Ctrl-PrtSc again.

To test this function, make sure your printer is turned on, press Ctrl-PrtSc, then enter the Directory command:

```
A><Ctrl-PrtSc>dir
```

DOS again displays the directory of the system disk, but this time each line is printed as it is displayed. (If you're using a LaserJet or similar printer, remember that you have to press the ON LINE and FORM FEED buttons to get a printed copy.)

The directory is displayed more slowly than when you use the Directory command alone, because DOS waits until a line is printed before displaying and printing the next line. You can cancel the Directory command before the complete directory is printed by pressing Ctrl-Break. Remember to press Ctrl-PrtSc as well, to end the simultaneous displaying and printing.

If you want to print something without printing the command that creates the display, type the command first, then press Ctrl-PrtSc, and then press Enter. For example, when you printed the directory in the preceding example, the Directory command was the first line printed. To avoid printing the command, type:

```
A>dir<Ctrl-PrtSc>
```

Now printing begins with the first line of the directory; the Directory command isn't printed. Cancel the command by pressing Ctrl-Break.

Be sure to press Ctrl-PrtSc again to stop printing; otherwise, DOS continues to print everything it displays, even if you go on to an entirely different task.

Pressing Ctrl-P has the same effect as pressing Ctrl-PrtSc.

Shift-PrtSc versus Ctrl-PrtSc

These two methods of printing from the screen work differently and have different uses. Shift-PrtSc prints everything on the screen and stops. Ctrl-PrtSc, as you just saw, alternates displaying and printing, line by line. If everything you want is on the screen, use Shift-PrtSc; it's faster. But if you want to keep a running record of a series of commands and responses, or you want to print something longer than one screenful, use Ctrl-PrtSc.

Ctrl-PrtSc is better for printing long displays, because you can press it once to tell DOS to start simultaneous displaying and printing. Then you simply enter a command—such as the Directory command—to create the display, and press Ctrl-PrtSc again when you want to stop printing. If you use Shift-PrtSc for printing displays more than one screen long, you have to display the first screen, print it, then display the second screen, print it, and so forth until everything you want has been printed.

Restarting the System

Suppose you find yourself in a situation where your computer is not responding as you think it should, or it complains about something you don't know how to handle, or you decide it would be best to scrap what you're doing and start over from the beginning. You don't have to turn the power switch off and on to restart your system; you can do it by pressing Ctrl-Alt-Del.

Try it. (If you're using IBM's version 3.3 with no fixed disk, first replace the Operating diskette in drive A with the Startup diskette.)

Hold down both Ctrl and Alt and press Del.

The screen clears, the drive lights blink, the system beeps, and DOS is loaded just as it was when you turned the power on. Restarting with Ctrl-Alt-Del takes less time, though, because the computer doesn't test all its devices and memory as it does whenever you switch the power off and on.

If your system doesn't keep the time and date for you, notice that the date is once again 1-01-1980 and DOS is prompting you to enter the current date; restarting DOS resets the date and time. If the date prompt isn't on the screen, type *date* and press the Enter key.

Type the following to set the date to April 27, 1988:

```
Current date is Tue  1-01-1980
Enter new date (mm-dd-yy) 4-27-88
```

If the time prompt isn't displayed, type *time* and press Enter. Now type the following to set the time to 4:25 P.M.:

```
Current time is  0:00:35.09
Enter new time: 16:25
```

DOS displays its startup message and the system prompt.

A SHORT DIVERSION

The system prompt (A> or C>) is an economical way for DOS to show you the current drive and to let you know that you can enter a command. But the combination of a letter (for the current drive) and the greater-than sign (>) is only one possible system prompt. An advanced DOS command, Prompt, lets you change the system prompt to almost anything you want.

For example, you might prefer a more courteous machine. Type the following and press Enter (<space> means press the spacebar):

```
A>prompt May I help you?<space><Enter>
```

Now the system prompt isn't quite so cryptic:

```
May I help you? _
```

Each time DOS returns to the command level, it displays this polite phrase. Try it by pressing the Enter key once or twice to cause DOS to display the system prompt again. Although your new prompt looks quite different from A> (and actually conveys less information), the meaning is the same: DOS is at the command level, ready for you to enter a command.

To see just how much you can cram into the system prompt, type the following example as a single line (again, <space> means press the spacebar). Although the example is shown on two separate lines, don't press the Enter key until you come to <Enter> at the end of the third line:

```
May I help you? prompt The time is<space>$t$_ The date is<space>
$d$_ The current disk is<space>$n$_ Your command:<space><Enter>
```

Now the system prompt is three lines of data followed by a request for a command:

```
The time is 16:26:03.54
The date is Wed  4-27-1988
The current disk is A
Your command: _
```

You would probably quickly tire of all this, but the exercise shows how much flexibility DOS gives you. You don't have to take advantage of it all, but it's there if you want it.

To return the system prompt to its normal form, simply type the Prompt command by itself:

```
The time is 16:26:03.54
The date is Wed  4-27-1988
The current disk is A
Your command: prompt
```

It's back to the familiar A>.

CHAPTER SUMMARY

Each diskette has a directory that lists the name, extension, and size of each file, and the date and time the file was created or last changed. You can see the directory by typing *dir* and pressing Enter.

- If you're using 5.25-inch diskettes and IBM's release of version 3.3 of DOS on a computer without a fixed disk, you start the computer with the diskette labeled *Startup,* then replace it with the diskette labeled *Operating.*
- The Escape key cancels a line you have typed.
- Ctrl-Num Lock freezes the display. Ctrl-S has the same effect.
- Ctrl-Break cancels a command. Ctrl-C has the same effect.
- Ctrl-PrtSc turns simultaneous displaying and printing on and off. Ctrl-P has the same effect.
- Ctrl-Alt-Del restarts DOS.

Now that you're more familiar with the keyboard, the next chapter gives you a closer look at diskettes and files.

CHAPTER

4

A LOOK AT FILES AND DISKETTES

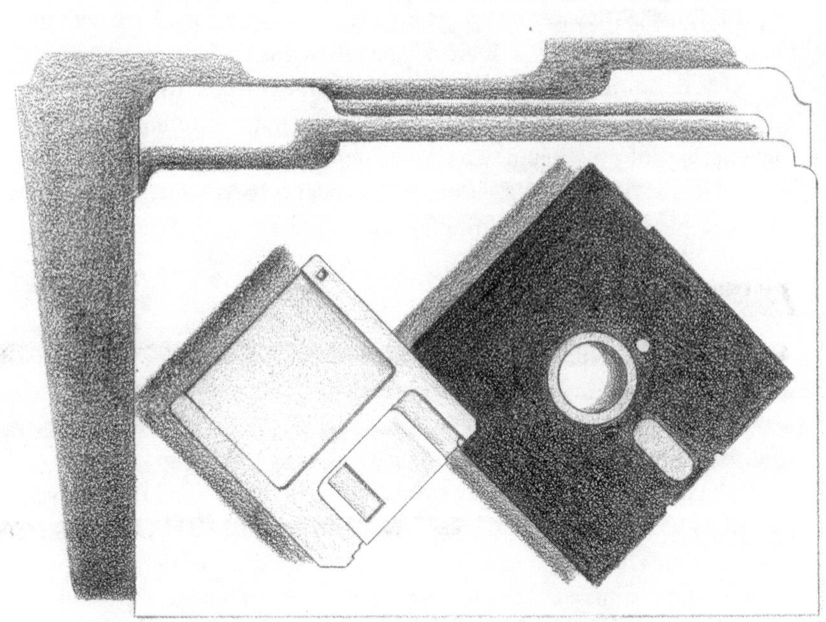

The computer's memory is temporary; it is cleared each time you turn off the computer. The only way you can save data permanently is to store the data in a file on a disk. When DOS needs data that is stored in a file, it reads the data from the disk into memory. If you change the data and want to keep the changed version, you must store the revised version on disk before turning off the system.

TYPES OF FILES

In general, a file contains either a program or data. A *program* is a set of instructions for the computer. *Data* is the text and numbers, such as a project proposal, a table of tax rates, or a list of customers, that the program needs to do your work.

Two types of files are important to your work: text files and command files. They are quite different, so it's important to look more closely at the kind of information these files contain and at how the files are used.

Text Files

Text files are data files that contain characters you can read (everyday letters, numbers, and symbols). Word-processing programs store their documents in text files, as does Edlin, the DOS text editor. Many files you use in your work with the computer—and all the files that you will create and use in this book—are text files.

The definition of a text file may seem self-evident at first, but it actually introduces you to an important characteristic of computer information storage. Your computer keeps information in two very different forms: One is text, the characters contained in text files; the other is machine-readable code, which looks meaningless to most people but is quite meaningful to computers.

Command Files

Command files contain the instructions DOS needs to carry out commands. These instructions can be a program, such as Diskcopy, or, as you will see in Chapter 12, "Creating Your Own Commands," they can be a series of DOS commands that you put together to perform a specific task, then store in a text file.

Not all DOS commands are stored in separate command files, however. Some commands, such as the Directory command, are built into the main body of DOS. When you load DOS into memory, you load these commands with it. When you want to use these commands, DOS has them on tap for immediate use—it does not need to look up a separate command file to carry them out.

These built-in commands are called *permanent,* or *internal,* commands. In contrast, the commands that are kept in command files until they are requested by you are called *temporary,* or *external,* commands. When you use a permanent command,

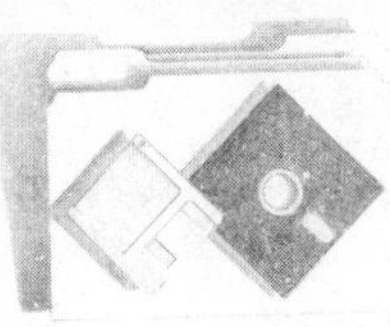

you simply request the command and DOS carries it out. When you use a temporary command, DOS must load the command file from disk into memory before it can carry out the command.

An application program, such as a word processor, is stored in a command file; it stores your work, such as documents, in data files.

HOW FILES ARE NAMED

No matter the type of file, each file must have a file name. Recall that a file name can be up to eight characters long. You can use almost any character on the keyboard when you name your files, but it's a good idea to give your files names, such as BUDGET or LETTER2, that describe their contents.

To identify a file more completely, a three-character suffix called the file *extension* can be added to the file name; this suffix is separated from the file name by a period. So that you and DOS can tell your files apart, each file on a disk must have either a different name or a different extension; REPORT.JAN and REPORT.FEB, for example, are different files to DOS, even though their file names are the same.

Specifying the Drive

When you name a file in a command, DOS must know which drive contains the disk with the file on it. If you don't specify a drive letter, DOS looks on the disk in the current drive (the drive letter shown in the system prompt). If the disk containing the file is not in the current drive, you can precede the file name with the letter of the drive and a colon. For example, if you specify the file as *b:report.doc*, DOS looks for it in drive B.

PREPARING FOR THE EXAMPLES

The following pages show a number of examples to help you become more comfortable with files and diskettes. With DOS, as with most other computer applications, doing is often the easiest and most effective way of learning.

If you have a fixed disk, make sure the latch on drive A is open, turn on the computer, and go through the startup routine until you see the system prompt (C>). (If you just finished Chapter 3, open the latch on drive A and restart the system by pressing Ctrl-Alt-Del.) Now put your copy of the DOS system diskette—Operating diskette if you're using IBM's version 3.3—in drive A; you'll use it for some of the examples.

If your system has diskette drives only, put your copy of the DOS system diskette in drive A, turn on the computer, and go through the startup routine until you see the system prompt (A>). If you're using IBM's version 3.3, remove the diskette from drive A and put in the diskette labeled Operating.

Don't Worry About Memorizing

You'll use several commands in this chapter, but you needn't remember exactly how to use each one; all the commands are described in more detail in the remaining chapters of the book. The purpose of this chapter is to introduce you to files and diskettes.

QUALIFYING A COMMAND

Up to now, all the commands you have entered consisted of a single word or abbreviation, such as *time* or *dir.* Most commands, however, let you add one or more qualifiers to make the action of the command more specific. These qualifiers are called *parameters.*

Some commands require parameters; others allow you to add parameters if you want. The Directory command, for example, does not require parameters, but it lets you add the name of the specific file you want to see; you'll use some such parameters in the following examples. The descriptions of the commands in later chapters show their parameters, both required and optional.

DISPLAYING SPECIFIC DIRECTORY ENTRIES

In the previous chapter you used the Directory command to display the directory entries of all files on the system disk. You can display the directory entry of a single file, or the directory entries for a selected set of files, by adding a parameter to the Directory command.

Displaying the Directory Entry of a Single File

To display the directory entry for a specific file, you simply type the file name (and extension, if there is one) after the command name. For example, you copied the system diskette with the Diskcopy command. Its command file is DISKCOPY.COM. To display the directory entry for DISKCOPY.COM, type the following command, including the blank following the command name. (If you're not using a fixed disk, you needn't include the drive letter. You can omit *a:* here and in the remaining examples.)

```
C>dir a:diskcopy.com
```

DOS displays only the directory entry of the file you specified:

```
 Volume in drive A has no label
 Directory of  A:\

DISKCOPY COM     6295   3-18-87  12:00p
        1 File(s)     55296 bytes free

C>_
```

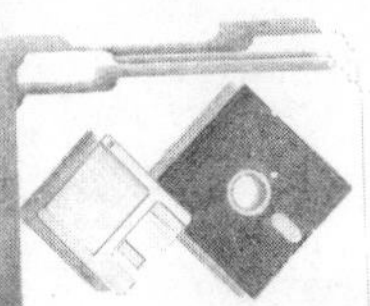

If the file you name isn't on the disk, or if you don't type the file name exactly as it is stored, DOS responds *File not found.*

Displaying the Directory Entries of a Set of Files

What if you remember most of a file name, or the file name but not the extension? DOS helps you out by giving you two wildcard characters, * and ?, that you can substitute for actual characters in a file name. Like wild cards in a poker game, the wildcard characters can represent any other character. They differ only in that ? can substitute for one character, while * can substitute for more than one character.

Suppose you remember only that a file's name begins with the letter F. It takes only a moment to check all the files that begin with F.

Use the DOS directory as an example. Type the following command. (Remember, if you're not using a fixed disk, you can omit the *a:*.)

```
C>dir a:f*
```

DOS displays the directory entries of all file names that begin with F:

```
 Volume in drive A has no label
 Directory of  A:\

FIND     EXE      6434   3-17-87  12:00p
FORMAT   COM     11616   3-18-87  12:00p
        2 File(s)      55296 bytes free

C>_
```

Wildcard characters can simplify the task of keeping track of your files. Chapter 5, "Managing Your Files," includes several examples of using wildcard characters with different commands.

Now it's time to stop practicing with the system disk and create some files of your own.

PREPARING A DISKETTE FOR USE

As mentioned earlier, before DOS can store a file on a new diskette, it must prepare the diskette for use. This preparation, in which DOS writes certain information for its own use on the diskette, is called *formatting*. DOS did the formatting for you automatically when you used the Diskcopy command, but you can explicitly tell DOS to do this with the Format command. You'll need two formatted diskettes for the examples in this book. Now is a good time to format them, so get out two blank diskettes and two blank labels before proceeding.

Type the following:

```
C>format b:
```

This command tells DOS to format the diskette in drive B.

Formatting a diskette erases any files that may be stored on it, so DOS gives you a chance to make sure you haven't put the wrong diskette in the specified drive by displaying a message, then waiting for you to type something:

```
Insert new diskette for drive B:
and strike ENTER when ready_
```

If you discover that you put in the wrong diskette, no problem: Just take out the wrong one and put in the right one before you press the Enter key.

If you can't find a diskette that you want to format, and you want to cancel the command, again, no problem: You don't have to turn the system off; just press Ctrl-Break.

But you do want to format the diskette now. If you have one diskette drive, your DOS diskette should still be in drive A. Replace it with a blank diskette and close the drive latch. If you have two diskette drives, place a blank diskette in drive B and close the latch.

Press Enter. DOS displays a message telling you formatting is in progress. Depending on your version of DOS, the message might be simply *Formatting...*, or it might be a constantly changing display that looks like this:

```
Head:    0 Cylinder:     1
```

In either case, the light on the drive goes on, and DOS begins writing on the diskette. When it has finished, DOS tells you *Format complete,* reports on the amount of available storage on the diskette, and asks if you want to format another:

```
Format complete
   1213952 bytes total disk space
   1213952 bytes available on disk

Format another (Y/N)?_
```

The numbers shown are for the 1.2 MB diskette drive on the IBM PC/AT and compatible machines. Depending on the type of diskette drives you have and the version of DOS you're using, the total disk space in your report might be 1,457,664, or 1,213,952 (as shown), or 730,112, or 362,496, or 322,560, or 179,712, or 160,256 bytes.

DOS is now waiting for you to say whether you want to format another diskette. Type *y*. The message asking you to put the diskette in drive B and strike Enter is repeated, so go through the same process to format the second diskette. When DOS finishes, it asks you again whether you want to format another.

Now type *n*. DOS displays the system prompt (C>), telling you the Format command is ended and that DOS is waiting for you to type another command.

You now have two formatted diskettes. It's time to put one of them to use by creating a file; if you removed the diskette you just formatted, put it in your diskette drive (drive B if you have two diskette drives).

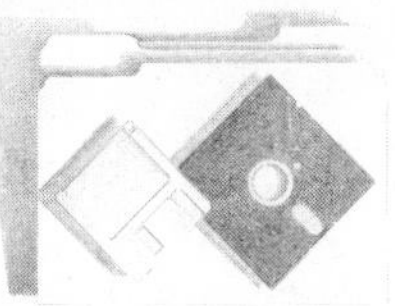

CREATING A TEXT FILE

An easy way to create a text file is by using the DOS Copy command. As you might guess from its name, the Copy command can be used to make a copy of a file. It can also be used to copy characters from the keyboard into a file.

DOS refers to the parts of your computer, such as the keyboard, display, and printer, as *devices.* To DOS, devices, like files, have names. The keyboard is known to DOS as CON (for CONsole).

You are going to create a file by telling DOS to copy what you type from the keyboard onto the blank diskette in drive B.

Note: If you have one diskette drive, recall that DOS treats it as both drive A and drive B. In the remaining examples, DOS will sometimes display Insert diskette for drive A: *or* Insert diskette for drive B:, *followed by* and strike any key when ready. *When you see this message, simply press the spacebar or any other key and continue with the example.*

To create a file named NOTE.DOC on the diskette in drive B, type the following example. End each line by pressing Enter; where you see a blank line, press Enter to tell DOS to insert an extra line:

```
C>copy con b:note.doc
October 16, 1987

Dear Fred,
Just a note to remind you
that our meeting is at 9.

Jack
```

That's the end of the file. To tell DOS that it's the end of the file, press Ctrl-Z (hold down the Control key and press Z), then press Enter:

```
<Ctrl-Z><Enter>
```

When you press Ctrl-Z, DOS displays ^Z (the ^, remember, represents the Control key). After you press Enter, DOS acknowledges that it copied a file:

```
        1 File(s) copied

C>_
```

To verify that the file is there, display the directory of the diskette in drive B:

```
C>dir b:
```

Sure enough, NOTE.DOC is on the diskette:

```
 Volume in drive B has no label
 Directory of  B:\

NOTE      DOC        94  10-16-87   2:54p
        1 File(s)    1213440 bytes free

C>_
```

This method of creating a text file is quick and convenient, and it is used in examples throughout the book.

Displaying a Text File

Because you can read the characters in text files, you'll often want to display one on the screen. It's even easier to display a text file than it is to create it. Just use the DOS Type command. To display your file, type the following:

```
C>type b:note.doc
```

DOS quickly displays each line and returns to the command level:

```
October 16, 1987

Dear Fred,
Just a note to remind you
that our meeting is at 9.

Jack

C>_
```

This is the quickest way to see what's in a file; you'll probably use the Type command frequently. Displaying a file isn't always helpful, though, because not all files are text files; they don't all contain readable characters. See for yourself. If you have only one diskette drive, replace your practice diskette with the copy of the DOS system diskette (Operating diskette with IBM's version 3.3). Now type the following to display the contents of the DOS command file named SORT.EXE:

```
C>type a:sort.exe
```

Yes, the display is correct. It's hard to tell from that jumble what is in the file, because the file contains a program stored in machine code, not as a text file.

If you have only one diskette drive, replace the DOS diskette with your practice diskette before continuing. (Don't worry; under normal circumstances, you won't have to exchange diskettes this often.)

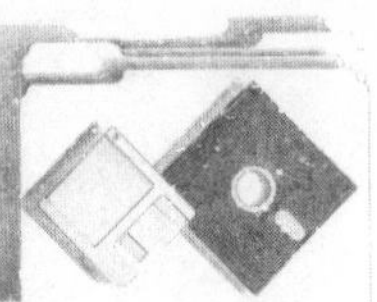

Printing a Text File

One of the main reasons you write documents, of course, is to have a printed copy. You can print your file by copying it to the printer. You've already copied from the keyboard to a disk. Now, copy from the disk to the printer. The printer is known to DOS as PRN. Make certain the printer is turned on, and type the following:

```
C>copy b:note.doc prn
```

The file is printed. When you print a file, you'll probably want to position the paper by hand before you enter the command, so that the printing will begin where you want it to on the page.

There's an easier way, however, to print a file: the Print command. To print your file with the Print command, type the following:

```
C>print b:note.doc
```

DOS responds:

```
Name of list device [PRN]: _
```

Press the Enter key. DOS displays the following two messages and prints your file:

```
Resident part of PRINT installed

    B:\NOTE.DOC is currently being printed

C>_
```

These messages are explained in more detail in Chapter 5, "Managing Your Files."

The Print command makes most printers advance to the next page after printing. Although this file is too short to show it, you can continue to use the system to do other work while the Print command is printing a file.

Copying a Text File

The Copy command is one of the more versatile DOS commands. You have already used it to create and print a text file. The Copy command also duplicates files.

To copy the file named NOTE.DOC into another file named LETTER.DOC, type:

```
C>copy b:note.doc b:letter.doc
```

When you press Enter, DOS copies the file; then it acknowledges that it did so:

```
        1 File(s) copied

C>_
```

Display the directory of the diskette in drive B again to verify the copy:

```
C>dir b:
```

Now you have two text files:

```
 Volume in drive B has no label
 Directory of  B:\

NOTE      DOC        94  10-16-87   2:54p
LETTER    DOC        94  10-16-87   2:54p
        2 File(s)   1212928 bytes free

C>_
```

If you wanted, you could make changes to one file and still have a copy of the original version on disk. You'll find the Copy command quite useful when you need several files that differ only slightly, or when you have several small files that can be combined in different ways to create other files: often-used paragraphs, for example, that can be recombined in different letters, contracts, or other documents.

Erasing a Text File

Just as you get rid of paper files, you can erase disk files. To erase NOTE.DOC from the diskette in drive B, type:

```
C>erase b:note.doc

C>_
```

Now check the directory one more time:

```
C>dir b:

 Volume in drive B has no label
 Directory of  B:\

LETTER    DOC        94  10-16-87   2:54p
        1 File(s)   1213440 bytes free

C>_
```

It's gone.

SOME ADVANCED FEATURES

Several commands and features give you much greater control over the way DOS does its work. For example, you can:

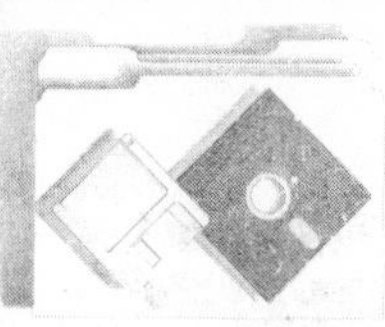

- Sort lines of data—for example, sort alphabetically the list of directory entries produced by the Directory command.
- View a long display one screenful at a time, without having to freeze the display by pressing Ctrl-Num Lock.
- Tell DOS to send the results, or *output*, of a command to the printer instead of to the display, simply by adding a few characters to the command.
- Search lines of data for a series of characters.

The examples in this section give you a glimpse of these advanced features; the features are described in detail, with many additional examples, in later chapters.

You'll notice that these advanced features cause more disk activity and take a bit longer than the other DOS commands. That's because DOS creates temporary files to help it carry out the advanced features.

Sorting Lines of Data

You have probably arranged card files or lists in some sequence, such as alphabetic or numeric order. The Sort command sorts, or arranges, lines of data such as a list of names for you. To see how this works, sort the lines of the text file B:LETTER.DOC. Type the following:

```
C>sort < b:letter.doc
```

The less-than symbol (<) tells DOS to send a copy of the file B:LETTER.DOC to the Sort command, which then displays the lines of the file rearranged (sorted) into alphabetic order:

```
Dear Fred,
Jack
Just a note to remind you
October 16, 1987
that our meeting is at 9.

C>_
```

Although you probably don't want to sort the lines of your letters, you can put whatever you like in a text file—for example, a list of customers or employees. The Sort command is a powerful addition to your kit of computer tools.

Viewing a Long Display One Screenful at a Time

When you displayed the directory of the system diskette in Chapter 3, the first few lines scrolled off the top of the screen because the display was too long to fit. You saw that you can freeze the display by pressing Ctrl-Num Lock. There's an easier way to stop scrolling: The More command displays one screenful, with -- *More* -- at the bottom of the screen, then waits for you to press any key to continue to the next screenful. Display the directory of the system disk again, this time using the More command.

If you have a fixed disk, place your copy of the DOS system diskette (Operating diskette if you have IBM's version 3.3) in drive A and type the following. Type the vertical bar by holding down a Shift key and pressing the key labeled with a ¦ character; remember, if you have two diskette drives, you can omit the *a:* in the command:

```
C>dir a: ¦ more
```

DOS displays the first screenful, but the last few lines aren't displayed yet (notice the -- *More* -- in the last line):

```
 Volume in drive A has no label
 Directory of  A:\

APPEND   EXE     5825   3-17-87  12:00p
ASSIGN   COM     1561   3-17-87  12:00p
ATTRIB   EXE     9529   3-17-87  12:00p
BACKUP   COM    31913   3-18-87  12:00p
BASIC    COM     1063   3-17-87  12:00p
BASICA   COM    36403   3-17-87  12:00p
CHKDSK   COM     9850   3-18-87  12:00p
COMMAND  COM    25307   3-17-87  12:00p
COMP     COM     4214   3-17-87  12:00p
DEBUG    COM    15897   3-17-87  12:00p
DISKCOMP COM     5879   3-17-87  12:00p
DISKCOPY COM     6295   3-17-87  12:00p
EDLIN    COM     7526   3-17-87  12:00p
FIND     EXE     6434   3-17-87  12:00p
FORMAT   COM    11616   3-18-87  12:00p
GRAFTABL COM     6128   3-17-87  12:00p
GRAPHICS COM     3300   3-17-87  12:00p
JOIN     EXE     8969   3-17-87  12:00p
LABEL    COM     2377   3-17-87  12:00p
MORE     COM      313   3-17-87  12:00p
-- More --
```

To see the rest of the directory, press any key. DOS displays the remaining lines:

```
PRINT    COM     9026   3-17-87  12:00p
RECOVER  COM     4299   3-18-87  12:00p
RESTORE  COM    34643   3-17-87  12:00p
SHARE    EXE     8608   3-17-87  12:00p
SORT     EXE     1977   3-17-87  12:00p
SUBST    EXE     9909   3-17-87  12:00p
TREE     COM     3571   3-17-87  12:00p
XCOPY    EXE    11247   3-17-87  12:00p
BASIC    PIF      369   3-17-87  12:00p
BASICA   PIF      369   3-17-87  12:00p
MORTGAGE BAS     6251   3-17-87  12:00p
       31 File(s)     55296 bytes free
```

The More command displays long output one screenful at a time, giving you a chance to view it all at your convenience.

Note: When you use the More command, you might see directory entries for files with odd names, such as 1106002B and 11060104 or %PIPE1.$$$ and %PIPE2.$$$. These are temporary files that DOS creates, then erases when it no longer needs them.

Sending Command Output to the Printer

In earlier examples, you printed the output of the Directory command by pressing Shift-PrtSc and Ctrl-PrtSc. There's a more direct way to print the output of a command: Simply follow the command with a greater-than symbol (>) and the name of the printer, PRN. To print the directory of the disk in the current drive, make sure the printer is turned on and type:

```
C>dir > prn
```

If you don't want to wait for the whole directory to be printed, cancel the printing by pressing Ctrl-Break.

This same technique can be used to send the output of a command to some other device or to a file, by substituting the device name or file name for PRN.

Finding a Series of Characters in a File

How many times have you searched through a pile of letters or notes, looking for a particular item or reference? If you have to look through DOS files or the output of DOS commands, the Find command will do the looking for you. For example, suppose you want to see the directory entries of all DOS files with SK in their names. Try the following (the quotation marks tell DOS which letters—known technically as a *character string*, or just *string*—to look for).

If you have a fixed disk, first make sure that your copy of the system (or Operating) diskette is in drive A. Type:

```
C>dir a: | find "SK"
```

DOS displays only the entries with SK in their names:

```
CHKDSK   COM     9850   3-18-87  12:00p
DISKCOMP COM     5879   3-17-87  12:00p
DISKCOPY COM     6295   3-17-87  12:00p

C>_
```

The Find command is even more useful when you use it to search for a series of characters in a text file. If a file contains a list of names and telephone numbers, for example, you can quickly display one particular entry, or all entries that contain a particular series of characters (such as an area code), or even all entries that *don't* contain a particular series of characters. Chapter 13, "Taking Control of Your System," shows you how to create such an automated index of names and telephone numbers with nothing but DOS commands.

Combining Features

These advanced features of DOS can also be used together in a single command, giving you even more flexibility in controlling DOS. Combining these features makes it possible to do a great deal with just one command. For example, suppose you want to print the directory entries of all files on the disk in drive A whose names include the letter F; further, you want the entries sorted according to the size of the files. Type the following:

```
C>dir a: ¦ find "F" ¦ sort /+16 > prn
```

This whole command translates easily into: Go to drive A, look at the directory, find all files with the letter F in their names, sort those files starting at the 16th column (where the size begins), and send the results to the printer. DOS does as it is told; it prints the directory entries of the sorted files in order, from the smallest (369 bytes) to the largest (11616 bytes):

```
BASIC    PIF      369   3-17-87  12:00p
BASICA   PIF      369   3-17-87  12:00p
GRAFTABL COM     6128   3-17-87  12:00p
FIND     EXE     6434   3-17-87  12:00p
FORMAT   COM    11616   3-18-87  12:00p
        31 File(s)     55296 bytes free
```

You may rarely search your directories this carefully, but such combinations make DOS a powerful tool for handling text files.

CHAPTER SUMMARY

This chapter concludes the portion of the book designed to give you a feel for running DOS, including some of its advanced features. The key points to remember include:

- The computer's memory is cleared each time you turn the system off. To save your work permanently, you must store it in a file on a disk.
- A text file contains ordinary characters you can read.
- A command file contains instructions that DOS uses to carry out a command.

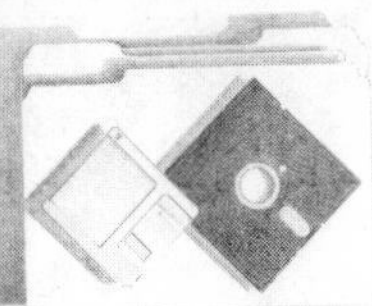

- A file name can be up to eight characters long; you can add an extension of up to three characters, separated from the file name by a period.
- Each file on a disk must have a different name or a different extension.

The remainder of the book shows you how to use DOS to manage your files, disks, and devices; use the text editor; and create your own commands.

PART 2

LEARNING TO USE DOS

Part 2 shows you how to use DOS to manage your work with the computer. The chapters in Part 2 include extensive examples that use real-life situations to illustrate each DOS command, but the information is organized so that you can quickly find a particular topic to refresh your memory.

The material in these chapters covers all versions of DOS. Chapter 9 covers the use of a fixed disk in detail.

Chapters 12 through 16 show you how to use the advanced features of DOS. Chapter 17 introduces you to networks.

CHAPTER 5

MANAGING YOUR FILES

The previous chapters defined a file as a named collection of related information stored on a disk, and showed you several ways to create, copy, display, print, and otherwise work with your computer files. This chapter describes the DOS filing system in detail, showing you more about how files are named and how you can use DOS to manage your computer files.

Note: A few of the examples in the remaining chapters of this book may look familiar, because they repeat some of the examples in Chapters 2, 3, and 4. This repetition is intentional, so that Chapters 5 through 16 present a complete guide to DOS commands. You won't have to refer back to Chapters 2, 3, or 4 for command descriptions.

THE DOS FILE COMMANDS

To be useful, a filing system—whether it contains disk files or paper files—must be kept orderly and up to date. Using the DOS file commands, you can manage your disk files much as you manage your paper files. This chapter covers the DOS commands you use most often on a day-to-day basis. It shows you how to:

- Display specific directory entries with the Directory command.
- Display a file with the Type command.
- Copy a file with the Copy command.
- Combine files with the Copy command.
- Send a copy of a file to a device with the Copy command.
- Remove a file from a disk with the Erase command.
- Change the name of a file with the Rename command.
- Compare two files with the Compare command.
- Print a file with the Print command.
- Control whether a file can be changed with the Attribute command.

FILE NAMES AND EXTENSIONS

As Chapter 4 pointed out, files are named so that you (and DOS) can tell them apart; each file on a disk must have a different name. You know that a file name can be up to eight characters long, made up of any letters or numbers; you can also use the following symbols:

! @ # $ % & ( ) - _ { } ` ' ~

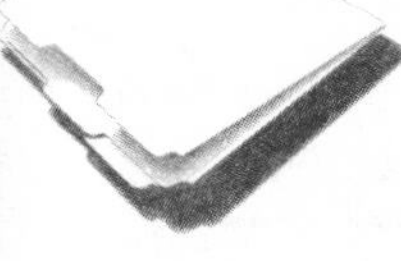

You can add a suffix—called an *extension*—to the file name to describe its contents more precisely. The extension can be up to three characters long and can include any of the characters that are valid for the file name. It must be separated from the name by a period. The extension distinguishes one file from another just as the name does: REPORT and REPORT.JAN, for example, are two different files, as are REPORT.JAN and REPORT.FEB. Figure 5-1 shows some valid and invalid file names.

These file names are valid	These are invalid...	because
B	1987BUDGET	Name too long
86BUDGET	BUDGET.1987	Extension too long
BUDGET.86	.87	No file name
BUDGET.87	SALES 86.DAT	Blank not allowed
BDGT(87)	$1,300.45	Comma not allowed

Figure 5-1. Some valid and invalid file names

Try to make file names and extensions as descriptive as possible. A short file name might be easy to type, but you can have difficulty remembering what the file contains if you haven't used it for a while. The more descriptive the name, the more easily you can identify the contents of the file.

Special Extensions

Figure 5-2 describes some extensions that have special meanings to DOS. These extensions either are created by DOS or cause DOS to assume the file contains a particular type of program or data. You should avoid giving your files any of these extensions.

Some application programs also use special extensions. For example, Microsoft Word, the Microsoft word processor, uses DOC to identify a document, BAK to identify a backup version of a document, and STY to identify a file that contains a style sheet of print specifications. You should avoid using any extensions that have special meaning for your application programs; these extensions are usually listed in the documentation that comes with each program.

Specifying the Drives

You can tell DOS to look for a file in a specific drive by typing the drive letter and a colon before the file name. If you specify a file as *b:report*, for example, DOS looks in drive B for a file named REPORT; if you specify the file as *report*, DOS looks for the file in the current drive.

Extension	Meaning to DOS
BAK	Short for *Backup*. Contains an earlier version of a text file. Edlin (the DOS text editor) and many word processors automatically make a backup copy of a file and give it this extension.
BAS	Short for *BASIC*. Contains a program written in the BASIC programming language. You can't run this program by typing its name; you can run it only while using the BASIC language.
BAT	Short for *Batch*. Identifies a text file you can create, which contains a set of DOS commands that are run when you type the name of the file.
COM	Short for *Command*. Identifies a command file that contains a program DOS runs when you type the file name.
CPI	Short for *Code Page Information*. Describes the characters that a device can use. Used in DOS version 3.3 and later.
EXE	Short for *Executable*. Like COM, identifies a command file that contains a program DOS runs when you type the file name.
INI	Short for *Initialize*. Describes how a program should start operating. Used by Microsoft Windows, Microsoft Word, the MS-DOS Manager, and other programs.
PIF	Short for *Program Information File*. Describes how an application program works; used by Microsoft Windows.
SYS	Short for *System*. Identifies a file that can be used only by DOS.

Figure 5-2. Special DOS file name extensions

PREPARING FOR THE EXAMPLES

If your system isn't running, start it (from the fixed disk if you're using one). If you are using 5.25-inch diskettes and IBM's release of version 3.3 on a system without a fixed disk, replace the Startup diskette in drive A with the Operating diskette.

You need one empty, formatted diskette for the examples in this chapter. Put the formatted diskette in the diskette drive (drive B if you have two diskette drives), and type the following to create a sample text file named REPORT.DOC on the diskette; be certain to press Enter at the end of each line. Where you see ^Z, either hold down the key labeled Ctrl and press Z or press the function key labeled F6:

```
C>copy con b:report.doc
This is a dummy file.
^Z
```

If you have only one diskette drive, DOS asks you to make sure the correct diskette is in the diskette drive:

```
Insert diskette for drive B: and strike
any key when ready
```

The correct diskette is in the drive, so just press the spacebar or any other key. DOS acknowledges:

```
        1 File(s) copied

C>_
```

Change the current drive to B by typing:

```
C>b:
```

DOS changes the system prompt to show that drive B is now the current drive:

```
B>_
```

Now you're ready to create some more sample files.

Creating the Sample Files

Type the following Copy commands (described in detail later in the chapter) to create some other sample files.

```
B>copy report.doc report.bak
        1 File(s) copied

B>copy report.doc bank.doc
        1 File(s) copied

B>copy report.doc budget.jan
        1 File(s) copied

B>copy report.doc budget.feb
        1 File(s) copied

B>copy report.doc budget.mar
        1 File(s) copied
```

Now check the directory.

```
B>dir
```

It should list six files:

```
 Volume in drive B has no label
 Directory of  B:\

REPORT   DOC        23  10-16-87   9:16a
REPORT   BAK        23  10-16-87   9:16a
BANK     DOC        23  10-16-87   9:16a
BUDGET   JAN        23  10-16-87   9:16a
BUDGET   FEB        23  10-16-87   9:16a
BUDGET   MAR        23  10-16-87   9:16a
        6 File(s)    1210880 bytes free
```

Remember, the time and date will vary according to the information you enter when you start DOS, but the file names and sizes (23 bytes) should be the same.

WILDCARD CHARACTERS

To make it easier to manage your disk files, most file commands let you use wildcard characters to handle several files at once. That way, when you want to do the same thing to several files—change their names, perhaps, or erase them—you don't have to enter a separate command for each file. You can use wildcard characters to tell DOS you mean a set of files with similar names or extensions. Just as a wild card in a poker game can represent any other card in the deck, a wildcard character can represent any other character in a file name or extension.

There are two wildcard characters, the asterisk (*) and the question mark (?). The following examples use the Directory command to illustrate ways you can use wildcard characters to specify groups of files.

Using the Asterisk Wildcard Character: *

The asterisk makes it easy to carry out commands on sets of files with similar names or extensions; it can represent up to all eight characters in a file name or up to all three characters in an extension. If you use the asterisk to represent the name or extension, you are specifying all file names or all extensions.

The following examples illustrate several ways to use the asterisk to find selected directory entries. You can use the asterisk with other DOS commands as well.

To specify all files named BUDGET, regardless of extension, type the following:

```
B>dir budget.*
```

DOS displays the directory entry of each sample file named BUDGET, regardless of its extension:

```
 Volume in drive B has no label
 Directory of  B:\

BUDGET   JAN        23  10-16-87   9:16a
BUDGET   FEB        23  10-16-87   9:16a
BUDGET   MAR        23  10-16-87   9:16a
        3 File(s)    1210880 bytes free
```

To specify all file names beginning with B, type the following:

```
B>dir b*
```

If you don't specify an extension, the Directory command displays the entry for each file that matches the name, regardless of extension (it's the equivalent of specifying the extension as *). There are four such files:

```
 Volume in drive B has no label
 Directory of  B:\

BANK      DOC        23  10-16-87   9:16a
BUDGET    JAN        23  10-16-87   9:16a
BUDGET    FEB        23  10-16-87   9:16a
BUDGET    MAR        23  10-16-87   9:16a
         4 File(s)   1210880 bytes free
```

To specify all files with the same extension, regardless of name, you replace the name with * . For example, to specify each file with the extension DOC, type:

```
B>dir *.doc
```

DOS displays just those entries:

```
 Volume in drive B has no label
 Directory of  B:\

REPORT    DOC        23  10-16-87   9:16a
BANK      DOC        23  10-16-87   9:16a
         2 File(s)   1210880 bytes free
```

Using the Question Mark Wildcard Character: ?

The question mark replaces only one character in a file name or extension. You'll probably use the asterisk more frequently, using the question mark only when one or two characters in the middle of a name or extension vary.

To see how the question mark works, type the following:

```
B>dir budget.?a?
```

This command specifies all files named BUDGET that have extensions beginning with any character, followed by the letter *a*, and ending with any character. DOS displays two entries:

```
 Volume in drive B has no label
 Directory of  B:\

BUDGET    JAN        23  10-16-87   9:16a
BUDGET    MAR        23  10-16-87   9:16a
         2 File(s)   1210800 bytes free
```

A Warning About Wildcard Characters

Be careful using wildcard characters with commands that can change files. Suppose you spent several days entering a year's worth of budget data into 12 files named BUDGET.JAN, BUDGET.FEB, BUDGET.MAR, and so on. On the same disk you also have three files you don't need named BUDGET.OLD, BUDGET.TST, and BUDGET.BAD. The disk is getting full, so you decide to delete the three unneeded files. It's 2 A.M., you're tired, and you're in a hurry, so you quickly type *erase budget.** and press Enter. You have told DOS to do more than you wanted.

You may realize immediately what you have done, or it may not dawn on you until you try to use one of the 12 good budget files and DOS replies *File not found.* You display the directory; there isn't a single file named BUDGET, because you told DOS to erase them all.

With commands that can change a file (Erase or Copy), use wildcard characters with extreme caution.

DISPLAYING DIRECTORY ENTRIES

As you have seen, the Directory command (dir) displays entries from the directory that DOS keeps on each disk. Each entry includes the name and extension of the file, its size in bytes, and the date and time it was created or last updated. You can use the Directory command to display all entries, or just the entries of selected files.

In the descriptions of the commands here and throughout the remaining chapters, you are shown the general form of the command—the name of the command and all its parameters—before you try the examples. If a parameter has an exact form, such as /W, the form is shown. If a parameter is something you specify, such as a file name, it is named and shown enclosed in angle brackets: for example, <filename>.

The Directory command has three qualifiers, or parameters: filename, /W, and /P. Written out, the command format, including the parameters, looks like this:

dir <filename> /W /P

When using the Directory command, if you:

- Include a <filename>, for example, *dir budget.jan,* DOS searches the disk in the current drive and displays the entry for that file. If DOS does not find the file, it displays *File not found.*
- Include both a drive letter and a <filename>, for example, *dir b:budget.jan,* DOS displays the directory entry for the file you specify from the disk in the drive you specify.
- Include a <filename> with wildcard characters, DOS displays the entries for all files whose name and extension match the wildcard characters; for example, you used *dir budget.** earlier to display the entries for BUDGET.JAN, BUDGET.FEB, and BUDGET.MAR.

- Omit a <filename>, but include a drive letter, for example, *dir b:*, DOS displays all the entries from the disk in the drive you specify.
- Omit a <filename>, for example, *dir*, DOS displays all directory entries on the disk in the current drive.

Because a list of directory entries can be quite long, the Directory command includes two parameters you can use to keep the list from scrolling off the screen:

- /W (Wide) tells DOS to display only the file names and extensions in five columns across the screen. This display contains less information than a complete directory listing, because it omits the file sizes, dates, and times, but it makes a long list of entries more compact.
- /P (Pause) tells DOS to display the entries one screenful at a time; a message at the bottom of the screen tells you to strike a key to continue.

Examples of Displaying Directory Entries

Because you have already used the Directory command several times, only the options are shown here. (Remember, if you're not using a fixed disk, type *a:* where the example shows *c:*. Also, if your system has only one diskette drive, DOS will prompt you several times to insert a diskette for drive A or drive B in the course of these examples. Just press Enter when DOS prompts you to put in the diskette.)

Displaying a Directory in Wide Format

If your system has only one diskette drive, remove the practice diskette and put in the DOS system diskette (the Operating diskette if you're using IBM's version 3.3). Now type the Directory command as follows:

```
B>dir a: /w
```

DOS arranges just the name and extension of each file in columns across the screen. (The following display shows the first three of the five columns.)

```
 Volume in drive A has no label
 Directory of  A:\

APPEND   EXE      ASSIGN   COM      ATTRIB   EXE...
BASICA   COM      CHKDSK   COM      COMMAND  COM...
DISKCOMP COM      DISKCOPY COM      EDLIN    COM...
GRAFTABL COM      GRAPHICS COM      JOIN     EXE...
PRINT    COM      RECOVER  COM      RESTORE  COM...
SUBST    EXE      TREE     COM      XCOPY    EXE...
MORTGAGE BAS
        31 File(s)      55296 bytes free
```

Remember, if you're using a different version of DOS, your display will be different.

Such a display doesn't contain as much information as the standard directory display, but it packs a lot of entries onto the screen. The wide format is particularly handy when all you want is a quick look at the names of the files on a crowded disk.

Pausing the Directory Display

To display the directory of the disk in drive A one screenful at a time by using the /P option, type:

```
B>dir a: /p
```

DOS displays the first 23 entries, then *Strike a key when ready . . .* To see the next screenful, press any key. This option lets you view the entire directory without using Ctrl-Num Lock to freeze the display periodically.

If your system has one diskette drive, replace the diskette in drive A with the practice diskette that contains the sample files you created earlier in this chapter.

DISPLAYING A FILE

Many of the files you use are text files, and there will be times when you want to check the contents of a file but don't need a printed copy. DOS gives you a quick way to see what's in a file: the Type command. (The name Type is a carryover from the days when most computers had only typewriter-like consoles.)

When you use the Type command, DOS displays the file without stopping; if the file is longer than one screenful and you want to read the entire file, freeze the display by pressing Ctrl-Num Lock.

The Type command has one parameter:

type <filename>

<filename> is the name of the file to be displayed. The Type command displays just one file at a time, so you can't use wildcard characters in the file name. If you do use a wildcard character, DOS displays *Invalid filename or file not found* and returns to command level. If the file you name doesn't exist, DOS displays *File not found* and, again, returns to command level.

An Example of Displaying a File

To display the file named REPORT.DOC on the diskette in the current drive, type:

```
B>type report.doc
```

DOS displays the file:

```
This is a dummy file.

B>
```

You'll probably use the Type command frequently to check your text files.

MAKING COPIES OF FILES

Just as you sometimes make copies of your paper files, you'll find yourself needing copies of your disk files.

You may want to share a file with a colleague who has a computer, you may want to alter the copy slightly to produce a different version, or you may want to store a copy for safekeeping. The Copy command can make a copy of a file on the same disk (with a different file name) or on a different disk (with any valid file name).

When used to make copies of files, the Copy command has two major parameters, <file1> and <file2>. The format of the Copy command is:

copy <file1> <file2>

<file1> is the name of the file to be copied (the *source* file) and <file2> is the name of the copy to be made (the *target* file). You can use wildcard characters to copy a set of files.

Note: Three additional, seldom-used parameters (/A, /B, and /V) are described in Appendix E, the DOS command reference.

When copying files, if you:

- Specify a <file1> that is not on the disk in the current drive and omit <file2>, DOS copies <file1> to the disk in the current drive and gives the copy the same name as the original. Example (if the current drive is B): *copy a:report.mar.*
- Specify only a drive letter as <file2>, the file is copied from the disk in the current drive to the disk in the drive you specify and is given the same name as <file1>. Example: *copy report.feb a:*
- Specify a <file1> that doesn't exist, DOS responds by displaying the file name you typed, followed by *File not found* and *0 File(s) copied*, and returns to command level.
- Specify a <file2> that doesn't exist, DOS creates it.
- Specify a <file2> that does exist, DOS replaces its contents with <file1>. This is the same as erasing the existing target file, so be careful not to give the target the same name as an existing file you want to keep.

The following practice session illustrates different ways to copy files; it also indicates the type of situation in which you might want to use each form of the command.

Examples of Copying Files

You want to change a document you already have on disk, but you want to keep the original, as well as the changed version. For example, to make a copy of the file REPORT.DOC on the same diskette and to name the copy RESULTS, type:

```
B>copy report.doc results
```

DOS acknowledges *1 File(s) copied.*

To verify that both files, REPORT.DOC and RESULTS, are on the diskette, display the directory by typing:

```
B>dir
```

DOS now shows seven files on the diskette:

```
 Volume in drive B has no label
 Directory of  B:\

REPORT   DOC        23  10-16-87   9:16a
REPORT   BAK        23  10-16-87   9:16a
BANK     DOC        23  10-16-87   9:16a
BUDGET   JAN        23  10-16-87   9:16a
BUDGET   FEB        23  10-16-87   9:16a
BUDGET   MAR        23  10-16-87   9:16a
RESULTS             23  10-16-87   9:27a
        7 File(s)    1210368 bytes free
```

Any time you want to verify the results of an example, use the Directory command to see what files are on the diskette.

Suppose you want to copy a file from another diskette and store it, under the same file name, on the diskette in the current drive.

For example, your current drive is drive B. To copy a file from drive A to the diskette in drive B, all you need to specify is the drive letter and name of the source file, because DOS assumes you want to copy the source file to the disk in the current drive and give the target file the same name.

The DOS diskette you use to start your system contains a number of external DOS command files, including FORMAT.COM, the file for the Format command. Copy FORMAT.COM to the disk in the current drive by typing the following:

```
B>copy a:format.com
```

If you have only one diskette drive, DOS prompts you to insert the diskette for drive A. Put in your copy of the system (or Startup) diskette and press Enter. DOS reads FORMAT.COM into memory, then prompts you to insert the diskette for drive B. Take out your copy of the system diskette and put the practice diskette back in.

DOS copies FORMAT.COM to the diskette in drive B and gives it the same name.

Now suppose you want to change a file and store the new version under the same file name and on the same diskette as the original, but be able to distinguish between the two versions. Simply make a copy of the file on the same diskette, with the same

file name but a different extension. You can use the asterisk wildcard character to tell DOS to use the same file name. For example, to make a copy of BUDGET.MAR and call it BUDGET.APR, type the following:

```
B>copy budget.mar *.apr
```

DOS acknowledges that it copied one file.

You have several files named REPORT stored on disk. Suppose you want to keep the originals, but make copies of them all for a new project; to avoid confusion, you want to give the copies a new file name but keep the same extension. For example, to make a copy of each file named REPORT, giving each copy the name FORECAST, type the following:

```
B>copy report.* forecast.*
```

DOS displays the name of each source file as it makes the copies:

```
REPORT.DOC
REPORT.BAK
        2 File(s) copied
```

You can copy all the files on a diskette by specifying the source file as `*.*` and specifying the target as just a drive letter. This procedure is not the same as copying the diskette with the Diskcopy command; the difference is explained under the heading ''Copying a Complete Diskette'' in Chapter 6, ''Managing Your Diskettes.''

In addition to the Copy command, versions 3.2 and 3.3 of DOS include two additional commands for copying files selectively: Replace, which lets you copy only files that already exist on the target disk; and Xcopy, which lets you copy only files that haven't been backed up. These commands are described in Chapter 9, ''Managing Your Fixed Disk.''

SENDING FILES TO DEVICES

In Chapter 4, you printed a file by using the Copy command to send a copy of the file to the printer. You can also send a copy of a file to any other output device. If, for example, you copy a file to a communications connection, or *port,* on the computer, the file goes to whatever device is attached to the port—such as a telecommunications line to another computer.

When it is used to send a copy of a file to an output device, the Copy command has two parameters:

copy <filename> <device>

<filename> is the name of the file to be sent; <device> is the name of the device to which the file is to be sent.

Be sure <device> exists. If you try to send a file to a device that doesn't exist or isn't ready, DOS might stop running. You won't hurt anything, but you'll have to restart the system.

An Example of Sending Files to a Device

To send a copy of each sample file with the extension DOC to the printer, make certain your printer is turned on and type:

```
B>copy *.doc prn
```

DOS displays the name of each file as it sends the file to the printer:

```
REPORT.DOC
BANK.DOC
FORECAST.DOC
        1 File(s) copied
```

The files are printed with no separation between them. DOS reports only one file copied because, in effect, only one output file was created: the printed copy of the three files.

COMBINING FILES

Sometimes, it's useful to combine several files. Perhaps you have several short documents, and you decide it would be easier and more convenient to work with one document that includes all the shorter ones. If you have several sets of files with similar names or extensions, you can combine each set into a new file, creating several new files. The Copy command lets you copy several files into a new file without destroying the original versions.

When it is used to combine files, the Copy command has two parameters:

copy <source> <target>

<source> represents the files to be combined. You can use wildcard characters to name the source files to be combined, or you can list several file names, separating them with a plus sign (+). If any file in the list doesn't exist, DOS goes on to the next name without telling you the file doesn't exist.

<target> represents the file that results from combining the source files. If you specify a target, DOS combines the source files into the target file. If you don't specify a target, DOS combines all the source files into the first source file in the <source> list, changing its contents.

Examples of Combining Files

Suppose you have two files you want to use as the basis for a single new file, but you want to keep the originals intact. For example, to combine the files BANK.DOC and REPORT.DOC into a new file named BANKRPT.DOC, type:

```
B>copy bank.doc+report.doc bankrpt.doc
```

DOS displays the names of the source files as it copies them:

```
BANK.DOC
REPORT.DOC
        1 File(s) copied
```

Again, DOS reports one file copied because the command created only one file.

You can copy several files into an existing file. To combine BUDGET.JAN, BUDGET.FEB, and BUDGET.MAR into the first file, BUDGET.JAN, type:

```
B>copy budget.jan+budget.feb+budget.mar
```

DOS displays the name of each source file as it copies:

```
BUDGET.JAN
BUDGET.FEB
BUDGET.MAR
        1 File(s) copied
```

Now, suppose you've been keeping monthly budget files. It's the end of the year. You still need separate monthly files for comparison with next year's figures, but right now, you want to work with all the files together. To combine all the files named BUDGET into a file named ANNUAL.BGT, type:

```
B>copy budget.* annual.bgt
```

DOS responds:

```
BUDGET.JAN
BUDGET.FEB
BUDGET.MAR
BUDGET.APR
        1 File(s) copied
```

Or, suppose you want to combine pairs of files with the same file names, but different extensions. You can combine them under the same file names, with new extensions, and end up with both the original and combined versions.

If you have entered all the examples, among the files on the diskette in drive B are REPORT.DOC and REPORT.BAK, FORECAST.DOC, and FORECAST.BAK. To combine each pair of files with the same name and the extensions DOC and BAK into a single file with the same name and the extension MIX, type:

```
B>copy *.bak+*.doc *.mix
```

DOS displays the names of the files as it copies them:

```
REPORT.BAK
REPORT.DOC
FORECAST.BAK
FORECAST.DOC
        2 File(s) copied
```

This time DOS reports two files copied because the command created two files: REPORT.MIX and FORECAST.MIX.

ERASING FILES

Just as you have to clean out a file drawer once in a while, you'll occasionally have to clear your disks of files you no longer need. The Erase command (you can type it either as *erase* or as *del*, for *delete*) erases one or more files from a disk.

The Erase command has one parameter:

erase <filename>

<filename> is the name of the file to be erased. If you use wildcard characters, DOS erases all files that match <filename>. If the file doesn't exist, DOS displays *File not found* and returns to command level.

Warning: Whenever you type an Erase command that uses wildcard characters, double-check the command on the screen before you press the Enter key, because you don't get a second chance. Make sure you have specified the correct drive letter (if necessary), file name, and extension; be certain that you know exactly which files will be erased and that you want all of them to be erased.

There is only one exception to this warning: If you tell DOS to erase all the files on a disk by typing erase *.* *, DOS prompts* Are you sure (Y/N)? *before erasing the files. DOS erases the files only if you respond* y.

Examples of Erasing Files

To erase the file named BUDGET.APR on the diskette in the current drive, type:

```
B>erase budget.apr
```

As soon as you press the Enter key, the file's gone.

To erase all files with an extension of BAK on the diskette in the current drive, type the following:

```
B>erase *.bak
```

DOS erases REPORT.BAK and FORECAST.BAK and displays the system prompt.

Remember, you don't get a second chance, so make sure you have typed the correct file name and the correct drive letter and extension (if they are necessary) whenever you use wildcard characters with the Erase command.

Be particularly careful when you use the question mark in a file extension. To see why, create two additional test files by typing:

```
B>copy results *.1
      1 File(s) copied

B>copy results *.12
      1 File(s) copied
```

This gives you three files with the same name but different extensions: RESULTS, RESULTS.1, and RESULTS.12. Now type a Directory command, using a single question mark as the extension. Before you press Enter, decide which files you believe DOS will list.

```
B>dir results.?
```

DOS lists two files:

```
 Volume in drive B has no label
 Directory of  B:\

RESULTS              23  10-16-87    9:27a
RESULTS  1           23  10-16-87    9:39a
     2 File(s)    1195008 bytes free
```

If you expected to see only RESULTS.1, the response to this Directory command is a surprise. If you had typed an Erase command, instead of a Directory command, the files you see listed are the files DOS would have erased. An unexpected directory listing can be momentarily confusing, but unintentionally erasing files is definitely an unpleasant surprise.

To erase both the files you just created but leave your original RESULTS file untouched, type the following command:

```
B>erase results.1?
```

Typing *1* as the first character of the extension ensures that the file RESULTS isn't affected. Note, however, that even though you included a question mark (which takes the place of a single character) after the 1, DOS erased RESULTS.1 as well as RESULTS.12. Be careful whenever you use wildcard characters with commands that change or erase files.

CHANGING FILE NAMES

There will be times when you want to change the name of a file. You might simply change your mind, or perhaps you'll have changed the contents of a file so much that you want to give it a name that more closely describes its new contents. The Rename command changes a file's name or extension, or both. You can use wildcard characters to rename a set of files.

The Rename command has two parameters:

rename <oldname> <newname>

<oldname> is the name of an existing file. If the file doesn't exist, DOS displays *Duplicate file name or File not found* and returns to command level.

<newname> is the name you want to give to the file specified by <oldname>. If there is already a file with the new name, DOS displays *Duplicate file name or File not*

found and returns to command level. Two files on the same disk can't have the same name, and DOS would have to erase the existing file to carry out the command, so this built-in safeguard keeps you from inadvertently erasing one file in the process of renaming another.

You can abbreviate the Rename command as *ren.*

The Rename command simply changes the name of a file; it doesn't copy a file to a different disk. Both the old name and the new name must refer to the same drive. If you specify a drive letter with the new name, DOS responds *Invalid parameter.*

Examples of Changing File Names

To change the name of the file ANNUAL.BGT to FINAL on the disk in the current drive, type:

```
B>ren annual.bgt final
```

DOS changes the name and displays the system prompt.

To change the extension of the file BUDGET.MAR from MAR to 003, on the disk in the current drive, you can use the * wildcard character for the new file name. Type the following:

```
B>ren budget.mar *.003
```

The file is now named BUDGET.003.

To change the extension DOC to TXT for all files on the disk in the current drive, use the * for both the old and new file names. Type the following:

```
B>ren *.doc *.txt
```

Verify this change with the Directory command by typing:

```
B>dir *.txt
```

DOS shows four files, all of which used to have the extension DOC:

```
 Volume in drive B has no label
 Directory of  B:\

REPORT   TXT       23  10-16-87   9:16a
BANK     TXT       23  10-16-87   9:16a
FORECAST TXT       23  10-16-87   9:16a
BANKRPT  TXT       47  10-16-87  10:51a
        4 File(s)   1196032 bytes free
```

If you use the Directory command now to display the entries of all files with the extension DOC, DOS responds *File not found.*

PREPARING FOR THE REMAINING EXAMPLES

The remaining examples in this chapter show you how to use some external DOS commands. These commands are on your fixed disk, if you're using one, or on the DOS diskette in drive A. Before continuing with the examples, you must enable DOS to find the command files it needs.

If you're using a fixed disk, change the current drive to C by typing:

```
B>c:
```

and leave your practice diskette in drive B.

If you're not using a fixed disk, change the current drive to A by typing:

```
B>a:
```

and leave your practice diskette in drive B. If you're using IBM's version 3.3 on 5.25-inch diskettes, verify that the Operating diskette is in drive A.

Now the current drive is the one containing the command files DOS will need to carry out your requests, and drive B contains the diskette with the files on which DOS will act. To tell DOS where to find the practice files, you'll preface their file names with the drive letter, *b:*.

CONTROLLING WHETHER A FILE CAN BE CHANGED

Your disks will contain many files. Some, such as program files (including DOS, application programs, and programs you write yourself), you will seldom, if ever, erase. Although you probably have backup copies, some of these files may exist only on your working disks; erasing them could represent a serious loss.

Similarly, you will probably have other files, such as spreadsheets, for periodic calculations or reports, and word-processing style sheets or form letters, that you seldom change. Because these files can represent a significant investment of time and information, inadvertently changing them could also be a serious loss.

The Attribute (attrib) command lets you protect yourself from inadvertently erasing or changing a file. You do this by making the file *read-only,* which means that you (or anyone else using the file) can read it but cannot erase or change it. Before a read-only file can be changed or erased, the protection must be removed, again with the Attribute command.

Because you can affect the read-only status of a file with only one command, it's easy to temporarily protect files that may change later—the most recent version of a text file or spreadsheet, for example. This protection can be particularly useful if someone else is going to use the same disk or computer you do.

When used to control the read-only status of a file, the Attribute command has three parameters:

attrib +R –R <filename>

+R tells DOS to make <filename> read-only—that is, to deny all attempts to change or erase <filename>.

–R tells DOS to let <filename> be changed or erased.

<filename> is the name of the file whose read-only status is to be affected. If you enter the command with the <filename> only, DOS displays the name of the file and, if the file is read-only, displays an R to the left of the file name. You can check or change the read-only status of a series of files by using wildcard characters.

The display of the Directory command doesn't show whether a file is read-only; you must use the Attribute command.

Note: If you're using version 3.3 of DOS, you can use the Attribute command to affect the read-only status of groups of files stored in units called subdirectories. *(Subdirectories, and this use of the Attribute command, are described in Chapter 8, "A Tree of Files.") In addition, if you're using version 3.2 or 3.3 of DOS, you can also use the Attribute command to control the* archive *status of a file, which controls how the file is treated by the Backup and Xcopy commands, which you use to make archive copies of your files. (This use of the Attribute command is described in Chapter 9, "Managing Your Fixed Disk," as are the Backup and Xcopy commands.)*

Example of Controlling Whether a File Can Be Changed

Type the following command to tell DOS to display the status of the files with the extension TXT on the disk in the current drive:

```
C>attrib b:*.txt
```

DOS responds:

```
A        B:\REPORT.TXT
A        B:\BANK.TXT
A        B:\FORECAST.TXT
A        B:\BANKRPT.TXT
```

None of the file names are preceded by an R; this tells you none is read-only.

If you're not using version 3.2 or 3.3 of DOS, your display doesn't include the *A* to the left of each file name, and you can safely skip the rest of this paragraph. If you do see the *A*, the letter shows that the file's archive status is on; this means that the file has not been backed up by the Backup command or copied by the Xcopy command since it was created or last changed. The importance and use of a file's archive status is described in Chapter 9, "Managing Your Fixed Disk."

To make BANK.TXT read-only, type:

```
C>attrib +r b:bank.txt
```

DOS responds by displaying the system prompt. Now, when you check the status again, DOS shows that BANK.TXT is read-only. Type the following:

```
C>attrib b:*.txt

  A       B:\REPORT.TXT
  A    R  B:\BANK.TXT
  A       B:\FORECAST.TXT
  A       B:\BANKRPT.TXT
```

If you try to erase BANK.TXT, DOS displays an error message:

```
C>erase b:bank.txt
Access denied
```

The result would be the same if you edited the file with a word processor; when you tried to store the revised version, DOS would issue the error message. You could, however, save the revised version with a different name.

Remove the read-only protection and verify that it is gone by typing:

```
C>attrib -r b:bank.txt

C>attrib b:bank.txt

  A       B:\BANK.TXT
```

COMPARING FILES

Note: Some versions of DOS prior to version 3 do not include the Compare command. If you're not sure whether you have this command, check your DOS diskettes for the command file by typing dir comp.com. *If you don't have the Compare command, you have a similar command named FC (for* File Compare*); it is described in Appendix E.*

Sometimes you'll want to know whether two files are exactly the same. Suppose you have two files named BUDGET on different disks. They're the same length, but are they different budgets, or two copies of the same one? You could display or print both files and compare them, but that could take quite a while and you still might miss some small difference. It's quicker and more accurate to use Compare (comp).

The Compare command has two parameters:

comp <file1> <file2>

<file1> and <file2> are the file names of the files to be compared. If you omit <file2>, DOS prompts you for it. If you omit both <file1> and <file2>, DOS prompts you for both.

If the files are different lengths, DOS displays *Files are different sizes* and asks you if you want to compare any more files. If the files are the same length, the Compare command compares them byte-by-byte. If the files are identical, DOS tells you so by displaying *Files compare ok.*

If the files are the same length but DOS finds a difference, DOS displays a message that shows the characters that differ, and how far each is from the beginning of the file. If DOS finds 10 mismatches, it displays *10 Mismatches - ending compare*, and asks if you want to compare any more files.

Examples of Comparing Files

To compare REPORT.TXT with BUDGET.FEB, type:

```
C>comp b:report.txt b:budget.feb
```

The files are identical, so DOS replies as follows:

```
B:REPORT.TXT and B:BUDGET.FEB

Eof mark not found

Files compare ok

Compare more files (Y/N)? _
```

Don't be concerned by *Eof mark not found*—DOS is simply telling you that it didn't include your end-of-file indicator (^Z) as a character in the files. Type *y* to tell DOS you want to compare more files. DOS prompts you for the names of the files. To compare REPORT.TXT with REPORT.MIX, type the file names as follows:

```
Enter primary file name
b:report.txt

Enter 2nd file name or drive id
b:report.mix
```

DOS determines that the two files are different lengths, and it doesn't even begin to compare them:

```
B:REPORT.TXT and B:REPORT.MIX

Files are different sizes

Compare more files (Y/N)? _
```

Type *n* and DOS returns to command level.

You can use wildcard characters to compare two sets of files with one command. To compare all files with the extension TXT and all files with the same file name but the extension MIX, type the following:

```
C>comp b:*.txt b:*.mix
```

There are four files with the extension TXT, but only two with the extension MIX. DOS tells you which files don't exist and which ones it tried to compare:

```
B:REPORT.TXT and B:REPORT.MIX

Files are different sizes

B:BANK.TXT and B:BANK.MIX

B:BANK.MIX - File not found

B:FORECAST.TXT and B:FORECAST.MIX

Files are different sizes

B:BANKRPT.TXT and B:BANKRPT.MIX

B:BANKRPT.MIX - File not found

Compare more files (Y/N)? _
```

Type *n* to return DOS to command level.

Because all the sample files are identical, you'll have to create one that is different, but still the same length (23 bytes), to see how DOS notifies you about differences. To create a different file, named DIFF, type the following:

```
C>copy con b:diff
This is not the same.
^Z
        1 File(s) copied
```

Now compare REPORT.TXT with DIFF by typing:

```
C>comp b:report.txt b:diff
```

DOS quickly finds and reports 10 errors:

```
B:REPORT.TXT and B:DIFF

Compare error at OFFSET 8
File 1 = 61

File 2 = 6E

Compare error at OFFSET 9
File 1 = 20

File 2 = 6F

Compare error at OFFSET A
File 1 = 64

File 2 = 74
```

```
Compare error at OFFSET B
File 1 = 75

File 2 = 20

Compare error at OFFSET C
File 1 = 6D

File 2 = 74

Compare error at OFFSET D
File 1 = 6D

File 2 = 68

Compare error at OFFSET E
File 1 = 79

File 2 = 65

Compare error at OFFSET 10
File 1 = 66

File 2 = 73

Compare error at OFFSET 11
File 1 = 69

File 2 = 61

Compare error at OFFSET 12
File 1 = 6C

File 2 = 6D

10 Mismatches - ending compare

Compare more files (Y/N)? _
```

Type *n* to return DOS to command level.

The messages that show the differing characters and their locations use numbers that are combinations of the digits 0 through 9 and the letters A through F. These characters are from the base-16 number system usually called *hexadecimal,* in which A through F are used to represent the decimal numbers 10 through 15. If you must know what the differing characters are or must calculate their exact locations, you need a chart of the American Standard Code for Information Interchange (ASCII), which shows how characters are encoded, and you need a guide to hexadecimal arithmetic. The manuals that came with your computer might contain both. In addition, the book *Supercharging MS-DOS* (Microsoft Press, 1986) describes both the ASCII code and hexadecimal numbers.

PRINTING FILES

You can print files at the same time you're using the computer to do other things. The Print command keeps a list—called the *print queue*—of files to be printed, and it prints the files in the order in which they appear in the queue. The print queue normally can hold up to 10 files.

In addition to printing files, the Print command lets you change two characteristics of its operation: the size of the print queue and the printer that DOS uses. For a description of these uses of the Print command, see "Changing Operation of the Print Command" later in this chapter.

Because the computer can really do only one thing at a time, DOS prints when nothing else is happening, such as when you pause to think between keystrokes. You'll notice that printing slows and sometimes even stops when something else is going on—especially when DOS is using a disk drive.

You use the Print command to add a file to the print queue, delete a file from the queue, cancel all printing, and display the names of the files in the queue. When used to print a file, the Print command has four parameters:

print <filename> /P /C /T

<filename> is the name of the file to be added to or deleted from the print queue. You can enter more than one file name with a Print command; just type the list of file names, separating each from the next with a blank.

/P (for *print*) tells DOS to add <filename> to the print queue. DOS assumes this parameter if all you specify is <filename>.

/C (for *cancel*) tells DOS to remove <filename> from the print queue. If the file is being printed, printing stops and the paper is advanced to the top of the next page.

/T (for *terminate*) stops all printing. If a file is being printed, printing stops and the paper is advanced to the top of the next page. All files are removed from the print queue.

If you enter the Print command with no parameters, DOS displays the list of files in the print queue.

Examples of Printing a File

DOS advances the paper to the next page each time it prints a new file, so the examples here use several sheets of printer paper. Check what each example does before you try it, so that you can be ready to stop the printing process. You'll save both time and paper. First, a bit of preparation.

Most of the sample files you created in this chapter consist of a single line and would print too quickly for you to try using all the Print parameters in the following examples. Increase the size of the file REPORT.TXT using Edlin, the DOS text editor (it's described in Chapters 11 and 12). Type the following lines:

```
C>edlin b:report.txt
End of input file
*1,1,2,99c
*e
```

The Edlin command copies the first (and only) line 99 times, so REPORT.TXT now consists of 100 identical lines.

Command files don't contain printable characters, so erase FORMAT.COM from the diskette in drive B by typing the following (don't forget the *b:*):

```
C>erase b:format.com
```

Finally, make sure the printer is turned on and that the paper is adjusted to the top of a page. This completes the preparation for the Print command examples.

To print the file REPORT.TXT, type:

```
C>print b:report.txt
```

The first time you enter the Print command after starting the system, DOS prompts you for the name of the printer to use:

```
Name of list device [PRN]: _
```

The brackets around PRN mean that DOS will use the device named PRN if you press the Enter key. Unless you have more than one printer attached to your system, or you are using a printer with a serial interface, just press the Enter key. If you have never printed with your printer, press the Enter key.

When you respond to the prompt, DOS loads the Print command file, named PRINT.COM, from the system disk and keeps it in memory until you either turn the system off or restart DOS. Depending on your version of DOS, PRINT.COM increases the amount of memory that DOS uses by as much as 5600 bytes. DOS reports that the program is loaded:

```
Resident part of PRINT installed
```

and it displays the names and print status of the files in the print queue:

```
    B:\REPORT.TXT is currently being printed
```

There is one file in the print queue (REPORT.TXT), and it's now being printed.

When you printed a file in Chapter 4 by copying it to the printer, DOS didn't display the system prompt—and you couldn't use the system—until the file had been printed. This time, the system prompt returned as soon as printing started. As soon as DOS starts printing a file with the Print command, DOS is ready to accept another command from you.

Note: If you're using a laser printer, or if your computer is part of a network, the following descriptions of the /C and /T parameters don't apply. Check the network or laser printer manual to see how to stop printing a file or, in the case of a network, delete files from its print queue. The laser printer doesn't beep or advance to the next page at the times described in the following paragraphs. You may have to push the buttons labeled ON LINE *and* FORM FEED *to clear the page from the printer; check the manual for instructions. Laser printers are also very fast, so you may just prefer to skip these examples.*

If you decide you don't want to print a file after all, you can remove it from the print queue with the /C parameter; type the following command while REPORT.TXT is being printed:

```
C>print b:report.txt /c
```

DOS stops printing the file and prints the following message on the page:

```
File B:\REPORT.TXT Canceled by operator
```

It then advances the paper to the next page and beeps.

You can put more than one file in the print queue with a single Print command. To tell DOS to print both REPORT.TXT and BUDGET.JAN, type:

```
C>print b:report.txt b:budget.jan
```

DOS starts printing REPORT.TXT and displays the print queue:

```
B:\REPORT.TXT is currently being printed
B:\BUDGET.JAN is in queue
```

If you want to stop printing entirely, you can remove all files from the print queue with the /T parameter. Type the following, again while REPORT.TXT is being printed:

```
C>print /t
```

DOS stops printing the current file, prints *All files canceled by operator* at the point where it stopped printing, advances the paper to the next page, removes all remaining files from the queue, and beeps. It displays a terse acknowledgment:

```
PRINT queue is empty
```

You can also put several files in the print queue at once by using wildcard characters. To print all the files whose extension is TXT, type:

```
C>print b:*.txt
```

Now DOS tells you that there are four files in the queue:

```
B:\BANK.TXT is currently being printed
B:\REPORT.TXT is in queue
B:\FORECAST.TXT is in queue
B:\BANKRPT.TXT is in queue
```

DOS prints the files in the order shown. Stop all printing again by typing:

```
C>print /t
```

Again, DOS stops printing the current file, prints the cancellation message, advances the paper to the next page, beeps, removes all remaining files from the queue, and acknowledges on the screen *PRINT queue is empty.*

The following example uses several sheets of paper. If you are not using continuous form paper or an automatic sheet feeder, you shouldn't try this example, because it might print on the platen of your printer. Skip to the heading "Changing Operation of the Print Command."

The print queue normally holds up to 10 files. To fill it, tell DOS to print all the files on the diskette in drive B; there are 13 files, so DOS puts the first 10 in the queue. Type the following:

```
C>print b:*.*
```

DOS tells you the queue is full and displays the list of files in the queue:

```
PRINT queue is full

        B:\REPORT.BAK is currently being printed
        B:\DIFF is in queue
        B:\BANK.TXT is in queue
        B:\BUDGET.JAN is in queue
        B:\BUDGET.FEB is in queue
        B:\BUDGET.003 is in queue
        B:\RESULTS is in queue
        B:\REPORT.TXT is in queue
        B:\FORECAST.TXT is in queue
        B:\BANKRPT.TXT is in queue
```

You really don't need to print all these files. Stop all printing by typing:

```
C>print /t
```

DOS empties the queue and alerts you as before:

```
PRINT queue is empty
```

Changing Operation of the Print Command

DOS initially limits the print queue to 10 files, but you can increase the size of the queue and can also tell DOS to use a printer other than the standard printer, PRN (more details on printers are in Chapter 7, "Managing Your Devices").

You can change Print command operations only the first time you use the Print command during a session at your computer; if you try to use these options again before restarting DOS or turning the computer off, DOS displays the message *Invalid parameter* and ignores the command.

When used to change the size of the print queue or the name of the printer, the Print command has two parameters:

print /D:<printer> /Q:<size>

/D:<printer> tells DOS to use the printer named <printer>. If you omit /D:<printer>, DOS uses the standard printer named PRN.

/Q:<size> tells DOS the number of files the print queue can hold; the maximum number is 32. If you omit /Q:<size>, the print queue holds 10 files.

If you wanted to increase the size of the print queue to 15 files, you would type *print /q:15*. If you wanted to tell DOS to use the printer named LPT2, you would type *print /d:lpt2*. You can combine the /D and /Q parameters in the same Print command, but you cannot combine them with other parameters unless you are entering the Print command for the first time since starting DOS.

The Print command lets you print text files without losing the use of your system during printing; it can make both you and your system more productive.

Several infrequently used parameters that give you more precise control over how the print program interacts with DOS are described in Appendix E.

CHAPTER 6

MANAGING YOUR DISKETTES

Diskettes are the computer's filing cabinets. Managing your computer filing system includes not only keeping track of your files, as described in the previous chapter, but also taking care of your diskettes. There are many ways to prepare and store information on diskettes; the concepts underlying diskette handling, however, apply to all microcomputers.

Several DOS commands deal with entire diskettes, not with individual files. For example, you must prepare a new diskette for use; this process is called formatting (or, less commonly, initializing). Or, if you need an exact copy of a diskette, you don't copy each file separately; you copy the entire diskette with one command.

This chapter suggests ways to handle your diskettes, briefly describes how DOS stores files on diskettes, and shows you how to do the following:

- Prepare a diskette for use with the Format command.
- Create another system diskette with the Format command.
- Duplicate a diskette with the Diskcopy command.
- Compare the contents of two diskettes with the Diskcomp command.
- Analyze and report on the use of diskette storage space with the Check Disk command.
- Assign, change, or delete the volume label (identifying name) of a disk with the Label command.
- Display the volume label of a disk with the Volume command.

The Label and Volume commands can be used with either diskettes or a fixed disk. Two additional commands, Backup and Restore, can also be used with diskettes or a fixed disk to make backup copies of files and to restore them if they're needed. Because Backup and Restore are typically used to deal with the files on a fixed disk, these commands are described in Chapter 9, ''Managing Your Fixed Disk.''

HANDLING DISKETTES

Diskettes are remarkably durable, especially the 3.5-inch type in a hard plastic shell. The useful life of diskettes depends on how often you use them, of course, but even more important is how you treat them. Handle your diskettes with the same care you use when handling valuable recording tapes or photographs:

- Avoid touching the diskette surfaces that show through the openings in the protective jacket. Dirt, fingerprints, or dust can shorten the life of a diskette and can damage or destroy the data.

- Keep diskettes away from magnets and other sources of magnetic influence, such as telephones, electric motors, and television sets.
- Keep food and drinks away from diskettes. The same goes for cigarettes, cigars, pipes, and ashtrays.
- Don't fold, spindle, or mutilate diskettes. Don't pile other objects on them.
- Don't write on diskette labels with a pencil, ballpoint pen, or other sharp instrument; use a felt-tipped marker.
- Store your diskettes in a safe place when you're not using them. Protect them from extreme heat or cold, humidity, or contact with other objects.

Many products are available for storing diskettes, including plastic boxes, vinyl pockets that fit a three-ring binder, and hanging file folders. All offer good protection; they aren't necessary, but they make it easier for you to store your diskettes safely, rather than leaving them scattered around your desk.

Although an office is a mild environment compared to a factory or a shop floor, data on a diskette can be damaged by such innocuous objects as a paper clip that has been stored in a magnetic paper-clip holder, a magnetized letter opener, an electric pencil sharpener, or a telephone-answering machine. If you put a letter down on top of a diskette lying on your desk, it's all too easy to put a hot coffee cup or heavy object on the letter without realizing that the diskette is underneath.

The safest places for a diskette are in the computer and in protective storage. Information and time are two of your most valuable assets: A damaged diskette can cost you both, so protect your diskettes accordingly.

BACK UP YOUR DISKETTES

Even though you treat your diskettes with care, they can still be mislaid or damaged by accident, files can be inadvertently changed or erased, and eventually diskettes simply wear out. Making backup copies of your diskettes limits the amount of information and time you lose if something goes wrong. The time it takes to make these copies could be one of your better investments.

Unless a program diskette is copy protected so that you cannot duplicate the original, make a copy of the program before you ever use it—even if you plan to install the program on your fixed disk. Store the original diskette in a safe place, and use the copy. If something happens to the copy, make another copy from the original. Always keep the original stored safely.

Your collection of data files will grow as you use application programs, such as a word processor or spreadsheet. Back up a data diskette whenever the value of the information it contains—or the time it would take to re-create it—is greater than the value of a blank diskette and the few minutes it takes to make a copy.

As you found in Chapter 2, when you copied the DOS diskettes, it's easy to make a backup copy of a diskette. Keep your backup copies in a safe place and use your computer with the comforting thought that, should something unforeseen happen, you're protected.

HOW INFORMATION IS STORED ON A DISKETTE

Information is stored on a diskette much as music or video is recorded on tape. A description of how DOS uses a diskette helps you understand the commands you use to manage your diskettes.

What Is a Diskette?

What we call a diskette actually consists of two parts: a disk of thin plastic coated with magnetic material, and a protective plastic jacket or hard shell. Figure 6-1 shows a 5.25-inch diskette in its flexible jacket, and Figure 6-2 shows both the front and back of a 3.5-inch diskette in its hard shell.

The dashed lines in Figures 6-1 and 6-2 show how the coated disk lies inside the protective jacket. The magnetic coating itself is visible through the openings in the jacket of a 5.25-inch diskette (shaded in Figure 6-1). The spring-loaded shutter that normally covers the opening in a 3.5-inch diskette is moved aside by the diskette drive to provide access to the magnetic coating. The hole in the center of the disk goes around the drive motor, which spins the disk so that data can be written (recorded) or read (played back).

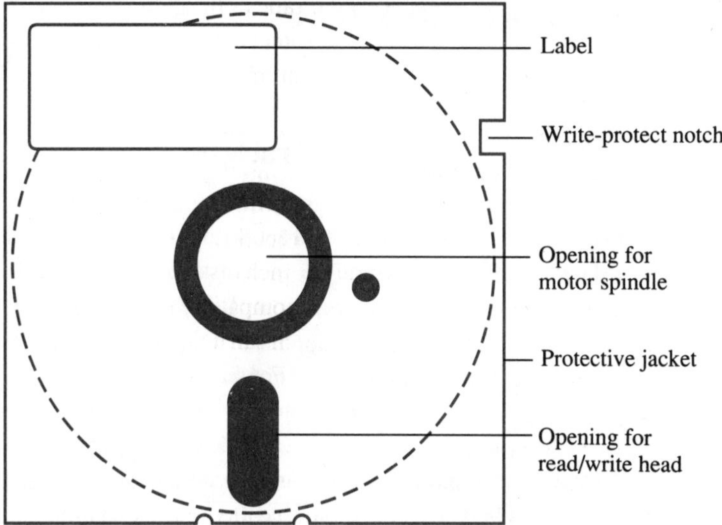

Figure 6-1. A 5.25-inch diskette

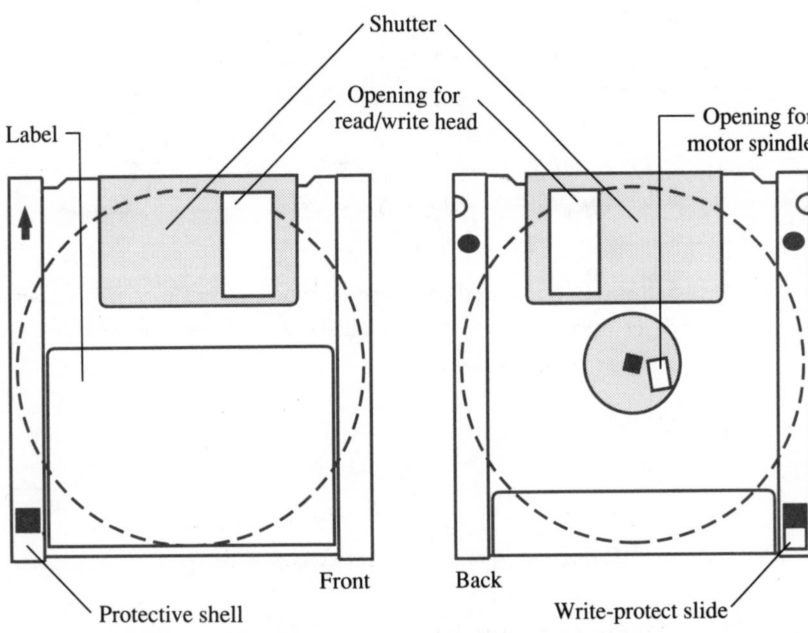

Figure 6-2. A 3.5-inch diskette

The write-protect notch or slide lets you protect all the files on a diskette from being erased or changed. To protect a 5.25-inch diskette, cover the write-protect notch with one of the small tabs of tape included with the box of diskettes. To protect a 3.5-inch diskette, move the write-protect slide up (toward the center of the diskette) until the hole through the diskette shell is covered. To permit files on the diskette to be changed or erased, remove the tape or move the slide down. Protect your DOS diskettes by covering the write-protect notch—protect each of your application program diskettes, too, unless the application program manual tells you otherwise.

How Does DOS Keep Track of Files?

Information is recorded on a diskette in narrow concentric circles called *tracks*; there are 40 such tracks on a standard 360-kilobyte (360 K) diskette and 80 tracks on the high-capacity 5.25-inch and 3.5-inch diskettes used on the IBM PC/AT, IBM PC Convertible, IBM PS/2 models, and compatible systems. A track is divided into smaller areas called *sectors,* each of which can hold 512 bytes. Figure 6-3 shows how tracks and sectors are laid out on a diskette. For simplicity, the illustration shows only four tracks.

The side, track, and sector numbers of the beginning of a file are stored as part of the directory entry for the file. You don't see this information when you use the Directory command, but DOS can find any sector on a diskette by its side, track, and sector numbers, just as you can find any seat in a stadium or a theater by its section, row, and seat numbers.

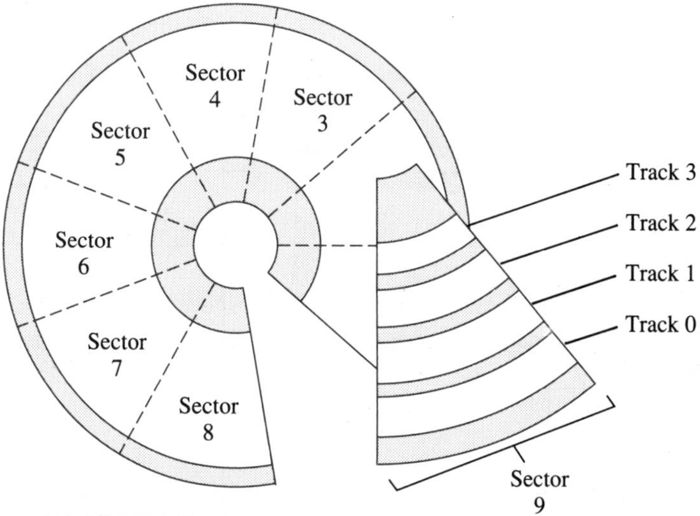

Figure 6-3. Tracks and sectors on a diskette

Diskette Capacity

Tracks on a standard diskette are numbered 0 through 39 (making 40 in all); sectors are numbered 1 through 9, for a total of 360 sectors (40 tracks times 9 sectors per track) on each side. Most personal computers that run DOS have double-sided drives, which use both sides of a diskette, but some earlier models had single-sided drives that used only one side. A standard double-sided (or 360 K) diskette has an actual capacity of 368,640 bytes (though not all of it is available for files); a single-sided (or 180 K) diskette has a capacity of 184,320 bytes.

The high-capacity 5.25-inch diskettes used on the IBM PC/AT and compatible systems have 80 tracks (numbered 0 through 79), each of which has 15 sectors. A sector still stores 512 bytes, so the two sides of a high-capacity (or 1.2 MB) diskette can hold 1,228,800 bytes.

The 3.5-inch diskettes used on the IBM PS/2 computers and compatible systems are also double-sided diskettes with 80 tracks per side. Depending on disk capacity, however, they have either 9 or 18 sectors per track—again with 512 bytes per sector. The 9-sectored (or 720 K) diskettes can hold 737,280 bytes; the 18-sectored (or 1.44 MB) diskettes can hold 1,474,560 bytes.

Volume Label

Any disk can be assigned a name, or *volume label,* to identify its contents. The volume label can be up to 11 characters long, and you can use the same characters allowed in a file name, plus a space. DOS stores the volume label on the disk and displays it when you use the Directory, Check Disk, Label, or Volume commands. The volume label is for identification only; you can't use it in a command to specify a disk.

PREPARING FOR THE EXAMPLES

The examples in this chapter require one diskette that doesn't contain any files you want to keep (the examples erase any data on the diskette). Put the diskette in your diskette drive; if you have two diskette drives, put the diskette in drive B.

PREPARING A DISKETTE FOR USE

As you've seen, the Format command prepares a diskette for use. The diskette can be either new or previously formatted. However, formatting erases any existing files, so be certain not to format a diskette that contains files you need.

In carrying out the Format command, DOS also checks for flaws on the recording surface of the diskette and marks any bad sectors so they won't be used. After formatting, DOS displays a message that tells you the maximum number of bytes the diskette can hold, how many bytes (if any) are defective, and how many bytes are available for storing files.

DOS knows whether drives are single sided or double sided, standard or high capacity, and formats the diskette accordingly. If you are using high-capacity drives, you can tell DOS to format, read, and write 360 K double-sided diskettes, but the diskettes you prepare in this way can be used only in another high-capacity drive; the tracks are too narrow to be read reliably by a standard double-sided drive.

Depending on the type of 5.25-inch diskette drive you have, DOS formats diskettes for 9 or 15 sectors per track. If your diskette drive normally formats 360 K diskettes, however, you can tell it to format a diskette with eight sectors per track so the diskette can be used with any version of DOS.

The Format command reserves space on the diskette for the directory, thus reducing the amount of storage available for files. Because the directories of single-sided and double-sided diskettes are different sizes, and because early versions of DOS created only eight (rather than nine) sectors per track, the storage capacity of your diskettes depends on both the type of diskette drive and the version of DOS you use. Figure 6-4, on the next page, shows the number of bytes available for all combinations of drives and number of sectors per track.

Format Command Parameters

When used to prepare a non-system (data) diskette, the Format command has five parameters:

format <drive> /V /1 /4 /8

<drive> is the letter, followed by a colon, of the drive that contains the diskette to be formatted (such as *b:*). With version 3.1 or earlier, if you omit <drive>, DOS formats the diskette in the current drive. If you're using version 3.2 or 3.3 and omit <drive>, DOS responds *Drive letter must be specified* and returns to the system prompt.

Size	Sides	Tracks per Side	Sectors per Track	Total Capacity	Available for Files	System Where Used
3.5"	2	80	18	1,474,560 (1.44 MB)	1,457,664	IBM PS/2 (except Model 30); DOS version 3.3 only
5.25"	2	80	15	1,228,800 (1.2 MB)	1,213,952	IBM PC/AT and compatibles; DOS version 3 only
3.5"	2	80	9	737,280 (720 K)	730,112	IBM PS/2 Model 30, IBM PC Convertible, and compatibles; DOS versions 3.2 and later
5.25"	2	40	9	368,640 (360 K)	362,496	IBM PC, PC/XT, and compatibles; DOS versions 2 and 3 only
5.25"	2	40	8	327,680 (320 K)	322,560	IBM PC, PC/XT, and compatibles; DOS versions 1, 2, and 3
5.25"	1	40	9	184,320 (180 K)	179,712	IBM PC, PC/XT, and compatibles; DOS versions 1, 2, and 3
5.25"	1	40	8	163,840 (160 K)	160,256	IBM PC, PC/XT, and compatibles; DOS versions 1, 2, and 3

Figure 6-4. Storage capacity of different diskettes

/V tells DOS you want to give the diskette a volume label.

/1 formats only one side of a diskette in a standard 360 K double-sided drive.

/4 formats only nine sectors per track on a double-sided diskette in a high-capacity drive.

/8 formats eight sectors per track.

Versions 3.2 and 3.3 require that you specify a drive letter, even if you want to format the disk in the current drive. Version 3.3 also adds parameters that let you format a diskette with less than its maximum capacity. You probably won't need this capability very often, so these parameters aren't described here, but they are included in the Format command description in Appendix E, the DOS command reference.

Warning: If you're not *using version 3.2 or 3.3 and you type a Format command without specifying a drive letter, DOS formats the disk in the current drive. If the current drive is a diskette drive that contains your system disk and you haven't covered the write-protect notch, DOS erases every file on your system diskette. If the current drive is a fixed disk, formatting erases every file on it: not just the DOS files, but every program and data file you have stored. Although newer versions of DOS provide some protection against inadvertently formatting the wrong disk, the consequences are severe enough that you should be certain you know which disk is going to be formatted before you press the Enter key after typing a Format command.*

Examples of Preparing a Diskette

If you're not using a fixed disk, your system prompt is A>, not C>, as shown in the examples. This difference has no effect on what you type or how DOS responds, so follow the examples as printed; just remember the difference in the system prompt.

Format the diskette in drive B and give it a volume label by typing the following:

```
C>format b: /v
```

DOS asks you to put the diskette in drive B:

```
Insert new diskette for drive B:
and strike ENTER when ready_
```

Make sure the right diskette is in the drive, then press Enter.

If you're using version 3.1 or an earlier version, DOS displays *Formatting...* while it formats the disk. If you're using version 3.2 or 3.3, DOS displays *Head: 0 Cylinder: 0* and changes the head and cylinder numbers to show you its progress (*cylinder* is another way of referring to a track).

When DOS has formatted the diskette, it displays *Format complete* and prompts you for the volume label:

```
Volume label (11 characters, ENTER for none)? _
```

Name this diskette DOSDISK by typing the following:

```
dosdisk
```

DOS displays the report of available storage on the diskette and asks if you want to format another. Reply *n*.

Display the directory of the disk: It's empty, but you can see the volume label on the first line.

```
C>dir b:

Volume in drive B is DOSDISK
Directory of  B:\

File not found
```

MAKING ANOTHER SYSTEM DISKETTE

You used the Diskcopy command to make backup copies of the DOS diskettes. The copies contained exactly the same files as the original. Sometimes, however, to leave room for a large application program, you might need a system diskette that doesn't include all the DOS command files.

You could copy your system diskette and erase the files you don't need, but there's a simpler way: The /S option of the Format command formats a diskette and copies the files that must be on a system diskette. These include COMMAND.COM and three hidden files that are necessary for DOS to operate and must be stored in specific locations on the diskette. A system diskette created in this way contains none of the command files for the DOS external commands, such as Format, but you can use this diskette to start DOS and to use any of the internal commands, such as the Directory command.

COPYING A COMPLETE DISKETTE

The Diskcopy command makes an exact duplicate of any diskette, including the hidden and system files on a system diskette. If the target diskette isn't formatted, IBM's version of DOS formats it before copying; Diskcopy in other versions of DOS may require formatted diskettes. Diskcopy works only with diskettes; you cannot use it to copy to or from a fixed disk.

The Diskcopy command has three parameters:

diskcopy <source> <target> /1

<source> is the letter, followed by a colon, of the drive that contains the diskette to be copied (such as *a:*).

<target> is the letter, followed by a colon, of the drive that contains the diskette that is to receive the copy (such as *b:*).

If you omit <target>, DOS copies from the diskette in <source> to the diskette in the current drive; if you omit <target> and you specify the current drive as <source>, DOS assumes you want to use only the current drive and prompts you to switch diskettes during the copy.

If you don't specify <source> or <target>, DOS assumes you want to use only the current drive and prompts you to switch diskettes during the copy.

/1 copies only the first side of a diskette if you have a system with double-sided drives.

DOS gives the target diskette the same number of sides and sectors as the source diskette. If the source diskette, for example, has nine sectors per track and the target diskette was formatted with eight, DOS formats the target diskette with nine sectors per track before copying.

Examples of Copying a Diskette

You copied the system diskette in Chapter 2, but make another copy here; you'll need it in a moment for another example. Follow the instructions under the heading that describes your system.

If You Have One Diskette Drive

Because you have only one diskette drive, DOS must use it for both the source and target diskettes, prompting you to exchange diskettes as required. The diskette you just formatted is in the diskette drive. Replace it with your copy of the DOS system diskette. (If you're using IBM's release of version 3.3, use the Operating diskette.)

To copy the diskette, type:

```
C>diskcopy a: b:
```

DOS prompts you to put in the source diskette:

```
Insert SOURCE diskette in drive A:

Press any key when ready . . .
```

You put the diskette in already, so press any key. DOS tells you how many tracks, sectors, and sides it's copying (just sectors and sides, if you're using version 2), then prompts you to put the target diskette in the drive:

```
Insert TARGET diskette in drive A:

Press any key when ready . . .
```

Remove the system diskette and put in the diskette you formatted in the previous example, then press a key. DOS might prompt you to exchange diskettes until it has copied the diskette. Then it asks if you want to copy another:

```
Copy another diskette (Y/N)?_
```

Reply *n*.

If You Have Two Diskette Drives

If you're using DOS on a system with a fixed disk and two diskette drives, put your copy of the DOS system diskette in drive A (use the Operating diskette if you have IBM's release of version 3.3). If you don't have a fixed disk, verify that the system (or Operating) diskette is in drive A.

To copy the diskette in drive A to the diskette you just formatted in drive B, type:

```
A>diskcopy a: b:
```

DOS prompts you to put in the diskettes. The correct diskettes are in the two drives, so just press a key. DOS tells you how many tracks, sectors, and sides it's copying (just sectors and sides in version 2), then asks if you want to copy another; reply *n*.

COMPARING TWO DISKETTES

Note: The command for comparing two diskettes might not be included in your version of DOS. You can check for it in your DOS manual, or you can check your DOS diskettes by typing dir diskcomp.com. *If you don't have the Diskcomp command, skip to the heading "Checking the Condition of a Disk."*

Sometimes you'll want to know whether two diskettes are identical—for example, you may have copied a diskette with the Diskcopy command, and you want to be certain the duplicate is an exact copy of the original. Diskcomp compares two diskettes sector-by-sector. The Diskcomp command can only be used with diskettes; you cannot use it to compare a fixed disk with a diskette.

*Note: Just because two diskettes contain the same files, they're not necessarily identical, because the files might be stored in different sectors. If you want to compare all the files on two diskettes, rather than the diskettes themselves, use the Compare (comp) command (described in Chapter 5) and specify all files (* .*).*

The Diskcomp command has four parameters:

diskcomp <drive1> <drive2> /1 /8

<drive1> and <drive2> are the drive letters, each followed by a colon, of the drives containing the diskettes to be compared (such as *a:* and *b:*). If you omit <drive2>, DOS compares the diskette in <drive1> to the diskette in the current drive.

If you omit both <drive1> and <drive2>, DOS assumes you want to use only the current drive and prompts you to switch diskettes during the comparison.

/1 compares only the first side of double-sided diskettes.

/8 limits the comparison to eight sectors, even if <drive1> contains a nine-sector diskette.

If DOS finds any differences, it displays the side and track of each; for example:

```
Compare error on side 0, track 33
```

Examples of Comparing Two Diskettes

Follow the instructions under the heading that describes your system.

If You Have One Diskette Drive

To compare the system diskette to the copy you just made, type:

```
C>diskcomp a: b:
```

DOS prompts you to put in the first diskette:

```
Insert FIRST diskette in drive A:

Press any key when ready . . .
```

Make sure the copy you just made is in the drive, then press a key. DOS prompts you to put in the second diskette:

```
Comparing 40 tracks
9 sectors per track, 2 side(s)

Insert SECOND diskette in drive A:

Press any key when ready . . .
```

Remove the diskette, put in the copy of the DOS diskette you made in Chapter 2, and then press a key. If necessary, DOS continues to prompt you to exchange diskettes until it finally tells you it's done and asks if you want to compare more diskettes:

```
Compare OK


Compare another diskette (Y/N) ?_
```

Reply *n*.

If You Have Two Diskette Drives

To compare the diskette in drive B (the copy you just made) to the diskette in drive A (the copy you made in Chapter 2), type:

```
A>diskcomp a: b:
```

DOS prompts you to put in the diskettes:

```
Insert FIRST diskette in drive A:

Insert SECOND diskette in drive B:

Press any key when ready . . .
```

The diskettes are already in the drives, so press a key. DOS reports how many tracks, sectors, and sides it is comparing, then reports the results of the comparison and asks if you want to compare more diskettes:

```
Comparing 40 tracks
9 sectors per track, 2 side(s)

Compare OK


Compare another diskette (Y/N) ?_
```

Reply *n*.

CHECKING THE CONDITION OF A DISK

Computers aren't infallible; malfunctions can produce errors in the directory of a disk. Such errors are rare, but the Check Disk (chkdsk) command helps by making sure that all files are recorded properly.

Check Disk analyzes the directory on a disk, comparing the directory entries with the locations and lengths of the files, and reports any errors it finds. The Check Disk report includes the following:

- The total amount of space on the disk.
- The number of files and directories and how much space they take up.
- How much space on the disk remains available for files.
- The size of the computer's memory and how many bytes remain free for use.

You can also ask the command to display the name of each file on the disk and to check whether any files are stored inefficiently.

If possible, DOS stores files in adjacent, or *contiguous,* sectors. As files are deleted and new files are stored, however, they can become fragmented (stored in nonadjacent sectors). A fragmented file isn't a cause for worry; the worst that can happen is that DOS will take slightly longer to read the file. If several files on a diskette are fragmented, you can restore them to contiguous sectors by copying all the files to an empty, formatted diskette with the Copy command. (Remember, don't use the Diskcopy command, because it makes a faithful sector-by-sector copy of the diskette, storing the files in exactly the same—nonadjacent—sectors in which they are stored on the original diskette.)

The Check Disk command has four parameters:

chkdsk <drive> <filename> /V /F

<drive> is the letter, followed by a colon, of the drive that contains the diskette to be checked. If you omit <drive>, DOS checks the diskette in the current drive.

<filename> is the name of the file whose storage you want DOS to check. DOS displays a message if the file is stored in noncontiguous sectors. You can use wildcard characters to check a set of files.

/V displays the name of each directory and file on the disk.

/F tells DOS to correct any errors it finds in the directory if you so specify when the error is found.

Examples of Checking a Disk

Whether you have one or two diskette drives, check the diskette in drive B by typing:

```
C>chkdsk b:
```

Press any key if DOS prompts you to insert a diskette in drive B.
DOS displays its report (the numbers you see might be different):

```
362496 bytes total disk space
     0 bytes in 1 hidden files
307200 bytes in 31 user files
 55296 bytes available on disk

655360 bytes total memory
570176 bytes free
```

To check the diskette in drive B, and to check whether all files on it are stored in contiguous sectors, type:

```
C>chkdsk b:*.*
```

DOS displays the same report as the preceding, but adds the following message:

```
All specified file(s) are contiguous
```

If any files were stored in noncontiguous sectors, DOS would display their names and the number of noncontiguous blocks of storage in place of this message.

To check the diskette in drive B and, at the same time, display the name of each file on it, type:

```
C>chkdsk b: /v
```

DOS displays the name of each file on the diskette, then appends its usual report of disk space and memory available. Because you are checking the copy of your system disk in this example, the list of files scrolls off the top of the screen; to view it all, you can freeze the display by pressing Ctrl-Num Lock.

Note: If you had organized the files on a diskette into groups called directories, the /V parameter of the Check Disk command would list the directories, as well as the files grouped within them. Directories are covered in Chapter 8, "A Tree of Files."

You can combine the Check Disk parameters in one command; for example, *chkdsk b:* .* /v* would check the diskette in drive B, check all files on it for fragmentation, and display the names of all files.

If the Check Disk command finds an error, it displays a message, such as *Allocation error for file, size adjusted,* followed by a file name and a prompt asking you whether to correct the error. If you specified the /F parameter, you can reply *y* to tell DOS to try to correct the error. Depending on the type of error, DOS may or may not be able to recover the data.

ASSIGNING OR CHANGING A DISK'S VOLUME LABEL

The Label command assigns, changes, or deletes the volume label of a diskette or fixed disk. It has two parameters:

label <drive> <newlabel>

<drive> is the letter, followed by a colon, of the drive (such as *b:*) that contains the disk whose volume label is to be altered.

<newlabel> is the volume label to be assigned to the disk in the drive specified by <drive>.

If you omit <drive>, DOS assumes you want to alter the label of the disk in the current drive. If you omit <newlabel>, DOS prompts you to enter the new label.

Examples of Changing a Disk's Volume Label

At the beginning of this chapter, you used the /V option of the Format command to assign the volume label DOSDISK to your practice diskette. Later, you copied DOS to the same diskette with the Diskcopy command. Diskcopy creates an exact duplicate of a source diskette, including the volume label, so your practice diskette is no longer named DOSDISK. To check this, type the following:

```
C>label b:
```

DOS responds:

```
Volume in drive B has no label

Volume label (11 characters, ENTER for none)? _
```

But volume labels are useful, so name the diskette DOSCOPY. Type:

```
doscopy
```

and press Enter.

If the diskette had a volume label and you wanted to delete it, you would reply to the prompt by pressing the Enter key without typing a name. DOS would then ask *Delete current volume label (Y/N)?* You would reply *y* to delete the volume label.

DISPLAYING A DISK'S VOLUME LABEL

The Volume (vol) command displays the volume label of a fixed disk or a diskette. If you assign descriptive volume labels to your diskettes when you format them, you can use the Volume command to make sure that you're using the correct diskettes. It's faster and easier than checking the directory.

The Volume command has one parameter:

vol <drive>

<drive> is the letter, followed by a colon, of the drive (such as *b:*) that contains the diskette whose volume label is to be displayed. If you omit <drive>, DOS displays the volume label of the disk in the current drive.

To display the volume label of the diskette in drive B, type:

```
C>vol b:
```

DOS displays the volume label:

```
Volume in drive B is DOSCOPY
```

If the diskette had no volume label, DOS would respond *Volume in drive B has no label.*

CHAPTER 7

MANAGING YOUR DEVICES

Data flows into and out of a computer system through pieces of equipment called *devices*. Devices are categorized by whether they handle data coming in (input) or going out (output), or both. The keyboard, for example, is an input device; the computer gets information from it. A printer is an output device; the computer sends information to it. A disk drive is both an input device and an output device; the computer can either read a file from a disk or write a file onto a disk.

Some devices, such as the keyboard, don't need much attention from you because DOS requires no special instructions to operate them. Other devices, however, such as a color display or a printer, sometimes require you to tell DOS how you want to use them. If you have both a monochrome display and a color display, for example, each time you start DOS it uses the monochrome display unless you tell it otherwise.

Color displays, printers, and the computer's communications channels, called *ports,* can all be used in a variety of ways. This chapter shows you how to do the following with the DOS device commands:

- Clear the screen with the Clear Screen command.
- Switch displays and control the color display with the Mode command.
- Control the width and line spacing of your printer with the Mode command.
- Define the settings of the communications ports with the Mode command.
- Copy from a device to a file or to another device with the Copy command.
- Make DOS able to print graphics with the Graphics command.
- Make DOS able to display special graphics characters on a color/graphics display in graphics mode with the Graftabl (Load Graphics Table) command.

DOS also includes a group of commands that let you change the keyboard layout, available characters, and other operating characteristics to match the requirements of other languages and countries. If you need to use your computer with more than one language, Appendix B, "DOS Is an International System," shows you how to use these commands.

DEVICE NAMES

Just as files have names, so do devices. You can use a device name in many DOS commands just as you would use a file name. DOS assigns all device names, however. You can't name a device yourself. Figure 7-1 shows the devices that make up a typical system, with the names assigned to them by DOS.

CON is short for *Console.* It is both an input device and an output device and refers to both the keyboard (input) and the display (output). Because the keyboard is input only and the display is output only, DOS can tell which one to use by the way you use the name CON in a command.

PRN is short for *Printer*. It is an output device and refers to the parallel printer that DOS uses unless you specify otherwise (much as DOS looks for files on the current drive unless you specify otherwise). You can attach as many as three parallel printers (named LPT1, LPT2, and LPT3); PRN means LPT1.

AUX is short for *Auxiliary*. It is for both input and output and refers to the communications port that DOS uses unless you instruct otherwise. You can attach one or two communications ports, named COM1 and COM2, with any version of DOS; if you're using version 3.3, you can attach up to four communications ports (COM1 through COM4). Unless you or a program specifies otherwise, DOS assumes that AUX means COM1. On a typical system, COM1 could be used for a modem, and COM2 could be used for a serial printer—or vice versa.

DOS reserves these names for use with devices only; you cannot give any of these names to a file.

PREPARING FOR THE EXAMPLES

Devices often need very specific setup instructions and operating parameters. The examples in this chapter work with IBM and IBM-compatible personal computers. If you're not using one of these machines, you might need to use different instructions to manage your devices. Refer to your documentation for specific information.

When you try the examples, make sure the devices you name are attached to the system and are turned on. You won't hurt anything by entering a command naming a device that isn't present or isn't ready, but the command may cause an error that requires you to restart DOS.

If you're using 5.25-inch diskettes and IBM's release of version 3.3 on a system with no fixed disk, put the Startup diskette (*not* the Operating diskette) in drive A.

CLEARING THE SCREEN

Sometimes you might want to erase distracting clutter from the screen: old directory listings, perhaps, or the display of commands DOS has already completed for you. You can clean things up with the Clear Screen (cls) command, which erases everything on the screen and then displays the system prompt in the upper left corner.

The Clear Screen command has one form:

cls

To test it, type its name:

```
C>cls
```

The screen is cleared, except for the system prompt.

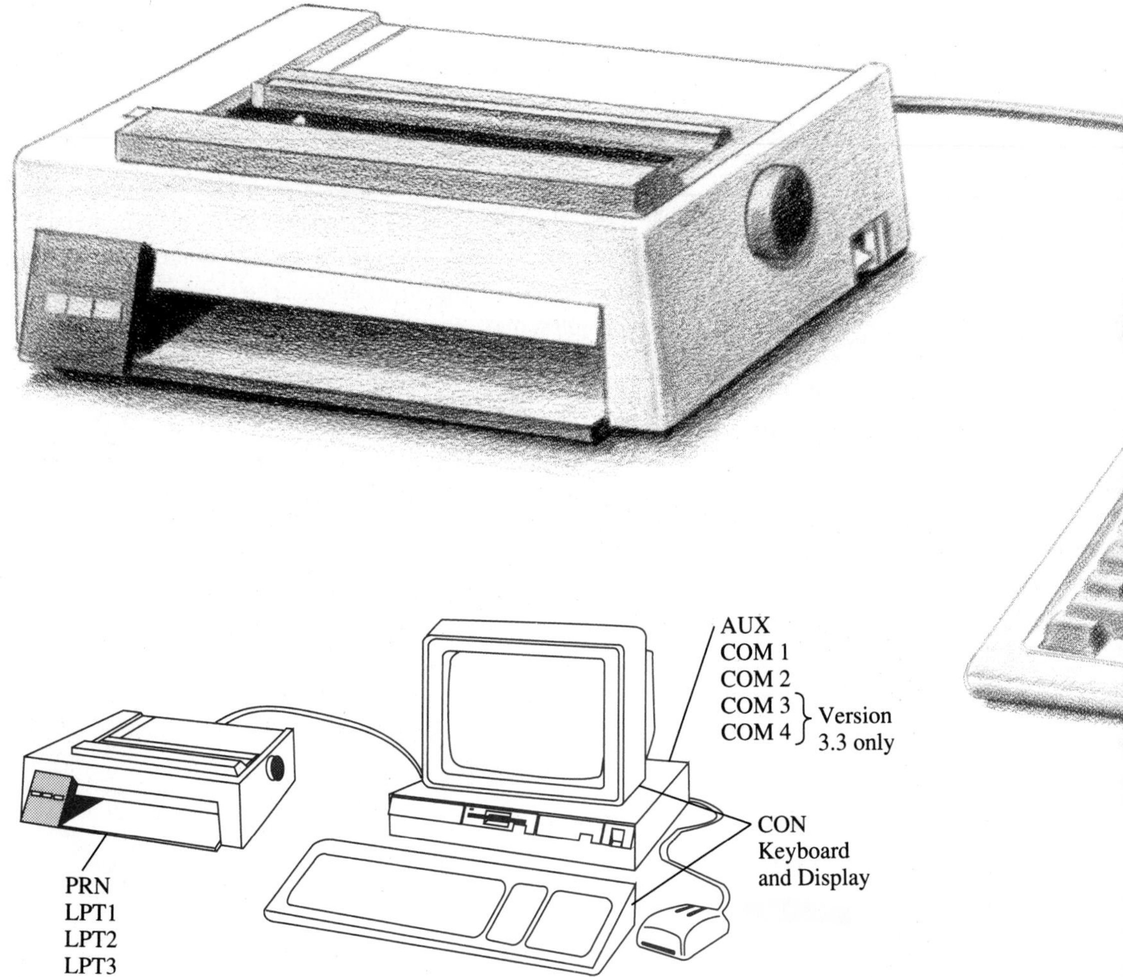

Figure 7-1. DOS device names

CONTROLLING THE DISPLAY

Several different displays and display adapters (the printed-circuit cards that are inserted into the system unit to operate the display) are used with IBM personal computers and compatible machines. Figure 7-2 describes the most commonly used types of displays and display adapters.

Short Name	IBM Product Name	Description
MDA	Monochrome Display Adapter	Text only, medium resolution, one color (usually green on a dark background). Introduced with the IBM PC.
CGA	Color/Graphics Adapter	Text and graphics, low resolution, up to 16 colors. Introduced with the IBM PC.
Hercules	None (works with monochrome display)	Displays graphics on monochrome display. (Not compatible with CGA. An application program must specifically support the Hercules board, but most major applications do because of its popularity.)
EGA	Enhanced Graphics Adapter	Text and graphics, medium resolution, up to 64 colors. Introduced with the IBM PC/AT.
MCGA	Multicolor Graphics Array	Text and graphics, low to medium resolution, up to 256 colors. Introduced with the IBM PS/2 models.
VGA	Video Graphics Array	Text and graphics, medium to high resolution, up to 256 colors. Introduced with the IBM PS/2 models.

Figure 7-2. IBM and IBM-compatible displays and adapters

The DOS Mode command has several display-related options. Which you use depends on the type of display you have and how much you want to see on the screen.

If you have a color display attached to a color/graphics adapter, you can use the Mode command to specify whether DOS displays 40 or 80 columns (characters) across the width of the screen.

When used to control the number of columns on a display attached to a color/graphics adapter, the Mode command has one form:

mode <method>

<method> is either 40 or 80.

To display 40 columns on a display attached to a color/graphics adapter, type:

```
C>mode 40
```

DOS clears the screen and displays the system prompt in large characters in the upper left corner of the screen.

SWITCHING AND CONTROLLING TWO DISPLAYS

If you have two displays, one attached to a monochrome display adapter and the other to a color/graphics adapter, DOS uses the monochrome display when you start the system. The Mode command lets you switch from one display to the other, specify the number of columns on the display attached to the color/graphics adapter, and specify whether DOS tries to display in color. If you have a non-color display attached to the color/graphics adapter, disabling color can make the display easier to read.

When used to switch and control displays, the Mode command has one form:

mode <method>

<method> is one of the following:

mono	Display attached to monochrome display adapter
bw40	Color display, 40 columns, color disabled
bw80	Color display, 80 columns, color disabled
co40	Color display, 40 columns, color enabled
co80	Color display, 80 columns, color enabled

Examples of Switching and Controlling Displays

If you're using a color display, you can type the following to switch to the monochrome display:

```
C>mode mono
```

DOS displays the system prompt on the monochrome display.

To specify the color display, 80 columns, and color enabled, type:

```
C>mode co80
```

DOS clears the screen and displays the system prompt in the upper left corner.

CONTROLLING THE PRINTER WIDTH AND SPACING

A dot-matrix printer normally prints a maximum of 80 characters per line, and six lines per inch. It can also print in a smaller type, called *condensed,* that fits 132 characters on a line. This ability to change widths is often useful for printing spreadsheets and other documents wider than 80 characters. The printer can also print eight lines per inch, to fit more lines on a page.

Note: If you have a letter-quality or laser printer, the documentation that came with the printer tells you how to define the printer to DOS and how to control the printer's characteristics, such as line and character spacing. The examples here most likely won't work, unless your laser printer can emulate an Epson dot-matrix printer.

If your printer is attached to a parallel port, you can use the Mode command to specify the line width (80 or 132) and spacing (6 or 8).

When used to control a dot-matrix printer attached to a parallel port, the Mode command has three parameters:

mode <printer> <width>,<spacing>

<printer> is the name of the printer, followed by a colon (*lpt1:*, *lpt2:*, or *lpt3:*).

<width> is either 80 or 132.

<spacing> is either 6 or 8 and must be preceded by a comma.

You must always include <printer>. If you omit <width>, DOS leaves the current width unchanged, but you must still type the comma before <spacing> to tell DOS that you omitted <width>. If you omit <spacing>, DOS leaves the current spacing unchanged.

Examples of Controlling a Dot-Matrix Printer

Make sure the printer is turned on before entering the following examples.

To cause a printer attached to LPT1 to print in small type (up to 132 characters per line if the printer can do so), type the following:

```
C>mode lpt1: 132
```

DOS replies:

```
LPT1: set for 132
```

To test the setting, simultaneously print and display the directory by typing:

```
C><Ctrl-PrtSc>dir
```

The directory is printed with the new line width. (You can cancel the Directory command by pressing Ctrl-Break.) Press Ctrl-PrtSc to stop simultaneous printing.

To set the spacing of the printer attached to LPT1 to eight lines per inch and leave the width unchanged, type:

```
C>mode lpt1: ,8
```

DOS replies:

```
Printer lines per inch set
```

To see the effect of this setting, again start printing and displaying the directory simultaneously by typing:

```
C><Ctrl-PrtSc>dir
```

This time the directory is printed both in small type (from the previous example) and with closer line spacing. Press Ctrl-PrtSc again to stop simultaneous printing.

To restore the printer to normal width and line spacing, type:

```
C>mode lpt1: 80,6
```

DOS replies:

```
LPT1: set for 80

Printer lines per inch set
```

The printer is back to its normal settings.

CONTROLLING THE SERIAL COMMUNICATIONS PORT

Serial communications is controlled by several characteristics, or communications parameters, that define how fast and in what form data is transmitted. Different devices often require different parameter settings; the parameters of your serial port must match those of the device or computer service with which you want to communicate. Before you can use a communications port, you must set these parameters with the Mode command.

The communications parameters you can set include:

- *Baud,* how quickly characters are sent or received.
- *Parity,* the kind of error-checking technique used.
- *Databits,* the number of electrical signals required to define a character.
- *Stopbits,* the number of electrical signals that mark the end of a character.

A more complete definition of these parameters is beyond the scope of this book. Figure 7-3 on the following page lists the parameters you can set with the Mode command. The documentation of the device or computer service you want to use shows the required setting; compare these settings with Figure 7-3 to see which, if any, parameters you must change.

When used to set the parameters of a serial communications port, the Mode command has one form:

mode <port> <baud>,<parity>,<databits>,<stopbits>

Name	Valid Settings	How You Specify	Value DOS Assumes
Baud	110, 150, 300, 600, 1200, 2400, 4800, 9600, 19,200*	You can abbreviate the first two digits (11 for 110, 24 for 2400)	None (you must set a value)
Parity	None Odd Even	N, O, or E	Even (E)
Databits	7 or 8	7 or 8	7
Stopbits	1 or 2	1 or 2	2 if baud = 110, 1 otherwise

* 19,200 is available in version 3.3 only and can be used only with a computer capable of that speed, such as some IBM PS/2 models.

Figure 7-3. Serial communications parameters

<port> is the name, followed by a colon, of the communications port—*com1:* or *com2:* (*com1:* through *com4:* if you're using version 3.3). The remaining parameters, separated by commas, are those described in Figure 7-3.

You must specify a value for <baud> each time you enter this Mode command. DOS assumes the values for the other parameters listed in the last column of Figure 7-3 unless you specifically change them; you needn't specify these parameters unless the device or service with which you want to communicate requires values different from those that DOS assumes.

If you omit any parameter from the Mode command, you must still type the comma that precedes it, to show DOS you omitted the parameter.

Examples of Controlling the Serial Port for Communications

These examples show you different uses of the Mode command. Don't enter them unless you have a serial communications port.

To set the baud rate for COM1 to 1200 and accept the default values for the other parameters, you would type:

```
C>mode com1: 1200
```

DOS replies by reporting the current setting of each parameter:

```
COM1: 1200,e,7,1,-
```

This report shows that <baud> is 1200, <parity> is even, <databits> is 7, and <stopbits> is 1. The hyphen at the end tells you DOS will not keep trying to send to a device that isn't ready, but will stop after a brief time.

To set <baud> for COM1 to 300, <parity> to odd, leave <databits> set to 7, and set <stopbits> to 2, you would type:

```
C>mode com1: 300,o,,2
```

Note the two commas before the 2, telling DOS that you omitted <databits>. DOS confirms the settings:

```
COM1: 300 ,o,7,2,-
```

CONNECTING A SERIAL PRINTER

If you want to use a serial printer attached to a communications port, you must use the Mode command to tell DOS to send printer output to the communications port instead of the regular (parallel) printer port; this is called *redirecting* the printer output.

Before you redirect the printer output, you must first set the parameters of the serial communications port to the values required by the printer, as described in the preceding topic.

When used to redirect printer output to a serial communications port, the Mode command has one form:

mode <printer>=<port>

<printer> is the name of the printer (*lpt1:*, *lpt2:*, or *lpt3:*) whose output is to be redirected.

<port> is the name of the serial communications port (*com1:* or *com2:* in all versions of DOS, *com1:* through *com4:* in version 3.3). You must enter both parameters.

Example of Connecting a Serial Printer

To redirect printer output from LPT1 to serial port COM1, you would first set the serial port to match the communications parameters of your printer, then type:

```
C>mode lpt1:=com1:
```

DOS would acknowledge:

```
LPT1: redirected to COM1:
```

Now all output that would normally go to LPT1: would be sent to COM1: instead. To cancel the redirection, restoring the printer output to LPT1:, you would type:

```
C>mode lpt1:
```

COPYING FROM A DEVICE TO A FILE OR ANOTHER DEVICE

As you saw in earlier examples, you can use the Copy command to copy from a device to a file. You have used this technique several times to create sample files by copying from the keyboard to a file, and you will find it handy for creating short text files.

You can also copy from one device to another. Copying from the keyboard to the printer, for example, is a quick and convenient way to print short notes or lists.

When you copy from one device to a file or another device, DOS continues to copy until it comes to the character (Ctrl-Z) that marks the end of a file. Whenever you copy from the keyboard, you can send this end-of-file character by pressing the key labeled F6 and then pressing the Enter key (or, as you've done before, by pressing Ctrl-Z and Enter).

When used to copy from a device to a file or another device, the Copy command has two parameters:

copy <source> <target>

<source> is the name of the source device.
<target> is the name of the target file or device.

Examples of Copying from a Device to a File or Another Device

To copy from the keyboard (CON) to the printer (PRN), make certain the printer is turned on and type:

```
C>copy con prn
```

Now everything you type will be both displayed and sent to the printer. Type a few lines, and then end the copy by pressing F6 or Ctrl-Z (shown as ^Z in the example because that's how DOS displays it):

```
These lines are being
copied from the
keyboard to the printer.
^Z
        1 File(s) copied

C>_
```

Note: If you're using a Hewlett-Packard LaserJet Plus or a similar laser printer, this example will produce a printed copy if you press the ON LINE *button and then the* FORM FEED *button. Be sure to do this after you type the example; otherwise, it might appear at the beginning of the next document you print.*

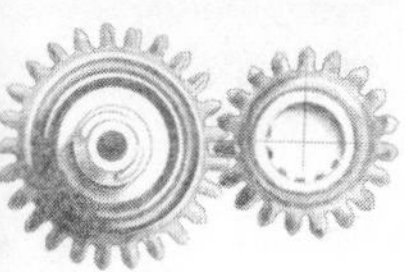

To copy from the serial communications port (AUX) to the printer (PRN), you would first set the serial port to match the communications parameters of whatever is attached to it, then you would type:

```
C>copy aux prn
```

Everything received at the communications port would be printed until the end-of-file character was received.

PRINTING GRAPHICS IMAGES

Pressing Shift-PrtSc prints the text displayed on either a monochrome or color display, but it does not print graphics images from a display that is attached to the color/graphics adapter. The Graphics command enables DOS to print these graphics images on any of several different printers.

You need enter the Graphics command only once. After you enter it, pressing Shift-PrtSc prints everything on the screen of the active display, including graphics images. Low-resolution graphics images are printed across the paper; color on non-color printers is simulated with shading. High-resolution graphics images are printed sideways (rotated 90 degrees) and enlarged.

The Graphics command loads a program that increases the amount of memory that DOS uses by about 2000 bytes.

The Graphics command has four parameters:

graphics <printer> /R /B /LCD

<printer> is one of the IBM printers, or a compatible model. It can be any of the following:

- For the IBM Personal Computer Color Printer, the options are: *color1* for a black ribbon; *color4* for a red-green-blue ribbon; *color8* for a cyan-magenta-yellow ribbon.
- For the IBM Personal Computer Compact Printer, specify *compact.*
- For an Epson-compatible printer, specify *graphics.*
- For the IBM PC Convertible Printer, specify *thermal* (version 3.3 only).

If you don't specify <printer>, DOS assumes *graphics.*

/R tells DOS to print the screen as you see it—in other words, light characters on a dark background.

/B tells DOS to print the background color if you have specified *color4* or *color8* for <printer>. If you don't specify /B, DOS doesn't print the background color.

/LCD tells DOS to print the contents of the liquid crystal display of the IBM PC Convertible computer.

When you enter the Graphics command, DOS loads the program, adds it to the parts of the system kept in memory, and displays the system prompt. You needn't enter the command again until the next time you start DOS.

If you're using a color display and have a printer that can print graphics, you can test the Graphics command by entering the command and appropriate parameters, then displaying a graphics image and pressing Shift-PrtSc.

DISPLAYING GRAPHICS CHARACTERS

Even when the color/graphics adapter is in graphics mode, it normally cannot display the 128 special characters that include accented characters, Greek letters, box-drawing graphics, and others. The Graftabl command enables DOS to display these characters when the color/graphics adapter is in graphics mode.

Like the Graphics command, you need enter the Graftabl command only once. After you enter it, the additional characters can be displayed on the screen. The Graftabl command loads a small program that increases the amount of memory that DOS uses by about 2000 bytes.

You don't need the Graftabl command in normal DOS operation, but there are certain times it can come in handy. For example, suppose you would like to display accented French or Spanish characters on the screen. If your display is connected to the color/graphics adapter, you would simply type *graftabl.* DOS would either respond with a brief *GRAPHIC CHARACTERS LOADED* or, in version 3.3, with the more detailed message:

```
No version of Graphic Character Set Table is already loaded.

USA version of Graphic Character Set Table has just been loaded.
```

In either case, all 128 special graphics characters would be available until you reset or turned off your computer. DOS includes more foreign-language capabilities; these are significantly expanded in version 3.3. For a detailed description of these capabilities, see Appendix B, "DOS Is an International System."

CHAPTER 8

A TREE OF FILES

As you have seen, when DOS formats a disk, it creates a directory that describes each of the files on the disk. The directory holds a fixed number of entries: 64 on a single-sided diskette, 112 on a double-sided diskette, 224 on a high-capacity diskette, and 512 or more on a fixed disk (the number varies with the size of the disk).

To make your computer filing system more flexible, DOS lets you create additional directories, called *subdirectories,* on a disk. The subdirectories divide the disk into different storage areas, each of which you can use as if it were a different disk.

To distinguish the main directory that DOS creates from the subdirectories that you create, the main directory is known as the *root directory* because a multilevel directory structure can grow from it.

As you add levels to your file structure, a block diagram would show it spreading from the root directory and branching to other directories, like a tree branches from its root. This type of file structure is often called a tree-structured file system, and is the reason for the name root directory. Despite this multilevel directory structure, you can still use a diskette created with version 1 of DOS (which didn't permit subdirectories) because later versions treat a version 1 disk as having a root directory only.

DEFINING A SUBDIRECTORY

A subdirectory is simply a file that contains directory entries; these entries are identical in form to the entries in the main directory, but there is no limit to the number of entries you can put in a subdirectory.

You name a subdirectory as you name any other file, but because the subdirectory defines other files, you cannot use the normal file commands to copy or erase a subdirectory. This chapter shows you how to use several commands that enable you to do the following:

- Create a subdirectory with the Make Directory command.
- Change or display the name of the current directory with the Change Directory command.
- Delete a subdirectory with the Remove Directory command.
- Display a list of all the directories on a disk with the Check Disk command.
- Tell DOS where to look for a command file, if it's not in the current directory, with the Path command.
- Tell DOS where to look for a data file, if it's not in the current directory, with the Append command (version 3.3 only).

Using these features of DOS, you can create and manage a computer filing system that is tailored to the way you work.

PREPARING FOR THE EXAMPLES

The examples in this chapter require one formatted diskette. If you're using a fixed disk or have a one-drive system, put the diskette in the diskette drive. If you're using two diskette drives, put the formatted diskette in drive B. If any files from earlier examples are stored on the diskette, erase them by typing the following; be sure to include the *b:*, or you will erase all the files on the current disk:

```
C>erase b:*.*
```

If you have only one diskette drive, DOS asks you to make sure the correct diskette is in the drive:

```
Insert diskette for drive B: and strike
any key when ready
```

Press any key.

DOS asks you to confirm that you want to erase all the files:

```
Are you sure (Y/N)?_
```

Before you respond, check the command you entered and be certain that you typed the drive letter (*b:*). If you didn't, press Ctrl-Break to cancel the Erase command, and retype the command correctly. If you did type the drive letter, respond *y*. Because a mistake here could cause the loss of valuable files, you must also press the Enter key after typing *y* before DOS will carry out the command.

After you have erased the files, change the current drive to B by typing:

```
C>b:
```

This completes the preparation.

CREATING A MULTILEVEL FILE STRUCTURE

Suppose you work at a small company and provide services to two departments, Marketing and Engineering. You keep all your papers in a file drawer. You keep miscellaneous items in the front of the drawer, and dividers labeled MKT and ENG separate the parts where you store papers that relate to each department. Figure 8-1 shows how the file drawer might look.

Now that you're going to be using a computer, you can set up your computer filing system to match your paper files by creating two subdirectories named MKT and ENG. You can store miscellaneous computer files in the main, or root, directory of the disk, and you can store the files relating to each department in separate subdirectories. Figure 8-2 shows the filing cabinet and a block diagram of this corresponding DOS file structure.

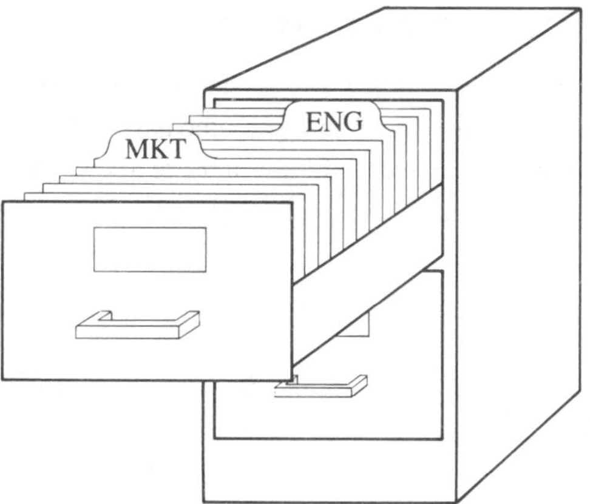

Figure 8-1. File drawer with dividers

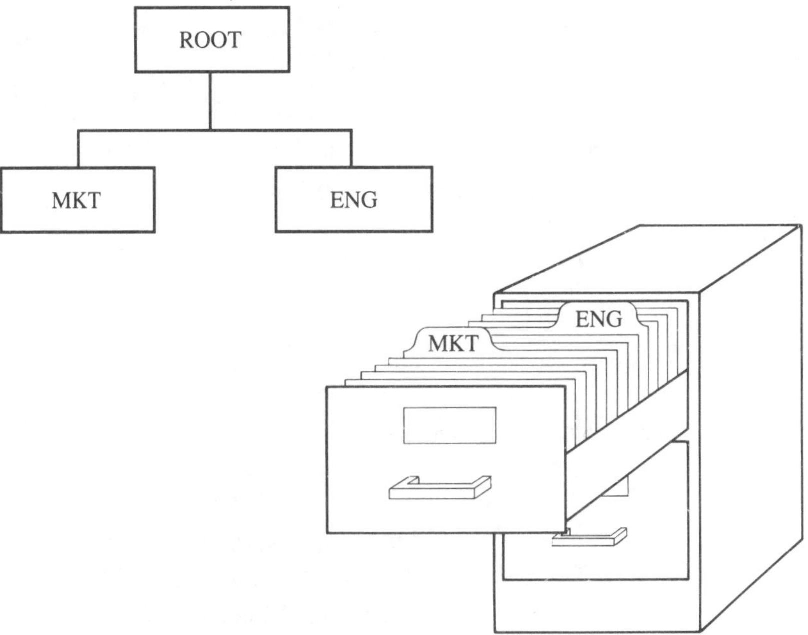

Figure 8-2. Two-level file systems

Creating a Subdirectory

The Make Directory (md, or mkdir) command creates a subdirectory. The only parameter you must include is the name of the subdirectory you want to create. The command is described later in more detail; for now, type the following to create two subdirectories named MKT and ENG:

```
B>md mkt

B>md eng
```

You can see the subdirectories you just created by displaying the entries in the root directory. Type:

```
B>dir
```

DOS shows two files named MKT and ENG:

```
 Volume in drive B has no label
 Directory of  B:\

MKT          <DIR>      10-16-87    8:14a
ENG          <DIR>      10-16-87    8:14a
        2 File(s)    1212928 bytes free
```

Note that the directory identifies the files as subdirectories by displaying <DIR> after their names. The backslash (\) in the second line of the display is the character that DOS uses to refer to the root directory of a disk. You've seen the backslash in earlier directory displays; you'll see more of it and its uses in later examples.

Because MKT is a subdirectory, you can display its contents with the Directory command, just as you can display the contents of the root directory. Type the following command:

```
B>dir mkt
```

DOS displays the contents of MKT:

```
 Volume in drive B has no label
 Directory of  B:\MKT

.            <DIR>      10-16-87    8:14a
..           <DIR>      10-16-87    8:14a
        2 File(s)    1212928 bytes free
```

Even though you just created it, MKT seems to contain subdirectories named . (one period) and .. (two periods). These really aren't subdirectories; they're abbreviations you use to refer to other directories. You'll see how these abbreviations are used a bit later.

The Path to a Directory

The second line of the preceding directory display tells you that you're looking at the directory of B:\MKT. The \ (backslash) refers to the root directory, and MKT is the name of the subdirectory whose contents you're displaying. Together, they are called the *path name* of the directory, or just the *path,* because they describe the path DOS follows to find the directory. The path names of the two subdirectories you created, \MKT and \ENG, tell DOS that the subdirectories are in the root directory.

You can also include a path name with a file name, to tell DOS where to find a file. The path name goes just before the file name (after the drive letter, if one is included) and is separated from the file name by a backslash. For example, if the subdirectory \MKT contained a file named BUDGET.JAN, the full path and file name would be \MKT\BUDGET.JAN.

The Current Directory

Just as DOS keeps track of the current drive, it also keeps track of the current directory. When you start DOS, the current drive is the drive from which the DOS programs were loaded; the current directory is the root directory of the current drive.

Just as you can change the current drive, you can change the current directory, so that you don't have to type the path name each time you want to work with a directory other than the current directory.

The Change Directory (cd, or chdir) command changes or displays the name of the current directory. If you enter the command with no parameter, it displays the name of the current directory. To see what the current directory is, type:

```
B>cd
```

The current directory is the root directory, so the response is short:

```
B:\
```

It tells you that any command you enter will apply to the root directory of the diskette in drive B, unless you specify a different path name. Change the current directory to the subdirectory named MKT by typing:

```
B>cd mkt
```

DOS acknowledges merely by displaying the system prompt, but if you display the current directory again by typing:

```
B>cd
```

DOS responds:

```
B:\MKT
```

Now any command you enter applies to the subdirectory MKT in the root directory. Type the Directory command again:

```
B>dir
```

DOS displays the entries in the subdirectory \MKT:

```
 Volume in drive B has no label
 Directory of  B:\MKT

.            <DIR>      10-16-87   8:14a
..           <DIR>      10-16-87   8:14a
        2 File(s)    1212928 bytes free
```

This is the same display you saw earlier when you typed *dir mkt*, but this time you didn't have to name the subdirectory because you had changed the current directory to \MKT.

Using Subdirectories

Your diskette now has the directory structure shown in Figure 8-2. You can use each of these directories as if it were a separate disk. The current directory is \MKT. Create a file in the root directory by typing the following lines:

```
B>copy con \sample.txt
This is a sample file.
^Z
        1 File(s) copied
```

Notice that you included the backslash to tell DOS to put the file in the root directory. You also use the backslash to display the contents of the root directory when it's not the current directory. Type the following:

```
B>dir \
```

Again DOS displays the entries in the root directory:

```
 Volume in drive B has no label
 Directory of  B:\

MKT          <DIR>      10-16-87   8:14a
ENG          <DIR>      10-16-87   8:14a
SAMPLE   TXT         24 10-16-87   8:17a
        3 File(s)    1212416 bytes free
```

The root directory contains two subdirectories and the file you just created.

Copying from One Directory to Another

Because you can treat directories as if they were separate disks, you can copy a file from one directory to another. Copy SAMPLE.TXT from the root directory of drive B to a file named ACCOUNT in the current directory (\MKT) by typing:

```
B>copy \sample.txt account
        1 File(s) copied
```

You included the path (the backslash, meaning the root directory) in front of SAMPLE.TXT to tell DOS where to find the file; you didn't include a path for ACCOUNT, because you were putting it in the current directory. Now display the current directory by typing the following:

```
B>dir

 Volume in drive B has no label
 Directory of  B:\MKT

.            <DIR>      10-16-87   8:14a
..           <DIR>      10-16-87   8:14a
ACCOUNT            24   10-16-87   8:17a
        3 File(s)    1211904 bytes free
```

The file is there. You can copy files from one directory to another as easily as you can copy them from one disk to another.

Just as DOS doesn't confuse two files with the same name on different disks, it doesn't confuse two files with the same name in different directories. DOS can tell the latter apart because their paths are different. You can demonstrate this by copying the file named ACCOUNT from \MKT to the subdirectory \ENG, giving it the same file name. Type the following:

```
B>copy account \eng
```

You didn't include the file name after the path name of the target directory because you wanted to give the copy the same name as the original. Assure yourself that the file was copied by displaying the directory of \ENG:

```
B>dir \eng

 Volume in drive B has no label
 Directory of  B:\ENG

.            <DIR>      10-16-87   8:14a
..           <DIR>      10-16-87   8:14a
ACCOUNT            24   10-16-87   8:17a
        3 File(s)    1211392 bytes free
```

You now have two files named ACCOUNT on the same disk; but they are in different subdirectories, and their different path names make them as different to DOS as if you had given them different file names.

Time Out for a Quick Review

Before completing your multilevel file structure, take a few minutes to review the following definitions. They summarize the terms and concepts introduced in the preceding examples.

Directory entry: A description of a file that includes the name, extension, and size of the file, and the date and time it was created or last updated.

Directory: A list of directory entries. You'll also see it used with a sense of place: "Which directory am I in?"

Root directory: The list of directory entries that DOS creates and maintains on each disk. It is called the root directory (or simply the root) because the entire directory structure on the disk grows from it. Because the root has no name to DOS, it is represented by a backslash (\).

Subdirectory: A file that contains directory entries. Like the term directory, it is also sometimes used with a sense of place: "Which subdirectory is that file in?"

Path name: The list of directory names that defines the path to a subdirectory. The directory names are separated by a backslash (\). The root directory is represented by a backslash at the beginning of the path. If a file name is included at the end of the path, it is separated from the last directory name by a backslash.

Current directory: The directory that DOS assumes you want to use unless you specify another in a command. The current directory is similar in concept and effect to the current drive.

ADDING MORE LEVELS TO YOUR FILE STRUCTURE

The subdirectories you create can contain any type of file, including other subdirectories. Like putting dividers between other dividers in a file drawer, this further structuring narrows the subject of a storage area. Suppose you do the following type of work for the Marketing and Engineering departments:

MARKETING	ENGINEERING
Word processing	Word processing
Budgets	Budgets
Customer lists	Project scheduling
Sales forecasts	

You decide to set up your file structure to match your work.

The following list shows the additional subdirectories you could create to match your computer files to the work you do (MKT and ENG are the departmental subdirectories you created earlier):

In MKT:	**In ENG:**
WP	WP
BUDGET	BUDGET
CUSTOMER	SCHEDULE
SALES	

You would then have created the file structure shown in Figure 8-3.

Making a Subdirectory
The MD Command

As you saw earlier, the Make Directory (md, or mkdir) command creates a subdirectory. The Make Directory command has two parameters:

md <drive><path>

<drive> is the letter, followed by a colon, of the drive (such as *b:*) that contains the disk on which the subdirectory is to be created. If you omit <drive>, DOS creates the subdirectory on the disk in the current drive.

<path> is the path name of the directory in which the subdirectory is to be created. If you omit <path>, the subdirectory is created in the current directory.

The current directory is \MKT. Check this by typing:

```
B>cd
```

DOS shows you the current directory:

```
B:\MKT
```

For the example in this chapter, you want four subdirectories in \MKT named WP, BUDGET, CUSTOMER, and SALES. Type the following Make Directory commands to create the subdirectories:

```
B>md wp

B>md budget

B>md customer

B>md sales
```

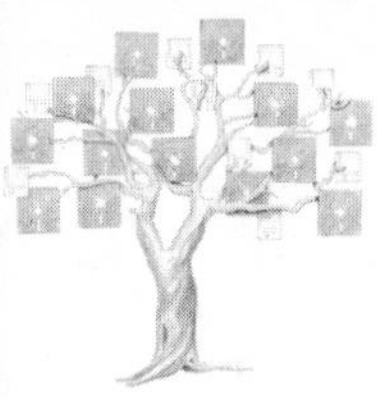

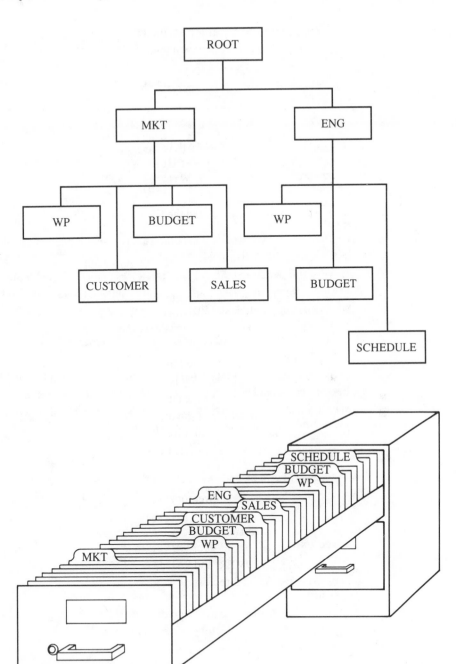

Figure 8-3. Three-level file systems

Display the directory of \MKT by typing:

```
B>dir

 Volume in drive B has no label
 Directory of  B:\MKT

.            <DIR>      10-16-87   8:14a
..           <DIR>      10-16-87   8:14a
ACCOUNT            24   10-16-87   8:17a
WP           <DIR>      10-16-87   8:21a
BUDGET       <DIR>      10-16-87   8:21a
CUSTOMER     <DIR>      10-16-87   8:21a
SALES        <DIR>      10-16-87   8:21a
        7 File(s)   1209344 bytes free
```

The directory shows the file you copied a few minutes ago (ACCOUNT) and the four subdirectories you just created.

Your file structure calls for subdirectories named WP and BUDGET in both \MKT and \ENG. Remember, DOS can distinguish between \MKT\WP and \ENG\WP, \MKT\BUDGET and \ENG\BUDGET, because their paths are different.

To create the subdirectory \ENG\WP, type:

```
B>md \eng\wp
```

You included the path (\ENG) because the current directory is \MKT. The Make Directory command doesn't change the current directory, so it's still \MKT, but you can verify that the subdirectory \ENG\WP was created by displaying the contents of \ENG. Include the path here, too, by typing:

```
B>dir \eng

 Volume in drive B has no label
 Directory of  B:\ENG

.            <DIR>      10-16-87   8:14a
..           <DIR>      10-16-87   8:14a
ACCOUNT            24   10-16-87   8:17a
WP           <DIR>      10-16-87   8:22a
        4 File(s)   1208832 bytes free
```

Now you're going to start moving around from subdirectory to subdirectory, so before creating the last two subdirectories in \ENG, here's a closer look at your navigator, the Change Directory command.

Changing the Current Directory The CD Command

You have already used the Change Directory (cd, or chdir) command to change and display the current directory. The Change Directory command has two parameters:

cd <drive><path>

<drive> is the letter, followed by a colon, of the drive (such as *b:*) that contains the disk on which the current directory is to be changed. If you omit <drive>, DOS changes the current directory on the disk in the current drive.

<path> is the path name of the directory that is to become the current directory. If you omit <path>, DOS displays the current directory on <drive>.

If you omit both <drive> and <path> (enter the command with no parameters), DOS displays the current directory of the disk in the current drive.

Changing the System Prompt

Although the Change Directory command lets you check the current directory quickly, there is a way to avoid having to check it at all. The system prompt shows the current drive, but you can change it to display other information, such as the current directory.

The Prompt command, which you met briefly in Chapter 3, is described more fully in Chapter 16, "Tailoring Your System." But for now, type the following. (Include a blank at the end of the line, just before you press the Enter key.)

```
B>prompt Current Directory is $p$_Command: <Enter>
```

Now the system prompt tells you the current drive and the current directory:

```
Current Directory is B:\MKT
Command: _
```

You could restore the system prompt to its more familiar form (the letter of the current drive followed by >) by entering the Prompt command with no parameters (*prompt*), but why not leave it this way for the rest of this chapter? The prompt takes up a bit more space, but it helps you keep track of where you are.

Using the Subdirectory Markers

Remember those markers (. and ..) listed in each subdirectory? They're designed to let you move quickly up and down a directory structure, particularly when several levels make the path names long.

The .. represents the directory that contains the current directory (sometimes called the *parent* of the current directory). The current directory is \MKT; to move the current directory up (toward the root directory) one level, type:

```
Current Directory is B:\MKT
Command: cd ..

Current Directory is B:\
Command: _
```

Now the system prompt shows you the current directory; as you can see, it has changed to the root directory, which is one level above \MKT.

To complete your file structure, you need two more subdirectories in \ENG. Change the current directory to \ENG and create \ENG\BUDGET and \ENG\SCHEDULE by typing the following:

```
Current Directory is B:\
Command: cd eng

Current Directory is B:\ENG
Command: md budget

Current Directory is B:\ENG
Command: md schedule
```

This completes the structure of your multilevel file system.

You have nine subdirectories, plus the root directory, any of which you can use as if it were a separate disk. To show you how easy it is, the next few examples have you put sample files in several of the subdirectories. Figure 8-4 shows how your final file system will look, including the path names of all directories (above the boxes) and the names of the files you'll add (inside the shaded boxes).

To create the sample files in \ENG\WP, first change the current directory to \ENG\WP and copy the file named ACCOUNT from \ENG, naming it LET1.DOC, by typing the following:

```
Current Directory is B:\ENG
Command: cd wp

Current Directory is B:\ENG\WP
Command: copy \eng\account let1.doc
        1 File(s) copied
```

Note that you must use \ENG in the command, even though \ENG\WP is a subdirectory of \ENG.

\

MKT <DIR>
ENG <DIR>
SAMPLE.TXT

\MKT

WP <DIR>
BUDGET <DIR>
CUSTOMER <DIR>
SALES <DIR>
ACCOUNT

\ENG

WP <DIR>
BUDGET <DIR>
SCHEDULE <DIR>
ACCOUNT

\MKT\WP

LET1.DOC
LET2.DOC
LET3.DOC
RPT1.DOC
RPT2.DOC
RPT3.DOC
LET1.STY
LET2.STY
LET3.STY

\MKT\BUDGET

BGT1.PLN
BGT2.PLN
BGT3.PLN

\ENG\WP

LET1.DOC
LET2.DOC
LET3.DOC

\MKT\CUSTOMER

\ENG\BUDGET

\MKT\SALES

\ENG\SCHEDULE

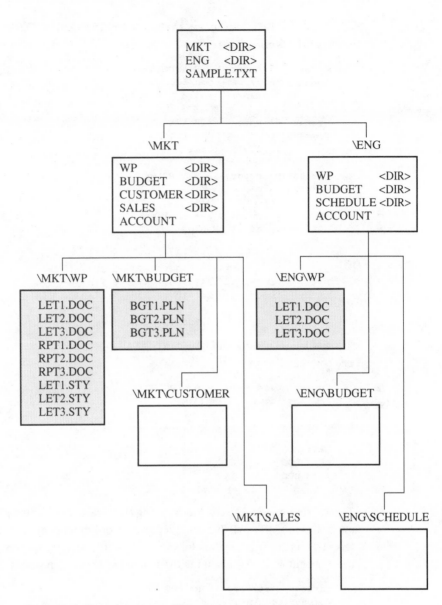

Figure 8-4. Two-department file structure

Now copy LET1.DOC twice, to create LET2.DOC and LET3.DOC, and display the directory by typing:

```
Current Directory is B:\ENG\WP
Command: copy let1.doc let2.doc
        1 File(s) copied

Current Directory is B:\ENG\WP
Command: copy let1.doc let3.doc
        1 File(s) copied

Current Directory is B:\ENG\WP
Command: dir

 Volume in drive B has no label
 Directory of  B:\ENG\WP

.            <DIR>      10-16-87   8:22a
..           <DIR>      10-16-87   8:22a
LET1     DOC        24  10-16-87   8:17a
LET2     DOC        24  10-16-87   8:17a
LET3     DOC        24  10-16-87   8:17a
        5 File(s)   1206272 bytes free
```

From this subdirectory, you can copy all three of these files to \MKT\WP with one command. Type the following:

```
Current Directory is B:\ENG\WP
Command: copy *.* \mkt\wp
```

DOS lists the source files as it copies them:

```
LET1.DOC
LET2.DOC
LET3.DOC
        3 File(s) copied
```

These files could be word-processing files that contain letters. Now create three more files in \MKT\WP that could represent word-processing files that contain reports. First, change the directory to \MKT\WP, then copy the three files whose names begin with LET, changing their names so they begin with RPT. Type:

```
Current Directory is B:\ENG\WP
Command: cd \mkt\wp

Current Directory is B:\MKT\WP
Command: copy let?.doc rpt?.doc
```

DOS again lists the source files as it makes the copies:

```
LET1.DOC
LET2.DOC
LET3.DOC
        3 File(s) copied
```

To complete the files in this subdirectory, copy the same three files again, this time changing their extension to STY, which could identify word-processing files that contain style sheets for formatting and printing documents. Type the following:

```
Current Directory is B:\MKT\WP
Command: copy let?.doc let?.sty
```

Now display the directory to verify that all nine files are there by typing:

```
Current Directory is B:\MKT\WP
Command: dir

 Volume in drive B has no label
 Directory of  B:\MKT\WP

.            <DIR>      10-16-87   8:21a
..           <DIR>      10-16-87   8:21a
LET1     DOC        24  10-16-87   8:17a
LET2     DOC        24  10-16-87   8:17a
LET3     DOC        24  10-16-87   8:17a
RPT1     DOC        24  10-16-87   8:17a
RPT2     DOC        24  10-16-87   8:17a
RPT3     DOC        24  10-16-87   8:17a
LET1     STY        24  10-16-87   8:17a
LET2     STY        24  10-16-87   8:17a
LET3     STY        24  10-16-87   8:17a
       11 File(s)    1201664 bytes free
```

To complete the file system, you need three files in \MKT\BUDGET named BGT1.PLN, BGT2.PLN, and BGT3.PLN. Use the Copy command to copy the files and change their names by typing the following:

```
Current Directory is B:\MKT\WP
Command: copy let?.doc \mkt\budget\bgt?.pln
```

DOS lists the source files as it makes the copies:

```
LET1.DOC
LET2.DOC
LET3.DOC
        3 File(s) copied
```

Your file system now has the directories and files shown in Figure 8-4.

Removing a Subdirectory The RD Command

As you work with a multilevel filing system, you may find that you no longer need a particular subdirectory, or that you want to combine the files from several subdirectories into one and then delete the unneeded subdirectories from your file structure. The Remove Directory (rd, or rmdir) command removes a subdirectory. A subdirectory cannot be removed if it contains any files or subdirectories.

The Remove Directory command has two parameters:

rd <drive><path>

<drive> is the letter, followed by a colon, of the drive that contains the disk with the subdirectory to be removed. You can omit <drive> if the subdirectory is on the disk in the current drive.

<path> is the path name of the subdirectory to be removed. You must specify <path> because DOS will not remove the current directory.

Suppose you decide you don't need the subdirectory \ENG\WP. Tell DOS to remove it by typing:

```
Current Directory is B:\MKT\WP
Command: rd \eng\wp
```

DOS responds *Invalid path, not directory, or directory not empty* because \ENG\WP isn't empty: You put three files, LET1.DOC, LET2.DOC, and LET3.DOC in it. You don't need the files, so you can erase them and then remove the directory.

This example points out the difference in the ways you handle files and subdirectories. As you saw in earlier chapters, you use the Erase command to erase a file from a disk. To remove a directory, however, you use the Remove Directory command.

In the next example, you will erase three files with the Erase command, and then remove a directory with the Remove Directory command. First, change the current directory to \ENG and delete the files with the Erase command by typing:

```
Current Directory is B:\MKT\WP
Command: cd \eng

Current Directory is B:\ENG
Command: erase wp\*.doc
```

You changed the current directory to \ENG, rather than to \ENG\WP, because DOS won't remove the current directory. Now that \ENG\WP is empty, enter the Remove Directory command and verify the change by displaying the directory. Type:

```
Current Directory is B:\ENG
Command: rd wp

Current Directory is B:\ENG
Command: dir

 Volume in drive B has no label
 Directory of  B:\ENG

.            <DIR>      10-16-87   8:14a
..           <DIR>      10-16-87   8:14a
ACCOUNT              24 10-16-87   8:17a
BUDGET       <DIR>      10-16-87   8:24a
SCHEDULE     <DIR>      10-16-87   8:24a
        5 File(s)    1202176 bytes free
```

The subdirectory \ENG\WP is gone.

If you want to remove a directory but need some of the files it contains, copy the files you need to another subdirectory, then erase all the files and remove the unneeded directory.

Displaying the Directory Structure The CHKDSK Command

If you create a file structure with several levels, you may not remember exactly what subdirectories you created or exactly where they are. You could display the contents of each directory on the disk to find the files marked <DIR>, but there's a quicker way. As described in Chapter 6, the Check Disk command includes an option (/V) that displays the name of each subdirectory and file on a disk. This option is included in versions 2 and 3 of DOS.

For example, suppose you want to display the directory structure of the diskette in drive B (the current drive). You can use Check Disk with the /V option, but Check Disk is an external DOS command.

Type the following command to see what happens if DOS can't find the command file it needs:

```
Current Directory is B:\ENG
Command: chkdsk /v
```

Depending on how your system is set up, DOS might respond:

```
Bad command or file name

Current Directory is B:\ENG
Command: _
```

If it displays the Check Disk report and a list of files, some of the following examples won't apply to you. Continue reading, but don't type any more examples until you come to the heading "Setting a Path and Displaying a Directory Structure."

But suppose you see the message *Bad command or file name*. What happened? DOS looked for the command file named CHKDSK in the current directory (\ENG) and didn't find it, because the DOS command files are on your fixed disk or, if you're using diskettes, on the diskette in drive A. You could change the current drive, type the command, then change the drive back, but that's an unnecessary inconvenience. DOS gives you a better solution: the Path command.

The Path to a Command The PATH Command

In a multilevel filing system, you'll probably change the current directory as you use the files in different subdirectories. But, as you just saw, you'll use command files too, such as the external DOS commands and application programs. When you type a command, DOS looks for the command file in the current directory. If you have changed the current directory, chances are the new current directory doesn't contain the command file you need.

The Path command lets you tell DOS where to look for a command file if it's not in the current directory. You can name one or more directories—the root directory or any subdirectory for the disk in any disk drive. This command lets you work in any subdirectory you want and still be able to use any command file.

The Path command has three parameters:

path <drive><path> ;

<drive> is the letter, followed by a colon, of the drive (such as B:) with the disk that contains the command file. If you omit <drive>, DOS looks on the disk in the current drive for the directory specified by <path>.

<path> is the path name of the directory that contains the command file.

You can specify several command paths in one command, separating them with semicolons. If you enter a Path command with no parameters (just type *path*), DOS displays the command paths you have defined. If you type *path* followed by only a semicolon, DOS cancels any command paths you have already defined.

If you have a fixed disk, you can use the Path command to let you use application programs, as well as external DOS commands, no matter what the current directory is. Suppose you use Microsoft Word, Lotus 1-2-3, R:BASE System V, and MaxThink, and your DOS files are in a directory named \DOS. Your Path command might look like:

```
path c:\dos;c:\word;c:\123;c:\rbfiles;c:\max
```

The order in which you specify the directory names determines the order in which DOS searches for the command file. By including the drive letter, you can use programs in any of these directories even if the current drive isn't C. You'll probably want to include a Path command in a special startup file named AUTOEXEC.BAT, which is described in Chapter 12, ''Creating Your Own Commands.'' Then you won't have to type a lengthy Path command each time you start your system.

Setting a Path and Displaying a Directory Structure

Now that you've been introduced to the Path command, you can complete the display you attempted earlier with the /V option of the Check Disk command.

If you're using diskettes, tell DOS to look in the root directory of drive A for command files by typing:

```
Current Directory is B:\ENG
Command: path a:\
```

(If you're using a fixed disk and the command worked when you typed it earlier, you can start typing the examples again.)

Enter the Check Disk command again to display the directory structure of the diskette in the current drive; the report is long, and part of it will scroll off the screen, but you're going to print it in a moment, so just let it go. Type the following:

```
Current Directory is B:\ENG
Command: chkdsk /v
```

DOS finds the command file it needs and reports on the directory structure of the diskette in drive B. The last few lines of the report are on the screen; here is the complete report:

```
Directory B:\
Directory B:\MKT
      B:\MKT\ACCOUNT
Directory B:\MKT\WP
      B:\MKT\WP\LET1.DOC
      B:\MKT\WP\LET2.DOC
      B:\MKT\WP\LET3.DOC
      B:\MKT\WP\RPT1.DOC
      B:\MKT\WP\RPT2.DOC
      B:\MKT\WP\RPT3.DOC
      B:\MKT\WP\LET1.STY
      B:\MKT\WP\LET2.STY
      B:\MKT\WP\LET3.STY
Directory B:\MKT\BUDGET
      B:\MKT\BUDGET\BGT1.PLN
      B:\MKT\BUDGET\BGT2.PLN
      B:\MKT\BUDGET\BGT3.PLN
Directory B:\MKT\CUSTOMER
Directory B:\MKT\SALES
Directory B:\ENG
      B:\ENG\ACCOUNT
Directory B:\ENG\BUDGET
Directory B:\ENG\SCHEDULE
      B:\SAMPLE.TXT

  1213952 bytes total disk space
     4096 bytes in 8 directories
     7680 bytes in 15 user files
  1201764 bytes available on disk

   655360 bytes total memory
   567200 bytes free
```

Before displaying its usual messages listing how much disk space and memory is available and being used, the Check Disk command lists each directory and file on the disk. The directories are identified by *Directory* preceding the path and file name; file names are indented six spaces below the name of the directory that contains them.

A printed copy of this report can be helpful, especially if your filing system has several levels. For a fixed disk with several hundred files, however, this list could be several pages long. That's fine if you really want to see where all your files are stored, but it can be a bit much if all you're interested in is the directory structure.

You've already seen how to send output to the printer with the greater-than symbol (>). Using techniques described in Chapter 13, "Taking Control of Your System," you can filter out all the file names from the output of the Chkdsk command, leaving just the subdirectory names, and send the output to the printer. Try it; make sure your printer is turned on and type the following (notice that a slash, not a backslash, precedes the *v*):

```
Current Directory is B:\ENG
Command: chkdsk /v ¦ find "Di" > prn
```

The printed list should show only the names of the directories (the lines that contain *Di*). Such a guide to your filing system can help you keep track of the files and subdirectories and use the system more effectively.

Note: The Tree command, included in the IBM version of DOS, produces output similar to the /V option of the Check Disk command. It is described in Appendix E, the DOS command reference.

The Path to a Data File
The APPEND Command

If you're using version 3.3, you can use the Append command to tell DOS where to look for a data file if it's not in the current directory. Just as with the Path command, you can name one or more directories on any disk drive.

The Append command has three parameters:

append <drive><path> ;

<drive> is the letter, followed by a colon, of the drive (such as *c:*) with the disk that contains the data files. If you omit <drive>, DOS looks in the directory specified by <path> on the current drive.

<path> is the path name of the directory that contains the data files.

You can specify several data paths in one command, separating them with semicolons. If you enter an Append command with no parameters (just type *append*), DOS displays the data paths you have defined. If you type *append* followed by just a semicolon, DOS cancels any data paths you have defined.

It's easy to try the Append command. The current directory is \ENG, and the file RPT1.DOC is in the directory \MKT\WP. First, try to display it by using the Type command:

```
Current Directory is \ENG
Command: type rpt1.doc
```

DOS replies *File not found* because RPT1.DOC isn't in the current directory. Now type two Append commands to set the data path to \MKT\WP and display the data path:

```
Current Directory is \ENG
Command: append \mkt\wp

Current Directory is \ENG
Command: append
APPEND=\MKT\WP
```

Now try the Type command again:

```
Current Directory is \ENG
Command: type rpt1.doc
This is a sample file.
```

This time DOS finds the file because you told it where to look. Cancel the data path by typing Append with just a semicolon, then check the data path again:

```
Current Directory is \ENG
Command: append ;

Current Directory is \ENG
Command: append
No Append
```

The Path and Append commands are valuable tools for improving the efficiency and convenience of using a fixed disk. Chapter 9, ''Managing Your Fixed Disk,'' describes their use in more detail, and Appendix E, the DOS command reference, includes a complete description of each.

If you're going to continue using your system, type the following to restore the system prompt:

```
Current Directory is \ENG
Command: prompt

B>
```

CHAPTER SUMMARY

Although this chapter introduced several new terms and concepts, it doesn't take many commands to set up a multilevel file system. The structure shown in Figure 8-3, for example, required only the following 11 commands (don't enter them, this list is just to show you the commands you entered):

md mkt	md sales
md eng	md \eng\wp
cd mkt	cd \eng
md wp	md budget
md budget	md schedule
md customer	

You might not create a file structure with this many levels on a diskette, although it's certainly possible if you use high-capacity diskettes. As you noticed, subdirectories require a great deal of work from the diskette drive. But you might find that two or three subdirectories reduce the number of diskettes you use, or that they let you use your system more efficiently. The examples in this chapter showed you how to use all the commands you need to create and manage a multilevel filing system.

If you're using a fixed disk, save the diskette that contains the file system you created in this chapter. You'll use it to copy sample files in the next chapter, "Managing Your Fixed Disk."

CHAPTER

MANAGING YOUR FIXED DISK

A fixed disk holds far more data than a diskette does, and DOS uses it much more quickly. As its name implies, you don't remove the disk; it is permanently fixed in the drive. Like a diskette, a fixed disk stores data in tracks and sectors; unlike a diskette, however, a fixed disk stores data on several magnetically coated, rigid metal—not plastic—disks that are enclosed in a nonremovable case.

A fixed-disk drive usually contains two or more separate disks that give it a total storage capacity of 10 to 30 megabytes, but fixed disks with even higher capacities are becoming more common. The IBM PS/2 Model 80, for example, comes with a fixed disk that can hold as much as 314 megabytes. This chapter focuses on how to use your fixed disk efficiently. If you don't have a fixed disk, you can skip to Chapter 10, "Creating and Editing Files of Text."

Managing your fixed disk requires more thought and planning than managing your diskettes, simply because of the sheer number of files involved. But properly organized and managed, your fixed disk is a fast and effective tool you use with a minimum of fuss. Two tasks are more important than any others in managing your fixed disk efficiently. One is setting up a filing system that lets you take advantage of the disk's capacity without losing track of all your files. The other is backing up the files periodically, both to protect yourself against loss of data in the event your fixed disk is inadvertently erased or damaged, and to clear out old files you no longer use regularly.

The previous chapter covered setting up a multilevel filing system. Everything you learned there applies to managing your fixed disk properly. This chapter covers the additional tasks of organizing directories and files on your fixed disk, using some commands that are tailored for keeping track of large numbers of files, and backing up files to diskettes and restoring them to the fixed disk.

In most ways, you treat a fixed disk as if it were a large diskette, using the DOS directory commands to create, change, and remove directories, and the DOS file commands to copy, erase, rename, and otherwise work with your files. The Volume and Label commands described in Chapter 6, "Managing Your Diskettes," can also be used with a fixed disk. But two diskette commands—Diskcopy and Diskcomp—don't work with the fixed disk because they are specifically designed to work only with entire diskettes.

Warning: It's possible to erase all the files on the fixed disk by inadvertently formatting it. A way to protect yourself against this is described under "Renaming the Format Command" in Chapter 16, "Tailoring Your System."

This chapter suggests some guidelines to simplify the job of managing your fixed disk; it shows you how to:

- Define and use a data path—similar to the command path, but for data files—using the Append command and its options.

- Control the archive attribute of a file with the Attribute command.
- Copy files selectively with the Replace and Xcopy commands.
- Back up files from one disk to another with the Backup command.
- Restore files from a backup disk with the Restore command.
- Put all the DOS files in a directory named \DOS and thus reduce clutter in the root directory.
- Install a new version of DOS on your fixed disk, using the System and Copy commands.

PUTTING APPLICATION PROGRAMS ON THE FIXED DISK

The examples in this chapter use part of the directory structure and sample data files you created in the previous chapter. When you actually set up a directory structure, you'll undoubtedly want to copy the command and data files of your application programs onto the fixed disk. Depending on how you set up your directories and how many application programs you use, you might put the application programs in the root directory, another subdirectory, or perhaps in a separate subdirectory for each application. Some application programs are copy protected and cannot be copied to the fixed disk. To use such an application program, you put the program diskette in drive A and use the Path command to tell DOS to look for command files on drive A, in addition to using the fixed disk. Check each application program's documentation for instructions on using the program with a fixed disk.

Note: Remember that DOS, too, is a collection of command files. And, like application program files, you can store the DOS files on your fixed disk in a variety of places—in the root directory, for example, or in a subdirectory named \DOS. It is not possible to predict how DOS has been installed on your fixed disk. If, however, all your DOS programs are in the root directory, you should consider moving them to a DOS directory so they'll be easy to find and won't clutter up your root directory and directory displays. Instructions for doing this are at the end of this chapter in the section "DOS and Your Fixed Disk." If you haven't yet prepared your fixed disk, turn to Appendix A, "Preparing Your Fixed Disk," and follow the instructions on installing DOS for the first time before you continue with this chapter.

PREPARING FOR THE EXAMPLES

The examples in this chapter rely on the information presented in the previous chapter, "A Tree of Files," and use the directory structure and files you created there. If you haven't completed those examples, do so before continuing.

The examples in this chapter require the sample subdirectories and files in Figure 9-1. You will create these on the fixed disk in a subdirectory named \TEMP, which will keep all your examples in one place for easy removal. If you already have a \TEMP directory, use a different—unique—name.

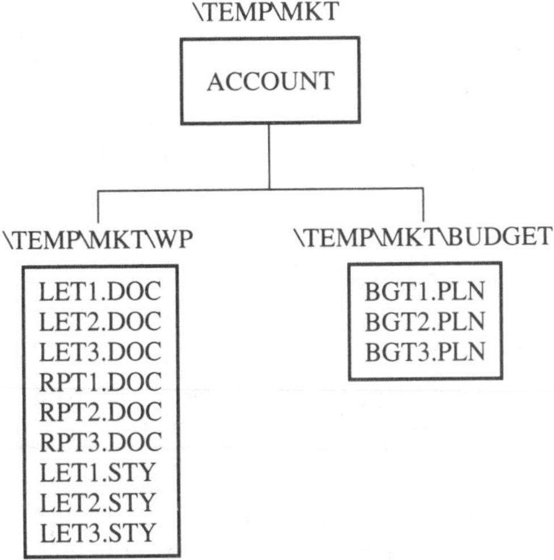

Figure 9-1. Subdirectories and files for fixed-disk examples

To keep track of where you are in your directory structure, change the prompt to an abbreviated version of the one you used in the last chapter by typing:

```
C>prompt $p$g<Enter>

C:\>
```

Now your system prompt shows both the current drive and the current directory.

To create the \TEMP subdirectory, type:

```
C:\>md temp
```

Moving Files to Your Fixed Disk

The remainder of your preparation depends on which version of DOS you're using. If you have version 3.2 or later, follow the instructions under the heading "Moving Files with the Xcopy Command." If you have a version of DOS prior to 3.2, follow the instructions under the heading "Moving Files with the Copy Command."

Moving Files with the Xcopy Command

If you're using version 3.2 or later of DOS, moving everything from your practice diskette to the \TEMP directory is simple. All you need is one Xcopy command,

which copies subdirectories and files from the source disk to the target disk. The Xcopy parameter you use here, /S, copies all subdirectories as well as all files. Xcopy is described in more detail later. For now, put the diskette that contains your sample files in drive A and type:

```
C:\>xcopy a: \temp /s
```

DOS responds:

```
Reading source file(s)...
A:SAMPLE.TXT
A:MKT\ACCOUNT
A:MKT\WP\LET1.DOC
A:MKT\WP\LET2.DOC
A:MKT\WP\LET3.DOC
A:MKT\WP\RPT1.DOC
A:MKT\WP\RPT2.DOC
A:MKT\WP\RPT3.DOC
A:MKT\WP\LET1.STY
A:MKT\WP\LET2.STY
A:MKT\WP\LET3.STY
A:MKT\BUDGET\BGT1.PLN
A:MKT\BUDGET\BGT2.PLN
A:MKT\BUDGET\BGT3.PLN
A:ENG\ACCOUNT
       15 File(s) copied
```

You don't need the file named SAMPLE.TXT, or the directory named \ENG and the file it contains, so remove them by typing:

```
C:\>erase \temp\sample.txt

C:\>erase \temp\eng\account

C:\>rd \temp\eng
```

Change your current directory to \TEMP:

```
C:\>cd temp

C:\TEMP>
```

You're through.

Moving Files with the Copy Command

Put the diskette that contains your sample files in drive A and type the following commands to duplicate the diskette's directory structure on your fixed disk:

```
C:\>md \temp\mkt

C:\>md \temp\mkt\wp

C:\>md \temp\mkt\budget
```

Now type the following to copy the files from the diskette to the fixed disk; press any key when DOS prompts you for the diskette for drive A:

```
C:\>copy a:\mkt\account \temp\mkt
        1 File(s) copied

C:\>copy a:\mkt\wp\*.* \temp\mkt\wp
A:\MKT\WP\LET1.DOC
A:\MKT\WP\LET2.DOC
A:\MKT\WP\LET3.DOC
A:\MKT\WP\RPT1.DOC
A:\MKT\WP\RPT2.DOC
A:\MKT\WP\RPT3.DOC
A:\MKT\WP\LET1.STY
A:\MKT\WP\LET2.STY
A:\MKT\WP\LET3.STY
        9 File(s) copied

C\>copy a:\mkt\budget\*.* \temp\mkt\budget
A:\MKT\BUDGET\BGT1.PLN
A:\MKT\BUDGET\BGT2.PLN
A:\MKT\BUDGET\BGT3.PLN
        3 File(s) copied
```

Now make \TEMP the current directory:

```
C:\>cd temp

C:\TEMP>
```

This completes the preparation.

DEFINING A DATA PATH

As you saw in the previous chapter, the Path command defines a path that tells DOS where to look for a command file if it's not in the current directory, and, if you're using 3.3 or a later version of DOS, the Append command defines a path that tells DOS where to look for a data file if it isn't in the current directory. (A command file, remember, is a nontext file whose extension is COM, EXE, or BAT; a data file is any file that doesn't have one of those extensions.)

When you define a command path with the Path command, DOS carries out the first command file it finds in the command path that matches the name of the command you type. Similarly, when you define a data path with the Append command, DOS applies the command you type to the first file it finds in the data path that matches the file name.

The first time you use the Append command you can specify two parameters, /X and /E, that control how the Append command works. After that first time, you can specify only the name of one or more directories that make up the data path.

The Append command has four possible parameters:

append /X /E <path> ;

/X increases the number of DOS commands that use the data path. You can specify /X only once—the first time you enter the Append command. If you specify /X, you cannot specify a data path in the same command; you must use an additional Append command to name the directories in the data path. If you specify /X, don't use the Xcopy, Backup, or Restore commands (described later in this chapter) while a data path is defined.

/E tells DOS to make the data path part of its working environment, just as it does the command path. You can specify /E only once—the first time you enter the Append command. If you specify /E, you cannot specify a data path in the same command; you must use an additional Append command to name the directories you want to include in the data paths.

<path> is the path name of the directory that is to be part of the data path. You can specify more than one <path>, separating them with semicolons. If the directory is on a drive other than the current drive, precede the path name with the drive letter followed by a colon (for example, *a:\mkt*).

If you type *append* followed by a semicolon only, DOS deletes the currently defined data path and limits its searches for data files to the current directory.

If you omit all parameters (type only *append*), DOS displays the data path in the same form as it displays the command path. If no data path is defined, DOS responds with the message *No Append.*

Examples of Defining a Data Path

To see the effect of the Append command, type the following commands to change the current directory to \MKT and display the directory entries of all files whose name begins with RPT:

```
C:\TEMP>cd mkt

C:\TEMP\MKT>dir rpt*

 Volume in drive C is FIXEDDISK
 Directory of  C:\TEMP\MKT

File not found
```

There is no file whose name begins with RPT in \TEMP\MKT, but there are three in TEMP\MKT\WP. Type the following three Append commands. The first specifies /X to make the data path available to more DOS commands, the second defines a data path that consists of the directory named \TEMP\MKT\WP, and the third displays the data path you specified:

```
C:\TEMP\MKT>append /x

C:\TEMP\MKT>append \temp\mkt\wp

C:\TEMP\MKT>append
APPEND=\TEMP\MKT\WP
```

Again display the directory entries of all files whose name begins with RPT:

```
C:\TEMP\MKT>dir rpt*

 Volume in drive C is FIXEDDISK
 Directory of  C:\TEMP\MKT

RPT1     DOC        24  10-16-87   8:17a
RPT2     DOC        24  10-16-87   8:17a
RPT3     DOC        24  10-16-87   8:17a
        3 File(s)   17317440 bytes free
```

Now DOS finds the files. But notice that the directory listing still shows the current directory (\TEMP\MKT), even though the files are in \TEMP\MKT\WP. Keep in mind that when you have a data path defined, DOS doesn't tell you the name of the directory in which it actually found the file. This can be a bit disorienting if you define a data path with many directories or if you have files with the same names stored in different directories.

Although DOS can locate any data file in the data path, there are some restrictions on how you can use those files. You can display them with the Type command or copy them with the Copy command. But if you try to erase a file in the data path, DOS responds *Access denied*; if you try to rename a file in the data path, DOS responds *Duplicate file name or file not found.*

And remember, if files in more than one directory in the data path match the file name you enter with a command, the command is carried out only on the first file (or set of files) that DOS finds in the data path directories.

The Append command is most useful for working with application programs that require access to data files (such as a spelling dictionary or a table of salary data) as well as access to program files. Just as the Path command lets you use an application program from any directory, even if it requires access to command files in a different directory, the Append command lets you use an application program from any directory, even if it requires access to both command and data files in other directories.

Note: Exercise some caution with application programs when you have defined a data path, because the effect is not always what you expect. Suppose the current directory

is \TEMP\MKT\WP and you have defined a data path that includes the directory \TEMP\ENG\WP. You edit a file named REPORT.DOC in TEMP\ENG\WP, then exit the word processor; it stores the edited version of REPORT.DOC in the current directory (\TEMP\MKT\WP), not *in \TEMP\ENG\WP. Now you've got two copies of REPORT.DOC: the unchanged original in \TEMP\ENG\WP—the one you meant to change—and the revised version in \TEMP\MKT\WP, where it doesn't even belong.*

CHANGING THE ARCHIVE ATTRIBUTE OF A FILE

In Chapter 5, following the heading "Controlling Whether a File Can Be Changed," you saw how to use the Attribute command to control the read-only attribute of a file or a group of files. If you're using 3.2 or a later version of DOS, you can also use the Attribute command to control the *archive attribute* of a file.

The archive attribute, like the read-only attribute, is a part of the directory entry that isn't displayed by the Directory command but can be examined or changed by DOS or any other program. This attribute is turned off by the Backup and Xcopy commands, which are described later in this chapter, and by some programs that back up files from a fixed disk. The attribute is turned on by Edlin, Microsoft Word, and most other programs that change a file.

The archive attribute therefore tells DOS (or any other program that checks it) whether a file has been changed since the last time it was backed up. The archive attribute is used principally by the Backup and Xcopy commands—and by backup programs—to determine which files must be backed up.

Because of the way it is stored in the directory entry, you may sometimes see the archive attribute called the *archive bit;* rest assured the terms refer to the same thing.

The Attribute command, which lets you control the read-only or archive attributes, can have six parameters:

attribute +R –R +A –A <filename> /S

+R turns on the read-only attribute (as you saw in Chapter 5), and –R turns it off.

+A turns on the archive attribute. This tells DOS (or any other program) that the file has been changed since it was backed up to an archival storage medium, such as a diskette or a tape. You can use this parameter with 3.2 and later versions.

–A turns off the archive attribute. This tells DOS (or any other program) that the file has not been changed since it was backed up for archival storage. You can use this parameter with 3.2 and later versions.

<filename> is the name of the file whose attributes are to be changed or displayed. You can use wildcard characters to specify a group of files.

/S tells DOS to apply the Attribute command to each subdirectory contained in <filename>. If you specify <filename> as the root directory of a disk and include /S, the Attribute command is applied to every subdirectory on the disk. You can use this parameter with version 3.3 only.

If you omit all parameters except <filename>, DOS displays the name or names of the files, with an A in column 3 if the file has the archive attribute and an R in column 8 if the file is read only.

Examples of Changing the Archive Attribute

First, change the current directory to \TEMP\MKT\WP and check the attributes of the files in the current directory by typing the following Change Directory and Attribute commands:

```
C:\TEMP\MKT>cd wp

C:\TEMP\MKT\WP>attrib *.*
  A        C:\TEMP\MKT\WP\LET1.DOC
  A        C:\TEMP\MKT\WP\LET2.DOC
  A        C:\TEMP\MKT\WP\LET3.DOC
  A        C:\TEMP\MKT\WP\RPT1.DOC
  A        C:\TEMP\MKT\WP\RPT2.DOC
  A        C:\TEMP\MKT\WP\RPT3.DOC
  A        C:\TEMP\MKT\WP\LET1.STY
  A        C:\TEMP\MKT\WP\LET2.STY
  A        C:\TEMP\MKT\WP\LET3.STY
```

DOS displays the name of each file with an A in column 3, because the files have never been backed up.

To turn off the archive attribute of all files with the extension DOC and check the result, type:

```
C:\TEMP\MKT\WP>attrib -a *.doc

C:\TEMP\MKT\WP>attrib *.*
           C:\TEMP\MKT\WP\LET1.DOC
           C:\TEMP\MKT\WP\LET2.DOC
           C:\TEMP\MKT\WP\LET3.DOC
           C:\TEMP\MKT\WP\RPT1.DOC
           C:\TEMP\MKT\WP\RPT2.DOC
           C:\TEMP\MKT\WP\RPT3.DOC
  A        C:\TEMP\MKT\WP\LET1.STY
  A        C:\TEMP\MKT\WP\LET2.STY
  A        C:\TEMP\MKT\WP\LET3.STY
```

Now only those files whose extension is STY have the archive attribute.

If you're using version 3.3 of DOS, you can use the /S parameter to apply the Attribute command to all subdirectories. To turn off the archive attribute of all files in

the directories \TEMP\MKT, \TEMP\MKT\WP, and \TEMP\MKT\BUDGET and then check the results in all three directories, type the following commands to change the directory to \TEMP\MKT, turn off the archive attribute of all files in all subdirectories, and check the attributes of all files in all subdirectories:

```
C:\TEMP\MKT\WP>cd ..

C:\TEMP\MKT>attrib -a *.* /s

C:\TEMP\MKT>attrib *.* /s
          C:\TEMP\MKT\WP\LET1.DOC
          C:\TEMP\MKT\WP\LET2.DOC
          C:\TEMP\MKT\WP\LET3.DOC
          C:\TEMP\MKT\WP\RPT1.DOC
          C:\TEMP\MKT\WP\RPT2.DOC
          C:\TEMP\MKT\WP\RPT3.DOC
          C:\TEMP\MKT\WP\LET1.STY
          C:\TEMP\MKT\WP\LET2.STY
          C:\TEMP\MKT\WP\LET3.STY
          C:\TEMP\MKT\BUDGET\BGT1.PLN
          C:\TEMP\MKT\BUDGET\BGT2.PLN
          C:\TEMP\MKT\BUDGET\BGT3.PLN
          C:\TEMP\MKT\ACCOUNT
```

The response to the second Attribute command shows that you turned off the archive attribute of all the files in \TEMP\MKT\WP, \TEMP\MKT\BUDGET, and \TEMP\MKT.

Type the following command to turn on the archive attributes of all files in all subdirectories in \TEMP\MKT. (Examples later in the chapter expect them to be on.)

```
C:\TEMP\MKT>attrib +a *.* /s
```

COPYING SELECTED FILES

In earlier chapters, you saw that you can copy files with similar names or extensions by using the Copy command and wildcard characters. If you're using 3.2 or a later version of DOS, you have even more flexibility in copying files:

- The Replace command lets you replace all files in every subdirectory of a target disk that have the same name as the files on a source disk. The Replace command also lets you copy only the files on a source disk that *don't* exist on the target disk or in a target directory.
- The Xcopy command, as you saw in preparing for this chapter's examples, lets you copy whole subdirectories and the files in them. It also lets you copy only files that have changed since they were last backed up, or those that have changed since a particular date.

Replacing Files on a Disk

The Replace command, like the Copy command, copies files from one disk or directory to another. Unlike the Copy command, however, a parameter of the Replace command lets you copy only files that don't exist on the target; this is called *adding* files because you don't copy any files that exist on both the source and target disks.

If, on the other hand, you don't tell DOS to copy only files that don't exist on the target, the Replace command copies all source files, including those that replace existing files on the target; hence, the name of the command.

As a further refinement, the Replace command also lets you copy files not only from the source directory, but also from all the subdirectories it contains.

The Replace command has seven parameters:

replace <source> <target> /A /S /R /P /W

<source> is the name of the file to be copied. You can use wildcard characters to replace a set of files that have similar file names or extensions.

<target> specifies where <source> is to be copied. You can include any combination of drive letter, path name, and file name.

/A (for *add*) copies only the files specified in <source> that don't exist in <target>. This lets you add files to <target> without replacing files that already exist. If you don't specify /A, all files specified in <source> are copied to <target>, just as if you had used the Copy command. If you specify /A, you cannot specify /S.

/S (for *search*) applies the Replace command to all subdirectories contained in <target>. If you specify <target> as the root directory of a disk, the command is applied to every subdirectory on the disk. If you specify /S, you cannot specify /A.

/R replaces files in <target> that are read only.

/P prompts you for confirmation before it replaces or adds each file.

/W (for *wait*) prompts you to press a key before the Replace command begins. This lets you put in the correct diskette before starting to replace or add files.

To see how the Replace command works, copy the file named LET1.DOC from \TEMP\MKT\WP to \TEMP\MKT\BUDGET and check the directory by typing:

```
C:\TEMP\MKT>copy wp\let1.doc budget
        1 File(s) copied

C:\TEMP\MKT>dir budget

 Volume in drive C is FIXEDDISK
 Directory of  C:\TEMP\MKT\BUDGET

.            <DIR>       10-16-87   8:21a
..           <DIR>       10-16-87   8:21a
BGT1     PLN         24  10-16-87   8:17a
BGT2     PLN         24  10-16-87   8:17a
BGT3     PLN         24  10-16-87   8:17a
LET1     DOC         24  10-16-87   8:17a
        6 File(s)   15157248 bytes free
```

Now use the Replace command with no parameters to copy all files whose name begins with LET and whose extension is DOC from \TEMP\MKT\WP to \TEMP\MKT\BUDGET by typing:

```
C:\TEMP\MKT>replace wp\let*.doc budget
```

DOS responds:

```
Replacing C:\TEMP\MKT\BUDGET\LET1.DOC

1 file(s) replaced
```

The Replace command copied only the file—the one you copied at the beginning of this example—that already existed in \TEMP\MKT\BUDGET. The message tells you that DOS *replaced* one existing file.

Now type the Replace command again, but this time include the /A parameter, which tells DOS to copy only those files that do not exist in the target; you're doing the opposite of what you did with the previous Replace command:

```
C:\TEMP\MKT>replace wp\let*.doc budget /a
```

DOS responds:

```
Adding C:\TEMP\MKT\BUDGET\LET2.DOC

Adding C:\TEMP\MKT\BUDGET\LET3.DOC

2 file(s) added
```

Sure enough, this time the Replace command copied the files that it didn't copy in the previous example. The message tells you that DOS *added* files to the target directory.

Copying Files with the Xcopy Command

In preparing for this chapter, you used the Xcopy command to move an entire directory structure from one disk to another. If the corresponding subdirectories don't exist on the target disk or directory, the Xcopy command creates them.

Unlike Copy and Replace, Xcopy can be used selectively to copy only files whose archive attribute is on, or to copy only files that have been changed since a date you specify.

The Xcopy command has 10 parameters:

xcopy <source> <target> /A /M /D:<date> /E /P /S /V /W

<source> is the name of the file to be copied. You can use wildcard characters to copy a set of files with similar file names or extensions.

<target> specifies where <source> is to be copied. You can include any combination of drive letter, path name, and file name.

/A copies only those files whose archive attribute is on, but leaves the archive attribute unchanged.

/M copies only those files whose archive attribute is on, but turns off the archive attribute. This tells DOS (or any other program) that the file hasn't been changed since it was last backed up and therefore doesn't need to be backed up again.

/D:<date> copies only files created or changed on or after <date>. (The date of creation or last change is the date shown in the directory entry for any file. Enter <date> just as you would for the Date command.)

/E creates subdirectories in <target> even if they're empty in <source>.

/P prompts for confirmation before each file specified in <source> is copied.

/S applies the Xcopy command to all subdirectories contained in <target>. If you specify <source> as the root directory of a disk, the Xcopy command is applied to every subdirectory on the disk.

/V verifies that the copy of the file on <target> was stored correctly. This can slow the operation of the Xcopy command somewhat, but it's good insurance if you're copying critical data and must be certain that it was copied correctly.

/W prompts you to press a key before the Xcopy command begins. This wait gives you a chance to put in the correct diskette before starting to copy files.

For this example, you create a temporary subdirectory named FRED in the root directory and dispose of it at the end of the example. First, change the current directory to \TEMP:

```
C:\TEMP\MKT>cd ..
```

Now type the following Make Directory command:

```
C:\TEMP>md \fred
```

and add the following sample file to \TEMP:

```
C:\TEMP>copy con test.doc
This is a test file.
^Z
        1 File(s) copied
```

All the files in \TEMP and its subdirectories have the archive attribute turned on. For the first Xcopy command, use the /A attribute to copy all the files in \TEMP whose extension is DOC and whose archive attribute is turned on:

```
C:\TEMP>xcopy *.doc \fred /a
```

DOS responds by displaying the name of each source file as it is copied:

```
Reading source file(s)...
TEST.DOC
        1 File(s) copied
```

DOS copied TEST.DOC, the only file in \TEMP whose extension is DOC. Verify this by displaying the directory of \FRED:

```
C:\TEMP>dir \fred

 Volume in drive C is FIXEDDISK
 Directory of  C:\FRED

.            <DIR>      10-16-87  12:28p
..           <DIR>      10-16-87  12:28p
TEST     DOC        22  10-16-87  12:35p
        3 File(s)  14096384 bytes free
```

Now type the same Xcopy command, but add the /S parameter to copy all files whose extension is DOC and whose archive attribute is turned on, not only in \TEMP but also in all its subdirectories:

```
C:\TEMP>xcopy *.doc \fred /a /s

Reading source file(s)...
TEST.DOC
\MKT\WP\LET1.DOC
\MKT\WP\LET2.DOC
\MKT\WP\LET3.DOC
\MKT\WP\RPT1.DOC
\MKT\WP\RPT2.DOC
\MKT\WP\RPT3.DOC
\MKT\BUDGET\LET1.DOC
\MKT\BUDGET\LET2.DOC
\MKT\BUDGET\LET3.DOC
    10 File(s) copied
```

This time DOS copied 10 files; it also copied the subdirectories named \MKT\WP and \MKT\BUDGET. Verify this by displaying the directory of \FRED\MKT:

```
C:\TEMP>dir \fred\mkt

 Volume in drive C is FIXEDDISK
 Directory of  C:\FRED\MKT

.            <DIR>      10-12-87  12:28p
..           <DIR>      10-12-87  12:28p
WP           <DIR>      10-12-87  12:39p
BUDGET       <DIR>      10-12-87  12:39p
        4 File(s)  14071808 bytes free
```

The Xcopy command created the subdirectories named WP and BUDGET in \FRED, then copied the files whose extension is DOC and whose archive attribute is on from \TEMP\MKT\WP to \FRED\MKT\WP and from \TEMP\MKT\BUDGET to \FRED\MKT\BUDGET.

The value of the archive attribute, however, is that it can tell you which files have changed since they were last backed up, if the archive attribute is turned off when a file is backed up and turned on when a file is changed. The /M parameter, like the /A parameter, tells Xcopy to copy only those files whose archive attribute is on; but it also turns the archive attribute off, so that you can mark the files as backed up. Type another Xcopy command to copy the files whose extension is DOC, but this time use /M instead of /A:

```
C:\TEMP>xcopy *.doc \fred /m /s
```

DOS responds just as it did to the previous Xcopy command, because it copied the same 10 files, but this time it turned their archive attribute off. It's easy to check this; retype the last Xcopy command:

```
C:\TEMP>xcopy *.doc \fred /m /s
        0 File(s) copied
```

This time no files were copied, because the previous command turned off the archive attributes of the files.

Now suppose you change one of the files. A new file's archive attribute is on, just as if it were an existing file you changed with Edlin or a word processor, so type the following to create a different version of \TEMP\TEST.DOC:

```
C:\TEMP>copy con test.doc
A new version of TEST.DOC.
^Z
        1 File(s) copied
```

Type the same Xcopy command you typed twice before; the first time it copied 10 files, the second time it copied no files, and this time it should copy one file:

```
C:\TEMP>xcopy *.doc \fred /m /s

Reading source file(s)...
TEST.DOC
        1 File(s) copied
```

You copied only the file whose archive attribute was on.

Type the following commands to dispose of the files and directories you added for this example:

```
C:\TEMP>erase \fred\mkt\wp\*.doc

C:\TEMP>rd \fred\mkt\wp

C:\TEMP>erase \fred\mkt\budget\*.doc

C:\TEMP>rd \fred\mkt\budget

C:\TEMP>rd \fred\mkt
```

```
C:\TEMP>erase \fred\test.doc
```

```
C:\TEMP>rd \fred
```

Change the current directory back to \TEMP\MKT:

```
C:\TEMP>cd mkt
```

and, finally, clean up your \TEMP\MKT\BUDGET directory for later examples:

```
C:\TEMP\MKT>erase budget\let*.doc
```

DEVELOPING A BACKUP PROCEDURE

It could take a drawerful of diskettes to back up all the files on a fixed disk: If your average file were 10,000 bytes long (about 6½ double-spaced typed pages), a full 10 MB fixed disk would have more than 1000 files, and you would need almost thirty 360 K diskettes to back them all up. A full 30 MB fixed disk could require almost ninety 360 K diskettes, or about twenty-five high-capacity (1.2 MB) diskettes.

But you don't have to back up all your files. You needn't back up program files, for example, because you've already got the original DOS and application-program diskettes. Some data files, such as a spelling dictionary, don't usually change, so it isn't necessary to back them up, either.

How often you back up your other data files, such as word-processed documents and spreadsheets, depends on how often they change. For example, spreadsheets might change often while the budget is being prepared, but remain unchanged the rest of the year. The backup procedures you use depend on how you use your computer. But no matter how you decide to back up your files, be certain to do so regularly. A system failure can happen, but if you back up your files regularly, such a failure will be more of an inconvenience than a disaster.

BACKING UP FILES

The Backup command lets you select files on the basis of their path name, file name, whether they have been changed since the last backup, or whether they have been changed since a particular date. The options can be combined, so you can back up files in just about any way you like.

The Backup command has 10 parameters:

backup <path><filename> <drive> /A /S /M /F /D:<date> /T:<time> /L:<logfile>

<path> is the path name of the directory from which files are to be backed up. If you don't specify <path>, DOS backs up files from the current directory.

<filename> is the name of the file to be backed up. You can use wildcard characters to back up a set of files. If you don't specify <filename>, DOS backs up all files in the specified directory.

<drive> is the letter, followed by a colon, of the drive (such as *a:*) that contains the diskette that receives the backup files. You must specify <drive>.

/A adds the backup files to the backup diskette, rather than erasing all files on the backup diskette as the command usually does before making the backup copies.

/S backs up files from all subdirectories.

/M backs up only the files that have been modified since the last backup.

/F formats the target disk if it isn't already formatted. The /F option of the Backup command uses the Format command file (FORMAT.COM) to format the target disk, so FORMAT.COM must be in either the current directory or a directory that is in the command path.

/D:<date> backs up all files that have changed since <date>. Enter <date> just as you would for the Date command.

/T:<time> backs up all files that have changed since <time> on <date>. Enter <time> just as you would for the Time command.

/L:<logfile> creates a log file on the disk in the source drive. The log file contains the date and time of the backup procedure and, for each file that is backed up, the path name, the file name, and the number (assigned by DOS) of the diskette that contains the file. If a log file already exists, the backup information is added at the end, creating a history of backups for the source drive. If you include /L but omit the colon and <logfile>, DOS names the log file BACKUP.LOG and stores it in the root directory of the source drive.

You can combine parameters in one Backup command.

Note: Although the Backup command exists in versions of DOS numbered 2.0 and later, not all the versions include all the parameters described here, nor are all the versions and releases of DOS compatible with one another. For a list of the options available to you, check the documentation that came with your version of DOS. To ensure that your backup procedure works smoothly, use the same version of DOS both to back up and to restore files.

Backing Up All the Files in a Directory

The simplest way to back up files is by directory. You back up all files in a directory by specifying just the path of the directory and the letter of the diskette drive that contains the backup diskette. Before you try the following examples, have a formatted blank diskette ready. Now, to back up all the files in \TEMP\MKT\BUDGET, type the following:

```
C:\TEMP\MKT>backup c:\temp\mkt\budget a:
```

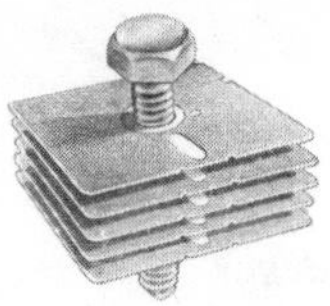

DOS beeps and displays a warning:

```
Insert backup diskette 01 in drive A:

Warning! Files in the target drive
A:\ root directory will be erased
Strike any key when ready
```

If you don't use the /A option, DOS erases any files in the backup diskette before it makes the backup copies. This warning gives you a chance to make certain the correct diskette is in the drive. Put your formatted blank diskette in drive A and press any key. DOS displays the name of each file as it makes the copies:

```
*** Backing up files to drive A: ***
Diskette Number: 01

\TEMP\MKT\BUDGET\BGT1.PLN
\TEMP\MKT\BUDGET\BGT2.PLN
\TEMP\MKT\BUDGET\BGT3.PLN
```

The directory of the backup diskette shows one file you might not expect. Type the following:

```
C:\TEMP\MKT>dir a:
```

If you're using 3.2 or an earlier version, DOS responds:

```
 Volume in drive A has no label
 Directory of  A:\

BACKUPID @@@       128  10-16-87   3:19p
BGT1     PLN       152  10-16-87   8:17a
BGT2     PLN       152  10-16-87   8:17a
BGT3     PLN       152  10-16-87   8:17a
        4 File(s)   358400 bytes free
```

BACKUPID.@@@ is a small file that DOS stores on a backup diskette to identify it. Also, note that the files you backed up are larger than the originals on the fixed disk; confirm this by typing:

```
C:\TEMP\MKT>dir \temp\mkt\budget

 Volume in drive C is FIXEDDISK
 Directory of  C:\temp\mkt\budget

.            <DIR>        10-17-87 12:11p
..           <DIR>        10-17-87 12:11p
BGT1     PLN         24   10-16-87  8:17a
BGT2     PLN         24   10-16-87  8:17a
BGT3     PLN         24   10-16-87  8:17a
        5 File(s)  17658400 bytes free
```

If you're using 3.2 or an earlier version, DOS adds 128 bytes at the beginning of each backup file. This addition contains the path and file name of the file that was backed up and is used by the Restore command when it restores files to the fixed disk. The Restore command deletes the path and file name information, so the restored version of the file is identical to the one you originally backed up. You'll work with the Restore command later in the chapter.

If you're using version 3.3, the DOS response to your directory command looks like this:

```
Volume in drive A is BACKUP   001
Directory of  A:\

  BACKUP   001         72  10-16-87    3:19p
  CONTROL  001        311  10-16-87    3:19p
          2 File(s)     360448 bytes free
```

If you're using version 3.3, DOS stores all the backed up files in the file named BACKUP.001 and all the path names in the file named CONTROL.001. (On a second backup diskette, the extensions would be 002; on a third backup diskette, they would be 003, and so forth.) Note that the size of BACKUP.001 corresponds to the total number of bytes in the three files it contains; CONTROL.001 contains all the extra information DOS needs to restore those files. This difference in the way backup files are stored means that the Restore command in version 3.3 works only with files backed up with the version 3.3 Backup command; the version 3.3 Restore command does not restore files backed up with earlier DOS versions.

If a Backup command fills the diskette before backing up all the files you specified, DOS prompts you to put in another diskette. It displays the same warning, but refers to the second diskette as BACKUP DISKETTE 02.

If another diskette is required, DOS prompts again, increasing the diskette number each time. If you were actually backing up files, you would label the diskette you just used with the contents and date and store it away in a safe place.

Backing Up All Subdirectories

You can back up the files in a directory and all its subdirectories with the /S option. For example, to back up all the files in \TEMP\MKT and its subdirectories (\TEMP\MKT\WP and \TEMP\MKT\BUDGET), specify \TEMP\MKT as the path and include the /S parameter by typing the following (be sure to use a backslash in \TEMP\MKT, but a forward slash in /S):

```
C:\TEMP\MKT>backup c:\temp\mkt a: /s
```

Again, DOS displays the warning; press any key to start the backup. DOS displays the file names as it makes the copies:

```
*** Backing up files to drive A: ***
Diskette Number: 01
\TEMP\MKT\ACCOUNT
\TEMP\MKT\WP\LET1.DOC
\TEMP\MKT\WP\LET2.DOC
\TEMP\MKT\WP\LET3.DOC
\TEMP\MKT\WP\RPT1.DOC
\TEMP\MKT\WP\RPT2.DOC
\TEMP\MKT\WP\RPT3.DOC
\TEMP\MKT\WP\LET1.STY
\TEMP\MKT\WP\LET2.STY
\TEMP\MKT\WP\LET3.STY
\TEMP\MKT\BUDGET\BGT1.PLN
\TEMP\MKT\BUDGET\BGT2.PLN
\TEMP\MKT\BUDGET\BGT3.PLN
```

This backup diskette contains all your marketing files, not just the files from one of the subdirectories. Note that you again backed up BGT1.PLN, BGT2.PLN, and BGT3.PLN. As the warning indicated, your prior backups were erased.

Backing Up Specific Files

You can back up specific files by including a file name with the Backup command. A word-processing directory, for example, might contain both documents, which can change frequently, and style sheets, which seldom change. You would back up the documents much more frequently than you would the style sheets. Type the following to change the current directory to \TEMP\MKT\WP and back up only the documents (files whose extension is DOC):

```
C:\TEMP\MKT>cd wp

C:\TEMP\MKT\WP>backup c:*.doc a:
```

DOS displays its usual warning, but wait a moment before you press any key to back up the files. It's good practice to store a printed list of the files on a backup diskette along with the diskette itself. That's easy; make sure your printer is on, and press Ctrl-PrtSc to start simultaneous printing. Now press any key. As usual, DOS displays the file names as it backs them up, but this time it prints the file names, too:

```
*** Backing up files to drive A: ***
Diskette Number: 01

\TEMP\MKT\WP\LET1.DOC
\TEMP\MKT\WP\LET2.DOC
\TEMP\MKT\WP\LET3.DOC
\TEMP\MKT\WP\RPT1.DOC
\TEMP\MKT\WP\RPT2.DOC
\TEMP\MKT\WP\RPT3.DOC
```

The files with an extension of STY were not backed up because you specified only those with an extension of DOC. You can store the printed list with the backup diskette. Remember to press Ctrl-PrtSc again to stop simultaneous printing.

Backing Up Only Files That Have Changed

As your files increase, you might want to be even more selective about the ones you back up. For example, a word-processing directory might contain hundreds of documents; backing them all up could take a lot of time and several diskettes. Two options of the Backup command let you back up only the files that have changed since a directory was backed up, or only the files that have changed since a particular date.

Selecting Files That Have Changed Since the Last Backup

The /M (Modify) option of the Backup command backs up only files that have changed since the directory was last backed up. To see this option, you need a file that has changed since you backed up \TEMP\MKT\WP in the last example. Create a short file by copying from the console:

```
C:\TEMP\MKT\WP>copy con new.doc
This file has changed
since the last backup.
^Z
        1 File(s) copied
```

Now tell DOS to back up only the files with an extension of DOC that have changed since the directory was last backed up:

```
C:\TEMP\MKT\WP>backup c:*.doc a: /m
```

DOS beeps its warning and, when you press a key, it displays the files backed up:

```
*** Backing up files to drive A: ***
Diskette Number: 01

\TEMP\MKT\WP\NEW.DOC
```

Only the new file is backed up.

Selecting Files That Have Changed Since a Particular Date

The /D:<date> option backs up only those files that have changed since a particular date. To see this, you'll need a file with a different date. Change the system date with the Date command. Type the following:

```
C:\TEMP\MKT\WP>date
Current date is Tue 10-16-1987
Enter new date (mm-dd-yy): 1-1-90
```

Now create a file named DATE.DOC by copying from the console:

```
C:\TEMP\MKT\WP>copy con date.doc
This file was last changed
on 1-1-90.
^Z
        1 File(s) copied
```

Use the /D:<date> option to back up the files that have changed since December 31, 1989 by typing:

```
C:\TEMP\MKT\WP>backup c:*.doc a: /d:12-31-89
```

After the warning, DOS displays the file it backs up:

```
*** Backing up files to drive A: ***
Diskette Number: 01

\TEMP\MKT\WP\DATE.DOC
```

Only the file changed after the date you specified is backed up. You can use the /T:<time> option to specify a time in addition to using the /D:<date> option to specify the date.

Adding Files to a Backup Diskette

Each form of the Backup command you have used so far starts by erasing any files on the backup diskette. There might be times, however, when you want to back up files from several different directories on one diskette or add a file or two to an existing backup diskette. The /A option adds a file to a backup diskette.

Your backup diskette now contains \TEMP\MKT\WP\DATE.DOC. To back up the files in \TEMP\MKT\BUDGET, adding them to the backup diskette, type the following command:

```
C:\TEMP\MKT\WP>backup c:\temp\mkt\budget a: /a
```

This time DOS doesn't need to warn you that it's going to erase any files from the backup diskette. If you're using version 3.3, DOS prompts:

```
Insert last backup diskette in drive A:
Strike any key when ready
```

Press a key to start the backup.

With all versions, DOS then starts backing up the files and displaying their names on the screen:

```
*** Backing up files to drive A: ***
Diskette Number: 01

\TEMP\MKT\BUDGET\BGT1.PLN
\TEMP\MKT\BUDGET\BGT2.PLN
\TEMP\MKT\BUDGET\BGT3.PLN
```

If your backup procedure involves periodically backing up a few files from several different directories, you can use the /A option to put all the backup files on one diskette. A word of caution about this technique: With versions of DOS through 3.2, if a file you add to a backup diskette has the same name and extension as a file already on the diskette, DOS changes the extension of the added file to @01, regardless of what it was before.

RESTORING FILES TO THE FIXED DISK

It's easy to restore a file from a backup diskette to the fixed disk. Simply put the backup diskette in the diskette drive and type the Restore command, specifying the name of the file to be restored. The Restore command needs the path and file name information added to files by the Backup command, so you can only restore files that were backed up with the Backup command. Remember, too, that the version 3.3 Restore command can restore only files backed up with the version 3.3 Backup command.

The Restore command has 11 parameters:

restore <drive> <path><filename> /S /P /M /N /B:<date> /A:<date> /E:<time> /L:<time>

<drive> is the letter, followed by a colon, of the drive (such as A:) that contains the backup diskette. You must include <drive>.

<path> is the path name of the directory to which the file is to be restored. If you omit <path>, the file is restored to the current directory.

<filename> is the name of the file to be restored. If you don't specify <filename>, all files backed up from the directory indicated by <path> are restored. You can use wildcard characters to restore a set of files. You must specify either <path> or <filename>.

/S restores files to all subdirectories.

/P tells DOS to prompt you for confirmation before restoring files that have changed since they were last backed up.

/M restores files that were *modified* (or deleted) since they were backed up.

/N restores files that have been deleted from the original source disk since they were backed up.

/B:<date> restores only those files that were changed on or *before* <date>. Enter <date> just as you would for the Date command.

/A:<date> restores only those files that were changed on or *after* <date>. Enter <date> just as you would for the Date command.

/E:<time> restores only those files that were changed at or *earlier than* <time> on <date>. Enter <time> just as you would for the Time command.

/L:<time> restores only those files that were changed at or *later than* <time> on <date>. Enter <time> just as you would for the Time command.

Note: Although the Restore command exists in versions of DOS numbered 2.0 and later, not all the versions include all the parameters described here. For a list of the options available to you, check the documentation that came with your version of DOS.

Warning: Don't use the Backup or Restore commands if you have entered an Assign, Join, or Substitute command to alter the way DOS interprets drive letters. Because these commands can mask the type of drive, DOS could damage or delete the files you specify in the commands or other files on the disk. For more information on Assign, Join, and Substitute, see "Commands for Occasional Use" in Chapter 16.

Preparing for the Restore Command Examples

Type the following to change the date, back up all the files in \TEMP\MKT\WP, and then erase all the files in \TEMP\MKT\WP:

```
C:\TEMP\MKT\WP>date
Current date is Mon 1-01-1990
Enter new date: 10-16-87

C:\TEMP\MKT\WP>backup c:\temp\mkt\wp a:

Insert backup diskette 01 in drive A:

Warning! Files in the target drive
A:\ root directory will be erased
Strike any key when ready

*** Backing up files to drive A: ***
Diskette Number: 01

\TEMP\MKT\WP\LET1.DOC
\TEMP\MKT\WP\LET2.DOC
\TEMP\MKT\WP\LET3.DOC
\TEMP\MKT\WP\RPT1.DOC
\TEMP\MKT\WP\RPT2.DOC
\TEMP\MKT\WP\RPT3.DOC
\TEMP\MKT\WP\LET1.STY
\TEMP\MKT\WP\LET2.STY
\TEMP\MKT\WP\LET3.STY
\TEMP\MKT\WP\NEW.DOC
\TEMP\MKT\WP\DATE.DOC

C:\TEMP\MKT\WP>erase *.*
Are you sure (Y/N)? y
```

This completes the preparation.

Restoring One File

Inadvertently erasing or changing a file is probably the most common reason for restoring a file. You restore a file by specifying the target drive, path name, and file name with the Restore command. (You must include the path name if you are restoring a file to a directory other than the current directory; the path name must be the same as the path from which the file was originally backed up.)

For example, to restore \TEMP\MKT\WP\LET1.STY, type:

```
C:\TEMP\MKT\WP>restore a: let1.sty
```

Note that the drive and path can be omitted because the file is being restored to the current directory.

DOS prompts you for the backup diskette:

```
Insert backup diskette 01 in drive A:
Strike any key when ready
```

The correct diskette is in the drive, so press any key. DOS displays the name of the restored file:

```
*** Files were backed up 10-16-1987 ***

*** Restoring files from drive A: ***
Diskette: 01
\TEMP\MKT\WP\LET1.STY
```

You can display the directory to verify that it's back.

Restoring a Set of Files

You can use wildcard characters to restore a set of files. To restore all the files whose extension is DOC that you backed up from the current directory (\TEMP\MKT\WP), type the following:

```
C:\TEMP\MKT\WP>restore a: *.doc
```

When DOS prompts you for the backup diskette, press any key. DOS displays the names of the files it restores. Again, you can display the directory to verify that the files were restored.

Restoring All the Files in a Directory

If you enter the Restore command with a path name but no file name, DOS restores all files belonging in that directory. For example, to restore all the files you backed up from \TEMP\MKT\WP, type:

```
C:\TEMP\MKT\WP>restore a:
```

Again, press any key when DOS prompts for the diskette. DOS restores all the files you backed up from \TEMP\MKT\WP, not just those whose extension is DOC.

Restoring All Subdirectories

Just as the /S option of the Backup command backs up the files in a directory and all its subdirectories, the /S option of the Restore command restores the files in a directory and all its subdirectories. To restore the files in \TEMP and all its subdirectories, you would type *restore a: \ temp*.* /s.*

Selecting Files to Be Restored

A file you restore replaces a file with the same name on the fixed disk. You might not want this replacement, especially if you have changed the file on the fixed disk since the backup diskette was made. You can protect yourself from unwanted changes by using the /P (*prompt*) option of the Restore command, which tells DOS to prompt for confirmation if the file on the fixed disk has changed since the backup was made.

Warning: If you're using version 3.2 or earlier and are restoring files that were backed up with a previous version of DOS, be sure to use the /P parameter. If DOS asks whether to restore files named MSDOS.SYS, IO.SYS, IBMBIO.COM, or IBMDOS.COM, reply n *(no). Otherwise, you would replace parts of your DOS program with portions of an earlier version, and DOS wouldn't start from your fixed disk.*

To see how the /P parameter works, change LET3.DOC and LET1.STY. First, copy from the console to create a new version of LET3.DOC:

```
C:\TEMP\MKT\WP>copy con let3.doc
The new version of let3.doc.
^Z
        1 File(s) copied
```

Copy this file to LET1.STY, making it a new file, too:

```
C:\TEMP\MKT\WP>copy let3.doc let1.sty
        1 File(s) copied
```

Now restore the entire directory with the /P option:

```
C:\TEMP\MKT\WP>restore a: \temp\mkt\wp\*.* /p
```

DOS asks for the diskette and begins restoring files in the usual way, until it finds a file on the fixed disk that has changed since its backup copy was made.

```
*** Files were backed up 10-16-1987 ***

*** Restoring files from drive A: ***
Diskette: 01

\TEMP\MKT\WP\LET1.DOC
\TEMP\MKT\WP\LET2.DOC
Warning! File LET3.DOC
was changed after it was backed up
Replace the file (Y/N)?
```

This message (yours might vary) gives you a chance to decide whether you want to restore the file. Suppose that you don't want to restore this file; type *n* and press Enter. DOS resumes displaying the names of the files it restores, starting with the one that follows LET3.DOC:

```
\TEMP\MKT\WP\RPT1.DOC
\TEMP\MKT\WP\RPT2.DOC
\TEMP\MKT\WP\RPT3.DOC
Warning! File LET1.STY
was changed after it was backed up
Replace the file (Y/N)?
```

Now suppose you do want to replace the version on the fixed disk with the backup version; type *y* and press Enter. DOS again resumes displaying the names of the files it restores, starting with LET1.STY:

```
\TEMP\MKT\WP\LET1.STY
\TEMP\MKT\WP\LET2.STY
\TEMP\MKT\WP\LET3.STY
\TEMP\MKT\WP\NEW.DOC
\TEMP\MKT\WP\DATE.DOC
```

This completes the examples for backing up and restoring files.

DELETING THE SAMPLE FILES AND DIRECTORIES

If you don't want to keep the files and subdirectories you created for these examples, the following commands erase the files and remove the directories. Be certain to type the Erase commands exactly as shown to avoid the possibility of erasing other files. If you created a temporary subdirectory with a name other than \TEMP, don't forget to type its name in place of \TEMP.

Change the current directory to \TEMP\MKT:

```
C:\TEMP\MKT\WP>cd \temp\mkt
```

Erase the file ACCOUNT in \TEMP\MKT:

```
C:\TEMP\MKT>erase account
```

Erase the files in \MKT\WP:

```
C:\TEMP\MKT>erase wp\*.*
Are you sure (Y/N)?y
```

Remove \TEMP\MKT\WP:

```
C:\TEMP\MKT>rd wp
```

Erase the files in \TEMP\MKT\BUDGET:

```
C:\TEMP\MKT>erase budget\*.*
```

Remove \TEMP\MKT\BUDGET:

```
C:\TEMP\MKT>rd budget
```

Change the current directory to \TEMP:

```
C:\TEMP\MKT>cd \temp
```

Remove \MKT:

```
C:\TEMP>rd mkt
```

Change the current directory to root:

```
C:\TEMP>cd \
```

Remove \TEMP:

```
C:\>rd \temp
```

The fixed disk now contains only the directories and files it had before you started the examples in this chapter.

The remainder of this chapter shows the system prompt as C>. If, as many people do, you prefer to have the system prompt show you the current directory, go on to the next section, but remember the difference between your prompt and what is shown in this book. If you prefer the normal C> displayed by DOS, type:

```
C:\>prompt
```

DOS AND YOUR FIXED DISK

Now that you're familiar with directories and the commands you use to manage them, it's time to look at your own system and see if you can put some of your knowledge to work. The final part of this chapter shows how you can organize your fixed disk to keep your root directory from becoming filled with an assortment of unrelated files.

Setting Up Your Directories

Because a fixed disk can hold so many files, it's important to create a directory structure that lets you keep track of your files and programs. You can set up your subdirectories to match the way you use your computer, organizing them by department or by application program, people's names, or any other way that's comfortable. The topic ''Setting Up a Filing System'' in Chapter 16 suggests several ways you might want to set up your directories.

Until you get a directory structure established, however, files have a tendency to collect in the root directory, making it difficult to find a file you need. If you reserve the root directory for nothing but subdirectories and files that must be there, finding your way around your fixed disk becomes much easier.

In addition to the DOS files, the root directory on your fixed disk might contain many other files. For example, files named CONFIG.SYS and AUTOEXEC.BAT are often created by application programs or are installed by the person who sets up your system. Depending on how your application programs have been copied onto the fixed disk, dozens of data files and program files might also be stored in the root directory of your fixed disk.

The only files that DOS requires to be in the root directory are COMMAND.COM, CONFIG.SYS, and AUTOEXEC.BAT. Some application programs also require files in the root directory; the documentation that came with the program should tell you about this, and the program itself may create the files when you install it.

The remainder of this chapter shows you how to put all the DOS files except COMMAND.COM in a subdirectory named \DOS in the root directory of your fixed disk. If your DOS files are already stored in a directory other than the root, you can either skip to the heading "Installing a New Version of DOS on Your Fixed Disk," or go on to the next chapter.

If your root directory contains many files in addition to the DOS files, the procedures described here use some DOS commands that are introduced in later chapters. If you like to know what you're doing before you do it, you might want to wait until you have completed several more chapters, then come back here to move the DOS files. It's up to you; read through the procedure and decide whether you want to do it now or later.

Depending on how your system is set up, you might also have to change the contents of the two files named AUTOEXEC.BAT and CONFIG.SYS in the root directory. This will mean using either a text editor, such as the DOS text editor Edlin, or a word processor that lets you store a file with no formatting commands in it (word processors describe such files as "unformatted," "text-only," or "nondocument"). The use of Edlin is described in Chapters 10 and 11. Again, if you prefer to wait, by all means do so. DOS will continue to function quite well in the meantime.

A Look at Your Fixed Disk

The following descriptions assume that your fixed disk is not shared, as on a network, and is dedicated to DOS—that is, it is not used by another operating system (such as the multiple-user operating system called XENIX). If your fixed disk is shared with other users or other operating systems, or if you aren't sure, check with the person who set up the disk before trying any of the procedures here.

If DOS and your fixed disk are yours to do with as you will, it's best to know what you're working with. So first, look at your root directory to see what's in it. Type:

```
C>dir /w
```

If DOS has simply been copied from your DOS diskettes to the root directory of your fixed disk, you see a fairly long display with a number of files that should be familiar by now. The display includes file names like this:

```
 Volume in drive C is FIXEDDISK
 Directory of  C:\

MANAGER          BIN              RUNNING      ...
DEVICE           CONFIG   SYS     AUTOEXEC BAK...
MKT              TEMP             WORD         ...
COMMAND  COM     AUTOEXEC BAT     CONFIG   BAK...
DIRS     BAT     APPEND   EXE     ASSIGN   COM...
BASIC    COM     BASICA   COM     CHKDSK   COM...
DISKCOMP COM     DISKCOPY COM     EDLIN    COM...
GRAFTABL COM     GRAPHICS COM     JOIN     EXE...
PRINT    COM     RECOVER  COM     RESTORE  COM...
SUBST    EXE     TREE     COM     XCOPY    EXE...
MORTGAGE BAS
       51 File(s)  12466176 bytes free
```

Notice that the display shows such DOS files as FORMAT.COM, PRINT.COM, DISKCOPY.COM, and so on—all are good indicators that your DOS files are in the root directory. If your directory looks like this, proceed with the instructions in the section that best describes what you see.

On the other hand, you might see something like this:

```
 Volume in drive C is FIXEDDISK
 Directory of  C:\

MANAGER          BIN              DOS          ...
RUNNING          DEVICE           CONFIG   SYS...
AUTOEXEC BAK     MKT              TEMP         ...
WORD             COMMAND  COM     AUTOEXEC BAT...
CONFIG   BAK     DIRS     BAT...
       22 File(s)  12763136 bytes free
```

If your display looks something like this, DOS is already in a directory of its own, and you can skip ahead, either to the next chapter or (for future reference) to the section on installing a new version of DOS.

Note: Although this display shows a directory named DOS, your DOS files might be in a directory with a different name, or they might be in a subdirectory of one of the directories shown on your screen. If you don't see the names of FORMAT.COM, DISKCOPY.COM, and other familiar DOS command files, try displaying the entries of a directory with a likely looking name, such as DOS or PROGRAMS. Another way to check is to type path *and display the entries in each directory that DOS shows in its response to the command.*

Moving the DOS Files from the Root Directory to \DOS

The following procedures leave all non-DOS files in the root directory. Because it's critical to store files in the correct directories, all Copy and Erase commands include both the drive letter and path name, whether or not they're normally required.

First, create a directory named \DOS in the root directory by typing the following Make Directory (md) command:

```
C>md \dos
```

Note: If you already have a directory named \DOS that contains something other than the DOS files, either use a name other than DOS in the procedure you follow or create a different directory, copy the files from your existing \DOS directory into it, and then delete the files from \DOS.

To move the DOS files, you must copy them to \DOS, then delete them from the root directory. The following three procedures describe how to go about it, depending on how many non-DOS files are already in the root directory and how familiar you are with their purpose. Choose the procedure whose title best describes the contents of your root directory and your understanding of their purpose.

Few Non-DOS Files: You Know What They Are

If your root directory contains only a few files other than the DOS command files, and you know what they are and what they contain:

1. Copy all the files in the root directory to \DOS. You'll need a list of the non-DOS files being copied, so if you want, turn on your printer and press Ctrl-PrtSc for simultaneous displaying and printing. Type:

   ```
   C>copy c:\*.* c:\dos
   ```

   Press Ctrl-PrtSc again to turn off printing.

2. Erase all the files in the root directory:

   ```
   C>erase c:\*.*
   ```

   Respond *y* when DOS asks *Are you sure?*

3. Copy the non-DOS files back to the root directory. This example shows three separate Copy commands, one for COMMAND.COM, one for CONFIG.SYS, and one for AUTOEXEC.BAT:

   ```
   C>copy c:\dos\command.com c:\

   C>copy c:\dos\config.sys c:\
   ```

```
C>copy c:\dos\autoexec.bat c:\
```

Type a similar Copy command for any other file you want to move back into the root directory.

4. Delete the non-DOS files from \DOS. Again, this example shows three Erase commands, one for COMMAND.COM, one for CONFIG.SYS, and one for AUTOEXEC.BAT:

```
C>erase c:\dos\command.com

C>erase c:\dos\config.sys

C>erase c:\dos\autoexec.bat
```

Type a similar Erase command for each file in \DOS that you copied back to the root directory. When you have erased all the non-DOS files from \DOS, a listing of the entries in your root directory should include the following:

```
 Volume in drive C is FIXEDDISK
 Directory of  C:\

DOS          <DIR>      10-16-87   1:53p
COMMAND  COM    25307    3-17-87  12:00p
AUTOEXEC BAT      762   10-16-87  10:57a
CONFIG   SYS      155   10-16-87   6:08a
```

In addition to the DOS directory and these files, your directory listing might show additional directories and some other files.

Go on to the heading "Changing CONFIG.SYS."

Many Non-DOS Files: You Know What They Are

If your root directory contains a lot of files in addition to the DOS command files, but you know what these files are, what they contain, and are certain which ones must remain:

1. Print a listing of the entries in the root directory:

```
C>dir c:\ > prn
```

Mark the files that must be in the root directory, such as COMMAND.COM, CONFIG.SYS, and AUTOEXEC.BAT, on the printed copy.

2. Copy the files you marked in Step 1 to \DOS. This example shows three Copy commands, for COMMAND.COM, CONFIG.SYS, and AUTOEXEC.BAT:

```
C>copy c:\command.com c:\dos

C>copy c:\config.sys c:\dos

C>copy c:\autoexec.bat c:\dos
```

Type a similar Copy command for any other file you want to keep in the root directory.

3. Now erase all the files in the root directory:

```
C>erase c:\*.*
```

Respond *y* when DOS asks *Are you sure?*

4. Copy the files that must be in the root directory from the \DOS directory back to the root directory:

```
C>copy c:\dos\*.* c:\
```

5. Erase the files from \DOS:

```
C>erase c:\dos\*.*
```

Respond *y* when DOS asks *Are you sure?*

6. Put the DOS Startup diskette (the diskette labeled DOS if you're using 3.2 or an earlier version) in drive A and copy all the files to \DOS:

```
C>copy a:*.* c:\dos
```

7. Copy COMMAND.COM from the system diskette to the root directory (DOS requires this file to be in the root directory of the disk from which it is started):

```
C>copy a:command.com c:\
```

8. Delete COMMAND.COM from \DOS (it only has to be in the root directory):

```
C>erase c:\dos\command.com
```

9. Put the DOS Operating diskette (the DOS diskette labeled Supplemental Programs if you're using 3.2 or an earlier version) in drive A and copy all the files to \DOS:

```
C>copy a:*.* c:\dos
```

When you have copied all the DOS files to \DOS, a listing of the entries in your root directory should include the following:

```
 Volume in drive C is FIXEDDISK
 Directory of  C:\

DOS          <DIR>      10-16-87   1:53p
COMMAND  COM    25307    3-17-87  12:00p
AUTOEXEC BAT      762   10-16-87  10:57a
CONFIG   SYS      155   10-16-87   6:08a
```

In addition to the \DOS directory and these files, your directory listing should include the other directories and files you kept there.

Go on to the heading "Changing CONFIG.SYS."

You're Not Sure What the Files In the Root Directory Are

If you don't know what the files in the root directory are or what they contain:

1. Put the DOS Startup diskette (the diskette labeled DOS if you're using 3.2 or an earlier version) in drive A and type the following command to store its directory listing in a temporary file named DOSDIR:

   ```
   C>dir a: > c:\dosdir
   ```

2. Put the DOS Operating diskette (the DOS diskette labeled Supplemental Programs if you're using 3.2 or an earlier version) in drive A and make sure the printer is ready to print. Now type the following commands to print a sorted directory listing of both DOS diskettes and to erase the temporary file:

   ```
   C>dir a: >> dosdir

   C>sort < dosdir > prn

   C>erase c:\dosdir
   ```

3. If necessary, move the paper to the top of a new page and print a sorted directory listing of the root directory of the fixed disk by typing the following command:

   ```
   C>dir c:\ ¦ sort > prn
   ```

   Now compare the two printed directories, marking each file name that appears in the listing of the root directory but not in the listing of the DOS diskettes.

4. Copy the files that you marked in Step 3 to \DOS. This example shows three Copy commands, for COMMAND.COM, CONFIG.SYS, and AUTOEXEC.BAT:

   ```
   C>copy c:\command.com c:\dos

   C>copy c:\config.sys c:\dos

   C>copy c:\autoexec.bat c:\dos
   ```

   Type a similar Copy command for each file you want to keep in the root directory. If you have many files with similar names or extensions that don't duplicate DOS file names or extensions, use wildcards to reduce the number of commands.

   For example, if several files have the extension DOC, type *copy c:* .doc c:\dos*. Be certain to mark all files on the listing that are copied by commands using wildcards. (DOS displays their names as it copies them.) That way, you can make sure that you've copied all the files you intend to keep in the root directory. When you've finished, you can double-check your work by printing a directory listing of \DOS (type *dir c:\dos > prn*) and comparing it with the listing you marked in step 3.

5. Now erase all the files in the root directory:

```
C>erase c:\*.*
```

Respond *y* when DOS asks *Are you sure?*

6. Copy the files that must be in the root directory from the \DOS directory back to the root directory:

```
C>copy c:\dos\*.* c:\
```

7. Erase the files from \DOS:

```
C>erase c:\dos\*.*
```

Respond *y* when DOS asks *Are you sure?*

8. Put the DOS Startup diskette (the diskette labeled DOS if you're using 3.2 or an earlier version) in drive A and copy all the files to \DOS:

```
C>copy a:*.* c:\dos
```

9. Copy COMMAND.COM from the system diskette to the root directory (DOS requires this file to be in the root directory of the disk from which it is started):

```
C>copy a:command.com c:\
```

10. Delete COMMAND.COM from \DOS (it only has to be in the root directory):

```
C>erase c:\dos\command.com
```

11. Put the DOS Operating diskette (the DOS diskette labeled Supplemental Programs if you're using 3.2 or an earlier version) in drive A and copy all the files to \DOS:

```
C>copy a:*.* c:\dos
```

When you have copied all the DOS files to \DOS, your root directory should look something like the display shown at the end of the preceding procedure.

Changing CONFIG.SYS

If there is a file named CONFIG.SYS in the root directory of your fixed disk, it might contain some Device commands that name DOS files. If it does, you must change these commands so that they refer to the new location of the DOS files (C:\DOS) instead of the root directory (C:\).

Check the contents of CONFIG.SYS by displaying it with a Type command:

```
C>type c:\config.sys
```

If DOS responds *File not found*, you have no file named CONFIG.SYS, so go on to "Testing the New DOS Directory."

If DOS displays the contents of the file, check each line to see if it is a Device command that names a DOS file; for example, *device=c:\vdisk.sys* or *device= c:\mouse.sys*. If it is, use your text editor or word processor (if it lets you store a file with no formatting commands) to change each Device command so that it refers to \DOS, not to the root directory. (The example Device commands shown earlier in the paragraph would become *device=c:\dos\vdisk.sys* and *device=c:\dos\mouse.sys*.)

Testing the New DOS Directory

Double-check your work by displaying the entries in the root directory to make sure it contains only subdirectories (entries identified by *<DIR>*), COMMAND.COM, and the files you left there:

```
C>dir c:\
```

Make certain that COMMAND.COM is included, because DOS won't start without it; if the file isn't in the root directory, put the DOS system diskette in drive A and copy COMMAND.COM to the root directory.

Next, check the directory of \DOS to make sure it contains the DOS files:

```
C>dir c:\dos
```

If you're not certain you can recognize the DOS files, look for such file names as FORMAT.COM, MODE.COM, or SORT.EXE, or compare the directory display to the directory list you printed earlier. If you didn't print one, put the DOS system diskette in drive A, display its directory, and compare the results. It isn't necessary to do a file-by-file check, just a general comparison. If the DOS files aren't in your DOS directory, or some are missing, copy them from the DOS diskettes to \DOS (Steps 6–9 of the second procedure).

Now it's time to make sure everything works. Open the latch on drive A and press Ctrl-Alt-Del to restart the system. DOS should start just as it did before.

If the system doesn't start properly, chances are that COMMAND.COM isn't in the root directory. Close the latch on drive A (so that DOS will start from the system diskette) and press Ctrl-Alt-Del again. When DOS is running, copy COMMAND.COM from the DOS diskette to the root directory on the fixed disk, and restart the system.

If DOS displays a message such as *Bad or missing VDISK.SYS*, a Device command in CONFIG.SYS probably still refers to the root directory instead of C:\DOS. Go back to the heading "Changing CONFIG.SYS" and follow the instructions there.

Adding \DOS to the Command Path

When your system is running with the DOS files in their new location, you have one more task: Put C:\DOS in the command path with the Path command, so that DOS can find its command files. You'll put this command in a file named AUTOEXEC.BAT— described under "Creating Your Own Startup Procedure" in Chapter 12—that contains commands DOS carries out each time the system is started.

First, check the contents of AUTOEXEC.BAT with the Type command:

```
C>type c:\autoexec.bat
```

If DOS responds *File not found*, type the following to create the file with the Path command you need:

```
C>copy con c:\autoexec.bat
path c:\dos
^Z
        1 File(s) copied
```

If DOS displays a series of commands in response to your Type command, edit the file using a text editor or a word processor. If there is no Path command, add the line *path c:\dos* to the file. If there is a Path command (such as *path c:* or *path c:\;c:\word*), add a semicolon and *c:\dos* to the end of the command and save the revised version of the AUTOEXEC.BAT file.

Now press Ctrl-Alt-Del to restart the system. When DOS displays the system prompt, check the command path by typing a Path command with no parameters:

```
C>path
```

DOS should respond by displaying the command path, which should include C:\DOS (for example, *PATH=C:\DOS* or *PATH=C:\;C:\WORD;C:\DOS*). If there is no path, or the path doesn't include C:\DOS, go back and repeat the instructions beginning with "Adding \DOS to the Command Path."

When you successfully add C:\DOS to the command path, DOS can find its command files no matter what the current directory is.

If the root directory in your fixed disk still contains application program files and data files, you should eventually move them to other directories. As you learn what more of the files are for and become more comfortable with the tree-structured filing system, you can create directories for these files, copy them to the new directories, and delete them from the root directory.

Installing a New Version of DOS On Your Fixed Disk

If DOS is installed on your fixed disk and you want to install a newer version, you must replace not only all the DOS command and data files, but also two hidden files that DOS requires. The System (sys) command transfers these two hidden files from the diskette in the drive from which you started DOS to the fixed disk drive.

After you have copied the two hidden files with the System command, you must copy all the DOS files from both DOS diskettes to the fixed disk. COMMAND.COM must be stored in the root directory of the fixed disk, but the other DOS files can be stored in any directory.

The example that follows shows you a complete procedure for installing a new version of DOS.

The System command has one parameter:

sys <drive>

<drive> is the letter, followed by a colon, of the disk that is to receive the DOS system files.

Example of Installing a New Version of DOS

This example shows you how to install version 3.3 of DOS on your fixed disk by copying the two hidden files, then copying the DOS files to either the root directory of the fixed disk or to a directory named \DOS (remember, COMMAND.COM must always be stored in the root directory). If you're installing a different version, the procedure is the same; just remember that references to the version 3.3 system diskette mean the system diskette for the new version you're installing.

Note: If your DOS files are in the root directory, but you want to put them in a directory named \DOS (or any directory other than the root), turn to the heading "Moving the DOS Files from the Root Directory to \DOS" earlier in this chapter and follow the instructions there before continuing with this example.

Installing a new version of DOS takes only a few commands:

1. Put the version 3.3 Startup diskette in drive A (if you're installing 3.2 or an earlier version, put in the diskette labeled DOS). Turn the computer on or, if it's already running, press Ctrl-Alt-Del to restart it.

2. Enter the date and time if DOS prompts for them. When DOS displays the system prompt, type the System command to copy the two hidden files:

   ```
   A>sys c:
   ```

   DOS responds *System transferred.*

3. Now you must copy the DOS command and data files to the fixed disk. To put all the DOS files in the root directory of the fixed disk, type the following Copy command (the number of files copied varies with different versions of DOS):

   ```
   A>copy *.* c:\
           22 File(s) copied
   ```

   To put COMMAND.COM in the root directory of the fixed disk and put the other DOS files in a separate directory (\DOS, in this example), type the following commands, substituting the name of your DOS directory, if it differs from \DOS:

   ```
   A>copy command.com c:\
            1 File(s) copied
   ```

```
A> copy *.* c:\dos
        22 File(s) copied

A> erase c:\dos\command.com
```

You deleted COMMAND.COM from C:\DOS because the second Copy command copied it, along with the other DOS files, to C:\DOS, and you don't need it there. It's quicker to copy all the files and then delete COMMAND.COM than it is to use several Copy commands to avoid copying COMMAND.COM.

4. If you're using 3.5-inch diskettes, you're through; go on to step 5. If you're using 5.25-inch diskettes, copy the remaining DOS files from the second (supplemental) DOS diskette to the directory named \DOS on the fixed disk. Take out the Startup diskette and put in the Operating diskette. (If you're installing 3.2 or an earlier version, take out the diskette labeled DOS and put in the diskette labeled Supplemental Programs.)

   If you're putting all the DOS files in the root directory of the fixed disk, type:

```
A> copy *.* c:\
        31 File(s) copied
```

   If you're putting the DOS files in a directory of their own, such as \DOS, type the following, substituting your directory name for \DOS if necessary:

```
A> copy *.* c:\dos
        31 files copied
```

5. That's it. Now open the latch on drive A, so that DOS will start from the fixed disk, and press Ctrl-Alt-Del. You should see the sign-on message of the new version you just installed.

CHAPTER SUMMARY

If you organize your file structure to match your work, a fixed disk quickly becomes an essential part of your computer system. If, in addition, you develop a backup procedure that protects only those files whose loss would cost you time or data, backing up your fixed disk takes just a little time and a few diskettes. The relatively small investments required to organize and safeguard your data will be returned many times over in ease of use and peace of mind, especially the first time an error—by the system or by you—causes the loss of a valuable file.

You can also create your own commands to back up the fixed disk. With the techniques described in Chapters 12, 14, and 15, backing up the fixed disk can become a routine part of using your computer, simplifying the job and guaranteeing consistency no matter who backs up the files on the fixed disk.

CHAPTER

10

CREATING AND EDITING FILES OF TEXT

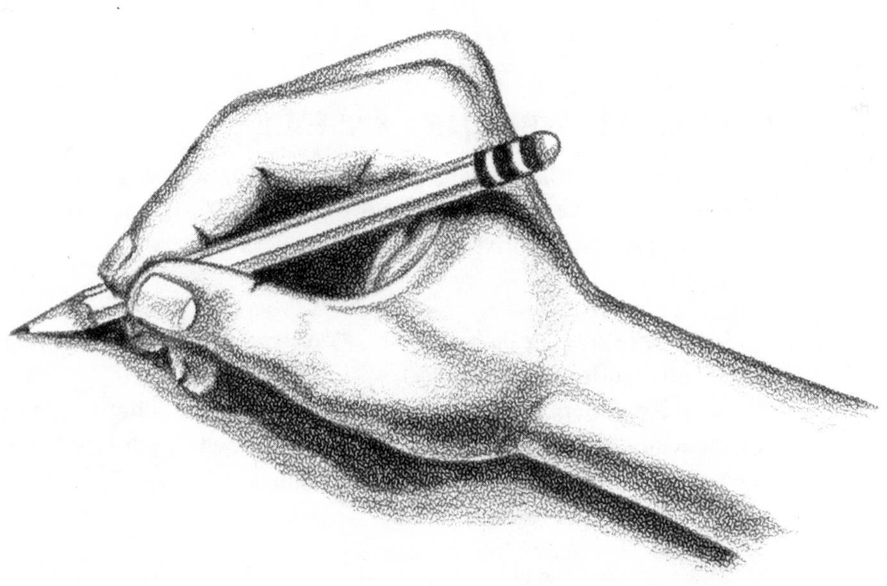

When you need to write a note or other short document, it's not always convenient to find a typewriter or to schedule the work with your word-processing people. You could use a word-processing program, but loading the program, writing the document, and printing the results might be more trouble than a short document is worth. What you need is a small, fast program that's easy to use. Edlin, the DOS text editor, is just such a program. After practicing the example in this chapter, you'll be able to use Edlin for those reminder lists, short notes, and memos, as well as for batch files (which you'll encounter in Chapter 12).

The example in this chapter presents a situation that could occur in any office: You're a project leader; your team has completed several spreadsheets, a 10-page proposal, and a cover letter. You have copied these files to a diskette and want the team to review the results one last time before the presentation next Monday. You're going to send a copy of the diskette to each team member, and you need a short memo to tell them what's on it.

Note: Edlin is a unique part of DOS with its own prompt and its own commands. The example in this and the following chapter shows you the evolution of a short text file named MEMO.TXT. To disrupt the example as little as possible, the descriptions of Edlin commands are included in the narrative portion of the text, but are not elaborated on as in the preceding chapters. Full descriptions of all Edlin commands and parameters are in the reference section in Appendix E of this book.

PREPARING FOR THE EXAMPLE

The example in this chapter requires one formatted diskette. If you have one diskette drive, put the diskette in it. If you have two diskette drives, put the diskette in drive B. Now change the current drive to drive B by typing:

```
C>b:
```

If you have only one diskette drive, DOS prompts you to insert a diskette. The diskette is in the drive, so press any key.

Edlin is an external command file. Whenever you use Edlin, DOS must be able to find the command program on disk. If you don't have a fixed disk, tell DOS to look for commands on the system disk in drive A by typing:

```
B>path a:\
```

This completes the preparation for the example.

CREATING A NEW TEXT FILE

When you type *edlin* followed by the name of a file in response to the system prompt, DOS copies the Edlin program into memory and starts the program running. Edlin

checks to see if the file you named exists. If the file exists, Edlin copies the file into memory and waits for you to enter any of several commands that say, in effect, "Edlin, do this to my file." If the file doesn't exist, Edlin assumes you want to create a file and give it the name you specified, and so it waits for you to enter an appropriate command.

To begin the example for this chapter, type the following to create a file called MEMO.TXT on the disk in drive B. Like DOS, Edlin accepts commands in either uppercase or lowercase letters:

```
B>edlin memo.txt
```

Edlin tells you that MEMO.TXT is a new file and waits for a command:

```
New file
*_
```

The asterisk (*) is the Edlin command prompt; it tells you that Edlin is ready for you to type an Edlin command, just as the DOS C> prompt tells you that DOS is ready for you to type a DOS command.

All you can do with a new file is insert lines. Most Edlin commands are single letters, so all you need type here is *i* (for Insert):

```
*i
```

Edlin responds with:

```
        1:*_
```

When you use Edlin, you work with a file line by line. To help you keep track of where you are, Edlin displays a line number at the beginning of each line. These line numbers are important, because many of the editing commands can be preceded by a line number or by starting and ending line numbers that define a range of lines you want to work with. The asterisk following the line number isn't part of the line; it shows you the *current line,* and it is no more a part of your document than the C> prompt or the cursor. Just as DOS remembers the current disk and uses it unless you specify otherwise, Edlin remembers the current line and uses it unless you specify otherwise.

In response to your Insert command, Edlin displays the number it will assign to the first line you enter, followed by the asterisk and the cursor. Because this is a new file, the first line number is 1. After you type the Insert command, Edlin adds each subsequent line you type to the file. You tell Edlin when to end each line by pressing Enter. Each time you press Enter, Edlin moves to the beginning of the next line and displays the new line number, the asterisk, and the cursor. When you want to stop adding lines, press Ctrl-Break (or Ctrl-C).

ENTERING LINES

It's time to enter the first few lines of the sample memo. If you make a typing error, you can backspace and correct it before pressing Enter. But don't worry if you enter a line with errors; as you'll learn, it's easy to correct them. Type the following lines, but not the line numbers; remember, they're automatically displayed by Edlin. <Ctrl-Break> means hold down the Ctrl key and press the Break key; <Enter> means press the Enter key without typing anything.

```
 1:*This diskette has 5 files on it:
 2:*FORECAST.PLN
 3:*OPTION1.PLN
 4:*OPTION2.PLN
 5:*LETTER.DOC
 6:*PROPOSAL.DOC
 7:*<Enter>
 8:*Please check the spreadsheets and print the
 9:*documents to make sure they agree with our
10:*assumptions.
11:*<Enter>
12:*Let's do this quickly, it's due Monday.
13:*<Ctrl-Break>

*_
```

Ctrl-Break shows on your screen as ^C and tells Edlin you don't want to insert any more lines, so Edlin moves the cursor to the beginning of a new line and displays its prompt, *, telling you it's waiting for another command.

DISPLAYING LINES

There are several reasons you might want to display your file:

- To see if you have included everything you meant to include.
- To check what you have done.
- To edit your file.

The List command (l) displays one line or a range of lines. If you type a line number followed by l, Edlin displays a maximum of 23 lines (one screenful), starting with the line you specify. To see the example you just typed, use the List command to display the document, starting at line 1. Type:

```
*1l
```

Edlin responds with:

```
1: This diskette has 5 files on it:
2: FORECAST.PLN
3: OPTION1.PLN
```

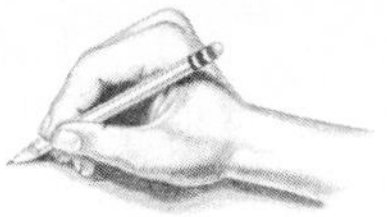

```
         4: OPTION2.PLN
         5: LETTER.DOC
         6: PROPOSAL.DOC
         7:
         8: Please check the spreadsheets and print the
         9: documents to make sure they agree with our
        10: assumptions.
        11:
        12: Let's do this quickly, it's due Monday.
*_
```

You can display a range of lines by preceding the l with the numbers, separated by a comma, of the first and last lines you want to see. For example, to display only lines 2 through 6, type:

```
* 2,6l
```

Edlin shows you:

```
         2: FORECAST.PLN
         3: OPTION1.PLN
         4: OPTION2.PLN
         5: LETTER.DOC
         6: PROPOSAL.DOC
*_
```

ADDING LINES TO A FILE

You can insert lines anywhere in an existing file by preceding the Insert command with a line number. Edlin inserts the new line or lines before the line you specify, and it automatically renumbers the lines following the insertion.

For example, to insert a blank line before the list of file names, type:

```
* 2i
         2:* <Enter>
         3:* <Ctrl-Break>

*_
```

To insert lines at the end of a document, use the Insert command and either specify a line number larger than the last line number or use the symbol #, which means "the line after the last line." To use # to add a signature line to your example, type:

```
* #i
        14:* <Enter>
        15:* Tom
        16:* <Ctrl-Break>

*_
```

Now suppose you decide to add a title to your memo. The beginning is line 1, so specify line 1 with the Insert command:

```
*1i
         1:*Final Project Review -- 10/16/87
         2:*<Enter>
         3:*To: Project team
         4:*<Enter>
         5:*<Ctrl-Break>

*_
```

Display the file now to see the insertions. Type:

```
*1l
```

Edlin shows you:

```
         1: Final Project Review -- 10/16/87
         2:
         3: To: Project team
         4:
         5:*This diskette has 5 files on it:
         6:
         7: FORECAST.PLN
         8: OPTION1.PLN
         9: OPTION2.PLN
        10: LETTER.DOC
        11: PROPOSAL.DOC
        12:
        13: Please check the spreadsheets and print the
        14: documents to make sure they agree with our
        15: assumptions.
        16:
        17: Let's do this quickly, it's due Monday.
        18:
        19: Tom
*_
```

Note that Edlin has renumbered all the lines.

ENDING AN EDITING SESSION

When you end an editing session with e (the End Edit command), Edlin stores your edited file on disk and returns you to DOS. After the file has been stored, DOS displays the system prompt (B>). Type the End Edit command:

```
*e
```

DOS stores the file on the disk and displays the system prompt:

```
B>_
```

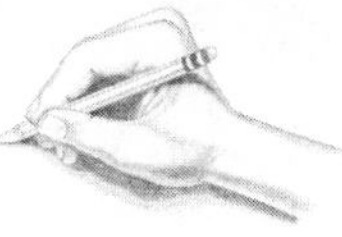

PRINTING A FILE

A file stored on diskette is of limited value if you can't print a copy of it, so DOS makes it easy to print a file. First, make sure the printer is turned on. Next, use the DOS Copy command to copy the practice file to the printer. Type the following:

```
B>copy memo.txt prn
```

DOS prints the file and tells you:

```
        1 File(s) copied
```

Your memo is ready for distribution. For many short jobs, that's all there is to it. Using Edlin, you can create and print a file in only a few minutes.

EDITING AN EXISTING TEXT FILE

There will be times you'll want to change an existing text file—perhaps to add items to a list, delete a sentence or two from a memo, or change some wording. Use Edlin now to edit your practice file. Type *edlin,* followed by the name of the file, MEMO.TXT:

```
B>edlin memo.txt
End of input file
*_
```

This time you're not creating a new file, so Edlin tells you that it has read to the end of your input file and copied the file into memory, and then it displays its prompt.

DELETING LINES

You can use Edlin to delete a line by typing the number of the line followed by d (the Delete command). For example, suppose you decide not to include line 10 (LETTER.DOC) in your memo. To delete the line, type:

```
*10d
```

Edlin acknowledges by moving to the next line and displaying the * prompt.

To delete several lines, precede the d with the numbers of the first and last lines to be deleted, separating the numbers with a comma (*number,number* represents the range of lines). To delete the heading (lines 1 through 4) in your practice memo, type:

```
*1,4d
```

To verify that the lines have been deleted, type:

```
*1l
```

Edlin responds with:

```
        1:*This diskette has 5 files on it:
        2:
        3: FORECAST.PLN
        4: OPTION1.PLN
        5: OPTION2.PLN
        6: PROPOSAL.DOC
        7:
        8: Please check the spreadsheets and print the
        9: documents to make sure they agree with our
       10: assumptions.
       11:
       12: Let's do this quickly, it's due Monday.
       13:
       14: Tom
*_
```

Again, notice that Edlin has renumbered the lines.

CANCELING AN EDITING SESSION

Suppose you change a file, then decide you really don't want the changes. You can cancel the editing session with q (the Quit command) and return to DOS. The revised version of your file won't be stored on disk.

So that you don't inadvertently cancel an editing session and lose your work, Edlin prompts you to confirm the Quit command. If you type *y*, Edlin returns you to DOS without storing the revised file. If you type any other character, Edlin ignores the Quit command. With this command, you don't have to press Enter after replying to the prompt.

For example, to cancel your editing session, type:

```
*q
```

Edlin responds:

```
Abort edit (Y/N)?_
```

Type *y*. Edlin returns you to DOS, and DOS displays its system prompt:

```
B>_
```

Edit the file again:

```
B>edlin memo.txt
End of input file
*_
```

Now, display it to verify that the lines you deleted earlier are still in the version stored on disk:

```
*1l
         1:*Final Project Review -- 10/16/87
         2:
         3: To: Project team
         4:
         5: This diskette has 5 files on it:
         6:
         7: FORECAST.PLN
         8: OPTION1.PLN
         9: OPTION2.PLN
        10: LETTER.DOC
        11: PROPOSAL.DOC
        12:
        13: Please check the spreadsheets and print the
        14: documents to make sure they agree with our
        15: assumptions.
        16:
        17: Let's do this quickly, it's due Monday.
        18:
        19: Tom
*_
```

It's the same version you stored with the End Edit command.

SEARCHING FOR A GROUP OF CHARACTERS

As a file gets longer, the List command becomes a less and less efficient way to locate and display a particular line. If your sample memo were 80, 90, or 100 lines long, for example, it would take several List commands to display it all, because the screen can display only 23 lines at a time.

You can locate a line much more quickly by telling Edlin to search for a unique group (*string*) of characters the line contains. But note the word "unique." You could become very frustrated if you specified a string of commonly occurring letter combinations, such as *the* or *ing*. Remember, Edlin makes no judgments. If you specified the string *the*, Edlin might dutifully show you every single *the, then, there, hither,* and *thither* in your document. To search for a string of characters, type the number of the line where Edlin should begin searching, then type *s* (for the Search command) and the string.

Suppose the sample memo was several pages long, the list of file names was on page 3, and you wanted to delete a file name. Instead of displaying several screenfuls of text to find the right line, you could use the Search command to find the first line containing the string PLN (the extension of the first three file names). Edlin displays the first line it finds that contains PLN.

Even though the memo is actually much shorter, perform this search anyway. To start searching at the beginning of the file for PLN (note the capitalization), type:

```
*1sPLN
```

Edlin displays the first line that contains PLN:

```
          7: FORECAST.PLN
*_
```

The line Edlin finds—or the line you choose—becomes the current line. In the preceding example, the current line is line 7. If no line contains the string you have specified, Edlin responds *Not found.*

Suppose you know that several lines contain the same string. You can amplify the Search command to tell Edlin to display a prompt, after it shows you each line, that asks whether this is the line you want. If you respond *y*, Edlin stops the search; if you reply *n*, Edlin searches for the next line that contains the string.

To tell Edlin you want to be shown this prompt, type a question mark before the *s*. For example, suppose you know that several lines contain PLN; you want to find OPTION2.PLN, but you're not sure which line it's on. To find OPTION2.PLN, type the following:

```
*1?sPLN
```

Edlin responds as follows. Type *n* or *y* as shown here:

```
          7:*FORECAST.PLN
O.K.? n
          8: OPTION1.PLN
O.K.? n
          9: OPTION2.PLN
O.K.? y
*_
```

As with most Edlin commands, you can specify a range of lines to search. If you know that you need to search only lines 2 through 5, you can limit the search by typing *2,5sPLN.* If you don't specify a starting line, Edlin starts searching from the line that follows the current line. If you don't specify an ending line, Edlin searches to the end of the file.

EDITING A LINE

Up to this point, you have been editing the memo by inserting and deleting entire lines. You can also edit individual lines, to change the wording or to correct typing errors. Edlin gives you two ways to change a line: You can use the Replace command (not the same as the DOS Replace command) or you can use the editing keys on your keyboard.

Replacing One String with Another

The Replace command (r), like the Search command, tells Edlin to look for a string of characters. Each time it finds the string, however, Edlin replaces the old string with a new string of characters you have included in the Replace command.

The format of the Replace command is much like the format of the Search command: a range of line numbers, *r* for *replace,* and then the string to search for. Because the Replace command replaces one string with another, the Replace command ends with the string that is to replace the old one. If you don't specify a replacement string of characters, Edlin deletes the string and replaces it with nothing. If you do specify a new string, you must separate the two strings. You do this by pressing F6 or Ctrl-Z.

Note: When you press F6 or Ctrl-Z, Edlin displays the keystroke as ^Z. But the symbols ^ and Z aren't actual characters. If you press the left arrow key, you erase both the ^ and the Z, because the pair represents one symbol. When you see ^Z in the following examples, press F6 or Ctrl-Z.

In the sample memo, suppose you remember that the extension of your word-processing files is TXT, not DOC. You could change each line that contains DOC, but it's faster to use the Replace command to change all the occurrences of DOC with one command. If you don't specify an ending line, Edlin assumes you mean the entire file. To change DOC to TXT throughout the practice file, type:

```
*1rDOC^ZTXT
```

Edlin displays each line it changes:

```
        10: LETTER.TXT
        11: PROPOSAL.TXT
*_
```

As with the Search command, the last line changed (line 11 in the example) becomes the current line. If no line contains the string, Edlin responds *Not found.*

But what if you want to change some, not all, occurrences of the first string? Again, as with the Search command, you can tell Edlin to prompt you for confirmation after it displays each line that would change. When Edlin prompts you for confirmation, it shows the changed version, but the change isn't permanent yet, so you can decide whether to make the change. If you type *n*, Edlin will scrap the new version and keep the original. You ask Edlin to display the prompt by typing *?* before the command name (r).

Suppose you want to change PLN to DIF, except in the line that refers to the file OPTION1.PLN; you want to leave that one unchanged. Because one occurrence of PLN is going to stay the same, you need to tell Edlin to prompt for confirmation. Type the following to make the changes:

```
*1?rPLN^ZDIF
        7: FORECAST.DIF
O.K.? y
        8: OPTION1.DIF
O.K.? n
        9: OPTION2.DIF
O.K.? y
*_
```

To look at the results, type:

```
*1l
        1: Final Project Review -- 10/16/87
        2:
        3: To: Project team
        4:
        5: This diskette has 5 files on it:
        6:
        7: FORECAST.DIF
        8: OPTION1.PLN
        9:*OPTION2.DIF
       10: LETTER.TXT
       11: PROPOSAL.TXT
       12:
       13: Please check the spreadsheets and print the
       14: documents to make sure they agree with our
       15: assumptions.
       16:
       17: Let's do this quickly, it's due Monday.
       18:
       19: Tom
*_
```

You can change the lines back by typing:

```
*1rDIF^ZPLN
        7: FORECAST.PLN
        9: OPTION2.PLN
```

and:

```
*1rTXT^ZDOC
       10: LETTER.DOC
       11: PROPOSAL.DOC
*_
```

The Replace command is one of Edlin's most powerful features, but use it with some care. You could change every occurrence of a string of characters in the entire file with one command—including some changes you didn't intend.

Remember, each occurrence of the string in a line is changed, so be sure you want all the changes you make. If you change a range of lines, check to make certain there aren't any occurrences that you don't want to change.

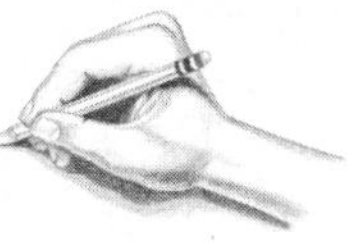

If you don't specify a starting line in the Replace command, Edlin starts with the line that follows the current line. If you don't specify an ending line, Edlin continues to the end of the file. To limit the changes to one line, specify the same line as both the beginning and the end of the range (for example, to change LETTER to MEMO in line 10, the command would be *10,10rLETTER^ZMEMO*).

Using the Editing Keys

Even when you change one or more lines with the Replace command, you're still probably thinking more in terms of the entire document than you are about individual lines. To make specific changes, you use several editing keys, which are shown on the representative keyboard in Figure 10-1.

Changing a Line

To tell Edlin you want to change a line, you type the line number and press Enter. Edlin displays the line, moves to the next line, displays the line number again, then waits for further instructions. You can then use the editing keys to copy the characters you want, skip the characters you don't want, or insert new characters. To help you become familiar with the editing keys, Figure 10-2 summarizes the keys and their functions. You may find it helpful to review this figure before going on to the next practice session.

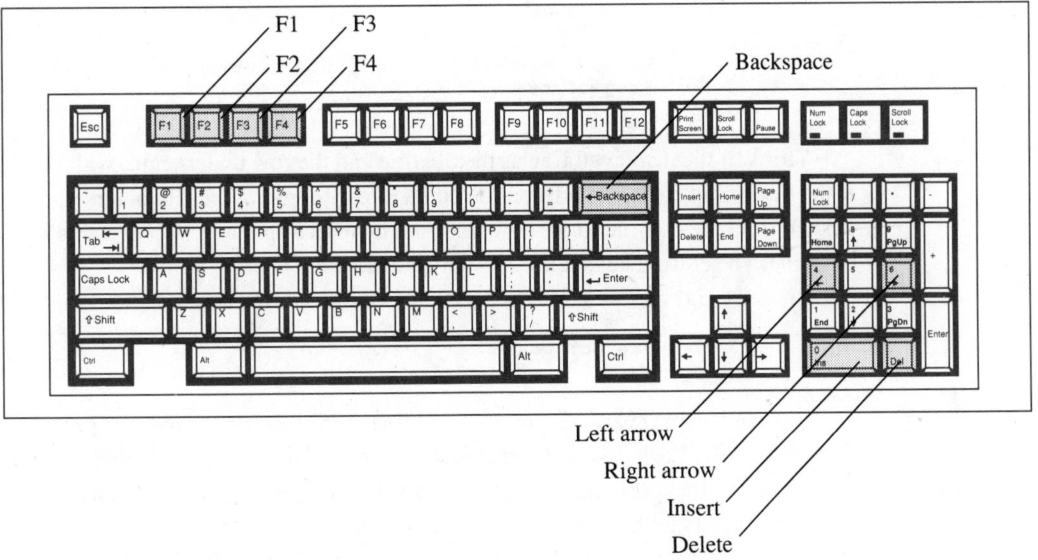

Figure 10-1. Editing keys

Key	Function
Right arrow	Copies one character.
Left arrow	Erases the last character you copied.
Ins	Causes characters you type to be inserted in the new line. Pressing Ins again stops the insert.
Del	Skips one character in the old line (effectively deleting it from the new line).
Backspace	Same as left arrow.
F1	Same as right arrow.
F2	Copies to a certain character in the old line (type the character after pressing F2).
F3	Copies the remaining characters in the line.
F4	Skips to a certain character in the old line (type the character after pressing F4).

Figure 10-2. Edlin editing key functions

Now use the editing keys to edit line 3 of the sample memo. To do this, type the line number, *3*, and press Enter:

```
*3
```

Edlin responds:

```
3:*To: Project team
3:*_
```

Think of the displayed line as the old line and the row underneath, with the cursor at the beginning, as the new line. You edit a line by copying the characters you want to keep from the old line to the new line, and by inserting any new characters in the new line. The editing keys tell Edlin which characters to copy.

Press the right arrow key. The first letter of the old line appears on the new line:

```
3:*To: Project team
3:*T_
```

You copied one character from the old line to the new line. Continue pressing the right arrow key. Each time you press it, you copy another character. When you reach the end of the line, pressing the right arrow key has no effect, because you have copied all the characters to the new line:

```
3:*To: Project team
3:*To: Project team_
```

If you pressed Enter now, you would be telling Edlin you had finished editing line 3. The line would remain unchanged, because you copied all the characters from the old line to the new without making any changes.

Press the left arrow key. The cursor moves one column to the left, erasing the last character you copied to the new line:

```
3:*To: Project team
3:*To: Project tea_
```

Continue pressing the left arrow key. Each time you press it, you erase another of the characters that you copied to the new line. When you reach the beginning of the line, you've erased all the characters you copied to the new line; you're now back where you started.

```
3:*To: Project team
3:*_
```

If you pressed Enter now, the line would again remain unchanged because you haven't copied any characters and Edlin assumes you don't want to change the line.

The F(unction) Keys

There are quicker ways to copy characters than by using the right arrow key.

F3: Press the key labeled F3. Because F3 copies all the original characters from the cursor location to the end of the line, all of the old line is copied to the new line. Hold down the left arrow key until the cursor is back to the beginning of the line.

F2: The F2 key copies all the characters in the original line up to a particular character you specify. F2 acts somewhat like a search command that works inside a line. To use it, press F2, then press the character at which you want the copy to stop. Edlin distinguishes between uppercase and lowercase letters, so be certain to press the exact character you want.

For example, suppose you want to change the word *Project* to *Product* in the example. To do this, you press F2 and j to copy all the characters up to the j, type *du* to replace *je*, then press F3 to copy the rest of the line. Press F2, then j:

```
3:*To: Project team
3:*To: Pro_
```

Now type *du*:

```
3:*To: Project team
3:*To: Produ_
```

The characters you type replace the corresponding characters in the old line, so in the new line, *du* has replaced *je*. Press F3 to copy the rest of the old line:

```
3:*To: Project team
3:*To: Product team_
```

Use the left arrow key to move the cursor back to the beginning of the line.

As you just saw, characters you type replace the corresponding characters from the old line. If you press the Insert key before typing the characters, however, Edlin inserts the characters into the new line without replacing any characters in the old line. To insert the word *New* after the word *To:* in line 3, for example, first copy *To:* by pressing the right arrow key four times (once for each character, including the blank after the colon):

```
3:*To: Project team
3:*To: _
```

Notice that line 3 still says *Project.* You didn't press Enter after changing it to *Product*, so the old line remains unchanged.

Now press the Insert key, type *New* (don't forget to add a blank after it), and press F3 to copy the rest of the old line:

```
3:*To: Project team
3:*To:New  Project team_
```

Use the left arrow key to move the cursor back to the left margin again.

Now suppose you want to delete one or more characters in your original line. You use the Delete key, which tells Edlin to eliminate the next character in the old line. Because the character isn't copied from the old line, it is deleted from the new one.

For example, to delete *To:* from line 3, press the Delete key four times (once for each character, plus the blank). Nothing seems to happen, but when you press F3 to copy the rest of the line, you see:

```
3:*To: Project team
3:*Project team_
```

You deleted *To:*, so it's not in the new line. Move the cursor back to the left margin again.

F4: But suppose you want to delete a number of characters. Isn't there a faster way? Yes, just as the F2 key copies to a specified character in the old line, the F4 key skips to a specified character in the old line, deleting the characters it skips, all at once. The way to use F4 is the same as for F2: Press F4, then the character at which you wish to stop. Again, Edlin distinguishes between uppercase and lowercase letters, so be certain to press the exact character you want.

To delete *To: Project* in line 3, for example, you could press the Delete key 12 times, but it's quicker to use F4. Press F4, then t to skip *To: Projec*. Press the Delete key twice to delete the t and the blank. Now press F3 to copy the rest of the line:

```
3:*To: Project team
3:*team_
```

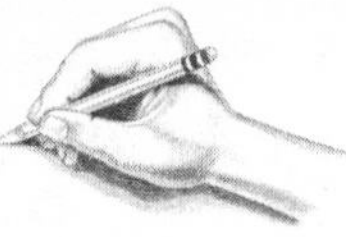

Remember, no matter how many changes you make, you can always cancel them by pressing Ctrl-Break before you press Enter. When you press Enter, the line is changed. Press Ctrl-Break to cancel the edit of line 3.

If you want to end your practice session here, type *e* to End Edit and return to DOS. Because the End Edit command saves your file on disk, you will be able to use the sample again in the next chapter, which covers more ways to revise an Edlin file.

CHAPTER SUMMARY

This concludes the first session with Edlin. The next chapter shows you how to revise a text file and describes several additional Edlin commands. If you're not going to continue with the next chapter right away, be sure to save the diskette that contains MEMO.TXT.

CHAPTER 11

USING EDLIN TO REVISE A FILE

The previous chapter showed you how to create a text file, type lines into it, and revise part or all of a line. Edlin would be useful even if this were all it could do, but there's more: Edlin includes several other ways to revise, or *edit,* a text file. This chapter shows you how to use these additional capabilities of Edlin, particularly for revising files. Using these features, you can:

- Display the file a screenful at a time with the Page command.
- Enter more than one Edlin command on a line by separating the commands with semicolons.
- Move one or more lines to another place in the file with the Move command.
- Copy one or more lines to another place in the file with the Edlin Copy command.
- Combine another file with the file you're editing with the Transfer command.

PREPARING FOR THE EXAMPLE

If you are continuing directly from Chapter 10, no preparation is needed. Go on to the heading "Printing Your File."

If you are starting a new session, you'll need the file you created in Chapter 10. Put the diskette that contains MEMO.TXT in your diskette drive (drive B if you have two diskette drives) and change the current drive to B by typing:

```
C>b:
```

On a system with a fixed disk, DOS will prompt for a diskette when you change the current drive. Press any key.

You must again tell DOS where to find the Edlin commands. For a system with two diskette drives and no fixed disk, type:

```
B>path a:\
```

Now type the following to edit MEMO.TXT:

```
B>edlin memo.txt
```

Edlin responds:

```
End of input file
*_
```

This completes the preparation for the example.

PRINTING YOUR FILE

Suppose you have completed your memo, but now decide to make some changes. The practice memo is short enough to change on the screen, but sometimes you'll want to print a file and mark the changes on the paper copy.

If you are working with Edlin, you don't have to return to DOS to print your file. You could press the Shift-PrtSc key combination, but this prints just one screenful (including commands and messages, as well as the file).

You can print the entire file by pressing Ctrl-PrtSc (which prints everything that is displayed) and displaying the file with the List command. Turn your printer on and type the following; remember, *1,#l* means list all lines from 1 to # (the line after the last line):

```
1,#l<Ctrl-PrtSc><Enter>
```

Your file is printed.

Before you type any other command, remember to press Ctrl-PrtSc again to stop simultaneous printing of everything you display.

REVISING YOUR MEMO

Assume you have finished the memo but decide to add instructions for reviewing the documents, and you want to make a few other changes to the memo as well. Figure 11-1 shows a copy of the file marked with the changes you plan to make; it won't take long to make these changes.

```
 1:*Final Project Review -- 10/16/87
 2:
 3: To: Project team
 4:      ======  ====  UPPERCASE
 5: This diskette has 5 files on it:
 6:
 7: FORECAST.PLN
 8: OPTION1.PLN   HIGHER SALES
 9: OPTION2.PLN   NO STAFF INCREASE
10: LETTER.DOC
11: PROPOSAL.DOC
12:
                                         MAKE
13: Please check the spreadsheets and print the
14: documents to make sure they agree with our
15: assumptions.
16:
17: Let's do this quickly, it's due Monday.
18:
19: Tom
            TO BE      YOU CAN REVIEW THE DOCUMENTS ON THE SCREEN.
          INSERTED     TO CHECK THE PROPOSAL, TYPE:
           BEFORE      TYPE B: PROPOSAL | MORE
          LINE 16      THIS DISPLAYS ONE SCREEN AT A TIME.
                       PRESS THE SPACE BAR TO DISPLAY THE
                       NEXT SCREEN, OR CTRL-BREAK TO STOP.
```

Figure 11-1. Sample memo marked with changes

First, to change *Project team* in line 3 to uppercase, type *3* to tell Edlin you want to edit line 3. When Edlin responds with the original line and the new line number, copy the first five characters by pressing the right arrow key five times; then type the uppercase characters to replace the lowercase ones:

```
*3
          3:*To: Project team
          3:*To: PROJECT TEAM
*_
```

Here is a quick way to confirm your change. Type the line number and press Enter. Edlin assumes you want to edit the line again and displays the newly revised line for you. Press Enter again. The second Enter tells Edlin to save the line without any further changes. Confirm the changes to line 3:

```
*3<Enter>
          3:*To: PROJECT TEAM
          3:*<Enter>
*_
```

Next, the revisions in Figure 11-1 show that you want to add descriptions to the file names in lines 8 and 9. To add text at the end of a line: Type the line number, press Enter, press F3 to copy the entire line, type the added text, and press Enter again. Add three blanks and the words *Higher sales* to line 8 as follows. Type:

```
*8
          8:*OPTION1.PLN
          8:
```

Press F3 to copy the line:

```
          8:*OPTION1.PLN
          8:*OPTION1.PLN
```

Press the spacebar three times, type *Higher sales*, and press Enter:

```
          8:*OPTION1.PLN
          8:*OPTION1.PLN   Higher sales
*_
```

When you have finished editing a line, you can press Enter when Edlin displays its next prompt and Edlin will assume you want to edit the next line. You want to add text at the end of line 9, so press Enter, press F3 to copy the entire line, and add three blanks followed by *No staff increase*:

```
*<Enter>
          9:*OPTION2.PLN
          9:*OPTION2.PLN   No staff increase
*_
```

Check your progress by listing the file:

```
*1l
         1: Final Project Review -- 10/16/87
         2:
         3: To: PROJECT TEAM
         4:
         5: This diskette has 5 files on it:
         6:
         7: FORECAST.PLN
         8: OPTION1.PLN   Higher sales
         9:*OPTION2.PLN   No staff increase
        10: LETTER.DOC
        11: PROPOSAL.DOC
        12:
        13: Please check the spreadsheets and print the
        14: documents to make sure they agree with our
        15: assumptions.
        16:
        17: Let's do this quickly, it's due Monday.
        18:
        19: Tom
*_
```

Now you want to delete the last two words, *print the*, of line 13 and replace them with one word, *make*. Type *13* and press Enter; press F3 to copy the entire line, then use the left arrow key to erase *print the*:

```
*13
        13:*Please check the spreadsheets and print the
        13:*Please check the spreadsheets and _
```

Type *make* and press Enter:

```
        13:*Please check the spreadsheets and print the
        13:*Please check the spreadsheets and make
*_
```

You want to delete more words, *documents to make*, at the beginning of the next line; press Enter to edit line 14:

```
*<Enter>
        14:*documents to make sure they agree with our
        14:*_
```

To make the change, you can either press the Delete key 18 times or skip to the second s (*sure*) in the line. It's faster to skip, so press F4 and press s. Nothing happens on the screen, because you haven't copied any characters yet. You want to skip to the second s, so press F4 and press s again. Press F3 to copy the rest of the line, but don't press Enter just yet:

```
        14:*documents to make sure they agree with our
        14:*sure they agree with our_
```

The words at the beginning have been deleted, and now the line is short enough to include the only word in the next line, *assumptions*.

To make your memo look nicer, type *assumptions* (don't forget a blank at the beginning and a period at the end) and press Enter:

```
        14:*documents to make sure they agree with our
        14:*sure they agree with our  assumptions.
*_
```

Line 15 contains only one word, *assumptions*, which you already moved up to the previous line. You've completed all the revisions up to this point; it's also where you want to insert instructions for displaying the files. Edit the line. It's the next line, so just press Enter and, instead of copying any characters, start entering the new text, which will replace the old:

```
* <Enter>
        15:*assumptions.
        15:* You can review the documents on the
*_
```

Now insert the remaining new lines before line 16. Type:

```
* 16i
        16:* screen. To check the proposal, type:
        17:* <Enter>
        18:* TYPE B:PROPOSAL ¦ MORE
        19:* <Enter>
        20:* This displays one screen at a time.
        21:* Press the spacebar to display the
        22:* next screen, or Ctrl-Break to stop.
        23:* <Ctrl-Break>
*_
```

Ctrl-Break in line 23 tells Edlin you have finished inserting lines. You have completed your revisions, so list the entire memo:

```
* 1l
         1: Final Project Review -- 10/16/87
         2:
         3: To: PROJECT TEAM
         4:
         5: This diskette has 5 files on it:
         6:
         7: FORECAST.PLN
         8: OPTION1.PLN   Higher sales
         9: OPTION2.PLN   No staff increase
        10: LETTER.DOC
        11: PROPOSAL.DOC
        12:
        13: Please check the spreadsheets and make
        14: sure they agree with our assumptions.
        15: You can review the documents on the
        16: screen. To check the proposal, type:
```

```
        17:
        18: TYPE B:PROPOSAL ¦ MORE
        19:
        20: This displays one screen at a time.
        21: Press the spacebar to display the
        22: next screen, or Ctrl-Break to stop.
        23:*
*_
```

The entire file won't quite fit on one screen. To see the rest, start displaying with the next line, 24:

```
*241
        24: Let's do this quickly, it's due Monday.
        25:
        26: Tom
*_
```

Your revised memo, complete with instructions, is ready for your team. Just store the memo, print a copy for each member of the project team, tuck one in each diskette envelope, and deliver them.

To save the memo, type:

```
*e
```

Edlin stores the file on disk and returns you to DOS:

```
B>
```

BACKUP FILES

When you edit an existing file, Edlin works with a copy that it has placed in your computer's memory. The original version remains, unchanged, on the disk. When you end an editing session on the working copy of an existing file, Edlin changes the extension of the unchanged original to BAK (for backup) and stores the revised version on the disk in addition to the BAK version. If there is already a file with the same name and an extension of BAK, Edlin erases the old BAK file before renaming the version it copied into memory for you to work with. If you need the original version, you can use the BAK file. (If you're using 3.2 or an earlier version, you'll have to change its extension, because Edlin in those versions won't edit a file with an extension of BAK. You can use the Rename command—for example, to change MEMO.BAK to MEMO.OLD by typing *ren memo.bak memo.old.*)

PAGING THROUGH A FILE

If you typed *e* to End Edit at the conclusion of the previous session, tell DOS you want to use Edlin to edit MEMO.TXT by typing:

```
B>edlin memo.txt
```

Edlin responds:

```
End of input file
*_
```

Earlier, you displayed the file screen by screen with the List command by increasing the line number by 23 (the number of lines per screen) each time (*1l* for the first screenful, then *24l* for the second screenful, and so on). The Page command (p) simplifies matters by letting you page through a file without keeping track of line numbers. Start with line 1 and page through the practice memo:

```
*1p
         1: Final Project Review -- 10/16/87
         2:
         3: To: PROJECT TEAM
         4:
         5: This diskette has 5 files on it:
         6:
         7: FORECAST.PLN
         8: OPTION1.PLN   Higher sales
         9: OPTION2.PLN   No staff increase
        10: LETTER.DOC
        11: PROPOSAL.DOC
        12:
        13: Please check the spreadsheets and make
        14: sure they agree with our assumptions.
        15: You can review the documents on the
        16: screen. To check the proposal, type:
        17:
        18: TYPE B:PROPOSAL ¦ MORE
        19:
        20: This displays one screen at a time.
        21: Press the spacebar to display the
        22: next screen, or Ctrl-Break to stop.
        23:*
*_
```

To see the next 23 lines (in this case, the lines remaining in the file), type:

```
*p
        24: Let's do this quickly, it's due Monday.
        25:
        26:*Tom
*_
```

If you don't specify a line number, the Page command displays the current line and the following 22 lines. The Page command changes the current line to the last line displayed, so you can page through a file just by typing *p* for each screenful.

ENTERING MORE THAN ONE COMMAND ON A LINE

If an action requires more than one command, you can put all the commands on the same line, separating the commands with semicolons. Edlin carries out each command as if it had been entered on a separate line. Some of the following examples use this technique.

MOVING LINES

You can move a paragraph or other block of lines from one place to another in the file with the Move (m) command. First, you specify the starting and ending line numbers of the block to be moved, then you specify the number of the line before which the block should be placed, separating the numbers with commas.

For example, suppose you want to move lines 5 through 12 from where they are to just before the last sentence (line 24). To move the lines and to verify the move, type the following, separating the commands with a semicolon:

```
*5,12,24m;1p
```

You see:

```
 1: Final Project Review -- 10/16/87
 2:
 3: To: PROJECT TEAM
 4:
 5: Please check the spreadsheets and make
 6: sure they agree with our assumptions.
 7: You can review the documents on the
 8: screen. To check the proposal, type:
 9:
10: TYPE B:PROPOSAL ¦ MORE
11:
12: This displays one screen at a time.
13: Press the spacebar to display the
14: next screen, or Ctrl-Break to stop.
15:
16: This diskette has 5 files on it:
17:
18: FORECAST.PLN
19: OPTION1.PLN   Higher sales
20: OPTION2.PLN   No staff increase
21: LETTER.DOC
22: PROPOSAL.DOC
23:*
*_
```

Note that Edlin renumbers the lines, just as when you insert or delete lines.

If you omit either the starting or ending line number, Edlin assumes you mean the current line. To move one line that is not the current line, specify it as both the beginning and end of the block (for example, to move line 26 to just before line 5, the command would be *26,26,5m*). After the lines are moved, the first line that was moved becomes the current line.

COPYING LINES

You can copy a block of lines to another place in the file with the Copy (c) command. To do so, specify the beginning and ending line numbers of the block and the number of the line before which the block is to be copied, just as you did with the Move command. Copy differs from Move in that the block you specify remains in its original location and is repeated in the new location.

For example, suppose you want to copy the line that begins with *This diskette has* plus the list of files (lines 16 through 22) to the end of the document so that you can use these lines as a label. Type the following Copy and Page commands to copy the lines and verify the copy (remember that # means the line that follows the last line):

```
*16,22,#c;16p
```

You see:

```
        16: This diskette has 5 files on it:
        17:
        18: FORECAST.PLN
        19: OPTION1.PLN   Higher sales
        20: OPTION2.PLN   No staff increase
        21: LETTER.DOC
        22: PROPOSAL.DOC
        23:
        24: Let's do this quickly, it's due Monday.
        25:
        26: Tom
        27: This diskette has 5 files on it:
        28:
        29: FORECAST.PLN
        30: OPTION1.PLN   Higher sales
        31: OPTION2.PLN   No staff increase
        32: LETTER.DOC
        33:*PROPOSAL.DOC
*_
```

You can make several copies of a block of lines with one Copy command by adding a comma and the number of copies just before the *c*. For example, to make five more copies of the same block of lines, type the following:

```
*16,22,#,5c;27p;p
```

If you omit the starting or ending line number, Edlin assumes the omitted line number is the current line. To copy one line other than the current line, specify it as both the start and end of the block. After the lines are copied, the last copy of the last line that was moved becomes the current line.

COPYING ANOTHER FILE

You can copy another file into the file you're editing. Suppose you have a file that contains the name and address of each member of the project team. If you want to include the address list in this memo, you don't have to type it again; you can merge the two files with the Transfer (t) command.

To see how this works, quit the edit of this file, use Edlin to create a small file named ADDRESS on the diskette in drive B, then return to editing MEMO.TXT and display the first 23 lines of the file. To do this, type:

```
* q
Abort edit (Y/N)?  y
B> edlin address
New file
* i
        1:* XXX ADDRESS LIST XXX
        2:* <Enter>
        3:* <Ctrl-Break>


* 1,1,2,3c;1p
        1: XXX ADDRESS LIST XXX
        2: XXX ADDRESS LIST XXX
        3: XXX ADDRESS LIST XXX
        4: XXX ADDRESS LIST XXX
        5:*
* e

B> edlin memo.txt
End of input file
* p
```

The first 23 lines of MEMO.TXT are on the screen.

To copy another file with the Transfer command, you specify the line before which the file is to be placed, then type *t* and the name of the file. Do not use commas.

To copy the file named ADDRESS to just before line 3 and see the result, type:

```
* 3taddress;1p
        1: Final Project Review -- 10/16/87
        2:
        3: XXX ADDRESS LIST XXX
        4: XXX ADDRESS LIST XXX
        5: XXX ADDRESS LIST XXX
        6: XXX ADDRESS LIST XXX
        7:
        8: To: PROJECT TEAM
        9:
       10: This diskette has 5 files on it:
       11:
       12: FORECAST.PLN
       13: OPTION1.PLN   Higher sales
       14: OPTION2.PLN   No staff increase
```

```
        15: LETTER.DOC
        16: PROPOSAL.DOC
        17:
        18: Please check the spreadsheets and make
        19: sure they agree with our assumptions.
        20: You can review the documents on the
        21: screen. To check the proposal, type:
        22:
        23:*TYPE B:PROPOSAL ¦ MORE
*_
```

If you don't specify the line number, Edlin copies the file to just above the current line and the first line of the copied file becomes the current line.

EDITING FILES TOO LARGE TO FIT INTO MEMORY

Although you'll probably find Edlin handy mostly for short documents, you can also use Edlin to edit very large files—even those that are larger than the amount of available memory. When you edit a very large file, Edlin starts loading the file into memory, stopping when it has filled 75 percent of the available memory; this leaves room for you to add to the file. If you insert enough additional text to fill the remaining 25 percent of available memory, or if you want to work with the part of the file that was not loaded, you can move the part of the file in memory onto disk, to make room for loading the next part of the file.

Two Edlin commands control this process: Write Lines (w), which stores (writes) the part of the file in memory (<number> of lines) onto disk; and Append Lines (a), which loads the next part of the file (<number> of lines) from disk into memory. The practice file is not large enough to demonstrate these commands, so simply keep them in mind for your own later use.

CHAPTER SUMMARY

Although Edlin is a simple text editor and lacks many of the features required of a word processor, its speed and simplicity make it an excellent tool for creating and revising short text files. The examples in Chapters 10 and 11 showed you how you can use Edlin to write a short memo. The remaining chapters of this book describe some of the advanced features of DOS, many of which require short files of text. You'll find that Edlin is admirably suited to taking advantage of these features.

CHAPTER 12

CREATING YOUR OWN COMMANDS

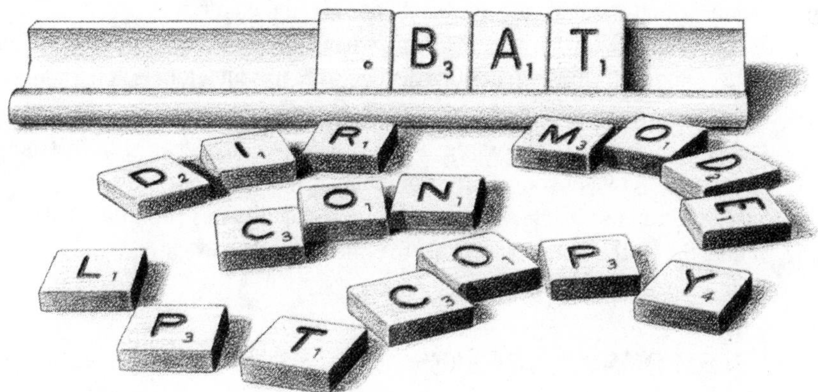

As the preceding chapters show, DOS gives you a great deal of control over your computer system. But DOS is necessarily general purpose, because many people use it for many different purposes. So that you can adapt the computer to your work, DOS lets you combine existing DOS commands to create your own special-purpose commands.

The technique is simple: To make your own command, you create a text file that contains DOS commands. You can give such a file—called a *batch file*—any valid name except the name of an existing command; the extension of the file must be BAT. To use your command, simply type the name of the batch file; DOS carries out the commands contained in the file as if you had typed each of them separately. Commands you create this way are called *batch commands.*

This chapter describes how to create batch files and how to carry out batch commands. It also describes the Remark command, which is intended for batch files, and it shows you how to modify the DOS startup procedure if there are certain commands you always carry out when you start your system.

A BATCH OF WHAT?

The term *batch* has its origins in the early days of large computers, when most work was done by submitting a deck of punched cards to the data-processing department. The punched cards had to contain all the instructions required for the program to run correctly. There was no chance to interact with the system. The data-processing personnel ran these jobs in batches and delivered the output.

In effect, you do the same thing when you use a batch command, because a batch file contains all the instructions needed to carry out a job. Batch, then, is used to describe a computer job that runs without interruption, as opposed to an interactive job—such as word processing—that consists of an exchange of instructions and responses between you and the computer.

You can use batch files to automate frequently used command sequences and to make the system more accessible to colleagues who use application programs but might not know DOS as well as you do.

HOW DOS SEARCHES FOR A COMMAND

If you type something when DOS is displaying the system prompt, DOS assumes you have typed a command name. It then follows a particular sequence in trying to carry out the command:

1. It checks to see if you typed the name of a built-in command, such as *dir* or *copy*. If you did, DOS runs the program that carries out that command.

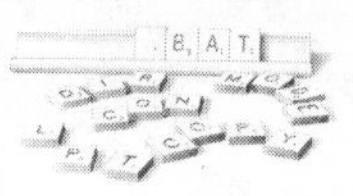

2. If what you typed isn't the name of a built-in command, DOS checks to see if you typed the name of a file with the extension COM or EXE (a command file). If you did, DOS loads the program contained in the file and runs it.
3. If what you typed isn't the name of a command file, DOS checks to see if you typed the name of a file with the extension BAT (a batch file). If you did, DOS carries out the commands in the batch file.

The sequence is important, because it explains why DOS won't carry out a command file with the same name as a built-in command, and why it won't carry out a batch file that has the same name as either a built-in command or a command file.

PREPARING FOR THE EXAMPLES

If you're using a fixed disk, create a directory named \RUNNING by typing the following:

```
C>md\running
```

Now change the current directory to \RUNNING by typing:

```
C>cd\running
```

Go on to the heading "Creating the Sample Files."

If you're not using a fixed disk, leave your system diskette in drive A and put a formatted disk in drive B. Type the following to change the current drive to B:

```
A>b:
B>_
```

The system prompt in the examples will be B>, not C>.

Creating the Sample Files

You will use three sample files in this chapter:

```
LETR1.DOC
LETR2.DOC
LETR3.DOC
```

Type the following to create the sample files (remember, press either F6 or Ctrl-Z, and then press Enter, where you see ^Z):

```
C>copy con letr1.doc
This is the sample file.
^Z
        1 File(s) copied

C>copy letr1.doc letr2.*
        1 File(s) copied
```

```
C>copy letr1.doc letr3.*
        1 File(s) copied

C>_
```

CREATING A BATCH FILE

A batch file is simply a text file, with an extension of BAT, that contains DOS commands. It's a simple matter to create a batch file. You can create one just as you create any other text file: Copy from the console to a text file, or use Edlin or a word processor (if it can store files without inserting its own formatting codes).

The examples in this chapter have you copy from the console to create short batch files. The only drawback to using this technique is that you can't go back to correct an error after you press Enter at the end of a line. If you make a typing error while entering an example, either press Ctrl-Break and re-enter the batch file, or use Edlin to correct the error in the file.

Suppose one of the application programs you use is a word processor, and you name the files that contain letters LETR1.DOC, LETR2.DOC, LETR3.DOC, and so forth. You use the Directory command fairly often to display the names of those particular files. Instead of typing *dir letr∗ .doc* each time, you could put the Directory command in a batch file named DIRLET.BAT.

Type the following to create the batch file:

```
C>copy con dirlet.bat
dir letr*.doc
^Z
        1 File(s) copied

C>_
```

The first line you typed names the batch file; the second line contains the command DOS carries out. Test your batch command by typing its name:

```
C>dirlet

C>dir letr*.doc

 Volume in drive C is FIXEDDISK
 Directory of  C:\RUNNING

LETR1    DOC       26  10-16-87  15:03p
LETR2    DOC       26  10-16-87  15:04p
LETR3    DOC       26  10-16-87  15:05p
        3 File(s)  11495424 bytes free
```

It's possible that you'll see a double prompt, like this:

```
C>
C>_
```

when your batch file finishes running. Don't worry about it. If you object to the duplication for esthetic reasons, press Ctrl-Z at the *end* of the last line of each batch file you copy from CON, instead of on a line by itself.

The first line displayed after you type your batch command is the Directory command that you entered into your batch file. DOS displays the commands in a batch file as they are carried out; it's as if you typed the command itself.

You could make the batch command even easier to type by naming the batch file just LDIR.BAT. In the long run, however, it's usually better to make the name long enough to give a good hint of what the command does, especially if you create a large number of batch files.

Displaying Messages from a Batch File

The Remark (rem) command doesn't cause DOS to do anything, but it is a valid command. You can include a message with the Remark command. The command form is:

rem <message>

Although this command isn't especially useful at the DOS command level, it lets you display a message from a batch file. To see how the Remark command works, create another version of DIRLET.BAT that displays a descriptive message; type the following:

```
C>copy con dirlet.bat
rem DIRECTORY OF LETTERS
dir letr*.doc
^Z
        1 File(s) copied
```

The new version of DIRLET.BAT replaces the first version you created a few minutes ago. Test this new version by typing:

```
C>dirlet
```

The Remark command you included causes DOS to display the message before it displays the directory:

```
C>rem DIRECTORY OF LETTERS

C>dir letr*.doc

 Volume in drive C is FIXEDDISK
 Directory of  C:\RUNNING

LETR1    DOC       26  10-16-87  15:03p
LETR2    DOC       26  10-16-87  15:04p
LETR3    DOC       26  10-16-87  15:05p
        3 File(s)  11495398 bytes free

C>_
```

Carrying Out the Same Batch Command with Different Data

You have seen that most DOS commands include one or more parameters that you can use to make your instructions more specific. When you enter a Directory command, for example, you can specify a file name to display some portion of the files on a disk and the /W option to display the wide form of the directory. The Copy command is another example. It requires two parameters: the name of the file to be copied, and the name to be given to the new copy.

Parameters let you use the same DOS command with different data. You can give your batch files the same capability with a feature called a *replaceable parameter*.

A replaceable parameter is a special symbol you put in a batch file. When you use the batch file, DOS replaces the symbol with a parameter you include when you type the batch command. The symbol consists of a percent sign followed by a one-digit number, such as %1. You can use the numbers 0 to 9 in replaceable parameters, and you can include more than one replaceable parameter in a batch file.

The number of the symbol identifies which parameter replaces the symbol. If a batch command takes two parameters, for example, DOS replaces %1, wherever it occurs in the batch file, with the first parameter you type with the batch command, and it replaces %2 with the second parameter you type. Replaceable parameters can be used anywhere in a batch command.

For example, suppose you wanted a batch command that would print a file by copying it to the printer. (You already have a DOS Print command, but go through the example anyway; it illustrates the use of replaceable parameters.) All the batch file needs is a Copy command and one replaceable parameter that identifies the file to be printed. The batch command is called *Prnt* to avoid confusion with the Print command. Type the following:

```
C>copy con prnt.bat
copy %1 prn
^Z
        1 File(s) copied
```

To test your Prnt batch command, make certain the printer is turned on and type the following:

```
C>prnt letr1.doc
```

DOS displays the command after replacing %1 with the batch-command parameter, LETR1.DOC, and prints the file:

```
C>copy letr1.doc prn
        1 File(s) copied
```

Figure 12-1 shows several versions of PRNT.BAT that you might create for printing other documents. Each version contains at least one replaceable parameter; the last

version contains two. To the left of each version is an example of how the batch command would be typed, and to the right are the corresponding commands that would be carried out after DOS replaced the replaceable parameters. The batch-command parameters, the replaceable parameters in each version of the batch file, and the result after DOS replaces them with the batch command parameters, are in *italics*.

Batch command you would type	Contents of PRNT.BAT	Commands that would be carried out
C>prnt *memo.doc*	copy *%1* prn	copy *memo.doc* prn
C>prnt *memo*	copy *%1*.doc prn	copy *memo*.doc prn
C>prnt *memo rept*	copy *%1*.doc prn	copy *memo*.doc prn
	copy *%2*.doc prn	copy *rept*.doc prn

Figure 12-1. Replaceable parameters in a batch file

Replaceable parameters make batch files much more flexible. Your batch commands needn't be limited to handling the same files or devices all the time—they can be used just like DOS commands to operate with any file or device.

Canceling a Batch Command

Just as with other DOS commands, you press Ctrl-Break to cancel a batch command. But when you cancel a batch command, DOS prompts you to confirm. To see this, create a short batch file named DIRS.BAT that displays the directory entries of the diskette in drive A and also the entries in the current directory.

If you're using a fixed disk, place your copy of the DOS system diskette in drive A. If you're using two diskette drives, the system diskette is already in drive A, so no preparation is needed. To create the batch file, type:

```
C>copy con dirs.bat
dir a:
dir
^Z
        1 File(s) copied
```

The Directory display of the system diskette is long enough to give you time to press Ctrl-Break. Type the name of the Dirs batch command, then press Ctrl-Break as soon as it starts displaying the file names:

```
C>dirs
```

```
C>dir a:

 Volume in drive A has no label
 Directory of  A:\

COMMAND  COM      25307  3-17-87 12:00p
ANSI     SYS       1678  3-17-87 12:00p
COUNTRY  SYS      11285  3-17-87 12:00p
DISPLAY  SYS      11290  3-17-87 12:00p
DRIVER   SYS       1196  3-17-^C

Terminate batch job (Y/N)? _
```

If you respond no, the command being carried out is canceled, but DOS continues with the next command in the batch file. Type *n*; DOS carries out the next command, which displays the current directory:

```
C>dir

 Volume in drive C is FIXEDDISK
 Directory of  C:\RUNNING

.            <DIR>        10-16-87  15:00p
..           <DIR>        10-16-87  15:00p
LETR1    DOC          26  10-16-87  15:03p
LETR2    DOC          26  10-16-87  15:04p
LETR3    DOC          26  10-16-87  15:05p
DIRLET   BAT          39  10-16-87  15:13p
PRNT     BAT          11  10-16-87  15:22p
DIRS     BAT          11  10-16-87  15:31p
        8 File(s)     11491328 bytes free
```

If you respond yes to the terminate question, DOS cancels the entire batch command and displays the system prompt. Type the Dirs batch command and cancel it again, but this time respond *y*:

```
C>dirs

C>dir a:

 Volume in drive A has no label
 Directory of A:\

COMMAND  COM      25307  3-17-87 12:00p
ANSI     SYS       1678  3-17-87 12:00p
COUNTRY  SYS      11285  3-17-87 12:00p
DISPLAY  SYS      11290  3-17-87 12:00p
DRIVER   S^C

Terminate batch job (Y/N)? y
```

DOS returns to the command level without completing the batch command.

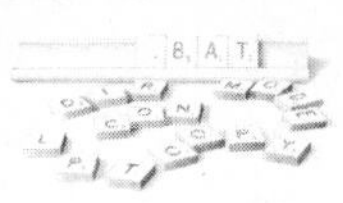

Creating Your Own Startup Procedure

Each time you start or restart the system, DOS goes through a startup procedure that, on many computers, includes prompting you for the current date and time and displaying the DOS version that you're using. If you want, you can substitute your own startup procedure by creating a special batch file named AUTOEXEC.BAT in the root directory of the disk from which you normally start DOS. Each time the system is started, DOS carries out the commands in AUTOEXEC.BAT.

A Quick Safety Check

If you already have a file named AUTOEXEC.BAT in your root directory, the following example will replace it, whether or not you want to. Even though you might not have created an AUTOEXEC.BAT file, the dealer from whom you purchased your computer or the person who set up your system might well may have created such a file—especially if your system has a fixed disk. You'd be unhappy to lose a familiar startup procedure you're using now.

It's easy to guard against this; type the following Directory command:

```
C>dir \autoexec.bat
```

If DOS replies *File not found*, go on to the heading "Creating AUTOEXEC.BAT." You don't have the file, so you won't hurt a thing by trying the example.

If, however, DOS displays a directory entry for a file named AUTOEXEC.BAT, you can protect it from inadvertent loss by renaming it before continuing with the example. Type the following:

```
C>ren \autoexec.bat autoexec.sav
```

You'll restore your original AUTOEXEC.BAT at the end of the example.

Creating AUTOEXEC.BAT

Whenever DOS completes its diagnostic tests, it checks to see whether there is a file named AUTOEXEC.BAT in the root directory of the system disk. If there is not, DOS completes its startup and displays the system prompt. If there is an AUTOEXEC.BAT file, DOS carries out the commands in it before displaying the system prompt.

If your system doesn't keep the time current when it's shut off, it's a good idea to keep the date and time current. You can put Date and Time commands in the AUTOEXEC.BAT file to ensure that you set the date and time correctly whenever you start or restart the system. Another useful addition to AUTOEXEC.BAT, especially if you keep your DOS and your programs in subdirectories, is a Path command that tells DOS where to find its external command files and your programs. Another good command to place in AUTOEXEC.BAT—again, especially useful if you use subdirectories—is a Prompt command like the one introduced in Chapter 9 that has the system prompt display both the current drive and the current directory.

Then, too, you can use AUTOEXEC.BAT for more specialized tasks. For example, suppose that each time you start the system you change to a particular directory on your fixed disk and list its contents. Or, if you're not using a fixed disk, suppose you change the current drive to drive B and then display the directory. You can tell DOS to carry out these commands each time you start the system by putting them in AUTOEXEC.BAT.

To test all of this, create an AUTOEXEC.BAT file that includes Date, Time, Path, and Prompt commands and also changes the current directory or drive and displays a directory listing. Create the file by copying from the console to the system disk.

If you're using a fixed disk, the Path command in this example uses the directory named \RUNNING that you created earlier and assumes that DOS is in a directory named \DOS. If you don't have a \DOS directory, don't worry; you won't harm your system. Type the following:

```
C>copy con \autoexec.bat
rem NEW STARTUP PROCEDURE
date
time
path c:\;c:\dos;c:\running
prompt $p$g
cd \running
dir
^Z
        1 File(s) copied
```

If you're not using a fixed disk, type the following:

```
B>copy con a:autoexec.bat
rem NEW STARTUP PROCEDURE
date
time
path a:\
prompt $p$g
b:
dir
^Z
        1 File(s) copied
```

You created the file in the root directory of the system disk, because that's where DOS always looks for AUTOEXEC.BAT. To test your startup procedure, you must restart the system.

Note: If you're using a fixed disk, be sure to open the door latch on the diskette drive so that DOS restarts from the fixed disk.

Now restart the system by pressing Ctrl-Alt-Del. The startup screen differs from what you have seen before. (If DOS displays the correct date and time, just press the Enter key.)

```
C>rem NEW STARTUP PROCEDURE

C>date
Current date is Tue  1-01-1980
Enter new date (mm-dd-yy): 10-16-87

C>time
Current time is  0:00:17.41
Enter new time: 16:50

C>path c:\;c:\dos;c:\running

C>prompt $p$g

C:\>cd running

C:\running>dir

 Volume in drive C is FIXEDDISK
 Directory of  C:\RUNNING

.            <DIR>      10-16-87  15:00p
..           <DIR>      10-16-87  15:00p
LETR1    DOC         26 10-16-87  15:03p
LETR2    DOC         26 10-16-87  15:04p
LETR3    DOC         26 10-16-87  15:05p
DIRLET   BAT         39 10-16-87  15:13p
PRNT     BAT         11 10-16-87  15:22p
DIRS     BAT         11 10-16-87  15:31p
        8 File(s)   11489280 bytes free

C:\RUNNING>
```

Your new startup procedure not only prompts for the date and time, as DOS normally does, it also tells DOS where to find the files it needs, changes the current directory or drive and tells you what it is, and then displays the entries in the current directory.

You can also use AUTOEXEC.BAT to handle special startup requirements. For example, if your system has equipment options that require special setup instructions with the Mode command, put the commands in AUTOEXEC.BAT so that you needn't type them each time you start or restart the system. Or, if your system has an electronic clock and calendar that require you to run a program to set the date and time, you can put the command in AUTOEXEC.BAT so that you don't have to enter the command each time you start the system.

If other people use the system to run an application program, such as a word processor or a spreadsheet, you can make a copy of the system diskette for them that includes an AUTOEXEC.BAT file ending with the command to start the application program automatically.

You can also use AUTOEXEC.BAT as a convenient way to restore the system to its normal state if you have temporarily changed some conditions, such as the setting of the serial-communications port or the characteristics of the color display.

If you renamed your existing AUTOEXEC.BAT file at the beginning of this example, type the following to restore it:

```
C>ren \autoexec.bat autoexec.run

C>ren \autoexec.sav autoexec.bat
```

Now your original AUTOEXEC.BAT will be executed the next time you start up your system; the version you created in the example is still in the root directory as AUTOEXEC.RUN, in case you want to experiment with it further.

If you didn't have an AUTOEXEC.BAT file to begin with, type the following to ensure that DOS will not carry out your example file the next time you start your system:

```
C>ren autoexec.bat autoexec.run
```

Finally, to rid your system of a possibly invalid Path command, restart your computer by pressing Ctrl-Alt-Del. If you have a fixed disk, change the current directory to \RUNNING (type *cd running*). If you don't have a fixed disk, change the current drive to B: (type *b:* at the system prompt).

Making a Chain of Batch Files

You can use a batch command in a batch file that defines another batch command. The second batch file could contain still another batch command. This is called *chaining,* because each batch file is linked to the next one.

When DOS carries out the last command in a batch file, it returns to the command level and displays the system prompt. If you put a chained batch command in another batch file, the chained batch command should be the last command in the first batch file, because any commands that follow it won't be carried out.

If you were to put a chained batch command in the middle of another batch file, DOS would carry out the commands in the first file, up to the chained batch command; then it would jump to the chained batch file, carry out its commands, and return to command level. Any commands that followed the chained batch command in the first batch file would not be carried out, because DOS does not return to a previous batch file.

For example, suppose you decide to create two batch commands:

- Dirprt, which displays the directory entry of a file, then prints the file.
- Disprt, which displays a file and then prints it.

Both batch commands end by printing the file. You have already entered a batch command named Prnt that prints a file; you can use it as a chained batch file in both the Dirprt and Disprt batch commands.

Type the following:

```
C>copy con dirprt.bat
dir %1
prnt %1
^Z
        1 File(s) copied

C>copy con disprt.bat
type %1
prnt %1
^Z
        1 File(s) copied
```

Make sure the printer is on and use your AUTOEXEC.RUN file as a sample to test the Dirprt batch command. AUTOEXEC.RUN is in the root directory of your system disk, so if you're not using a fixed disk, change the current drive to A by typing:

```
B>a:
```

Now test DIRPRT.BAT by typing:

```
C>dirprt \autoexec.run
```

First, DOS substitutes *autoexec.run* for %1, displays the Directory command in DIRPRT.BAT, and carries it out; your display differs slightly from the following if you're not using a fixed disk:

```
C>dir \autoexec.run

 Volume in drive C is FIXEDDISK
 Directory of  C:\

AUTOEXEC RUN        96 10-16-87  16:51p
        1 File(s) 11489280 bytes free
```

Next, DOS displays the Prnt batch command after again substituting *autoexec.run* for the replaceable parameter %1:

```
C>prnt \autoexec.run
```

Now DOS displays and carries out the Copy command (copy %1 prn) from PRNT.BAT, again substituting *autoexec.run* for %1:

```
C>copy \autoexec.run prn
        1 File(s) copied
```

The file is printed.

Test the Disprt batch command by typing:

```
C>disprt \autoexec.run
```

First, DOS displays the Type command in DISPRT.BAT and carries it out by listing the contents of AUTOEXEC.RUN:

```
C>type \autoexec.run
rem NEW STARTUP PROCEDURE
date
time
path c:\;c:\dos;c:\running
prompt $p$g
cd \running
dir
```

From here on, the Disprt batch command responds just as the Dirprt batch command did, because both batch files chain to PRNT.BAT:

```
C>prnt \autoexec.run

C>copy \autoexec.run prn
        1 File(s) copied
```

Again, the file is printed.

Chaining batch files is a good way to build powerful batch commands, because it lets you use one batch file in several different ways and reduces the chance of your batch files getting long and complicated.

If you're not using a fixed disk, change the current drive back to B by typing:

```
A>b:
```

Note: If you're using version 3.3, there's a way you can use a batch command anywhere in a batch file: It's the Call command, which is described in Chapter 15 under the heading "Using a Batch Command in a Batch File."

SOME USEFUL COMMANDS

This chapter concludes by describing a few batch commands you might find useful; they might also give you some ideas for other commands you could create. Each topic includes a description of what the command does, the contents of the batch file, and one or two examples of its use.

These examples are illustrative, not hands-on exercises, because you might not have the necessary files or devices to use them. But remember that they're here; you'll probably find a situation in which they can be helpful.

Printing a File

Earlier in the chapter you created the Prnt batch command, which prints a file by copying it to the printer. PRNT.BAT contains *copy %1 prn.* To use it, you type the name of the batch file followed by the name of the file to be printed. (For example, to print a file named REPORT.DOC, you would type *prnt report.doc.*)

As the examples in Figure 12-1 showed, you can make batch commands more specific by including common parts of a file name or extension in the batch file. For example, if you frequently print files whose extension is DOC, you could enter the command in the batch file as *copy %1.doc*; to print the file named REPORT.DOC you would only have to type *prnt report.*

Printing a File in Small Type

If your printer is compatible with Epson or IBM dot-matrix printers, you can use the Mode command to change to smaller type, so that 132 characters can be printed on a line. This type is handy for wide reports or spreadsheets, and putting the Mode and Copy commands in a batch file named SMALL.BAT makes them easy to use. SMALL.BAT contains:

```
mode lpt1: 132
copy %1 lpt1:
mode lpt1: 80
```

If your printer is attached to a different port, change *lptl* to *lpt2* or *lpt3*, as necessary. The Small command takes one parameter, the name of the file to be printed in small type. To use the Small command to print the file REPORT.DOC, you would type:

```
C>small report.doc
```

DOS would display the Mode and Copy commands and print the file in small type:

```
C>mode lpt1: 132

LPT1: set for 132

C>copy report.doc lpt1:
        1 File(s) copied

C>mode lpt1: 80

LPT1: set for 80
```

The second Mode command resets the printer to normal type.

Eliminating Old BAK Files

Because Edlin and many word processors create a backup file with an extension of BAK each time you edit a file, your disks can get crowded with files you might not need. The CLEANUP.BAT batch file described here would erase all the files in the current directory whose extension is BAK. CLEANUP.BAT contains:

```
erase %1*.bak
```

The Cleanup command takes one parameter, the directory name followed by a backslash. If you omit the parameter, the command cleans up the current directory.

You can clean up the disk in a different drive by preceding the path name with the drive letter and a colon. For example, to erase all files whose extension is BAK in the current directory, you would simply type *cleanup*. To erase all BAK files in the directory \MKT\WP, you would type *cleanup \mkt\wp*. Similarly, to erase all BAK files in the directory \LASTYEAR\RPT on the disk in drive A, you would type *cleanup a:\lastyear\rpt*. Finally, to erase all files whose extension is BAK in the current directory of the disk in drive B, you would type *C>cleanup b:*.

Batch files let you create your own commands to meet your needs. As you use DOS more, you'll probably find many uses for this capability. This chapter just introduces batch files. Chapters 13, 14, and 15 show you how to use several additional commands that make batch commands one of the most powerful features of DOS.

CHAPTER 13

TAKING CONTROL OF YOUR SYSTEM

Up to now, you have used the DOS commands in their standard form. DOS, however, gives you a great deal of flexibility in controlling the way some commands do their work for you.

This chapter describes where commands get their input and what they do with their output. It shows you how to control some commands and describes some additional commands that give you the building blocks for creating your own set of customized commands.

It is easy to visualize what happens with command output, so even though it might seem odd to discuss results before discussing causes, the next section on command output gives you a foundation for understanding command input as well.

REDIRECTING COMMAND OUTPUT

The result, or output, of most commands is some action, such as copying a file (with the Copy command) or controlling the operation of a device (with the Mode command). The output of a few commands, however, such as Directory, Check Disk, and Tree, is a report. Up to now, you have used these reports primarily as displays—DOS has sent them to the *standard output* device, the console. (Recall from Chapter 7 that DOS uses the name CON, or console, for both the keyboard, which is input only, and the display, which is output only.)

As you'll see in this chapter, DOS lets you send reports and other output to a different device, such as a printer, or to a file. This is called *redirecting* the output of the command; you did it a few times in previous chapters with such commands as *dir > prn.* The technique is simple: To redirect the output of a command that normally sends its results to standard output (the display), you type the command name followed by > and the name of the device or file to which the output is to be sent. The > looks something like an arrowhead pointing toward the alternate output device or file.

Using redirection it's easy, for example, to print a copy of the directory as you did in Chapter 4. To repeat that example, but this time with an understanding of what happens, make sure the printer is turned on and type the following (if you're not using a fixed disk, the system prompt will be A>):

```
C>dir > prn
```

The > tells DOS to redirect the output of the Directory command, and PRN tells DOS where to send it: to the printer. The directory should be printing now; if you want to cancel the printing, press Ctrl-Break.

REDIRECTING COMMAND INPUT

You've seen how quickly and easily you can redirect output to a device or a file. You can just as easily redirect input, in effect telling certain DOS commands to get their data from a source other than the one (often called *standard input*) they would normally use.

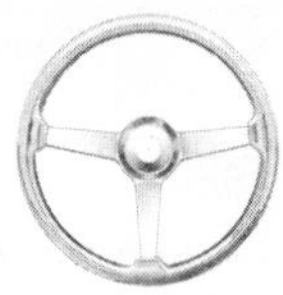

Together, redirected input and output are known as *redirection.* Although redirection sounds complicated, it is easy to understand, as the examples in this chapter show.

Three DOS commands, known collectively as *filter commands,* make particularly effective use of redirection.

FILTER COMMANDS

Filter commands take input from a device or a file, change the input in some way, and send the result to an output device or file. They are called filter commands because they work much like a filter in a water system, which takes the incoming water, changes it in some way, and sends it along the system.

DOS includes three filter commands that allow you to:

- Arrange lines in ascending or descending order with the Sort command.
- Search for a string of characters with the Find command.
- Temporarily halt the display after each 23 input lines (to give you a chance to read the screen) with the More command.

You can redirect both the input and the output of a filter command. The filter commands aren't really intended to be used with keyboard input. Rather, they are designed to get their input from a file or even from the output of another command. This chapter shows you how to use and combine the filter commands to create your own powerful, specialized commands.

PREPARING FOR THE EXAMPLES

Redirection and filter commands give you the elements of a simple file-management program. While they won't replace a file manager, they allow you to use DOS to search and sort simple lists without spending extra money or time on another program.

The examples in this chapter use a sample file that almost everyone needs: a list of names and telephone numbers. Too often, files of telephone numbers and business cards are out of date, incomplete, or in the other office. Questions arise: "Was that number in the telephone index or the business-card file?" Or "Did I file the number under Jones or under Accountants?" This example shows you how to let DOS keep track of your phone list and eliminate these questions.

If you're using a fixed disk, change the current directory to \RUNNING by typing the following:

```
C>cd \running
```

Go on to the heading "Entering the Sample File."

If you don't have a fixed disk, put a formatted diskette that has room for a few small files in drive B. Type the following commands to change the current drive to B and to set the command path to the root directory of the system diskette in drive A:

```
A>b:

B>path a:\
```

Entering the Sample File

The sample file is named PH. You'll create the file with Edlin. (You can use your word processor instead if, like Microsoft Word, it lets you save a document without inserting its own formatting codes.)

Each line of the file contains six items of data: last name, first name, area code, telephone number, a key word that identifies a category, and a short description. The key words are: *cust* for customer, *cons* for consultant, and *vend* for vendor. You will enter the items in specific columns, so you can sort the list by any item.

To create the file PH, type the following:

```
C>edlin ph
New file
*i
          1:*_
```

Edlin is waiting for you to enter something.

To help you get the items in the correct columns, the following entry shows the first line with a period marking each blank. Type the line as shown, but don't type the periods; press the spacebar once for each period:

```
1:*Jones.....Michele...(747).429-6360..cons.chemist
```

End the line by pressing the Enter key.

Now enter the remaining lines in the sample file, which is shown in Figure 13-1. Don't type the line numbers, and remember you already typed the first line.

```
 1: Jones     Michele   (747) 429-6360  cons chemist
 2: Smith     John      (747) 926-2945  vend furniture
 3: White     Alice     (747) 425-7692  cust accountant
 4: Green     Fred      (541) 926-4921  cust math teach
 5: Black     John      (747) 426-3385  cons mech eng pkg
 6: Smith     Ed        (541) 835-8747  vend caterer
 7: Jones     Alison    (747) 429-5584  cons chem engineer
 8: IBM       sales     (747) 463-2000  vend Dave Hill
 9: Jones     James     (747) 636-3541  cust architect
10: Black     Alice     (747) 426-7145  cust elec eng
```

Figure 13-1. Telephone and business-card list

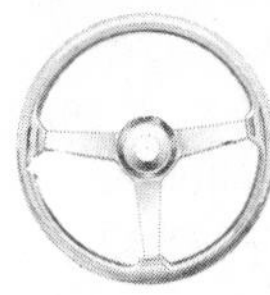

When you have typed all the lines, press Ctrl-Break to end the Insert command and type *e* (End Edit) to save the file. When DOS has stored the file, it displays the system prompt.

Now you're ready to use the file. To see the entry for Alice White, type:

```
C>find "Wh" ph

---------- ph
White     Alice     (747) 425-7692  cust accountant
```

That's fast, but it's just the beginning.

THE SORT FILTER COMMAND

The Sort filter command arranges, or sorts, lines of input and sends them to standard output (the display) unless you redirect the output—for example, to the printer. If you enter the command with no options, it sorts the lines of input in ascending order (alphabetically from A to Z, or numerically from lowest to highest number), starting the sort on the character in the first column.

The Sort command has two parameters:

sort /R /+<column>

/R (*Reverse*) sorts the lines in reverse order (Z to A, or highest to lowest number).

/+<column> sorts the lines starting at the specified column, rather than starting in the first column.

To sort a particular file, you can redirect the input of the Sort command by following the command name with < and the name of the file to be sorted; use a blank both before and after the <. If you don't redirect the input, the Sort command sorts lines that you type at the keyboard (standard input).

Sort Command Examples

Figure 13-2 shows the column number of each of the six items in the telephone list: last name, first name, area code, telephone number, key word, and description. You'll use these column numbers to sort the file in different ways.

```
1         11        21    27        37   42
Jones     Michele   (747) 429-6360  cons chemist
```

Figure 13-2. Column numbers of items in the telephone list

The simplest way to sort the file is in ascending order, starting in the first column (in the sample file, this sorts the entries by last name). Type:

```
C>sort < ph
```

DOS quickly displays the sorted result:

```
Black     Alice     (747) 426-7145  cust elec eng
Black     John      (747) 426-3385  cons mech eng pkg
Green     Fred      (541) 926-4921  cust math teach
IBM       sales     (747) 463-2000  vend Dave Hill
Jones     Alison    (747) 429-5584  cons chem engineer
Jones     James     (747) 636-3541  cust architect
Jones     Michele   (747) 429-6360  cons chemist
Smith     Ed        (541) 835-8747  vend caterer
Smith     John      (747) 926-2945  vend furniture
White     Alice     (747) 425-7692  cust accountant
```

The file itself isn't changed; what you see is simply the result of DOS reading, sorting, and displaying the lines of the file.

Note: If you typed sort ph *instead of* sort < ph, *nothing happened. DOS is waiting for you to type something: You left out the redirection symbol (<) that tells DOS where to find the lines to sort, so DOS is waiting for lines from standard input (the keyboard). You can correct this by pressing Ctrl-Z, then the Enter key, to end standard input. DOS displays the system prompt, and you can enter the Sort command again.*

To sort the file in reverse order, use the /R option:

```
C>sort /r < ph
```

It doesn't take DOS any longer to sort backward:

```
White     Alice     (747) 425-7692  cust accountant
Smith     John      (747) 926-2945  vend furniture
Smith     Ed        (541) 835-8747  vend caterer
Jones     Michele   (747) 429-6360  cons chemist
Jones     James     (747) 636-3541  cust architect
Jones     Alison    (747) 429-5584  cons chem engineer
IBM       sales     (747) 463-2000  vend Dave Hill
Green     Fred      (541) 926-4921  cust math teach
Black     John      (747) 426-3385  cons mech eng pkg
Black     Alice     (747) 426-7145  cust elec eng
```

Suppose you wanted to arrange the list by the key word—first the consultants, then the customers, then the vendors. The first letter of the key word is in column 37, so use the column option:

```
C>sort /+37 < ph
```

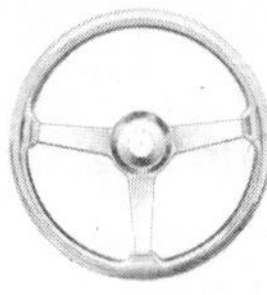

Now it's easy to pick out the different categories:

```
Jones    Alison    (747) 429-5584  cons chem engineer
Jones    Michele   (747) 429-6360  cons chemist
Black    John      (747) 426-3385  cons mech eng pkg
White    Alice     (747) 425-7692  cust accountant
Jones    James     (747) 636-3541  cust architect
Black    Alice     (747) 426-7145  cust elec eng
Green    Fred      (541) 926-4921  cust math teach
Smith    Ed        (541) 835-8747  vend caterer
IBM      sales     (747) 463-2000  vend Dave Hill
Smith    John      (747) 926-2945  vend furniture
```

Sorting is fast, easy, and useful.

THE FIND FILTER COMMAND

The Find filter command searches lines of input for a string of characters you specify. If you enter the command with no parameters other than the string, the Find command displays all lines that contain the string.

The Find command has five parameters:

find /V /C /N <"string"> <filename>

/V displays all lines that do not contain the string.

/C (*Count*) displays just the number of lines found, not the lines themselves.

/N (*Number*) displays the input line number with each line found.

<"string"> is the string of characters you want to find; it must be enclosed in quotation marks. The Find command distinguishes between uppercase and lowercase letters, so "cons" and "CONS", for example, are different strings.

<filename> is the name of the file to be searched. If you omit <filename>, the Find command searches standard input. You can include several different file names in a single Find command simply by separating the file names with blanks. If some of the files are not on the disk in the current drive, precede their file names with the letter, followed by a colon, of the drive containing the disk they are on.

Find Command Examples

To display the entries for all consultants in the file named PH, type the following:

```
C>find "cons" ph
```

The first line of output identifies the input file, PH. Each line that contains the string *cons* is displayed immediately after:

```
---------- ph
Jones    Michele   (747) 429-6360  cons chemist
Black    John      (747) 426-3385  cons mech eng pkg
Jones    Alison    (747) 429-5584  cons chem engineer
```

To see how the Find command works with more than one file, type the following to make two duplicate copies of PH:

```
C>copy ph ph1

C>copy ph ph2
```

Now type the Find command you used in the preceding example, but this time include PH1 and PH2:

```
C>find "cons" ph ph1 ph2
```

DOS displays the name of each file as it finds ''cons'' in PH, PH1, and PH2:

```
---------- ph
Jones     Michelle  (747) 429-6360  cons chemist
Black     John      (747) 426-3385  cons mech eng pkg
Jones     Alison    (747) 429-5584  cons chem engineer

---------- ph1
Jones     Michelle  (747) 429-6360  cons chemist
Black     John      (747) 426-3385  cons mech eng pkg
Jones     Alison    (747) 429-5584  cons chem engineer

---------- ph2
Jones     Michelle  (747) 429-6360  cons chemist
Black     John      (747) 426-3385  cons mech eng pkg
Jones     Alison    (747) 429-5584  cons chem engineer
```

Obviously, using the Find command to search for a character string in several files is more productive when the contents of the files differ, but this example shows the method, if not the full capability, of the command.

Return now to the original phone list, PH. If you just want to know how many consultants are in the list, use the /C (Count) option:

```
C>find /c "cons" ph
```

This time, the line that identifies the input file also shows the number of lines that contain the string:

```
---------- ph: 3
```

Three lines in the file contain *cons.*

As often happens in a real telephone index, the sample file uses different words or abbreviations to mean the same thing. Both *engineer* and *eng* are used, for example, to describe an engineer. Both words contain *eng*, however, so you can find all the engineers by typing the following:

```
C>find "eng" ph

---------- ph
Black     John      (747) 426-3385  cons mech eng pkg
Jones     Alison    (747) 429-5584  cons chem engineer
Black     Alice     (747) 426-7145  cust elec eng
```

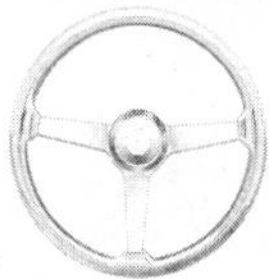

Finding Lines That *Don't* Contain the String

To display the entries *not* in the 747 area code, use the /V option:

```
C>find /v "(747" ph

---------- ph
Green      Fred        (541) 926-4921   cust math teach
Smith      Ed          (541) 835-8747   vend caterer
```

Including the left parenthesis with 747 distinguishes between entries with an area code of 747 and entries that might contain 747 in the phone number. Try the example without the left parenthesis:

```
C>find /v "747" ph

---------- ph
Green      Fred        (541) 926-4921   cust math teach
```

Ed Smith's telephone number is 926-8747, so his entry wasn't displayed even though his area code is 541. When you specify the characters to find, be sure to include enough to specify what you're looking for. In the sample file, for example, *"(7"* would be enough to specify the 747 area code; it wouldn't be enough, however, if the file contained another area code beginning with 7. And, as you saw, you must include the left parenthesis to distinguish an area code from some other set of numbers.

Including Line Numbers with the Output

To display the entries for people named Smith and to include the line numbers of the entries, use the /N option:

```
C>find /n "Smith" ph

---------- ph
[2]Smith      John        (747) 926-2945   vend furniture
[6]Smith      Ed          (541) 835-8747   vend caterer
```

The two entries displayed are the second and sixth lines of the sample file.

Combining Find Command Options

You can combine Find command options. For example, to display the entries not in the 747 area code and to include their line numbers, use both the /V and /N options:

```
C>find /v /n "(7" ph

---------- ph
[4]Green      Fred        (541) 926-4921   cust math teach
[6]Smith      Ed          (541) 835-8747   vend caterer
```

Note: If you are using version 2 of DOS, you see a blank line, [11], *at the bottom of the output. There are only 10 lines in the file, so what does that* [11] *mean? The last character in the file is the special code that marks the end of the file, the one that DOS displays as ^Z. The version 2 Find command counts this end-of-file marker as a separate line. Keep this in mind when you combine the /V option with either the /N option, as this example does, or the /C option, which counts that last line.*

MORE ON REDIRECTING

Earlier in this chapter, you redirected input to the Sort command by specifying the file PH. You can also redirect the output of a filter command. To print the entries for all vendors (redirect output from the display to the printer), type the following:

```
C>find "vend" ph > prn
```

The entries are printed. If your phone list has two or three hundred entries, this technique of using options and redirecting output is a quick way to print a copy showing a selected group of entries.

Redirecting Both Input and Output

You can redirect both input and output by following the command name with < and the name of the input file or device and then > and the name of the output file or device. Be sure to include blanks before and after both < and >.

For example, to print the sorted version of PH, check that your printer is on and then type the command:

```
C>sort < ph > prn
```

The input for the Sort command comes from the file PH, and the output is redirected to the printer. (Press Ctrl-Break if you don't want to wait for the file to be printed.)

DOS allows you to redirect both the input and output of a single command from and to the same file. That is, DOS does not report any error if, for example, you type the command *sort < ph > ph.* Doing this, however, can make the file unusable. If you want to sort a file and keep the same file name, use the following procedure:

- Redirect the output to a temporary file, such as PH-TMP. For example, to sort the PH in reverse order, you would type *sort /r < ph > ph-tmp.*
- If you're certain you no longer need it, delete the original file (*erase ph*). If you want to keep the original, give it a different name, such as OLDPH, with the Rename command (*ren ph oldph*).
- Then use the Rename command to give the temporary file the original file name (*ren ph-tmp ph*).
- The new version of PH would contain the telephone list sorted in reverse order. You could verify the contents by displaying PH with the Type command.

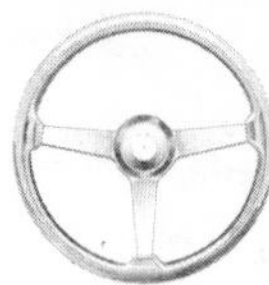

Adding Redirected Output to a File

When you redirect output to an existing file, the redirected output replaces the original file. But you can also *add* redirected output to the end of an existing file by using >>, instead of >. If the file doesn't exist, it is created, just as when you use >.

CONNECTING COMMANDS WITH A PIPE

A powerful way of using a filter command is to redirect the output of some other command to the input of the filter command. In effect, the two commands are connected, with the output of the first command feeding directly into the filter command. Continuing the analogy to a water system, this connection is called a *pipe*.

You tell DOS to pipe the output of one command to the input of another by typing ¦ between the names of the two commands; the ¦ provides the connection between the two commands. The More filter command provides a simple example.

The More Filter Command

The More filter command displays 23 lines (one screenful) and the line --*More*--, and then it pauses. When you press any key, More displays the next 23 lines and pauses again, continuing in the same way until all the input has been displayed.

The directory of the system disk is more than one screenful, so use it as an example; if you're using a fixed disk, place the system diskette in drive A. Type:

```
C>dir a: ¦ more
```

This command tells DOS to redirect the output of the Directory command to the input of the More command. The More command displays the first 23 lines of the directory and --*More*-- at the bottom of the screen. Press any key to see the rest of the directory, or press Ctrl-Break to cancel the More command and return to the system prompt. The More command lets you review a long output sequence or file without having to press Ctrl-Num Lock to start and stop the display.

Combining Filter Commands

You can pipe the output of one Find command to the input of another Find command to make a more specific search. A real-life list like the sample phone list, for example, might include several dozen customers. Suppose you want to display only the customers in the 747 area code. To do this, pipe the output of a Find command that searches for "cust" to another Find command that searches for "(7" by typing:

```
C>find "cust" ph ¦ find "(7"
White     Alice     (747) 425-7692  cust accountant
Jones     James     (747) 636-3541  cust architect
Black     Alice     (747) 426-7145  cust elec eng
```

If you check an earlier list of the file, you'll see that Fred Green is a customer, but his area code is 541, so the second Find command eliminated the entry for his name. Notice that the line that identifies the file (----------*ph*) isn't displayed. The first Find command pipes ----------*ph* as part of its output to the second Find command, but because the line does not contain the string "(7", it is not included as part of the output of the second Find command.

You can also pipe the output of the Find command to the Sort command. To see all the consultants sorted by last name, type the following:

```
C>find "cons" ph ¦ sort

---------- ph
Black      John      (747) 426-3385  cons mech eng pkg
Jones      Alison    (747) 429-5584  cons chem engineer
Jones      Michele   (747) 429-6360  cons chemist
```

You can combine as many commands as you like. Suppose you want to print a list of all customers in the 747 area code, sorted by telephone number. You can search PH for "cust", pipe that output to a Find command that searches for "(7", pipe that output to a Sort command that sorts at column 27 (the telephone number), and redirect the output to the printer. Type the following:

```
C>find "cust" ph ¦ find "(7" ¦ sort /+27 > prn

White      Alice     (747) 425-7692  cust accountant
Black      Alice     (747) 426-7145  cust elec eng
Jones      James     (747) 636-3541  cust architect
```

If your list included several dozen customers, this could be a handy way to organize a calling campaign.

The Difference Between > and ¦

Sometimes the distinction between > and ¦ isn't readily apparent, but the difference is easy to demonstrate. Sort is a filter command. To make the output of the Directory command the input to the Sort command, type the following:

```
C>dir ¦ sort
```

As you would expect, DOS displays the directory sorted in alphabetic order. (If the directory includes two files whose names look like 072F2321 or %PIPE1.$$$ and whose lengths are 0, don't be alarmed. These are temporary files DOS creates in order to pipe the output of one command to the input of another; DOS deletes the files when the commands are completed.)

Now type:

```
C>dir > sort
```

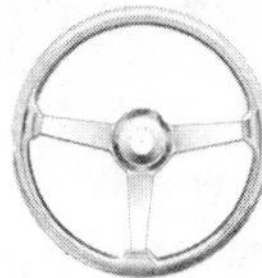

This time you don't see anything on the screen because you told DOS to redirect the output of the Directory command to a file named SORT. Confirm this by displaying the file with the Type command:

```
C>type sort
```

The file contains the directory, which is not sorted and contains no temporary files. It's an ordinary directory. You created a file named SORT when you redirected the output of the Directory command.

CHAPTER SUMMARY

As you can see, redirection, filter commands, and pipes let you create powerful, specific commands. The next two chapters show you how to combine these capabilities with the advanced batch commands to put the power of DOS to work for you.

CHAPTER

14

CREATING SMART COMMANDS

The previous two chapters showed how batch files, redirection, pipes, and filter commands let you build your own commands and change the way DOS commands work. This chapter shows how DOS gives you more control over the way it carries out the commands you build into a batch file. The techniques in this chapter help you create powerful commands tailored to your needs.

You can make your commands display their own instructions or warning messages. Or you can specify the circumstances under which DOS carries out one command—or a different sequence of commands altogether. You can even make the system pause until you tell it to proceed.

This chapter shows you how to develop a batch file that uses most of these capabilities. The next chapter extends the example, describes two additional batch commands, and shows several useful commands you can create. When you complete these two chapters, you'll be ready to apply the full power of DOS to your needs.

PREPARING FOR THE EXAMPLES

For these examples, you'll need one or two formatted diskettes and some sample files. If you completed the examples in Chapter 13, "Taking Control of Your System," use the diskette on which you stored the phone-list file. If you're not using a fixed disk, you also have to copy some command files onto one of your practice diskettes. Follow the instructions under the heading that describes your system.

If You're Using a Fixed Disk

If you're using a fixed disk, you need one formatted diskette; put it in drive A. Change the current directory to \RUNNING by typing:

```
C>cd \running
```

All the DOS commands you need are on the fixed disk. If the DOS files aren't in your command path, type a Path command to tell DOS where to find its command files. If they're in a directory named \DOS, for example, type *path = \dos.*

If You're Not Using a Fixed Disk

If you're not using a fixed disk, you need two formatted diskettes. Put the diskette with the phone list into drive B. You're going to take the system diskette out of drive A in a moment, so enter the following commands to copy the Find, Sort, and More commands to the practice diskette:

```
A>copy find.exe b:
        1 File(s) copied

A>copy sort.exe b:
        1 File(s) copied
```

```
A>copy more.com b:
        1 File(s) copied
```

The examples in this chapter have you modify a batch file several times. You use Edlin commands to make the changes, so copy the Edlin program to drive B by typing the following:

```
A>copy edlin.com b:
        1 File(s) copied
```

Now remove the system diskette from drive A and replace it with the second formatted diskette. Change the current drive to B by typing:

```
A>b:

B>_
```

As you follow the examples, remember that the system prompt will be B>, not C>.

Creating the Sample Files

You will use six sample files in the next two chapters:

P.DOC	Q.DOC
P.BAK	Q.BAK
P.OLD	Q.OLD

Type the following to create the files (press F6 and Enter where you see ^Z):

```
C>copy con p.doc
This is a sample file.
^Z
        1 File(s) copied

C>copy p.doc p.bak
        1 File(s) copied

C>copy p.doc p.old
        1 File(s) copied

C>copy p.* q.*
P.DOC
P.BAK
P.OLD
        3 File(s) copied
```

If you're creating these files on a diskette, you'll need this diskette in the next chapter, so title it BATCH COMMANDS (if it's already labeled for the phone-list file, just add the new words). This completes the preparation for the examples.

CREATING AN ARCHIVE COMMAND

Disk files proliferate as you use your computer. You'll probably archive files from time to time, copying them to long-term storage diskettes and then erasing them from your working disks, just as you occasionally remove documents from your paper files and put them in long-term storage.

Although DOS includes the Backup and Restore commands to help you archive old files, this chapter shows you how to use the DOS batch commands to develop an Archive command that everyone can use, whether or not they're comfortable using DOS commands.

Starting with just a Copy command, you expand the batch file to display instructions, provide a safeguard against inadvertently erasing a previously archived file, and erase the file after it is archived.

The diskette in drive A represents the archive diskette, the one you store in a safe place. Your fixed disk or the diskette in drive B represents the working disk that contains files you want to archive.

Your Archive command will be a file named ARCHIVE.BAT. The initial version contains only a Copy command. To create the file, type the following:

```
C>copy con archive.bat
copy %1 a:%1
^Z
        1 File(s) copied
```

This file is the starting point for your Archive command. It requires only one parameter, the name of the file to be archived. The Copy command copies this file (%1 in the Copy command) to the diskette in drive A, giving it the same name (a:%1) as the original. To see how the batch file works, make certain the archive diskette is in drive A; archive P.DOC by typing:

```
C>archive p.doc
```

DOS responds by displaying and carrying out the Copy command in the batch file:

```
C>copy p.doc a:p.doc
        1 File(s) copied
```

This isn't much, but then it's only a starting point. You'll add significantly to this simple command as you go through the examples in this chapter.

MODIFYING THE SAMPLE BATCH FILE

This chapter describes four batch commands: Echo, Pause, If, and Goto. Each command description explains the purpose of the batch command, then adds it to ARCHIVE.BAT. The modified version of the batch file is shown with the changed or added lines shaded, then instructions are given for making the changes with Edlin.

CONTROLLING SYSTEM MESSAGES

The Echo command controls whether commands in a batch file are displayed, and it lets you display your own messages. It has three parameters:

echo on off <message>

on causes commands to be displayed as they are carried out (this is called "turning echo on"). Echo is on unless you turn it off.

off causes commands not to be displayed as they are carried out (this is called "turning echo off"). Eliminating the commands from the display can make a batch file easier to use by reducing clutter on the screen.

<message> is a string of characters, such as a reminder or a warning, that you want to display. <message> is displayed whether echo is turned on or off.

You can include only one parameter with an Echo command. If you omit all parameters (just type *echo*), DOS displays the status of echo (either *ECHO is on* or *ECHO is off*).

The first changes to your Archive command add an Echo command at the beginning to turn echo off and another Echo command after it to display a title message.

Here is the modified version of ARCHIVE.BAT (the Edlin line numbers are displayed only for reference):

```
1: echo off
2: echo Archive Procedure
3: copy %1 a:%1
```

Using Edlin, type these commands to make the change:

```
C>edlin archive.bat
End of input file
*i
         1:*echo off
         2:*echo Archive Procedure
         3:*<Ctrl-Break>
*e
```

To archive P.DOC with your new Archive command, type the name of the batch file and the name of the file to be archived:

```
C>archive p.doc
```

Because echo is always on when DOS starts carrying out the commands in a batch file, DOS displays the first Echo command, which turns echo off. Then it carries out the second Echo command, which displays the title, *Archive Procedure*. Finally, it carries out the Copy command from the original ARCHIVE.BAT and copies the file:

```
C>echo off
Archive Procedure
         1 File(s) copied
```

Messages produced by a command itself (such as *1 File(s) copied* in the preceding example) are displayed whether echo is on or off.

If you're using version 3.3, you can prevent any command from being echoed by preceding it with the @ symbol. This means that you can eliminate even that first *echo off* message by changing the first line of ARCHIVE.BAT to *@echo off.* If you're using version 3.3, edit the file again to add the @ symbol at the beginning of line 1. From now on, all the examples will show the @ symbol; if you're not using version 3.3, simply ignore it.

Your Archive command is starting to take shape. It's time to add some instructions for the person who uses it.

MAKING THE SYSTEM PAUSE

Some DOS commands, such as Format and Diskcopy, display a message and wait for you to respond, giving you a chance to confirm your intention, or to complete preparation by inserting a diskette or by turning on the printer. You can have your batch files do the same; use the Pause command, which displays the message *Strike a key when ready . . .* and makes the system wait until you press any key.

The Pause command has one parameter:

pause <message>

<message> is a string of characters, such as a reminder or a warning, that you want the Pause command to display. <message> is displayed only if echo is on.

You'll add a Pause command to ARCHIVE.BAT now. You'll also add a message—a reminder to make certain the archive diskette is in drive A before the file is copied.

But wait: Any message you include as a parameter with the Pause command is displayed only if echo is on, and you have turned echo off in line 1 of ARCHIVE.BAT.

You can still use the Pause command, however. Instead of using the message capability of the Pause command, just use an Echo command to display the reminder, then add a Pause command without a message. This approach is a bit more work than simply adding a message after the Pause command, but the result is a command that's easier to use because you avoid cluttering the display with all the commands that DOS would display if you were to turn echo on.

The modified version of ARCHIVE.BAT is:

```
1: @echo off
2: echo Archive Procedure
3: echo Make sure archive diskette is in drive A
4: pause
5: copy %1 a:%1
```

Remember, if you're not using version 3.3, ignore the @ in line 1.

The Edlin commands to make this change are:

```
C>edlin archive.bat
End of input file
*3i
     3:*echo Make sure archive diskette is in drive A
     4:*pause
     5:*<Ctrl-Break>
*e
```

Test this version by typing:

```
C>archive p.doc

Archive Procedure
Make sure archive diskette is in drive A
Strike a key when ready . . . _
```

The Echo command displays the reminder, then the Pause command displays its message telling you to strike a key and the system waits. Complete the command by pressing any key. DOS copies the file and acknowledges:

```
        1 File(s) copied
```

CONTROLLING WHICH COMMANDS ARE CARRIED OUT

Besides carrying out DOS commands as though you had typed them individually, batch files let you specify that a command should be carried out only if some condition (such as whether a file exists) is true. This capability makes your batch files more flexible, letting you adapt them to a variety of situations.

The If command specifies the condition to be checked and the DOS command to be carried out. It has three parameters:

if not <condition> <command>

not qualifies the If command so that <command> is carried out only if <condition> is not true.

<condition> is the condition to check. It has two commonly used forms:

exist<filename> checks whether the named file exists. You can include a path name, if necessary. If <filename> exists, the condition is true.

<string1>==<string2> compares the two character strings you specify. If they are identical, the condition is true. Note that there are two equal signs.

<command> is any DOS command.

You'll add an If command to ARCHIVE.BAT to control when a warning message is displayed.

Adding Protection to Your Archive Command

When you copy a file with the Copy command, you tell DOS the name of the original and the name to be given to the new copy. DOS checks to see if there is already a file with the same name as the copy on the target disk; if there is, DOS erases the existing file and replaces it with the copy. What if you didn't realize that a file with the same name existed on the disk? You might inadvertently lose a valuable file.

To protect yourself against such an oversight, you will include two more commands in ARCHIVE.BAT. First, you will add an If command that checks to see whether the file to be archived already exists on the archive diskette in drive A. If it does, an Echo command in the second part of the If command displays a warning message telling you that you can cancel the command by pressing Ctrl-Break.

Then you'll add a Pause command to give you time to read the warning message and, if necessary, cancel the Archive command by pressing Ctrl-Break. Here is the modified version of ARCHIVE.BAT:

```
1: @echo off
2: echo Archive Procedure
3: echo Make sure archive diskette is in drive A
4: pause
5: if exist a:%1 echo a:%1 exists. Press
   CTRL-BREAK to cancel, or
6: pause
7: copy %1 a:%1
```

Here are the Edlin commands to make this change. Type line 5 on one line, even though it is shown on two in the text:

```
C>edlin archive.bat
End of input file
*5i
        5:*if exist a:%1 echo a:%1 exists. Press
           CTRL-BREAK to cancel, or

        6:*pause
        7:*<Ctrl-Break>
*e
```

Test this version of your Archive command by typing:

```
C>archive p.doc

Archive Procedure
Make sure archive diskette is in drive A
Strike a key when ready . . . _
```

Press any key to continue the command:

```
a:p.doc exists. Press CTRL-BREAK to cancel, or
Strike a key when ready . . . _
```

Don't press any key yet.

You might not want to replace the copy of the file in drive A. Press Ctrl-Break to cancel the command. DOS asks whether you really mean it:

```
Terminate batch job (Y/N)? _
```

Type *y* to confirm. DOS cancels the rest of your Archive command and displays the system prompt without copying the file. If you had not pressed Ctrl-Break, the file would have been copied as before, erasing the previously archived version of P.DOC.

Smoothing a Rough Edge

Your Archive command is getting more useful; you've protected yourself from inadvertently erasing an existing file. But there's a problem now. See what happens if the name of the file to be archived isn't the name of a file already on the diskette in drive A. Erase P.DOC from drive A and archive it again:

```
C>erase a:p.doc

C>archive p.doc

Archive Procedure
Make sure archive diskette is in drive A
Strike a key when ready . . . _
```

Fine so far. Press the spacebar to continue:

```
Strike a key when ready . . . _
```

That's not too good. The system comes right back and pauses again, even though everything is OK, because the Pause command that follows the If command is always carried out. Press the spacebar again:

```
        1 File(s) copied
```

DOS copies the file as it should. Your Archive command is working properly, but the two pauses could be confusing, especially if someone else uses your batch command. How can you fix this?

You could delete the first Pause command, but if you did, you wouldn't have a chance to make certain that the correct diskette has been placed in drive A. That's not a very good solution.

Or you could delete the second Pause command and change the If command, making the "file exists" warning a Pause message instead of an Echo message, as it is now. But then, recall that you would have to delete the command *echo off* at the beginning of the batch file so that the message following the new Pause command would be displayed. And that would mean all your commands in the file would be displayed. This solution would make the response to your Archive command somewhat cluttered and confusing, so it isn't very good, either.

There is, however, a way to change your Archive command so that the second Pause command is carried out only if the file to be archived is on the diskette in drive A. This solution requires using another command for batch files, the Goto command.

CHANGING THE SEQUENCE OF COMMANDS

The batch files you have created up to now carry out the DOS commands they contain in the order in which the commands appear. Your batch commands would be more flexible if you could control the order in which the commands are carried out. The Goto command gives you this control by telling DOS to go to a specific line in the command file, rather than to the next command in the sequence.

You tell DOS where to go in the batch file by specifying a *label.* A label identifies a line in a batch file; it consists of a colon (:) immediately followed by a string of characters (such as *start*). A label is not a command. It merely identifies a location in a batch file. When DOS goes to a label, it carries out whatever commands follow the label.

The Goto command has one parameter:

goto <label>

<label> is the label that identifies the line in the batch file where DOS is to go.

The Goto command is often used as part of an If command. For example, the If command checks some condition. If the condition is not true, DOS carries out the next command; if the condition is true, DOS carries out the Goto command and moves to some other part of the batch file.

Remember the problem with your Archive command? If the file to be archived is already on the diskette in drive A, you want to display a warning message and pause; otherwise, you just want to copy the file. This situation is tailor-made for an If command that includes a Goto command.

The modified version of ARCHIVE.BAT is:

```
@echo off
echo Archive Procedure
echo Make sure archive diskette is in drive A
pause
if not exist a:%1 goto safe
echo a:%1 exists. Press CTRL-BREAK to cancel, or
pause
:safe
copy %1 a:%1
```

These changes warrant a bit more explanation:

- The If command still checks whether the name of the file to be archived exists on the diskette in drive A. Now, however, the command includes the parameter

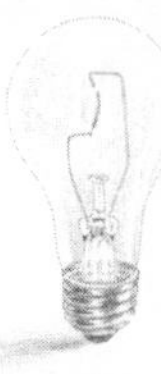

not, which means that the command in the second part of the If command is carried out only if the condition is not true (that is, if the file does *not* exist on the diskette in drive A).

- The second part of the If command—the command to be carried out if the condition is true—is changed to a Goto command that tells DOS to skip to a label called *:safe*.
- If the file to be archived doesn't exist on the diskette in drive A, the Goto command is carried out and DOS jumps to the label *:safe*, skipping the Echo and Pause commands. The Copy command following *:safe* copies the file.
- If the file to be archived does exist on the diskette in drive A, the Goto command is not carried out and DOS continues on to the Echo and Pause commands. If you don't cancel by pressing Ctrl-Break, DOS carries out the Copy command. In this instance, DOS ignores the line that contains the label *:safe* because the only purpose of the label is to identify a location in a batch file.

Use the following Edlin commands to make these changes. The symbol → means press the right arrow key; <Ins> means press the Insert key; <F2> means press the F2 function key; <F4> means press the F4 function key. Although lines 5 and 6 are shown on two lines, Edlin displays them on one line:

```
C>edlin archive.bat
End of input file
*5,5,6c
*5
         5:*if exist a:%1 echo a:%1 exists. Press CTRL-BREAK
            to cancel, or
         5:*→→→<Ins>not <F2>egoto safe
*6
         6:*if exist a:%1 echo a:%1 exists. Press CTRL-BREAK
            to cancel, or
         6:*<F4>e<F4>e<F3>
*8i
         8:*:safe
         9:*<Ctrl-Break>
*e
```

P.DOC is on the diskette in drive A (you archived it a bit earlier), so first see if this version of your Archive command warns you that the file exists. Type the following:

```
C>archive p.doc
Archive Procedure
Make sure archive diskette is in drive A
Strike a key when ready . . . _
```

Press any key to continue the command:

```
a:p.doc exists. Press CTRL-BREAK to cancel, or
Strike a key when ready . . . _
```

There's the warning. Press any key to complete the command:

```
        1 File(s) copied
```

But the problem came up when the file wasn't on the archive diskette: You got the second pause anyway. Test your revised Archive command in this situation by archiving P.BAK, which hasn't yet been archived:

```
C>archive p.bak
Archive Procedure
Make sure archive diskette is in drive A
Strike a key when ready . . . _
```

Press any key to continue:

```
        1 File(s) copied
```

Problem solved. Because P.BAK wasn't on the archive diskette in drive A, the Goto command was carried out; it caused DOS to skip over the intervening Echo and Pause commands and to copy the file.

Your Archive command works properly. You had to do a little more work to avoid the double pause, but now the command is less confusing and easier to use. You'll probably encounter this kind of circumstance fairly often as you create batch commands. Just remember: It takes a little more time to make a command easy to use, but the investment is usually worthwhile, especially if someone other than you will use the command.

Using Wildcard Characters with a Batch File

You can use wildcard characters to archive a series of files with your Archive command. Type the following command to archive all the files named P:

```
C>archive p.*
Archive Procedure
Make sure archive diskette is in drive A
Strike a key when ready . . . _
```

Press any key:

```
a:p.* exists. Press CTRL-BREAK to cancel, or
Strike a key when ready . . . _
```

You archived P.DOC and P.BAK in earlier examples, so they're on the archive diskette. The Archive command doesn't identify the specific file that exists, but it does give you a chance to cancel if you don't want to erase the file.

Press Ctrl-Break to cancel the rest of the command, and respond to the DOS prompt for confirmation with *y*:

```
Terminate batch job (Y/N)? y
```

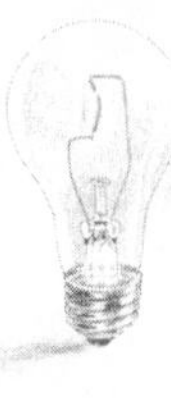

If you had pressed any key other than Ctrl-Break, all the files named P would have been copied to the diskette in drive A, replacing any that were already there.

Erasing the Original of an Archived File

Archiving not only involves copying a file to an archive diskette, it also means deleting the original. Your Archive command only copies; now it's time to make it delete, too. But just as it's prudent to check whether the file exists on the archive diskette before you make the copy, it's also prudent to check again before erasing the original, just to be sure the file was copied to the archive diskette.

You need only one additional If command to check whether the file to be archived is on the archive diskette and, if it is, to erase the original from the working disk. Here is this modified version of ARCHIVE.BAT:

```
@echo off
echo Archive Procedure
echo Make sure archive diskette is in drive A
pause
if not exist a:%1 goto safe
echo a:%1 exists. Press CTRL-BREAK to cancel, or
pause
:safe
copy %1 a:%1
if exist a:%1 erase %1
```

The Edlin commands to make this change are:

```
C>edlin archive.bat
End of input file
*10i
        10:*if exist a:%1 erase %1
        11:*<Ctrl-Break>
*e
```

The screen responses of this version of your Archive command are the same as in the previous version, but the new command erases the original file after copying it. Test it by archiving P.DOC again:

```
C>archive p.doc
Archive Procedure
Make sure archive diskette is in drive A
Strike a key when ready . . . _
```

Press any key to continue:

```
a:p.doc exists. Press CTRL-BREAK to cancel, or
Strike a key when ready . . . _
```

You want to copy the file to the archive diskette, so press any key:

```
        1 File(s) copied
```

See if the original version of P.DOC is still on your working diskette by typing:

```
C>dir p.doc

 Volume in drive C is FIXEDDISK
 Directory of  C:\RUNNING

File not found
```

The original is gone. Your Archive command does copy the specified file to the archive diskette and then delete the original.

Functionally, the command is complete.

DRESSING UP YOUR ARCHIVE COMMAND

The value of your batch files depends not only on what they do, but also on how easy it is to use them correctly. This ease of use is particularly important if you use a batch file only occasionally, or if someone else uses it; it's vital if the batch file erases other files, as your Archive command does.

That's why, for example, your Archive command starts by turning echo off: An uncluttered screen helps to make the responses less confusing. You can also do some other things to make a batch file easy to use:

- Clear the screen.
- Use the Echo command to display messages that report on progress or results.
- Use blanks or insert tabs so you can position messages displayed by the Echo command where they are prominent on the screen.
- Use the Echo command to include blank lines that further improve the readability of the screen.

You can also use the Remark command to put notes to yourself in the batch file. As long as echo is off, these remarks aren't displayed. Remarks can help you remember how a batch file works, in case you have to change it or you want to create a similar command using the same technique. Remarks are especially useful if the batch file is long or if it's one you may not look at very often.

Echoing a Blank Line

Up to now, you have used the Echo command either to turn echo off or to display a message. You can also use the Echo command to display a blank line—something you'll probably want to do fairly often to improve the appearance or readability of the screen display.

You've seen that you turn echo on or off by following *echo* with either *on* or *off*. If you follow *echo* with some other words, they are displayed as a message, and if you simply type *echo*, DOS tells you whether echo is on or off. How do you tell DOS to echo a blank line? In most releases of DOS, you type *echo*, press the spacebar once, hold down the key labeled Alt, type the number 255 on the numeric keypad (*not* the numbers in the top row of the keyboard), then release the Alt key. The cursor moves over one column, but you shouldn't see any new characters displayed. This action is represented by <Alt-255> in the examples. Whenever you see <Alt-255>, hold down the Alt key, press the 2 key on the numeric keypad, press the 5 key on the numeric keypad twice, then release the Alt key. If your version of DOS is one that does not understand <Alt-255>, there's an alternative way to echo a blank line: Type *echo*, press the spacebar once, and then press Enter.

The following changes don't add any capability to your Archive command, but they do make it easier for someone to understand what's happening. The changes are described in more detail in a moment. Here is the modified version of ARCHIVE.BAT:

```
 1: @echo off
 2: cls
 3: REM THREE TABS IN FOLLOWING ECHO COMMAND
 4: echo<tab><tab><tab>***ARCHIVE PROCEDURE***
 5: echo <Alt-255>
 6: echo Make sure archive diskette is in drive A
 7: pause
 8: REM BRANCH AROUND WARNING IF FILE NOT ARCHIVED
 9: if not exist a:%1 goto safe
10: echo <Alt-255>
11: REM CTRL-G SOUNDS A BEEP
12: echo ^Ga:%1 exists. Press CTRL-BREAK to cancel, or
13: pause
14: :safe
15: copy %1 a:%1
16: if exist a:%1 erase %1
17: echo <Alt-255>
18: echo %1 archived
```

The purpose of each change is as follows:

- In line 2, the Clear Screen command starts your Archive command off with a blank screen, giving you complete control over what is displayed.
- In line 3, the Remark command reminds you that the space at the beginning of the Echo command in line 4 is created by pressing the tab key three times.
- In line 4, the title (***ARCHIVE PROCEDURE***) is made more prominent and is displayed in the center of the screen by the insertion of three tabs.
- In line 5, an Echo command displays a blank line below the title. The <Alt-255> represents holding down the key labeled Alt, typing the number 255 on the numeric keypad, then releasing the Alt key.

- In line 8, the Remark command explains the purpose of the Goto command included in line 9.
- In line 10, another Echo command displays a blank line to make the warning message in line 12 more visible.
- In line 11, the Remark command explains how the beep is sounded by the Echo command in line 12.
- In line 12, the ^G (sometimes displayed as G^ in version 3.1 of DOS) in the message displayed by the Echo command represents a character called Ctrl-G, which causes the system to beep and calls attention to the warning. To enter Ctrl-G, hold down the Ctrl key and press G.
- In line 17, the Echo command displays another blank line, to make the message in line 18 more visible.
- In line 18, the Echo command displays a message that tells which file has been archived.

Here are the Edlin commands to make these changes. Type line 4 as a single line:

```
C>edlin archive.bat
End of input file
*2i
        2:*cls
        3:REM THREE TABS IN FOLLOWING ECHO COMMAND
        4:*<Ctrl-Break>

*4
        4:*echo Archive Procedure
        4:*→→→→<space><tab><tab><tab>***ARCHIVE
           PROCEDURE***
*5i
        5:*echo<space><Alt-255>
        6:*<Ctrl-Break>
*8i
        8:*REM BRANCH AROUND WARNING IF FILE NOT ARCHIVED
        9:*<Ctrl-Break>

*10i
       10:*echo<space><Alt-255>
       11:*REM CTRL-G SOUNDS A BEEP
       12:*<Ctrl-Break>

*12
       12:*echo a:%1 exists. Press CTRL-BREAK to cancel, or
       12:*→→→→→<Ins><Ctrl-G><F3>
*#i
       17:*echo<space><Alt-255>
       18:*echo %1 archived
       19:*<Ctrl-Break>

*1l
```

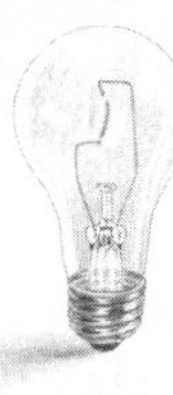

The final command displays the entire file. Compare your display with the modified form of ARCHIVE.BAT shown earlier. If there are any differences, correct them before saving the revised version. (If you have trouble with any of the special keys used in line 12, simply type the entire new line.) When the file is correct, save it by typing *e*.

Although you haven't changed anything your Archive command does, its screen responses are quite different now. Test the new version by archiving P.OLD (which isn't on the archive diskette):

```
C>archive p.old
```

Because ARCHIVE.BAT now starts by clearing the screen, everything you see from this point on is displayed by your Archive command. When the command prompts you to check the diskette in drive A, press any key to continue. The screen now looks like this:

```
                    ***ARCHIVE PROCEDURE***

Make sure archive diskette is in drive A
Strike a key when ready . . .
        1 File(s) copied

p.old archived
```

Test ARCHIVE.BAT again to see how it responds when the file already exists on the archive diskette. P.DOC and P.OLD are no longer on the disk in drive C (you archived them after making the change that erases the file), so archive P.BAK. Type the following, pressing any key to continue the command after each pause:

```
C>archive p.bak
```

The screen looks like this:

```
                    ***ARCHIVE PROCEDURE***
Make sure archive diskette is in drive A
Strike a key when ready . . .

a:p.bak exists. Press CTRL-BREAK to cancel, or
Strike a key when ready . . .
        1 File(s) copied

p.bak archived
```

ARCHIVE.BAT is quite a bit longer than when you began, but your Archive command doesn't look much like a homemade command any more. Although you needn't always go to such lengths when you create a command, it's nice to know that a little extra effort can make your work look professional. If others will use the batch files you create, the investment of your effort can quickly pay off in shorter training time, more efficient use of the system, and fewer mistakes.

CHAPTER SUMMARY

This chapter covered a lot of ground. Experimenting is the best way to put what you learned here into practice. Just be certain to use diskettes that don't contain files you need until you're sure your batch commands are working properly.

The next chapter describes two additional batch commands that let you create even more flexible batch files, and it shows you several useful batch commands you can use to start your personal collection. You need the archive diskette in drive A. Remove this diskette and label it ARCHIVED FILES.

CHAPTER

15

CREATING MORE SMART COMMANDS

The previous chapter showed you how to use the advanced capability of batch files. Knowing how to create batch files is only half the job, however; the other half is finding uses for them. This chapter shows you how to create some commands to search through the phone-list file you created in Chapter 13; it also describes two advanced batch commands and shows several useful batch files to give you some ideas for your own use.

PREPARING FOR THE EXAMPLES

For the first examples in this chapter, you need the phone-list file (PH) that you created in Chapter 13, ''Taking Control of Your System.'' If you haven't gone through the examples in Chapters 13 and 14, you should do so before proceeding.

If you're using a fixed disk, PH should already be in the directory named \RUNNING. Change the current directory to \RUNNING by typing:

```
C>cd \running
```

If you're using diskettes, put the diskette that contains the PH file in drive B and change the current drive to B. The system prompt will be B>, not C>, as shown in the examples.

COMMANDS TO SEARCH THROUGH A FILE

In Chapter 13, you created a file of names, addresses, and telephone numbers, and you used the Find and Sort commands to display entries. You can also put the Find and Sort commands in batch files to create your own search commands and achieve some of the capabilities of a simple record-management program.

For example, the simplest search uses the Find command to display all records that contain a particular string. Create a batch file named SHOW.BAT by typing the following (but ignore the @ symbol at the beginning of the Echo command if you're not using version 3.3):

```
C>copy con show.bat
@echo off
find "%1" ph
^Z
        1 File(s) copied
```

This batch file gives you a Show command that displays all records from PH that contain the string you specify as the parameter to your Show command. To search the phone list, type *show* followed by the string. For example, to display the entries for all consultants (entries that contain the string *cons*), type:

```
C>show cons
```

DOS displays all entries for consultants:

```
---------- ph
Jones      Michele    (747) 429-6360  cons chemist
Black      John       (747) 426-3385  cons mech eng pkg
Jones      Alison     (747) 429-5584  cons chem engineer
```

If you're not using version 3.3, DOS displays *C>echo off* before the list of entries.

This is easier than typing *find "cons" ph.* Read on; you'll find that you can use batch files to make more powerful searches just as easily.

Compound Searches

As the examples in "Taking Control of Your System" showed, you can also combine Find commands to search for records that contain various combinations of character strings, such as all consultants named Jones or all entries outside the 747 area code. Putting these Find commands in a batch file saves even more typing than the Show command you just created.

For example, suppose you want to create a command to show all entries that contain both one string and another. As you saw in Chapter 14, this requires two Find commands, with the output of the first piped to the second. You could call such a command Showand; create a file named SHOWAND.BAT by typing:

```
C>copy con showand.bat
@echo off
find "%1" ph ¦ find "%2"
^Z
        1 File(s) copied
```

This batch command takes two parameters: the two strings the Find command searches for. Now you can search the phone list for entries that contain two strings as easily as you can search it for entries containing one string; just type *showand* followed by the two strings. For example, to display all consultants named Jones, type:

```
C>showand cons Jones
```

DOS displays the records that contain both strings:

```
Jones      Michele    (747) 429-6360  cons chemist
Jones      Alison     (747) 429-5584  cons chem engineer
```

This is definitely easier than typing *find "cons" ph ¦ find "Jones"*.

What if you want to create a command that shows all entries except those that contain a particular string? Use a Find command with the /V parameter. You could call this command Showxcpt; create SHOWXCPT.BAT by typing the following:

```
C>copy con showxcpt.bat
@echo off
find /v "%1" ph
^Z
        1 File(s) copied
```

This batch command requires one parameter, the string you don't want to see. For example, to display all entries not in the 747 area code, type the following:

```
C>showxcpt (7
```

DOS displays all lines from PH that don't contain (7:

```
---------- ph
Green      Fred        (541) 926-4921  cust math teach
Smith      Ed          (541) 835-8747  vend caterer
```

These three batch files—SHOW, SHOWAND, and SHOWXCPT—let you search a file quickly in several ways. You can combine all three searches into a single command just by changing SHOW.BAT.

Chaining Batch Files to Create Powerful Commands

As Chapter 12, "Creating Your Own Commands," described, you can chain batch files, using the name of one batch file as a command in another batch file. When you do this, DOS carries out the commands in the second batch file as if you had typed its name; if the second batch file contains the name of a third batch file, DOS carries out its commands, and so on.

You can modify SHOW.BAT to cover all three types of searches you just performed by chaining it to either SHOWAND.BAT or SHOWXCPT.BAT. When you do this, the parameters you type with the revised SHOW command must specify the type of search as well as the string or strings to search for.

You're creating your own Show command with the following parameters:

show xcpt and <string1> <string2>

xcpt searches for entries that don't contain a string.

and searches for entries that contain two strings.

<string1> and <string2> are the strings to search for. If you include *and*, you must include both <string1> and <string2>; otherwise just include <string1>.

If you don't specify either *xcpt* or *and*, your Show command searches for all entries that contain string1.

This more powerful version of SHOW.BAT is still fairly short; type the following:

```
C>copy con show.bat
@echo off
if %1==xcpt showxcpt %2
if %1==and showand %2 %3
find "%1" ph
^Z
        1 File(s) copied
```

The first If command checks whether the first parameter (%1) typed with the Show command is *xcpt* (recall that the == compares two strings to see if they are identical). If %1 is the same as *xcpt*, SHOWXCPT.BAT is carried out. The second parameter (%2) you type with the Show command is the string to search for; it is the single parameter that SHOWXCPT.BAT requires.

The second If command checks whether the first parameter typed with the Show command is *and*. If it is, SHOWAND.BAT is carried out. The second and third parameters (%2 and %3) typed with the Show command are the two strings to search for; they are the two parameters that SHOWAND.BAT requires.

If the first parameter (%1) typed with the Show command is neither *xcpt* nor *and*, the Find command is carried out to perform a simple search.

Except for the Echo command, only one of the commands in SHOW.BAT is carried out in any particular search. Figure 15-1 shows the contents of SHOW.BAT and an example of each type of search you can make. For each example, the figure lists the

Contents of SHOW.BAT:

```
@echo off
if %1==xcpt showxcpt %2
if %1==and showand %2 %3
find "%1" ph
```

```
C>show cust

@echo off
if cust==xcpt showxcpt
if cust==and showand
find "cust" ph

C>show xcpt cust

@echo off
if xcpt==xcpt showxcpt cust -----> showxcpt cust
if xcpt==and showand cust
find "xcpt" ph                     @echo off
                                   find /v "cust" ph

C>show and cust Jones

@echo off
if and==xcpt showxcpt cust
if and==and showand cust Jones --> showand cust Jones
find "and" ph
                                   @echo off
                                   find "cust" ph | find "Jones"
```

Figure 15-1. Chaining batch files

Show command as you would type it, and substitutes values for the replaceable parameters in SHOW.BAT. The command in SHOW.BAT that is carried out is not shaded. An arrow to the right represents chaining to SHOWXCPT or SHOWAND; the contents of each chained batch file, with values substituted for its replaceable parameters, are shown below the chained batch file.

Now you can make any of the three types of searches with the Show command. The simple search works as it did in the earlier Show command. For example, to display all entries that contain Jones, type:

```
C>show Jones

---------- ph
Jones      Michele     (747) 429-6360  cons chemist
Jones      Alison      (747) 429-5584  cons chem engineer
Jones      James       (747) 636-3541  cust architect
```

To display all entries that don't contain a particular string, type *xcpt* as the first parameter. For example, to display all entries outside the 747 area code, type:

```
C>show xcpt (7

---------- ph
Green      Fred        (541) 926-4921  cust math teach
Smith      Ed          (541) 835-8747  vend caterer
```

Or, to search for two strings, type *and* as the first parameter. For example, to display all entries that contain both *Jones* and *eng*, type:

```
C>show and Jones eng

Jones      Alison      (747) 429-5584  cons chem engineer
```

If you put your telephone numbers and business cards in a text file like this, these three batch files put the contents of the file at your fingertips. Not only can you search for an entry quickly, you can easily display groups of related entries.

You can use this same technique with other data files that might not justify a full database program, but whose contents are a constant part of your work; some more examples are shown in Chapter 16, ''Tailoring Your System.'' This application, like the use of Edlin, is another example of DOS making your computer more valuable without using any additional software.

SOME USEFUL BATCH FILES

To give you some ideas about the sort of batch commands that might help you from day to day, several useful batch files are shown here. These are not step-by-step examples; each description gives the purpose of the batch file, shows its contents, explains how it works, and describes how you would use it.

An effective way to become familiar with batch commands is to experiment. You could enter the following batch files, for example, then experiment with them, making changes and seeing the effects of the changes. Just be sure to use disks that don't contain irreplaceable copies of files you need.

You can create the batch files by copying from the console to a file or by using Edlin. Where line numbers are shown in the listings, they're just for reference; don't enter them. Most of the batch files include one or more Echo commands to add a blank line to the display (for readability); they appear as *echo <Alt-255>*. To make them work properly, hold down the Alt key, press 255 on the numeric keypad, release the Alt key, and then press Enter; if this doesn't work, type *echo*, press the spacebar, and press Enter.

Cleaning Up Disk Storage

Because Edlin and many word processors create a backup file with the extension BAK each time you edit a file, your disks can get crowded with backup files you don't need. The CLEANUP.BAT batch file described here replaces one you created earlier; it displays the directory entries of all files with an extension of BAK and then pauses. At that point, you can cancel the command by pressing Ctrl-Break; if you press any key to proceed, the command erases the files.

CLEANUP.BAT contains:

```
1: @echo off
2: cls
3: echo ***Will erase the following files:***
4: dir %1*.bak
5: echo <Alt-255>
6: echo ^GPress Ctrl-Break to cancel, or
7: pause
8: erase %1*.bak
```

Notice that there is no blank between *%1* and **.bak* in lines 4 and 8; this lets you specify a drive letter or a path name as a parameter with the file name, but be sure to end a path name with a backslash (\).

The *^G* in line 6 (displayed as G^ in some versions of DOS) is Ctrl-G, which sounds a beep. To enter it, hold down the Control key and press G.

To erase all BAK files from the current directory on the disk in the current drive, type *cleanup* and press any key when the Pause command prompts you.

To erase all BAK files from another directory, type the path name followed by \ as a parameter; you can also precede the path name with a drive letter and colon (for example, *cleanup a:* or *cleanup \mkt\wp*).

Directory of Subdirectories

The Directory command displays *<DIR>* instead of the file size to identify a subdirectory. If a directory contains many files, picking out the subdirectories can be a bit difficult. The DIRSUB batch file described here lets you display only the entries for subdirectories.

DIRSUB.BAT contains:

```
1: @echo off
2: echo ***Subdirectories in %1***
3: echo <Alt-255>
4: dir %1 | find "<"
```

In this file, the output of the Directory command is piped to a Find command that displays all directory lines that contain a less-than sign (<).

You can type one parameter (%1) with the Dirsub command to specify the directory whose entries are to be displayed. The parameter can include any of the following: a drive letter and colon, a path name, or a file name. If you don't include a parameter, this Dirsub command displays the subdirectories in the current directory.

To see the subdirectories in the current directory, you would type *dirsub.* To see the subdirectories in the current directory of drive B, you would type *dirsub b:* To see the subdirectories in \MKT\WP, you would type *dirsub \mkt\wp.*

The special entries . and .. are in all directories except the root. You can modify DIRSUB.BAT so that it doesn't display these entries by changing line 4 of the batch file to the following:

```
dir %1 | find "<" | find /v "."
```

Now the output of the Find command is piped to a second Find command that uses the /V parameter to eliminate all lines that contain a period. You would use this version of the Dirsub command just as you would use the earlier version.

Moving Files from One Directory to Another

In a tree-structured file system, you'll sometimes want to move files from one directory to another. You can do this by copying the file to the new directory with the Copy command, then erasing the original with the Erase command. MOVE.BAT combines these into one command.

MOVE.BAT contains:

```
@echo off
copy %1 %2
cls
echo Files in target directory:
echo <Alt-255>
```

```
 6: dir %2
 7: echo <Alt-255>
 8: echo If files to be moved are not in directory,
 9: echo press Ctrl-Break to cancel. Otherwise
10: pause
11: erase %1
```

Here is how the batch file works, line by line:

- In line 1, the Echo command turns echo off.
- In line 2, the Copy command copies the files to the target directory.
- In line 3, the Clear Screen command clears the screen.
- In lines 4 and 5, Echo commands display a message and a blank line.
- In line 6, the Directory command displays the contents of the target directory.
- In lines 7 through 9, Echo commands display a blank line and a warning message.
- In line 10, the Pause command makes the system pause to let you cancel the Erase command in line 11 if the files you moved are not displayed in the listing of the target directory.

You have created a command with two parameters:

move <source> <target>

<source> is the name of the file to be moved (copied and then deleted). You can include a drive letter and path name. If you use wildcard characters in the file name, DOS displays the name of each file it copies.

<target> is the name of the directory to which the <source> files are to be copied. If you omit <target>, the files are copied to the current directory.

For example, assume that the current directory is \MKT\WP. To move the file REPORT.DOC to the directory \ENG\WP, you would type *move report.doc \eng\wp*. To move the file BUDGET.JAN from \ENG\WP to \MKT\WP, you type *move \eng\wp\budget.jan*. To move all files from \MKT\WP to \WORD\MKT, you would type *move *.* \word\mkt*.

THREE ADVANCED BATCH COMMANDS

Note: The batch commands you have worked with up to this point are sufficient for you to create useful batch files, like the search commands for the phone-list file that are tailored to your own needs. Rather than continue with the rest of this chapter right now, you might want to put the book aside for a while and experiment, then return to learn the last three batch commands this book discusses.

The three remaining batch commands, Shift, For, and Call, give you even more control over how your batch files work. They're somewhat more complicated than the other batch commands, but the examples should make their use clear.

Preparing for the Advanced Examples

The remaining examples in the chapter require the P files you archived in Chapter 14. Put the diskette you labeled ARCHIVED FILES in drive A.

Shifting the List of Parameters

The Shift command moves the list of parameters you type with a batch command one position to the left. For example, suppose you type a Shift command with three parameters. After the Shift command is carried out once, what was %3 becomes %2 and what was %2 becomes %1; what was %1 is gone. After a second Shift command, what started out as %3 is %1; what started as %2 and %1 are both gone.

This command lets a short batch file handle any number of parameters; the following sample batch file illustrates the technique. ARCH1.BAT archives any number of files. Here are its contents; remember, the line numbers are just for reference:

```
1: @echo off
2: :start
3: if "%1"=="" goto done
4: echo ***Archiving %1***
5: if not exist a:%1 copy %1 a:
6: shift
7: goto start
8: :done
```

Here's a line-by-line description of how it works:

- As usual, the first line is an Echo command to turn echo off.
- In line 2, the label *:start* marks the beginning of the commands that will be repeated for each parameter.
- In line 3, the If command checks to see whether a parameter was entered for %1. It does this by comparing %1 with two quotation marks enclosing nothing at all (“ ”). You're telling DOS to compare the first parameter (if one was typed) with nothing, or no parameter. When the comparison is true, meaning there are no more parameters, the Goto command sends DOS to the label *:done*.
- In line 4, the Echo command displays the name of the file that is being archived.
- In line 5, the If command checks whether the file to be archived exists on drive A; if it doesn't, the Copy command copies the file from the current drive to drive A. (The batch file assumes drive C or drive B is the current drive.)

- In line 6, the Shift command moves the list of parameters one position left.
- In line 7, the Goto command sends DOS back to the label *:start.*
- In line 8, the label *:done* marks the end of the command file.

To use this batch file you type *arch1*, then the names of the files to be archived. The command stops when %1 equals " "—in other words, when there are no more file names to be substituted for %1.

To test the command, copy the file named P.OLD, which you archived in Chapter 14, from the diskette in drive A to the current drive by typing:

```
C>copy a:p.old
```

Now archive P.OLD, Q.DOC, and Q.OLD by typing:

```
C>arch1 p.old q.doc q.old

***Archiving p.old***
***Archiving q.doc***
        1 File(s) copied

***Archiving q.old***
        1 File(s) copied
```

The confirming messages show that DOS did not copy the file that was already on the diskette in drive A (P.OLD), but that it did copy the files that weren't on the diskette (both Q.DOC and Q.OLD).

This short Archive command doesn't display instructions or warnings like the batch file you created in Chapter 14, but it does show how you can use the Shift command to write a batch file that handles any number of parameters. The technique is simple: Do something with %1, shift the parameters, then use a Goto command to send DOS back to the beginning to do it all over again. Just make sure you define a way to stop the process, or DOS will carry out the command forever.

Carrying Out a Command More than Once

Sometimes you might want DOS to carry out a command more than once in a batch file, such as once for each file that matches a file name with wildcard characters. The For command does just that. Like the If command, the For command has two parts: The first part defines how often a command is to be carried out, and the second part is the command to be carried out.

The For command is somewhat more complex than the other batch commands. If you don't fully understand the description of its parameters, read on and try the examples. As with many other aspects of using a computer, it's easier to use the For command than it is to read about it.

The For command has three parameters:

for %%p in (<set>) do <command>

The words *in* and *do* are required in the command; they are not parameters.

%%p is a replaceable parameter used inside the For command. DOS assigns to it, in turn, each value included in (<set>).

(<set>) is the list of possible values that can be given to %%p. You separate the values with blanks, and must enclose the entire list in parentheses—for example, *(1 2 3)*. You can also specify a set of values with a file name that includes wildcard characters—for example, *b:* .DOC*.

<command> is any DOS command other than another For command. You can use both batch-command parameters (such as %1) and the For command replaceable parameter (%%p) in <command>.

It's all less complicated than it sounds. When DOS carries out a For command, it assigns to %%p, in turn, each value that you specify in (<set>), then it carries out <command>. Each time it carries out <command>, DOS first substitutes for %%p the current value taken from (<set>).

A brief example shows how the For command works. The following batch command carries out an Echo command three times, displaying each of the three words enclosed in parentheses. Create FOR1.BAT by typing:

```
C>copy con for1.bat
for %%p in (able baker charlie) do echo %%p
^Z
        1 File(s) copied
```

In this For command, *(able baker charlie)* is (<set>) and *echo %%p* is <command>. The For command tells DOS to carry out the Echo command once for each word in parentheses, substituting, in turn, *able*, *baker*, and *charlie* for %%p. Test it by typing:

```
C>for1
```

For a change, this batch file doesn't begin by turning echo off, so DOS displays each command it carries out, starting with the For command:

```
C>for %p in (able baker charlie) do echo %p
```

DOS then displays and carries out the Echo command once for each value in the set, each time substituting the next value from the set for the replaceable parameter in the Echo command:

```
C>echo able
able

C>echo baker
baker

C>echo charlie
charlie
```

Instead of specifying actual values in the set, you can use replaceable parameters, such as %1. This technique works just like any other batch command, but can be confusing because now you can have %1 and %%p in the same command. Here's the difference: %1 refers to the first parameter typed with the batch command, %2 refers to the second parameter typed with the batch command, and so forth; %%p refers to the value selected from the set enclosed in parentheses within the For command.

The next example shows you the difference. Here, the words to be displayed are typed as parameters of the batch command, instead of being included as part of the For command. Create FOR2.BAT by typing:

```
C>copy con for2.bat
for %%p in (%1 %2 %3) do echo %%p
^Z
        1 File(s) copied
```

This For command tells DOS to carry out the Echo command (*echo %%p*) once for each value in parentheses, substituting for %%p the first, then the second, and finally the third parameter you type with the For2 command. Test it by typing:

```
C>for2 dog easy fox
```

DOS displays each command it carries out. First it displays the For command:

```
C>for %p in (dog easy fox) do echo %p
```

Note that DOS has substituted values for all replaceable parameters. The set in parentheses is now *(dog easy fox)*, because those are the three parameters you typed; they have replaced *(%1 %2 %3)*. As you may have noticed in the preceding display, DOS has also dropped one of the percent signs from %%p. DOS removes the first percent sign when it substitutes the parameters you type with the command for %1, %2, and so forth. It does, however, leave one percent sign to show that a value must still be substituted for %p.

DOS then displays and carries out three Echo commands, each time substituting one value from the set in parentheses for %p:

```
C>echo dog
dog

C>echo easy
easy

C>echo fox
fox
```

If you wish, you can specify the set in a For command with a file name and wildcard characters. DOS then assigns to %%p, in turn, each file name that matches the wildcard characters. You can use this technique to create a simple Archive batch file using only a For command. The following command doesn't display instructions and warnings, but it does show you how much can be done with a single batch command.

Create a batch file named ARCH2.BAT by typing the following:

```
C>copy con arch2.bat
for %%p in (%1) do if not exist a:%%p copy %%p a:
^Z
        1 File(s) copied
```

Q.DOC and Q.OLD are on the diskette in drive A (you copied them in the example of the Shift command). Use them to test ARCH2.BAT by archiving all Q files:

```
C>arch2 q.*
```

DOS displays each command it carries out, starting with the For command. (Remember, you have not turned echo off):

```
C>for %p in (q.*) do if not exist a:%p copy %p a:
```

DOS then displays and carries out three If commands, each time substituting a file name that matches the set enclosed in parentheses for the replaceable parameter in the If command:

```
C>if not exist a:Q.DOC copy Q.DOC a:

C>if not exist a:Q.BAK copy Q.BAK a:
        1 File(s) copied

C>if not exist a:Q.OLD copy Q.OLD a:
```

The messages displayed by the Copy command confirm that DOS didn't copy either Q.DOC or Q.OLD because they were already on the archive diskette, but did copy Q.BAK which hadn't been archived.

The For command gives you a quick way to carry out a DOS command several times. As shown in some of the sample batch files that conclude this chapter, the For command makes it possible to create powerful batch commands.

Using a Batch Command in a Batch File

Earlier in this chapter, in the final version of SHOW.BAT, you used batch commands (Showand and Showxcpt) in a batch file. DOS returned to the system prompt after carrying out these batch commands, even though neither was actually the last command in SHOW.BAT; the last command was Find. You can use this capability, called *chaining,* with any version of DOS.

If you're using version 3.3, however, you can also use the Call command in a batch file to tell DOS to carry out the commands in another batch file and then come back to continue with the next command in the original batch file instead of returning to the system prompt. This lets you use a batch command of your own making in a batch file, just as you would use a DOS command.

The Call command has two parameters:

call <batchfile> <parameters>

<batchfile> is the name of a batch command that you want DOS to carry out from within the calling batch file.

<parameters> represents any parameters that <batchfile> requires.

Two short batch files demonstrate the usefulness of the Call command. First, create a batch file named ECHOIT.BAT by typing the following:

```
C>copy con echoit.bat
@echo off
echo %1
^Z
        1 File(s) copied
```

ECHOIT.BAT simply echoes the parameter you enter with it. For example, to echo *fred*, type the following:

```
C>echoit fred
fred

C>_
```

Now create another batch file named ECHOALL.BAT that uses a For command to carry out ECHOIT.BAT for each of up to three parameters:

```
C>copy con echoall.bat
@echo off
for %%p in (%1 %2 %3) do call echoit %%p
^Z
        1 File(s) copied
```

The For command carries out the Call command for each of up to three parameters that can be entered with the Echoall batch command. The Call command carries out the batch command ECHOIT.BAT, specifying, in turn, each parameter entered with the Echoall batch command.

Now type the following to echo the words *xray*, *yankee*, and *zulu*:

```
C>echoall xray yankee zulu
xray
yankee
zulu
C>_
```

If you hadn't included the Call command, DOS would have carried out ECHOIT.BAT once to display the first parameter (*xray*), then returned to the system prompt.

SOME MORE USEFUL BATCH FILES

The following batch files use the advanced batch commands. Again, they aren't step-by-step examples; they're working samples to give you an idea of what can be done with the full set of batch commands. You can enter the batch files by copying from the console or by using Edlin. The line numbers shown are for reference only.

Displaying a Series of Small Text Files

If you work with many small text files, such as batch files or boilerplate paragraphs for word-processed documents, it's handy to be able to review several files with one command, rather than having to print or display them one at a time. The batch file shown here, REVIEW.BAT, uses the Shift, Type, and Pause commands to display any number of files one at a time. As before, recall that <Alt-255> echoes a blank line. REVIEW.BAT contains:

```
 1: @echo off
 2: :start
 3: if "%1"=="" goto done
 4: cls
 5: echo<spacebar><tab><tab>***FILENAME: %1***
 6: echo <Alt-255>
 7: type %1
 8: echo <Alt-255>
 9: echo <Alt-255>
10: pause
11: shift
12: goto start
13: :done
```

This batch file uses the same technique as the earlier examples of the Shift command. The Echo command in line 5 displays the file name (moved toward the center of the screen with two tabs), so that you'll know what file is displayed. Lines 8 and 9 display two blank lines to separate the file from the Pause command message.

With this Review command, you type the names of the files as parameters. To display several files with the extension DOC, for example, you type *review 1.doc 2.doc 3.doc*. DOS clears the screen and displays the first file, then displays the Pause command message and waits for you to press any key before clearing the screen and displaying the next file. When the If command in line 3 finds the first null parameter (" "), DOS returns to command level.

Searching Files for a String of Characters

Have you ever searched through your paper files to find a specific letter or reference? Or wondered how many letters you wrote about a particular subject or how often you use a particular word? These three short batch files give you several ways to scan a file or set of files for lines that contain a string of characters.

Displaying All Lines That Contain a String

To help you find all lines that contain a particular string, SCAN.BAT lets you specify the file to be searched and one string to search for. It displays each line in the file that contains the string. You can also use wildcard characters to search a set of files. Here are the contents of SCAN.BAT:

```
1: @echo off
2: cls
3: echo<space><tab><tab>***LINES IN %1 THAT CONTAIN %2***
4: echo <Alt-255>
5: for %%p in (%1) do find " %2 " %%p
```

All the work here is done in the last line of the batch file. The earlier lines clear the screen and display a title. The For command in line 5 actually carries out the Find command for each file name that matches the first parameter that you type with the Scan command; the Find command is the one that searches for the string that you type as the second parameter.

To display each line that contained the word *sales* in all files with an extension of DOC, you would type *scan *.doc sales*. DOS would clear the screen and display each line containing the word *sales* preceded and followed by a blank (" %2 ").

Displaying the Number of Lines Containing the String

COUNT.BAT is a slightly modified version of SCAN.BAT that displays the number of lines in the file that contain the string, but doesn't display the lines themselves.

Here are the contents of COUNT.BAT (changes from SCAN.BAT are shaded):

```
1: @echo off
2: cls
3: echo<space><tab><tab>***NUMBER OF LINES IN %1 THAT CONTAIN %2***
4: echo <Alt-255>
5: for %%p in (%1) do find /c " %2 " %%p
```

The only two changes are in the title displayed by the Echo command (line 3) and the addition of the /C parameter to the Find command (line 5).

As an example, to see how many lines in all files with an extension of DOC in the current directory contained the word *night*, you would type *count *.doc night*. The Count command would clear the screen and display the number of lines in each file that contained the word *night*.

Searching for Several Strings

Another batch file, SCANALL.BAT, again gives a count of lines, but it uses a different approach. The file or set of files to be searched is named in the batch file, but you can type however many strings you want as parameters to search for. This approach is particularly useful if you frequently search the same set of files, such as your word-processing files. SCANALL.BAT contains:

```
 1: @echo off
 2: :start
 3: if "%1"=="" goto done
 4: cls
 5: echo<space><tab><tab>***LINES IN *.DOC THAT CONTAIN %1***
 6: echo <Alt-255>
 7: for %%p in (*.doc) do find /c " %1 " %%p
 8: echo <Alt-255>
 9: pause
10: shift
11: goto start
12: :done
```

This batch file uses both the For and Shift commands to search several files for several strings. A line-by-line description is in order:

- Line 1 turns echo off.
- The label *:start* identifies the beginning of the commands to be repeated (it is the destination of the Goto command in line 11).
- The If command checks whether the parameter is null. If it is, the Goto command sends DOS to the end of the batch file (line 12).
- Line 4 clears the screen.
- The Echo commands in lines 5 and 6 display a title and a blank line.
- The For command in line 7 searches each file with an extension of DOC and displays the number of lines that contain the string (" %1 ") specified in the first parameter you type when you use the Scanall command.
- Like line 6, line 8 displays a blank line.
- The Pause command displays its message and waits for a key to be pressed.
- Line 10 shifts the parameters one position to the left.
- The Goto command sends DOS to the label *:start.*
- The label *:done* identifies the end of the batch file (the destination of the Goto command in line 3).

To use the Scanall command, type the words to be searched for as parameters. Remember, the Find command distinguishes between uppercase and lowercase letters. If, for example, you wanted to search for the words *sales*, *January*, and *region*, you would type *scanall sales January region.*

The Scanall command would clear the screen, search all the files whose extension is DOC for the word *sales*, display the number of lines, and then pause. When you pressed any key, it would scan all the files for the word *January*, would again display the results, and so forth for each word you specified. Try it with your own words and several dozen word-processing files; you'll be surprised at how quickly this command searches all the files, particularly if you're using a fixed disk.

If you wanted to display the lines containing the strings, rather than just the count, you could simply omit the /C parameter from the Find command in the batch file. This command could produce a lot of output. To print a record of it, you could press Ctrl-PrtSc after you entered the command, but before you pressed the Enter key, to start simultaneously printing and displaying the results.

Displaying a Sorted Directory

In Chapter 4 you displayed the directory sorted by file name. Because the items in a directory entry always begin in the same column, you can sort the directory entries four ways; all but one use the column parameter (/+<number>) of the Sort command to sort starting at the column where the information begins:

- Name—starts in column 1, so does not require the column parameter.
- Extension—starts in column 10.
- Size—starts in column 16.
- Time—starts in column 34.

Although the directory entry includes the date, you can't sort by date unless the date is shown as year-month-day, because January of one year would appear in the list before December of the preceding year (that is, 1-1-1988 would *precede* 12-31-1987). Most of the world (Japan excepted) shows either the day or the month first, so these examples don't sort by date.

The benefits of sorting a directory alphabetically by file name or by extension are obvious. In addition, if you need to delete some files to make space on a disk, or you're just interested in the relative sizes of files, sorting by size is useful. Even sorting by time can be helpful if you've updated a group of files and want to check on which you revised last.

You can create a command to display a directory sorted any of these ways with five short batch files: Four actually sort and display the directory, and one (the command that you type) chains to the correct one of the other four.

First, copy from the console, as you have done before, to create the following one-line batch files; their names tell how they sort the directory:

DIRNAME.BAT:

```
dir %1 | sort | find "-" | more
```

DIREXT.BAT:

```
dir %1 ¦ sort /+10 ¦ find "-" ¦ more
```

DIRSIZE.BAT

```
dir %1 ¦ sort /+16 ¦ find "-" ¦ more
```

DIRTIME.BAT

```
dir %1 ¦ sort /+34 ¦ find "-" ¦ more
```

Each of these batch files sorts and displays the directory specified in the parameter %1 and pipes the output of the Sort command to a Find command that selects only the lines that contain a hyphen (file entries only). The output of the Find command is then piped to the More command to handle directories more than one screen long. If no parameter is specified, the batch command sorts and displays the current directory. The only difference among the batch files is the column in which sorting begins.

You now need the batch file that chains to the correct one of the previous four. Name the file DIRSORT.BAT; it contains:

```
1: @echo off
2: for %%p in (name ext size time) do if "%1"=="%%p" dir%%p %2
3: echo First parameter must be name, ext, size, or time
```

Be sure *not* to put a blank between *dir* and *%%p* in line 2, or the result won't be a valid file name for any of the chained batch files. The quotation marks around %1 and %%p prevent DOS from displaying an error message if no parameter is typed with the command.

In the DIRSORT batch file, the For command sets %%p to each of the words, in turn, in the set in parentheses, then carries out the If command, which compares %%p to the first parameter typed with the Dirsort command. If there is a match, the If command adds the value of %%p to *dir* to produce the name of one of the four sort batch files, and chains to that batch file (for example, *dir* + *name* would become *dirname*). The second parameter (%2), if any, typed with the Dirsort command is the %1 parameter (the directory name) for the chained batch file.

If the first parameter you type with the Dirsort command isn't one of the four words in the set in parentheses, the condition in the If command is not true. Then the Echo command in the next line is carried out, displaying a message that lists the correct parameters, and the Dirsort batch command ends without chaining to one of the files that displays a sorted directory.

To display a sorted directory, you would type the Dirsort command with one or two parameters: The first, which is required, would specify how to sort and could only be *name*, *ext*, *size*, or *time*; the second parameter, which is optional, would be the drive letter, path name, or name of the directory to be displayed. If you didn't include the second parameter, the command would display the current directory of the disk in the current drive.

For example, to display the current directory, sorted by size, of the disk in the current drive, you would type *dirsort size*. To display the root directory, sorted by name, of the disk in drive A, you would type *dirsort name a:*

CHAPTER SUMMARY

These batch files should give you a good start on a collection of special-purpose commands, as well as some ideas for creating more of your own. This is where the flexibility of DOS really becomes apparent: The wide range of DOS commands and capabilities is only the starting point for putting DOS to work. With redirection, filter commands, and batch files, you can combine all the other DOS commands into a set of custom-tailored commands, to make your personal computer truly personal.

CHAPTER 16

TAILORING YOUR SYSTEM

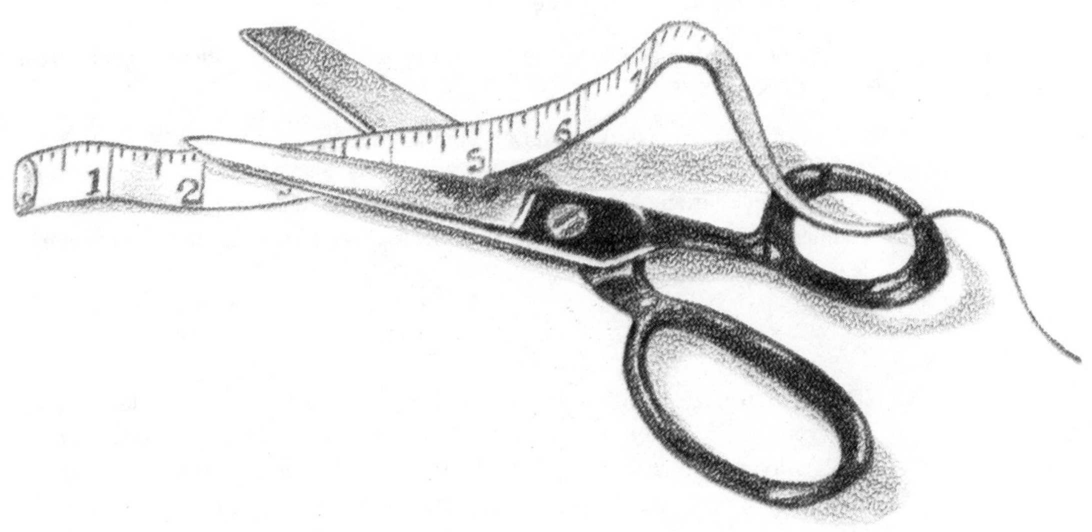

If you have tried the examples in the book, you have used all the major features of DOS. Although it may seem that DOS sometimes offers more options than you need, those options give you flexibility in tailoring DOS; they let you adapt the computer to yourself rather than adapt yourself to the computer.

This chapter shows several ways you can tailor DOS to your needs or preferences. Not only does this tailoring make DOS fit your work needs better, some of the techniques described here can also make your system immediately useful without your having to buy application programs. Some of these techniques can also make the system more accessible to people who may need to use the computer, but who don't have your experience with DOS. And tailoring can also make it easier to achieve consistency in such procedures as backing up a fixed disk when several people use the computer.

This chapter describes:

- Ways to set up a filing system that matches the way the computer is used.
- Batch commands that simplify using a multilevel filing system.
- Batch commands that automate backing up a fixed disk.
- Several simple record-management schemes similar to the telephone index described in Chapters 13 and 15.
- Commands that help you tailor your system hardware with the DOS file named CONFIG.SYS.
- Some less frequently used DOS commands.

Examples are included, but they are not step-by-step exercises. The intent of this chapter is to give you some ideas about how to tailor DOS by applying what you have learned in previous chapters.

SETTING UP A FILING SYSTEM

The multilevel file system described in Chapter 8, "A Tree of Files," lets you organize your files to match your work. A file structure is affected by such factors as the application programs that are used, how many people use the computer, and how many departments are involved. This section shows several different file structures, each organized to focus on a different approach to using the computer. Because every real-life situation is different, these are guides, not exact models.

It doesn't take long to set up a file system—all you need are a few Make Directory commands—but changing a file structure after dozens or hundreds of files have been created can be time-consuming. A few minutes' thought ahead of time can result in a file structure that suits the way the computer will be used.

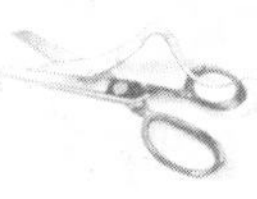

In the following examples, the computer system is assumed to have a fixed disk, on which a directory named DOS contains the DOS command files. The root directory is assumed to contain an AUTOEXEC.BAT file with a Path command that sets the command path at startup to \DOS and all other program directories in the file structure. General-purpose batch files and any other files that are needed by anyone using the system regardless of the current directory are also assumed to be in the root directory, though they, too, could be in directories of their own, with appropriate command paths added to AUTOEXEC.BAT.

An Application-Based File System

If a computer is used for several applications—as it would be by an independent professional or a small business—a natural way to organize the file structure is by application program. Figure 16-1 shows how a file system might be set up by an independent professional who uses the machine with a word processor, a spreadsheet program, and a database manager.

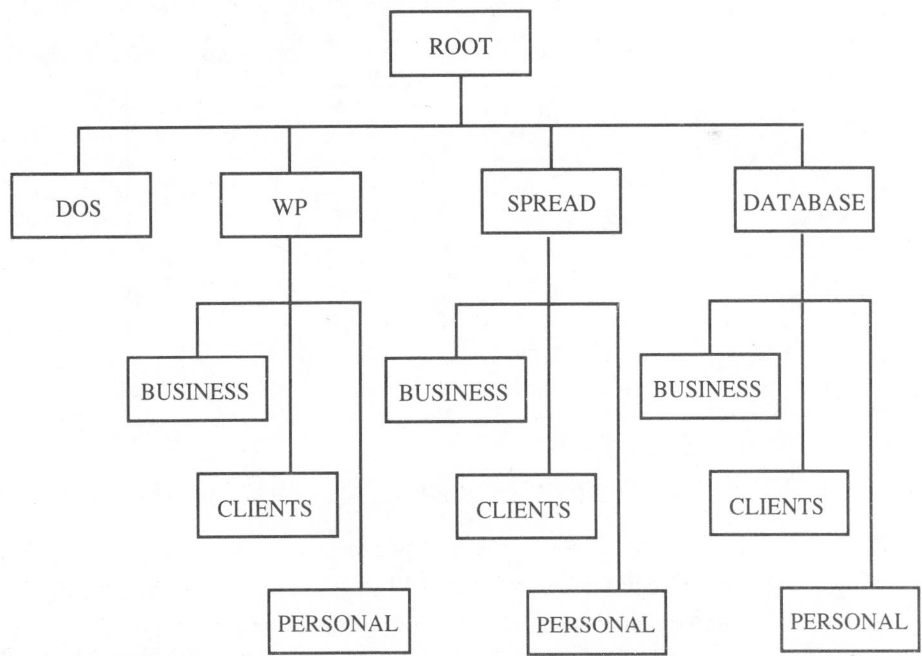

Figure 16-1. Application-based file structure for an independent professional

The first level of directories contains the DOS directory and three others (WP, SPREAD, and DATABASE) for the application programs. The next level (BUSINESS, CLIENTS, and PERSONAL) holds the data files for the applications.

With this file structure, when someone does some word processing, for example, the current directory is set to the directory that contains the document files (such as \WP\BUSINESS or \WP\PERSONAL) so that a path name does not have to be typed each time the person wants to start work on a different file. The Path command in AUTOEXEC.BAT provides access to the root directory (for general-purpose batch files), \DOS (for DOS commands), and \WP (for the word-processing program).

On the other hand, the file system for a computer used in a small business might define the second and subsequent directory levels to correspond to the departments that use the applications, rather than to the data files for the applications. Figure 16-2 shows how such a file system might be set up.

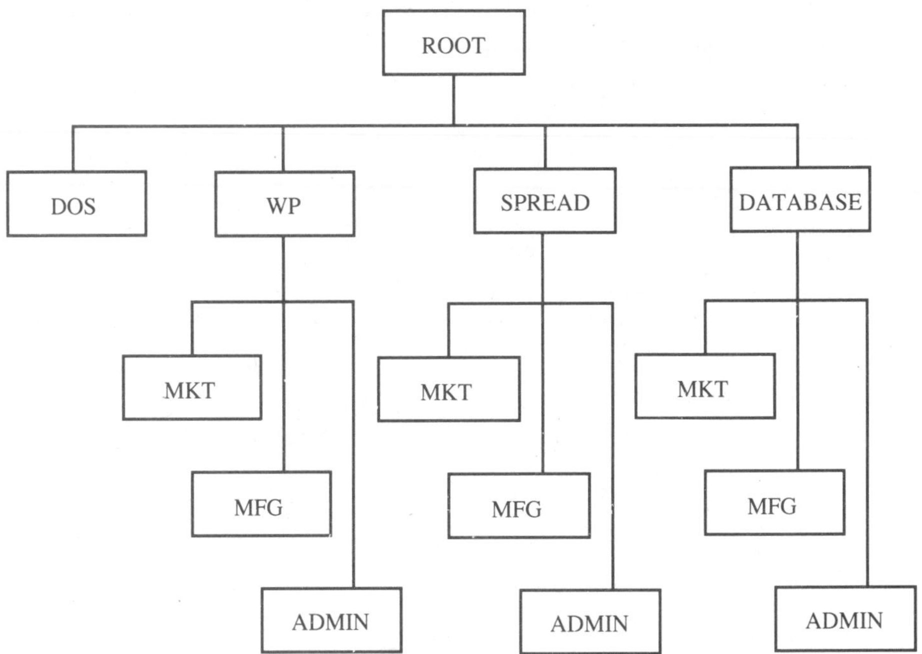

Figure 16-2. Application-based file structure for a small business

A Department-Based File System

Rather than beginning with the application program, as the preceding examples do, files can also be organized to emphasize the departments that use the machine. Figure 16-3 shows a file system for a machine used by the Marketing, Manufacturing, and Administration departments of a company. The application programs are the same as in the previous examples, but stored in subdirectories under \PROGRAMS. They are used jointly by all three departments. Because each program is in a subdirectory of its own, and the Path command in AUTOEXEC.BAT sets the command path to the \PROGRAM directories, any department can request any program.

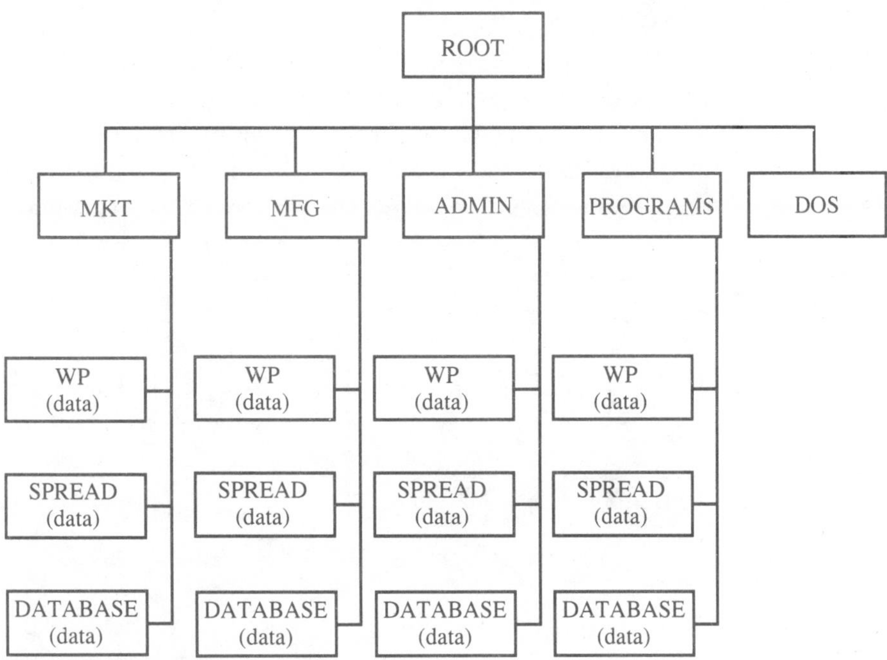

Figure 16-3. Department-based file structure

As much as anything else, the choice of how to organize files depends on how the people who use the computer view their work. If they think primarily in terms of what they're doing (''I do word processing''), the application-based structure might be the most comfortable. If they think in terms of who they do it for (''I'm the Marketing Administrative Assistant''), the department-based structure might be more appropriate. Neither structure is more efficient than the other; each simply reflects a different way of looking at the file system.

A User-Based File System

If several people use the computer, a file structure that emphasizes the users might be most appropriate, especially if the people use the machine for different applications. Figure 16-4, shown on the following page, outlines a directory structure for a system used by three people.

Again, directories are defined for the same application programs used in the other sample file structures. If the computer is used by people with varying degrees of familiarity with DOS, and if not all users need each application, this type of file structure can make use of the system seem more natural, especially if you create some batch commands that simplify using the directories.

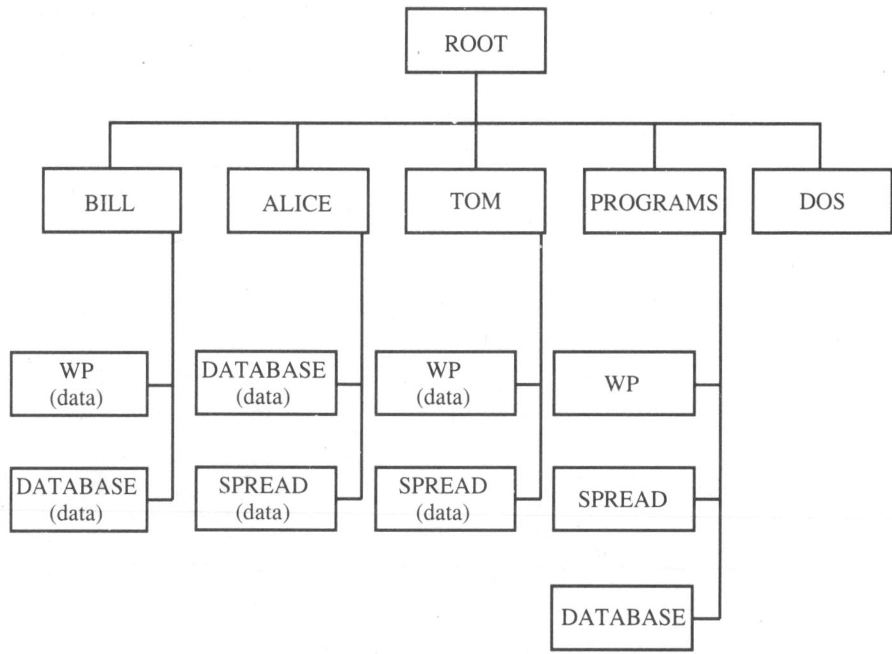

Figure 16-4. User-based file structure

Batch Files to Use Directories

Batch files designed for using directories can be simple or elaborate, depending on who will use them and how much time you want to invest in creating them. Creating separate directories for the people who use the system, for departments, and for application programs simplifies the appearance of the system and makes it easier to keep track of files. Separate directories, however, can also mean that you have to change directories more often. You can automate the use of directories with batch files; this technique makes it simple for all users to work with a structured filing system, even if they are not familiar with DOS. If you make certain the command search path always includes the directory in which they're stored, the batch files for using directories can be accessible from any directory or subdirectory. Switching from one directory and application program to another is always just a matter of typing a single command.

In its simplest form, a batch file to use a directory simply changes the current directory. For example, suppose you have the file structure shown in Figure 16-3, and you want a batch file called WORDMKT.BAT in the root directory to help manage word processing for the Marketing department.

A basic, but functional, version of WORDMKT.BAT could look like the following example (line numbers here and throughout the chapter are for reference only):

```
@echo off
cd \mkt\wp
```

The Change Directory command sets the current directory to \MKT\WP, which contains the Marketing word-processing files. To use your word-processing program with the Marketing data files, you would just type *wordmkt.*

You could create a similar batch file for each directory that contains data files, and then use any directory just by typing the name of the appropriate batch file. Figure 16-5 shows the directories in Figure 16-3 that contain data files and indicates how the corresponding batch files might be named.

Directory that Contains Data Files	Directory that Contains Program	Name of Batch File
\MKT\WP	\PROGRAMS\WP	WORDMKT.BAT
\MKT\SPREAD	\PROGRAMS\SPREAD	SPMKT.BAT
\MKT\DATABASE	\PROGRAMS\DATABASE	DBMKT.BAT
\MFG\WP	\PROGRAMS\WP	WORDMFG.BAT
\MFG\SPREAD	\PROGRAMS\SPREAD	SPMFG.BAT
\MFG\DATABASE	\PROGRAMS\DATABASE	DBMFG.BAT
\ADMIN\WP	\PROGRAMS\WP	WORDADM.BAT
\ADMIN\SPREAD	\PROGRAMS\SPREAD	SPADM.BAT
\ADMIN\DATABASE	\PROGRAMS\DATABASE	DBADM.BAT

Figure 16-5. Directories and batch files for a department-based file structure

To produce the other batch files, you simply change the Change Directory command to point to the corresponding directories that contain the data files. For example, the batch command (SPMFG.BAT) to do spreadsheets for the Manufacturing department could contain:

```
@echo off
cd \mfg\spread
```

With these batch files, anyone could then type *wordmkt* and edit a few Marketing documents, type *spadm* and work on some spreadsheets for the Administration department, then type *dbmfg* and update the Manufacturing inventory database, all without worrying about—or even knowing about—the correct directory.

A set of batch files like these makes the multilevel filing system not only more flexible, but also easier to use.

Improving the Appearance of the Batch Files

To dress up the appearance of your batch files for using directories, you could clear the screen and display the directory one screenful at a time. The Change Directory command would be unchanged; this modified version of WORDMKT.BAT would look like the following:

```
@echo off
cd \mkt\wp
cls
dir /w | more
```

The /W parameter of the Directory command is used here in case the directory is long; the More command is used in case the directory is *very* long.

Creating Your Own Menu System

If someone unfamiliar with DOS will be using the system, you can use batch files to create a menu system that quickly moves the less-experienced user to the correct directory. For example, suppose you have the file structure shown in Figure 16-3; the batch files described here let someone turn on the system and, by typing *mkt*, see the following display:

```
                    *** MARKETING ***

Applications: Word processing
              Spreadsheet
              Database

Enter W, S, or D

_
```

If the user types *w*, the following type of directory format screen is displayed (the entries are hypothetical):

```
          *** MARKETING--WORD PROCESSING ***
Document files:

 Volume in drive C is FIXEDDISK
 Directory of  C:\MKT\WP

.                ..                 TAXMEMO  DOC...
THP0315  DOC     BUDGET    DOC      INVEN01  DOC...
SLSLTR   DOC     THP0311   DOC      CONFNOT  DOC...
LETR04   DOC     SLSMEMO   DOC      LETR07   DOC...
INVEN04  DOC     INVEN02   DOC      SVCREC   DOC...
LETR06   DOC
       26 File(s)   17162384 bytes free

C>_
```

Displays of this kind would require four batch files for each department: For the Marketing department, there would be one (MKT.BAT) in the root directory and three (W.BAT, S.BAT, and D.BAT) in \MKT. First, here are the contents of MKT.BAT:

```
@echo off
cd \mkt
cls
REM THREE TABS AT BEGINNING OF FOLLOWING ECHO COMMAND
echo <tab><tab><tab>*** MARKETING ***
echo <Alt-255>
echo Applications: Word processing
echo               Spreadsheet
echo               Database
echo <Alt-255>
echo Enter W, S, or D
prompt $a
```

As you can see, most of the commands are Echo commands. The batch file is straightforward: It turns off echo, changes the directory to \MKT, clears the screen, and displays the menu and choices. Then the Prompt command (described later in this chapter) makes the system prompt (C>) invisible, so the user sees only the cursor, and the system returns to command level. MKT.BAT has ended even though, as the sample screen showed, it appears to be waiting for a reply to the prompt *Enter W, S, or D.*

If the user types *w* (for word processing), DOS carries out the batch file W.BAT in \MKT. Its contents are:

```
@echo off
cls
cd wp
REM TWO TABS IN FOLLOWING ECHO COMMAND
echo <tab><tab>*** MARKETING--WORD PROCESSING ***
echo Document files:
prompt
dir *.doc /w
```

This batch file produces the second sample display (the response to the menu selection). It, too, is straightforward. It turns echo off, clears the screen, changes the directory to \MKT\WP, displays the titles, resets the system prompt to C>, and displays in wide format the directory entries of all files with an extension of DOC.

To complete the menu system in \MKT, you need two batch files similar to W.BAT, one for your spreadsheet and one for your database program. The contents of S.BAT for the spreadsheet are:

```
@echo off
cls
cd spread
REM TWO TABS IN FOLLOWING ECHO COMMAND
echo <tab><tab>*** MARKETING--SPREADSHEET ***
echo Spreadsheet files:
prompt
dir *.pln /w
```

In the preceding and following lists, the changes from W.BAT are shaded. You can see that the format is the same. In this example, spreadsheet files are given the extension PLN. To complete the menu system, here are the contents of D.BAT:

```
@echo off
cls
cd database
REM TWO TABS IN FOLLOWING ECHO COMMAND
echo <tab><tab>*** MARKETING--DATABASE ***
echo Database files:
prompt
dir *.dat /w
```

By clearing the screen, displaying your own titles, displaying directory entries, and otherwise controlling the appearance of the system, you can use batch files like these to make the system appear custom-tailored for your own company or department, or even for an individual user. One person who understands how to use the flexibility and power of DOS can make the system easier to use and more productive for everyone else. Batch commands are the key.

AUTOMATING BACKUP OF A FIXED DISK

Chapter 9, "Managing Your Fixed Disk," described how to decide which files need backing up, and when, in order to reduce the number of backup diskettes you need. You can also reduce the amount of time required to back up files.

Suppose you have the file structure shown in Figure 16-3. You decide that each month you should back up all the Marketing and Manufacturing files (all files in \MKT and \MFG and their subdirectories), and each week you should back up all Marketing word-processing documents (files with an extension of DOC) and Manufacturing spreadsheets (files with an extension of PLN) that have changed since the previous week. You can create two batch files—MNTHBKUP.BAT and WEEKBKUP.BAT—that contain the required Backup commands.

The contents of MNTHBKUP.BAT are:

```
@echo off
cls
echo *** MONTHLY FILE BACKUP ***
echo <Alt-255>
echo Put a formatted diskette in drive A
pause
backup \mkt a: /s
backup \mfg a: /s /a
echo LABEL DISKETTE "BACKUP" AND THE MONTH
```

The batch file starts by clearing the screen, displaying a title, and instructing the user to put the backup diskette in drive A. The first Backup command backs up all files from \MKT and all its subdirectories. Any previously existing files on the

backup diskette are erased. The second Backup command backs up all files from \MFG and all its subdirectories, adding them to the files backed up from \MKT.

The form of WEEKBKUP.BAT is similar:

```
@echo off
cls
echo ***WEEKLY DOCUMENT BACKUP***
echo <Alt-255>
echo Put a formatted diskette in drive A
pause
backup \mkt\wp\*.doc a: /m
backup \mfg\spread\*.pln a: /m /a
echo LABEL DISKETTE "BACKUP" AND MONDAY'S DATE
```

Like MNTHBKUP.BAT, WEEKBKUP.BAT starts by clearing the screen, displaying a title, and making sure the correct diskette goes in drive A. The first Backup command backs up all files with the extension DOC from \MKT\WP that have been modified since the last backup. Any previously existing files on the backup diskette are erased. The second Backup command backs up all files with the extension PLN from \MFG\SPREAD.

Unless your system is heavily used, only one backup diskette per week is required to back up the changed files of both departments. Because the monthly backup backs up all files, you can reuse the weekly backup diskettes in the following month.

With batch files like these, anyone who uses the system can back up files without knowing how to use the Backup command. All they have to do is type *weekbkup* once a week and *mnthbkup* once a month and follow the instructions on the screen. If your AUTOEXEC.BAT file sets the command search path to the directory containing the batch files, you or anyone else can use these batch files no matter what the current directory is.

RENAMING THE FORMAT COMMAND

If you're not using version 3, it's possible to erase all files on the fixed disk by inadvertently formatting it. The scenario goes like this: The fixed disk (drive C) is the current drive; you want to format a diskette, so you put it in drive A and type *format* but forget to add *a:* to the command. You have told DOS to format the disk in the current drive (the fixed disk). DOS displays its message warning you that formatting the disk erases all files. Believing that the disk to be formatted is the diskette in drive A, you press the Enter key. DOS dutifully formats the fixed disk, removing everything stored on it.

Although it's not likely you would make both these errors (forget to type *a:* and tell DOS to go ahead without checking), and even though version 3 of DOS gives an explicit warning if the disk to be formatted is a fixed disk, the consequences are severe enough that you should consider protecting yourself against the possibility. The technique is fairly simple: Rename the Format command file and create a batch file named FORMAT that always formats the diskette in drive A. The following commands do it (assuming the current directory is the directory on the fixed disk that contains the DOS files):

```
C>rename format.com xformat.com
C>copy con format.bat
xformat a: %1 %2 %3
^Z
        1 File(s) copied
```

To format a diskette in drive A with this batch file, you just type *format*; there's no chance of formatting the disk in the current drive.

To use any parameters of the Format command other than the drive letter, include them with your new Format command. To format a system diskette in drive A, for example, you would type *format /s.*

If you want to format a diskette in a drive other than A, just enter the Format command with the usual parameters, but remember to type the command as *xformat*, because you renamed the command file.

USING DOS AS A RECORD-MANAGEMENT PROGRAM

Chapters 13 and 15 showed you how to use filter commands and batch files to search a telephone list. This procedure can also be used to keep track of any small to medium-sized file—say, from 50 to 200 entries. Although this technique doesn't replace a record-management or file-management program, it's simple and quick, and the price is right: You don't need anything except DOS.

The following topics describe other types of information you can keep track of in the same way. Using the same sort of batch files you created in Chapter 15, you can quickly locate any entry or group of entries in your record files.

The descriptions here don't include examples; they simply describe the information included in each line and the columns in which the items of information begin (so that you can sort them). As with any batch files, the best way to get comfortable with this technique and apply it to your own needs is to experiment. These examples give you a starting point.

Keeping Track of Your Computer Files

As you use the computer, your collection of computer files will grow and grow. If you use a word processor, for example, keeping track of all the letters and other documents you create can be a problem. Using wildcard characters with the Directory command makes a particular file easier to find, but you still might have to do some searching to answer such questions as, "How many letters did I write in October to the regional sales office?" or "When did we respond to that request from the National Science Foundation?"

You can solve this problem by creating an index file that describes all your word-processing files. You could use the same technique to keep track of any large collection of files.

Figure 16-6 shows the items of information and the columns in which they begin, to give you the format for an index file that keeps track of word-processing files.

Columns 1 through 3 contain the initials of the originator of the document (THP).

Columns 5 through 12 contain the file name (MFGLET31). All files are assumed to have the same extension.

Columns 14 through 21 contain the date the document was created (10/16/87).

Columns 23 through 79 contain a brief description of the document.

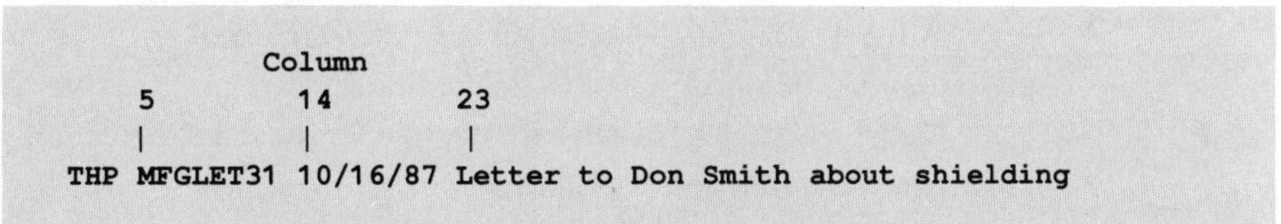

```
           Column
    5        14       23
    |        |        |
THP MFGLET31 10/16/87 Letter to Don Smith about shielding
```

Figure 16-6. Word-processing index file

Keep this index file up to date as you create word-processing files, and you can quickly find files and answer questions with batch files like SHOW.BAT, SHOWAND.BAT, and SHOWXCPT.BAT, which you created in Chapter 15.

To answer:	Type:
When did we respond to that request from the National Science Foundation?	show NSF
What letters did I write to the regional sales office in October?	show and sales 10/

Want a list of all the documents about the new inventory system, or a list of all letters sent in March? If you keep your index up to date, the answers are just a command away.

Simple Bibliographic Index

If your work requires a lot of reading, you're probably frustrated at times by how easy it is to forget where you saw something. If research is important to your job, but it is not significant enough to justify purchasing and learning to use a database manager or a bibliographic retrieval program, this simple technique might be the answer.

Again, the answer is to create an index file and search it with batch commands. Figure 16-7 shows the items of information and the columns in which they begin, to give you the format for an index file that keeps track of magazine articles, books, and other sources of reference material.

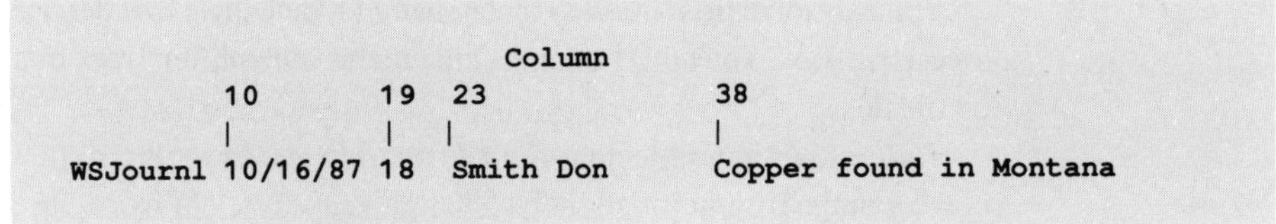

Figure 16-7. Bibliographic index file

Columns 1 through 8 contain the abbreviated title of the journal, book, or other reference source.

Columns 10 through 17 contain the date of the reference.

Columns 19 through 21 contain the page number.

Columns 23 through 36 contain the author's name.

Columns 38 through 79 contain the title or description of the reference.

Again, with batch files like the ones you created in Chapter 15, you can find bibliographic references with one command:

To answer:	Type:
Where did I see that article on kinesthesia?	show kine
I remember an article last June about laser surgery.	show and 6/ laser

The time it takes to keep this index up to date pays off in the ability to find valuable information much more quickly.

Capital Inventory

If you're an independent professional or you operate a small business, you could easily have a much larger investment in capital goods than you realize. Your accountant and insurance agent probably emphasize the importance of keeping an up-to-date inventory of capital goods, but it's easy to put off this sort of record keeping.

Figure 16-8 shows a simple index file that lets you keep track of your capital goods. It's no substitute for a complete inventory system, but it's a start, and one that lets you quickly search and sort your inventory.

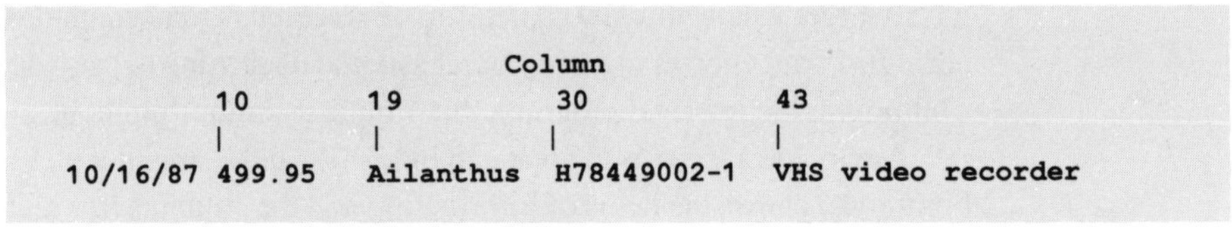

Figure 16-8. Capital inventory index file

Columns 1 through 8 contain the date of the acquisition.

Columns 10 through 17 contain the cost of acquisition.

Columns 19 through 28 contain the manufacturer's name.

Columns 30 through 41 contain the serial number.

Columns 43 through 79 contain the description.

Here, too, with batch files like the ones you created in Chapter 15, you can keep track of your inventory with one command:

To answer:	Type:
When did we get the copy machine?	show copy
What did we buy before 1987?	show xcpt /87

This technique can also be used to keep track of your personal inventory for insurance purposes; with a bit of modification, it could also be used for collections, such as coins, stamps, or first editions.

CHANGING YOUR SYSTEM CONFIGURATION

Unlike the other DOS commands, which tell DOS *what* to do, the configuration commands tell DOS *how* to do something, such as use a device or communicate with a disk drive. These commands are required infrequently, usually only when you add a device to your computer system (thereby changing its setup, or *configuration*).

Unlike other DOS commands, you don't type the configuration commands at the keyboard; you put them in a special file called CONFIG.SYS, which must be in the root directory of your DOS disk. DOS carries out these commands only when it is started; if you change a command in CONFIG.SYS, you must restart DOS for the command to take effect.

Some application programs or accessory devices require certain commands in CONFIG.SYS. The documentation of the application program or device usually includes step-by-step instructions.

If you need a configuration command and your DOS disk already has a file named CONFIG.SYS in the root directory, use Edlin or some other text editor to add the configuration command to the file. If your DOS disk doesn't have a CONFIG.SYS file in the root directory, use a text editor to create the file and put the configuration command in it. If you need only one or two configuration commands, however, you can use the Copy command to copy from the console to CONFIG.SYS, just as you created the sample files in earlier chapters.

The Device Command and Device Drivers

The Device configuration command specifies a program (a command file with an extension of SYS) that tells DOS how to use a particular device. Such a program is called a *device driver*. The form of the Device command is:

device=<device>

If you have a Microsoft Mouse, for example, the file named MOUSE.SYS is the device driver that tells DOS how to interpret the mouse movements. To tell DOS to use MOUSE.SYS, you would insert a line with the Device command *device=mouse.sys* in your CONFIG.SYS file.

Simulating a Disk Drive in Memory with VDISK.SYS

Note: The ability to simulate a disk drive in memory is made possible by a file named VDISK.SYS in IBM's releases of DOS beginning with version 3.0. This capability is available in versions 3.2 and 3.3 of MS-DOS, in a file named RAMDRIVE.SYS. Check your documentation if you are uncertain whether your version of DOS includes either VDISK.SYS or RAMDRIVE.SYS.

DOS reads from and writes to diskettes quickly, and it uses a fixed disk even more quickly; both devices are mechanical, however, and quite slow compared to the computer's electronic memory. Starting with some versions numbered 3.0, DOS lets you set aside a portion of the computer's memory for use as a simulated disk, making it possible for disk operations to be performed at memory speeds.

This simulated disk is called a *virtual* disk, because it's virtually the same as having another disk drive. It's also often called a *RAM disk* or *RAM drive,* because the "disk" exists in your computer's memory (RAM), rather than as a solid piece of hardware. VDISK.SYS or RAMDRIVE.SYS is the device driver that defines a virtual disk drive.

A virtual disk behaves like any other disk: It has a drive letter and a directory, and you can specify it in any command that uses a disk. It is much faster than a real disk drive, however, and the difference is especially noticeable when you use commands, such as Copy, that work with disk drives, or when you use application programs that access the disk frequently, as many word processors and database programs do. To use a virtual disk drive, you copy the files you need from a physical disk to the virtual drive after DOS has started, then copy them back to the disk after you have completed the work. Copying them back is particularly important, because any changes you make to the files are recorded only in memory when you are using a virtual disk, and the contents of memory disappear whenever you turn off your computer.

DOS assigns the next available drive letter to the virtual disk drive. On a two-drive system, the next available letter is usually C; on a system with one diskette drive and a fixed disk, the next available letter is usually D.

Although a real disk drive has a fixed capacity, such as 360 K or 1.44 MB, a virtual disk can have whatever capacity you want, within certain limits: It must be at least 1 K if you're using VDISK.SYS or 16 K if you're using RAMDRIVE.SYS, and there must be at least 64 K of memory remaining for program use after the virtual disk is defined. If your computer has enough memory, you can define more than one virtual disk by including more than one virtual-disk Device command in CONFIG.SYS.

If your computer is equipped with extended memory (above 1 MB, as in the IBM PC/AT or IBM PS/2 models 50 and 60 or compatible computers) or if it contains an expanded-memory board that increases the amount of available memory according to the Lotus/Intel/Microsoft Expanded Memory Specification, you can tell DOS to use this additional memory for your virtual disk, while leaving your computer's more conventional memory space for programs to use.

As fast and efficient as it is, the remarkable speedup offered by virtual disks can have some drawbacks. If your computer doesn't have extended memory or an expanded-memory board, or if you don't tell DOS to use this additional memory (with the /E and /A options described shortly), the memory used for a virtual disk reduces the amount of memory available to programs. Furthermore, the contents of a virtual disk are lost each time you turn the computer off.

Make certain that your virtual disk leaves enough memory for the programs you use, and be sure to copy the files you want to keep onto a real disk before you turn the computer off. When you work with an application program, you can automate this process by using a batch file to copy your working files to the virtual disk, start the application program, and then copy the revised working files back to the real drive after you leave the application program.

The Device command to define a virtual disk has the following parameters.

For IBM versions 3.0 and later:

device=vdisk.sys <size> <sector> <directory> /E

For MS-DOS versions 3.2 and later:

device=ramdrive.sys <size> <sector> <directory> /E /A

VDISK.SYS or RAMDRIVE.SYS is the name of the device-driver program. If it isn't in the root directory of the DOS disk, you must include the drive letter and path name of its directory.

<size> is the size, in kilobytes, of the virtual disk. The minimum is 1 K if your device driver is named VDISK.SYS and 16 K if it is named RAMDRIVE.SYS. The maximum is the total available memory on your computer. If you omit <size> or specify an incorrect value, DOS sets <size> to 64.

<sector> is the size, in bytes, of each sector on the virtual disk. You can specify 128, 256, or 512 with either VDISK.SYS or RAMDRIVE.SYS; you can also specify 1024 with RAMDRIVE.SYS. If you omit <sector> or specify an incorrect value, DOS sets <sector> to 128.

<directory> is the number of directory entries allowed in the root directory of the virtual disk. For device=VDISK.SYS, you can specify any value from 2 to 512; for device=RAMDRIVE.SYS, you can specify 3 to 1024. Each directory entry takes up 32 bytes of the virtual disk. If you omit <directory> or specify an incorrect value, DOS sets <directory> to 64.

/E can be used only with a computer that contains extended memory above 1 MB. It tells DOS to use this extended memory for the virtual disk. Using extended memory for a virtual disk leaves the maximum amount of memory available for programs. Currently, this parameter can be used only with the IBM PC/AT and computers compatible with it. If you use /E, you cannot use /A.

/A is used with a computer that contains an expanded-memory board that meets the Lotus/Intel/Microsoft Expanded Memory Specification. Like the /E option, /A leaves the maximum amount of memory available for programs. If you use /A, you cannot use /E.

DOS may adjust some of the numbers you specify. If the <size> you specify doesn't leave at least 64 K of memory available, DOS reduces <size> so that 64 K of memory is available for programs.

If the number of directory entries you specify, times 32 bytes per entry, leaves a partial sector remaining, DOS adjusts the number of directory entries upward to fill that final sector completely.

If there isn't enough memory to create the virtual disk as you specify it, DOS doesn't create the virtual disk.

Example of Simulating a Disk Drive in Memory

Suppose your computer has a fixed disk, one diskette drive, and 640 K of memory, and your word processor is Microsoft Word. You want to use a virtual disk to speed your word-processing sessions, and you also want to be sure not to forget to copy the edited files back from the virtual disk after you finish your work. You decide that you can afford to use 180 K of memory for the virtual disk, that each sector should be 512 bytes, and that you need only 32 entries in the root directory of the virtual disk.

First, using Edlin or another text editor, you would put one of the following Device configuration commands in CONFIG.SYS (which one depends on the name of your virtual-disk device driver):

```
device=vdisk.sys 180 512 32
```

or

```
device=ramdrive.sys 180 512 32
```

Because DOS treats the diskette drive as both A and B and the fixed disk is drive C, the virtual drive would be drive D. (If the system had two diskette drives and no fixed disk, the virtual drive would be C.)

Then you would create the following batch file named WP.BAT in the root directory of your system disk:

```
1: @echo off
2: cd \wp
3: copy %1 d:
4: d:
5: word
6: c:
7: copy d:%1
8: erase d:%1
9: cd \
```

Now suppose you start your system and want to edit a file named REPORT.DOC. You type:

```
C>wp report.doc
```

The batch file does the following:

- In line 1, it turns echo off.
- In line 2, it changes the current directory to the word-processing directory.
- In line 3, it copies REPORT.DOC to the virtual disk drive.
- In line 4, it changes the current drive to the virtual drive.
- In line 5, it starts the word-processing program.
- In line 6, after you quit the word-processing program, it changes the current drive back to drive C.
- In line 7, it copies REPORT.DOC (which you edited and saved in the word-processing program) to the fixed disk.
- In line 8, it deletes REPORT.DOC from the virtual disk.
- In line 9, it changes the directory back to the root directory of the fixed disk, leaving you just where you were when you entered the batch command.

You could use this same batch file to edit a set of files with similar file names or extensions by using a wildcard character. For example, to work with all the files whose file name starts with LET and whose extension is DOC, you would type:

```
C>wp let*.doc
```

Notice, however, that this would copy all the files that match the file name (*let*.doc*) to the virtual disk and then back to the real one, whether or not you changed them.

You could also copy program files to a virtual disk to reduce the time required to load and start executing a program. This is usually helpful only if you use a very large program that must periodically return to the program disk to load additional portions, or if you routinely use several different programs and switch back and forth.

How you use a virtual disk depends to a great extent on how much memory your computer has and what sort of work you do with it. As with many other DOS commands, you may need to do a bit of experimenting before you find the most useful way for you.

Controlling the Display with ANSI.SYS

DOS includes a device driver called ANSI.SYS. ANSI is an acronym for American National Standards Institute. ANSI.SYS defines a standard set of methods for managing a display, including how to display and erase characters, move the cursor, and select colors. Some programs require your system disk to have a CONFIG.SYS file that contains the command *device=ansi.sys*.

Some Other Configuration Commands

Several other configuration commands control internal operating characteristics of your system, and usually deal with how DOS handles files or reads disks. Some application programs or devices include detailed instructions for adding or changing configuration commands. These configuration commands are described in more detail in Appendix E.

Buffers

The Buffers configuration command defines the number of work areas in memory (*buffers*) that DOS uses to handle reading from and writing to a disk. The effect of this configuration command on system performance depends on the type of disk drive you use and the types of programs that you use. The form of the Buffers command is:

buffers=<number>

Unless otherwise instructed, versions of DOS through 3.2 use two or three buffers, depending on your system and the amount of memory it has. If you're using version 3.3, DOS might use more buffers. You can, of course, override these values by including a Buffers configuration command in CONFIG.SYS. For optimum performance, some programs require you to set buffers to a higher number than DOS assumes. FASTBACK, for example, needs 40. For a list of the values that DOS uses, see the description of the Buffers command in Appendix E.

Files

The Files configuration command tells DOS how many files it can use at one time. Unless otherwise instructed, DOS can use a maximum of eight files at a time. The form of the Files command is:

files=<number>

Lastdrive

The Lastdrive configuration command specifies the highest drive letter that DOS recognizes as valid. If CONFIG.SYS doesn't contain a Lastdrive command, the highest drive letter DOS recognizes is E. This command is usually used to specify a higher letter (up to Z) if DOS needs more than five drive letters. This might happen because the computer is part of a network, because it uses many virtual disk drives, or because a large fixed disk is divided into sections, each of which is referred to by a different drive letter. The form of the Lastdrive command is:

lastdrive=<letter>

COMMANDS FOR OCCASIONAL USE

This book has described all the commands you routinely use to operate DOS. There are a few remaining commands you might occasionally need, and there are several commands that you won't need unless you plan to do some programming or to use some of the advanced capabilities of DOS. The less commonly used commands are described briefly here, and in more detail in Appendix E.

Displaying the DOS Version Number

The Version command displays the number of the version of DOS you're using. If you use more than one version, or if you are using someone else's machine, this gives you a quick way to check the version.

The Version command has no parameters:

ver

If you're using IBM's version 3.3, for example, DOS replies *IBM Personal Computer DOS Version 3.30* in response to the command.

Changing the System Prompt

As shown in examples in earlier chapters, you can change the system prompt with the Prompt command to display much more than just the current drive letter. The change takes effect as soon as you enter the command.

The Prompt command has one parameter:

prompt <string>

<string> is a string of characters that defines the new system prompt. You can use any characters you want. You can also cause the new prompt to include one or more items of useful information by including a dollar sign and one of the following characters, to specify what you want the prompt to contain:

Character	Produces
d	The current date
p	The current directory
n	The current drive
t	The current time
v	The DOS version number
g	A greater-than sign (>)
l	A less-than sign (<)
b	A vertical bar (¦)
q	An equal sign (=)
e	An Escape character
h	A backspace
$	A dollar sign ($)
_	A signal to end the current line and start a new one. (The character is an underscore, not a hyphen.)

You can include as many combinations of $, followed by a character, as you wish. DOS ignores any combination of $ followed by a character that is not in the preceding list. You saw an example of this earlier in this chapter: In the batch file MKT.BAT, the system prompt was set to nothing (made invisible) with the command *prompt $a.*

If you enter the Prompt command with no parameter (just type *prompt*), DOS restores the prompt to the standard DOS version: the letter of the current drive followed by a greater-than sign (for example, C>).

The Prompt command takes effect immediately, so it's easy to experiment. You saw how to change the system prompt to a courteous request (*May I help you?*) in Chapter 3 and you changed it to a two-line display of the current directory in Chapter 8. Don't be afraid to experiment, because all you need do to restore the system prompt to its standard form is type *prompt.*

Several examples follow. Notice how the system prompt changes each time to show the effect of the previous Prompt command. Press the spacebar before pressing the Enter key to end each command, to leave a blank space between the end of the system prompt and the beginning of the command that you type next.

To define the system prompt as the current drive and directory, type:

```
C>prompt $p

C:\mkt\wp _
```

The example assumes that the current drive is C and that the directory is \MKT\WP. To define the system prompt as two lines that show the date and time, type:

```
C:\mkt\wp prompt $d$_$t

Fri 10-16-1987
14:57:10.11 _
```

The time and date will vary, depending on how you have set them in your system. Press the Enter key several times to see that DOS keeps the time current.

Finally, combining several of the options shows just how much you can include in a prompt:

```
Fri 10-16-1987
15:02:10.11 prompt $v$_$d $t$_Current directory $q $p$_Command:

IBM Personal Computer DOS Version  3.30
Fri 10-16-1987 15:02:57.68
Current directory = C:\MKT\WP
Command:_
```

The Prompt command lets you easily tailor the system prompt to the balance of brevity and information that you prefer. When you design a system prompt that you like, put it in AUTOEXEC.BAT and you'll never have to type it again; DOS will carry out the command every time you start the system.

Speeding Up File Access

Note: The Fastopen command described here is available only in version 3.3 of DOS. If you have a different version of DOS, skip to the next section, "Altering the Way DOS Interprets Drive Letters."

Each time you (or an application program) need a file, DOS might first need to search for the subdirectory that contains the file, then search the directory entries for the file itself. On a fixed disk with hundreds or thousands of files, all this searching can take some time.

The Fastopen command tells DOS to keep track (in memory) of the locations of subdirectories and files as it uses them; the next time it's asked for a file or subdirectory, DOS checks in memory before it searches the disk. If the file or subdirectory is in memory, DOS can go directly to it on the disk instead of searching for it.

If you or your application programs tend to use the same files or directories over and over, the Fastopen command can make DOS visibly faster.

The Fastopen command works only with fixed disks and must be re-entered each time you start DOS; it has two parameters:

fastopen <drive>=<files>

<drive> is the drive letter, followed by a colon, of the fixed disk whose files and subdirectories you want DOS to keep track of (for example, *c:*).

<files> is the number of files and subdirectories whose location DOS is to keep in memory; it must be preceded by an equal sign. If you don't specify <files>, DOS keeps track of the last 10 files and subdirectories (34 in IBM's version 3.3). You can specify a value for <files> from 10 to 999.

For example, if you had one fixed disk, drive C, and wanted DOS to keep track of the last 20 files and subdirectories used, you would type *fastopen c:=20*. If you routinely wanted to use these values with the Fastopen command, you would put it in AUTOEXEC.BAT.

Altering the Way DOS Interprets Drive Letters

Warning: The following three commands (Assign, Substitute, and Join) let you change the way DOS interprets drive letters. These commands restrict your use of other DOS commands, such as Backup, Restore, and Print, that deal with disks and files. Use the next three commands sparingly, and check the descriptions of the other disk and file commands in your DOS manual to make certain you understand the restrictions. The Substitute and Join commands must not be used on a network.

Assigning a Drive Letter to a Different Drive

Some application programs require that you put the diskettes with your data files in one particular drive. This can be inconvenient if you're using a fixed disk and prefer to use it for your data files. The Assign command gives you a solution: It lets you tell DOS to make a drive letter refer to a different drive (for example, to tell DOS to use the fixed disk, drive C, whenever it receives a request for drive B).

Because the Assign command affects all requests for a drive, you should use it with caution—especially if you are using a fixed disk. Always bear in mind that some DOS commands, such as Erase, delete existing files from the disk in the specified drive. If you use one of these commands after you have used Assign, you could inadvertently lose valuable programs or data files. Only three commands, Format, Diskcopy, and Diskcomp, ignore drive reassignments specified with Assign.

The Assign command has two parameters:

assign <drive1>=<drive2>

<drive1> is the letter of the drive to be assigned to a different drive.

<drive2> is the letter of the drive that is to be used in place of <drive1>.

If you omit both <drive1> and <drive2>, DOS cancels any assignments.

For example, suppose you have a graphics program that requires all data files to be on drive B, but you want to use your fixed disk (drive C) for data files. To tell DOS to assign all requests for drive B to drive C instead, you would type *assign b=c*.

The assignment affects all requests for the drive, including any commands you enter other than Format, Diskcopy, and Diskcomp. If you assign drive B to drive C as in the previous example, and then type *dir b:*, DOS displays the directory of the fixed disk. The assignment remains in effect until you restart DOS or cancel the assignment by typing *assign*.

Treating a Directory as if It Were a Disk

The Substitute (subst) command lets you treat a directory as if it were a separate disk. If your directory structure includes long path names, or if you use application programs that accept a drive letter but not a path name, you can use the Substitute command to tell DOS to treat all future references to a particular drive as references to a directory on the disk in a different drive.

After naming a drive letter in a Substitute command or in a Join command (described next), you cannot refer to that drive letter in any other command, so you will probably want to use a drive letter that doesn't refer to an existing drive. In order to do this, you must tell DOS to accept more drive letters than there are disk drives. You do this by putting a Lastdrive command in the CONFIG.SYS file in the root directory of your DOS system disk. The Substitute command has two parameters:

subst <drive> <pathname> /D

<drive> is the letter, followed by a colon, to be used to refer to <pathname>.

<pathname> is the path name of the directory to be referred to by <drive>.

/D deletes any substitutions that involve <drive>. If you include /D, you cannot include <pathname>.

If you omit all parameters (just type *subst*), DOS displays a list of any substitutions in effect.

For example, suppose you find yourself frequently referring to a directory whose path name is C:\MPLAN\SALES\FORECAST, and you would like to use a shorter synonym. To substitute *x:* for the path name, you would make certain that your CONFIG.SYS file contained a Lastdrive command that specified the letter x, then type *subst x: c:\mplan\sales\forecast*. The substitution would remain in effect until you restarted DOS or canceled the substitution by typing *subst x: /d*.

Treating a Disk as if It Were a Directory

The Join command lets you treat a disk drive as a directory on the disk in a different drive. If you use an application program that stores its data files on the program disk, you can use the Join command to tell DOS to treat another drive as if it were a directory on the program disk. The Join command has three parameters:

join <drive> <pathname> /D

<drive> is the letter, followed by a colon, of the drive to be connected to the directory specified by <pathname>. It cannot be the current drive.

<pathname> is the path name of the directory to which <drive> is to be joined. It must be an empty subdirectory in the root directory of the disk to which <drive> is to be joined.

/D deletes any joins that involve <drive>. If you include /D, you cannot include <pathname>.

If you omit all parameters (just type *join*), DOS displays a list of any joins in effect. Once you specify a drive letter as <drive> in a Join command, you cannot use that letter to refer to a drive.

For example, suppose you have an application program that takes up most of a diskette and you need a lot of disk space for data files.

If you put the application program diskette in drive A and a blank diskette in drive B, you could tell DOS to treat the blank diskette in drive B as a directory named \DATA on the diskette in drive A by typing *join b: a:\data.* The join would remain in effect until you restarted DOS or canceled the join by typing *join b: /d.*

CHAPTER 17

DOS AND LOCAL AREA NETWORKS

Personal computers have become commonplace in offices and the home, but advances in software and hardware continue to increase their capability and create more uses for them. One of these developments, the *local area network,* makes it possible to connect a number of personal computers and let the people who use them share such expensive options as large fixed disks and laser printers.

Because they are so effective in allowing computer users to share hardware, software, and even data, local area networks are becoming increasingly common in all types of work situations: small businesses; departments of large businesses; offices of independent professionals, such as architects, doctors, engineers, and lawyers; academic departments; government offices—anywhere, in fact, that several computers are used by persons with common goals.

WHAT IS A LOCAL AREA NETWORK?

A local area network is a group of personal computers located in the same general area—one building, perhaps, or one floor of a large building—connected by a common cable and running the same network program. The network program moves files back and forth among the computers in the network. When you print a file on the network printer, for example, it is the network program that locates the file and, if necessary, sends it to the computer to which the network printer is attached; there, the network program stores the file on disk and prints it when the printer is available.

A number of networks and network programs are available, each with its own operating characteristics. This chapter briefly describes the program known as Microsoft Networks, which works with DOS versions 3.1 and later, and is used with a range of network hardware on IBM and non-IBM computers. Microsoft Networks lets you use most DOS commands described in this book with little or no change.

WHY USE A NETWORK?

Suppose your company bought personal computers for you and a half dozen of your colleagues. The computers would certainly give you more powerful tools to use in your work, but this arrangement has two potential shortcomings:

- Separate options, such as printers and fixed disk drives, are expensive to provide for each computer.
- It's awkward for several users to work with the same program and data diskettes at the same time.

Although the cost of hardware decreases each year, providing a printer or fixed disk for every machine isn't always practical—especially if different printers (such as dot-matrix, letter-quality, and laser) are used for different types of documents (such

as rough drafts, correspondence, and reports). If only one machine is connected to a particular printer, other users must bring to it a diskette that contains the files they want to print, then either interrupt the user of that machine or wait until it's free—not a convenient solution.

Sharing information creates its own problems. If several users work with the same database, such as customer records or inventory, they must either share a computer or move the data to their own computers. Sharing a computer is obviously inconvenient. Moving a data diskette around is equally inconvenient. Duplicating the data on each machine is more convenient, but could require several expensive fixed disks and creates the potential for even more problems:

- If one user changes the database, that copy is different from everyone else's, and the other users won't have the new data until their copies are changed. In the meantime, they might well make changes to their copies. Now all the copies could be different. Who makes all these changes on the master copy? When is it done, and how can that person be sure all the changes are made?
- If users note the changes they make, but the master database isn't updated immediately, the changes aren't available to everyone until the master copy is brought up to date. How is the master copy changed and distributed? How often should this be done?

Because using inaccurate data can be even more damaging than not having timely access to it, these questions can't be ignored. The larger and more complex the database you work with, the more important it is to follow strict procedures for updating the data and making the changes available to everyone. Unfortunately, the larger and more complex the database, the more likely it is that something will go wrong and result in the distribution of inaccurate data.

Enter the network. If the database is stored on a shared disk in a local area network, all users have access to the same data; if one user changes the data, all other users have rapid access to the new version. No extra fixed disk, no complicated procedures, no chance of mismatched copies of the data.

Microsoft Networks can make a group of computers much more effective, and it can make valuable data much easier to protect when many people must use it. Using the network, however, is no more difficult than using DOS. In fact, using your computer with Microsoft Networks is virtually indistinguishable from just using your computer by itself.

Some New Terms

The concept of a network adds some new terms to your computer vocabulary:

Network resources: The fixed disks and printers shared by the computers in a local area network.

Server: A computer in a local area network that provides network resources to the others. Because of its function and the volume of information it handles, it must have a fixed disk. Many networks include more than one server.

Workstation: A network computer that uses network resources.

Network manager: The person who installs (or arranges for installation of) the network, identifies workstations to the network, and manages the operation of the network server or servers.

Network name: The name (chosen by the user of a network computer, and assigned by the network manager) by which each workstation and server in a network is known. The network name enables the network program to match tasks to the appropriate sending and receiving computers. When used in commands, the network name is usually preceded by two backslashes (\\).

Local: A file or device located on the computer you're using in the network.

Remote: A file or device located on a computer other than the one you're using in a network. Remote in this sense does not necessarily mean far away.

WHAT DO YOU NEED FOR A NETWORK?

Networks require hardware and software, but setting up a network can cost much less than the computers in the network. Because a network is made up of sophisticated equipment and software, some planning and preparation are required before it's ready to be used. The equipment and its installation can be broken into three categories:

- Hardware
- Software
- Testing

Network Hardware

Each workstation and server requires a network-interface board, which is similar to a display adapter or a memory-expansion board. This board goes inside the computer case, but installing this board is no more complicated than inserting any other accessory board. The Microsoft Networks software can be used with network-interface boards from many different manufacturers.

After the network boards have been installed, the computers must be linked by a cable that plugs into the rear of each interface board. The type of cable and the connectors used depend on which network-interface boards you choose. Sometimes, as when installing the cable means pulling it through walls, the job is probably better left to a skilled professional.

Network Software

Just hooking some computers together with a cable doesn't make a network: You must have programs to move data back and forth between the server and the workstations, direct traffic through the wires, and let computers connect and disconnect from the network—all in an orderly way.

Microsoft Networks is a collection of such programs, as DOS is a collection of housekeeping and file-handling programs. Each server and workstation in a network must have a system disk that contains DOS version 3.1 or later and the Microsoft Networks programs. To install the software, the network manager:

- Creates a file on the Microsoft Networks disk that contains the network name of each computer in the network. (The network manual describes the exact procedures.)
- Copies the appropriate Microsoft Networks program and data files to each server's and workstation's system disk.
- Adds a few lines to the DOS CONFIG.SYS file (or creates the file if it doesn't exist) on each server's and workstation's system disk.

After these steps have been completed, a network system disk has been created for each server and workstation. This disk can be used to start both MS-DOS and Microsoft Networks.

Testing the Network

To test the network hardware and software, the network manager starts each server and workstation with its network system disk, then types *echotest* at each. The ECHOTEST program sends a message from each server (if there is more than one) to each workstation; the workstations receive the message and then send it back (echo it) to each server.

The ECHOTEST program displays how many times the message is echoed by each computer, and runs until it's stopped. After each computer has echoed about 300 times—this takes about a minute—it's safe to assume that the network is ready to begin operation.

HOW DO YOU USE THE NETWORK?

Using a computer with Microsoft Networks isn't much different from just using a computer. You'll probably spend most of your time using application programs, such as a word processor, and occasionally use DOS commands to manage your files and do other general work. The network itself requires only a few additional commands, most of which you can put in a batch file to be carried out once at the beginning of a network session.

After you have connected to the network, it doesn't matter whether the files and printers you use are local or remote. You can edit files, print files, and generally treat the shared fixed disks and printers as if they were attached to your computer. However, because resources on a network are shared, you cannot use the following DOS commands: Chkdsk, Format, Diskcopy, Join, Recover, Print, Diskcomp, Fdisk, Substitute, Label, and System.

While connected to the network, you use Microsoft Networks commands to do the following:

- Start your workstation.
- Use the servers and printers.
- Temporarily disconnect from the network.
- Print a file on the network printer.

Starting Your Workstation

When the server is running, all you need do to join your workstation to the network is to start DOS in the normal way, then enter the Net Start Redirector (net start rdr) command to tell the network program who you are and that you want to use the network. This command runs a program that reroutes, or redirects, any requests for remote files or printers to the server.

For example, if the network name of your workstation were LISA, you would connect to the network by typing *net start rdr lisa.* If you use the network regularly, you or your network manager would probably put this command in an AUTOEXEC.BAT file to join your workstation to the network each time you start DOS.

Using Servers and Printers

After you have joined your workstation to the network, you can use any of the directories or printers that are available to computers on the network. You identify the directory or printer you wish to use by assigning it a drive letter or printer name with the Net Use command. (If the drive letter or printer name already exists on your own computer, the letter or name becomes unavailable to you until you disconnect from the network directory or printer.)

For example, suppose the server's network name is HOME and it has made available a directory named LETTERS. To use this directory, you would assign it the letter of a drive—D, perhaps. To use LETTERS, you would type *net use d:\\home\letters.* You can now treat LETTERS just as if it were another drive (D) attached to your computer: If you type *d:*, DOS changes the system prompt to D>, and drive D—the shared directory—becomes the current drive.

Similarly, if a server named HOME made available a printer named DOT, you could use the printer by entering *net use lpt1: \\home\dot*. If you already had a printer named LPT1 attached to your computer, however, you could not use it after entering this Net Use command.

You can disconnect from a network directory or printer with the /D option of the Net Use command. To disconnect from the directory in the previous example, you would type *net use d: /d*. If you're not sure which network directories and printer you're using, you can display a list by typing *net use*.

If you use the same network directories and printer in your sessions on the network, you can put the appropriate Net Use commands immediately after the Net Start Redirector command in an AUTOEXEC.BAT file and completely automate your connection to the network.

Temporarily Disconnecting From the Network

Because you cannot use a local device if you used its name in a Net Use command, there may be times when you need to disconnect from a network directory or printer temporarily. The Net Pause command disconnects either the network disk drive or the network printer to which you're connected, until you resume the network connection with the Net Continue command.

Suppose you have a printer named LPT1 attached to your workstation but, as in the preceding example, you're connected to the network printer with the name LPT1. Now you want to print a document on your own (local) printer. To do so, temporarily disconnect from the network printer by typing *net pause prdr* (*prdr* is short for *print redirection*). Print the file on your printer, then reconnect to the network printer by typing *net continue prdr*. Similarly, you can temporarily disconnect from network servers by typing *net pause drdr* (*disk redirection*) and reconnect by typing *net continue drdr*.

Printing a File on the Network Printer

After you have connected to a network printer, you can print a file on it with the Net Print command. To continue the preceding example, if you connected to the network printer using the name LPT1, you could print a file named SUMMARY.DOC on the network printer by typing *net print summary.doc lpt1*. (The file could be on a disk attached to your computer or on a disk attached to the server.)

You can also use the Net Print command to display the list of files waiting to be printed on the network printer (the print queue). To display the contents of the print queue on a server named HOME, for example, you would type *net print \\home*.

Other Commands

Microsoft Networks includes a few other commands for general network use:

- The Append command, like the DOS Append command, tells the network where to find a non-command file if it isn't in the current directory.
- The Net Name command displays the network name of the workstation.
- The Net Help command displays descriptions of the network commands.

In practice, however, the only network command you're likely to type whenever you want to use it is Net Print. You'll probably put the commands to join the network and connect to the shared directories and printer in a batch file, to be executed once at the beginning of a session. If you put them in an AUTOEXEC.BAT file, you could just start DOS and would be linked to the network without any further ado.

A NEW USER: THE NETWORK MANAGER

Because the network involves several computer systems and requires communication and cooperation among the users, one person is usually given the responsibility of coordinating the installation and ongoing use of the network. This person is the network manager.

After installing and testing the network, the network manager is responsible for starting and stopping the servers, making the shared directories and printers available, adding and deleting workstations and servers, and responding to requests for help from network users.

The remainder of this chapter is partly for the network manager, but is primarily intended to give you a feel for the tasks handled by your manager. The following sections briefly describe how the network manager uses a separate set of commands to:

- Start the network.
- Make directories and printers available.
- Check the status of the network.
- Stop and restart the network.
- Manage the network printer.

(The Net Help command can be used to display a description of the network manager's commands as well as the network user's commands.)

Note: The following commands should be used only by the network manager.

Starting the Network

After DOS is started on the server, the network manager starts the network with the Net Start Server command. For example, if the network name of the server is HOME, the command to start the network would be *net start server \\home*. This command, like a network user's Net Start Redirector and Net Use commands, would probably be in an AUTOEXEC.BAT file so the network would start each time DOS was started.

Making Directories and Printers Available

Once the network is started, the network manager uses the Net Share command to tell Microsoft Networks which directories and printers to make available to the workstations. Each directory or printer to be shared requires a Net Share command; in addition to the path name of the directory, or the device name of the printer, the manager also specifies the network name, which is usually shorter than a path name and can be made more descriptive.

For example, to make the directory named C:\WORD\SALES\CORRESP available to users and give it the network name LETTERS, the command at the server with those directories would be *net share letters=c:\word\sales\corresp*. To make available the printer named LPT1 and give it the network name DOT, the command would be *net share dot=lpt1:*

The Net Share command can also control access to directories and printers by assigning passwords. In addition, it can control whether the files in a directory are read-only and whether network users can create new files in the directory.

If the same directories and printer (or printers) are available to users each session, the Net Share commands can be placed in the server's AUTOEXEC.BAT file and Microsoft Networks can be told to carry out the commands in the file whenever the server is started or restarted. This completely automates starting the network.

Checking the Status of the Network

Several commands let the network manager monitor the network while it is running:

- The Net Status command displays a list of the shared directories and printers, the number of files waiting to be printed by the network printer, and some general information about the network configuration.
- The Net File command displays how many workstations are using each file that is available.
- The Net Error command displays the 15 most recent network errors and tells when they occurred.

Starting and Stopping the Network

The server computer can't just be turned off to stop the network. Microsoft Networks must carry out a series of shutdown tasks in an orderly fashion. If the network is stopped while workstations are still connected to it, the users at those workstations could lose work and files could be damaged, so the network manager must always make sure no one is using the network at the time it is shut down.

The Net Stop command stops the network. Before the Net Stop command is entered, however, the Net Status command should be used to make sure no workstations are active. If any are, the users at those workstations must be notified and the manager should wait for them to disconnect. When no workstations are active, typing *net stop* tells Microsoft Networks to shut down. After a few moments, DOS displays the system prompt, the network is stopped, and the server computer can be turned off.

If the network is stopped temporarily, for example, to add or delete a workstation, the Net Restart command starts the network and returns it to the same state it was in when the Net Stop command was entered.

Managing the Network Printer

So that the network printer can keep up with print requests from all workstations on the network, files to be printed are stored in a separate directory on the server's fixed disk. This is the network's print queue. Microsoft Networks includes several commands for managing this queue:

- The Net Print command displays the name, size, and first few words of each file in the queue. The command is typed *net print.*
- The Net Print Cancel command stops printing the file currently being printed. The command is typed *net print cancel.*
- The Net Print Restart command stops printing the file currently being printed, but puts it back in the print queue, rather than canceling it completely as the Net Print Cancel command does. The command is typed *net print restart.*
- The Net Print Kill command removes a file from the queue. To remove a file named PQ1001 from the print queue, the command would be *net print kill pq1001.*
- The Net Print On/Off command stops and restarts the printer. To stop the printer, the command would be *net print off.* To restart it, the command would be *net print on.*

- The Net Separator On/Off command controls whether a separate page that identifies a file by its name and workstation is printed at the beginning of each print job. To print the separator page, the command is *net separator on*. To eliminate the separator page, the command is *net separator off*.

PART 3

APPENDIXES

Five appendixes are included in Part 3. Appendixes A through D provide material you need only occasionally or for background information. For example, Appendix A, ''Preparing Your Fixed Disk,'' might be needed only once or twice in the lifetime of your computer; Appendix D, the Glossary, defines commonly used terms and those presented in the main portions of the book.

Appendix E serves a very different purpose. A comprehensive reference to DOS and Edlin commands, it provides easy-to-find answers to questions about the form or use of a command. Cross-references to Part 2 guide you to the discussions in Chapters 5 through 16.

APPENDIX

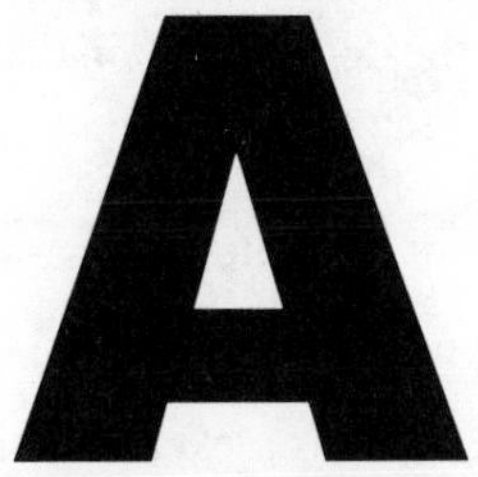

PREPARING YOUR FIXED DISK

The instructions in this appendix show you how to prepare your fixed disk so that DOS can be started from it and only DOS can use it. These instructions are for the IBM Personal Computer XT, AT, PS/2, and computers compatible with these models. See the documentation that came with DOS and with your computer if one of the following applies to you:

- You have a different computer.
- You want to run both DOS and another operating system from your fixed disk.
- Your fixed disk is 32 MB or less and you want to divide it into more than one section (partition) devoted to DOS.

To prepare the fixed disk, you must:

- Identify the fixed disk to DOS with the Fdisk command.
- Format the fixed disk with the Format command.
- Copy the DOS system files from the system diskette to the fixed disk with the Copy command.

IDENTIFYING THE FIXED DISK TO DOS

The DOS Fdisk command starts the Fdisk program, which helps you set up your fixed disk for the first time or change the way DOS uses it. Fdisk is called a *menu-driven* program because it displays a series of screens from which you choose, much as you choose from a restaurant menu. Each menu choice you make causes Fdisk to display another menu, and so the procedure continues until you finish setting up (*configuring*) or changing the configuration of your fixed disk.

To use Fdisk to identify your fixed disk to DOS:

1. Put the DOS system diskette in drive A (the lefthand or upper diskette drive) and turn the system on or restart it by pressing Ctrl-Alt-Del. DOS might prompt you for the correct date and time:

   ```
   Current date is Tue 1-01-1980
   Enter new date (mm-dd-yy): _
   ```

   If you don't see this prompt, skip to step 4.

2. If DOS displays the correct date, just press Enter. Otherwise, type today's date in numeric form, using the date format DOS displays in its *Enter new date* request. (In the United States, for example, you would enter October 16, 1987 as 10-16-87.) Press the Enter key after you type the date. DOS prompts you for the time:

   ```
   Current time is  0:01:30.00
   Enter new time: _
   ```

The current time DOS displays will differ, depending on how long your system has been on.

3. If DOS displays the correct time, just press Enter. Otherwise, type the current time, using a 24-hour clock. (For example, you would enter 2:30 P.M. as 14:30.) Press the Enter key after you enter the time. Now DOS displays the system prompt, telling you that it is ready for you to enter a command:

   ```
   A>_
   ```

4. Type the Fdisk command:

   ```
   A>fdisk
   ```

   DOS fills the screen with the first menu of choices for the Fdisk command:

   ```
   IBM Personal Computer
   Fixed Disk Setup Program Version 3.30
   (C)Copyright IBM Corp. 1983,1987

   FDISK Options

   Current Fixed Disk Drive: 1

   Choose one of the following:

       1.  Create DOS partition
       2.  Change Active Partition
       3.  Delete DOS partition
       4.  Display Partition Information

   Enter choice: [1]

   Press ESC to return to DOS
   ```

   (If you have more than one fixed disk, DOS displays a fifth menu option, *Select Next Fixed Disk Drive*. Disregard it for now.)

5. Press the Enter key (this selects item 1). If the fixed disk has not been prepared, DOS displays another prompt:

   ```
   Create DOS Partition

   Current Fixed Disk Drive: 1

       1. Create Primary DOS Partition
       2. Create Extended DOS Partition

   Enter choice: [1]

   Press ESC to return to FDISK Options
   ```

6. Press the Enter key to choose option 1. If the fixed disk has already been prepared by someone else, DOS responds *Primary DOS partition already exists* and *Press ESC to return to FDISK Options*. Press Esc once to return to the Fdisk menu and press Esc again to return to DOS. Go on to the heading "Formatting the Fixed Disk." Otherwise, DOS responds:

```
Create Primary DOS Partition

Current Fixed Disk Drive: 1

Do you wish to use the maximum size
for a DOS partition and make the DOS
partition active (Y/N).........?[Y]

Press ESC to return to FDISK Options
```

   Your primary DOS partition is the one DOS will start from and can be as large as 32 MB. As mentioned at the beginning of this appendix, these instructions assume you want DOS to use all of your fixed disk (up to 32 MB) as your primary disk drive, so press Enter to select Y (yes). DOS responds:

```
System will now restart

Insert DOS diskette in drive A:
Press any key when ready . . .
```

7. The DOS system diskette is already in drive A, so press any key. DOS is restarted and displays the date prompt. Set the date and time again as in steps 2 and 3.

   If your fixed disk is 32 MB or less, go on to the heading "Formatting the Fixed Disk."

8. If your fixed disk is larger than 32 MB, you have more disk space that you must identify to DOS. To do this, use the Fdisk command again:

```
A>fdisk
```

   DOS displays the same screen of options it did in step 4.

9. Again, press the Enter key to select item 1 (*Create DOS partition*). DOS displays the same screen of options it did in step 5.

10. This time, type 2 to choose *Create Extended DOS Partition* and press Enter. Fdisk shows a display like this:

```
Create Extended DOS Partition

Current Fixed Disk Drive: 1

Partition Status  Type  Start  End Size
 C: 1        A   PRI DOS    0  731  732
```

```
Total disk space is 979 cylinders.
Maximum space available for partition
is 531 cylinders.

Enter partition size............[ 247]

Press ESC to return to FDISK Options
```

The partition size Fdisk displays is the amount of remaining space on the fixed disk. Assuming that it is less than 32 MB and you want to devote all of it to your extended DOS partition, press Enter to accept the proposed size and press the Escape key. Fdisk then asks you how many cylinders of this extended partition you want to assign to a logical drive (''logical'' because it's not a physically separate piece of equipment). In this case, the logical drive is drive D:

```
Create Logical DOS Drive(s)

No logical drives defined

Total partition size is  247 cylinders.

Maximum space available for logical
drive is  247 cylinders.

Enter logical drive size........: [247]

Press ESC to return to FDISK Options
```

Press Enter to assign all of this space and press the Escape key twice to end the Fdisk program.

Press any key to restart your system and, if necessary, enter the correct time and date as you did earlier.

FORMATTING THE FIXED DISK

Note: Formatting the fixed disk erases any files that may be stored on it, so follow this procedure only if the fixed disk has not yet been formatted or if you don't need any of the files stored on it.

1. Type the Format command:

   ```
   A>format c: /s /v
   ```

   DOS displays a message before starting to format the disk, giving you a chance to cancel the command because formatting erases any files on the disk.

2. Press *y* and then press Enter. The light on the fixed disk goes on; DOS displays a constantly changing message telling you the head and cylinder number being

formatted and prepares the fixed disk for use. This takes several minutes. When DOS finishes, it responds:

```
Format complete
System transferred

Volume label (11 characters, ENTER for none)?
```

DOS is waiting for you to type an identifying name, or volume label, for the disk. The volume label is displayed each time you display the directory of the fixed disk; you can change this name with the Label command.

3. Type any name of up to 11 characters and press Enter. This completes formatting your primary DOS partition. DOS responds by displaying the system prompt:

```
A>_
```

4. If you devoted your entire fixed disk to DOS, go on to the heading "Copying the DOS System Files to the Fixed Disk." If your fixed disk is larger than 32 MB, and you created both primary and extended DOS partitions, repeat the formatting procedure for the extended DOS partition, this time without transferring the DOS system files:

```
A>format d: /v
```

Make sure you give this partition a volume label different from the one you gave to your primary DOS partition.

COPYING THE DOS SYSTEM FILES TO THE FIXED DISK

With the DOS system diskette still in drive A, create a directory especially for DOS on drive C:

```
A>md c:\dos
```

Now copy the DOS files from the system diskette in drive A to your DOS directory. Type:

```
A>copy *.* c:\dos
```

This process takes about two minutes. DOS displays the names of the files as it copies them. When all the files have been copied, DOS again displays the system prompt:

```
A>_
```

Remove the DOS system diskette from drive A and store it in a safe place. Now copy the remaining DOS files. Insert your second DOS diskette (labeled Operating or Supplemental Programs) in drive A and repeat the command (*copy *.* c:\dos*).

Finally, you need to tell DOS where to look for the files it needs whenever you start it from drive C. Do this by creating a special file named AUTOEXEC.BAT, which DOS looks for whenever it starts up. Type the following, entering ^Z by holding down the key labeled Ctrl and pressing Z. If you make a mistake before pressing Enter at the end of a line, backspace to the error and correct it. If you notice an error after you press Enter, press the keys labeled Ctrl and Break and try again; if you notice an error after pressing Ctrl and Z, retype the whole thing:

```
A>copy con c:\autoexec.bat
path c:\dos
^Z
```

DOS responds *1 File(s) copied.* You're done.

TESTING THE FIXED DISK

To make sure the procedures were successful, restart DOS from the fixed disk. Open the door of drive A so that DOS won't try to start from that drive, then restart DOS by pressing Ctrl-Alt-Del (hold down the keys marked Ctrl and Alt, and press the key marked Del).

If all went well, the system prompt is C> rather than A>, showing you that the fixed disk is the current drive.

If DOS doesn't restart properly, press Ctrl-Alt-Del again, making sure you are holding both the Ctrl and Alt keys down while you press the Del key. If DOS still doesn't restart properly, repeat the procedures in this appendix.

APPENDIX B

DOS IS AN INTERNATIONAL SYSTEM

Even though many languages share the basic Roman alphabet, they use different characters. These differences include both accented Roman characters, such as é, è, ë, or ê, and those that are altogether different, such as ¿ or £.

Different countries, regardless of language, also represent the numeric form of a date in different ways. In most North American and European countries, the numeric form of a date is shown in a day-month-year sequence (for example, 16-10-87 for October 16, 1987). In the United States, however, the sequence is month-day-year (10-16-87), and in Japan it is year-month-day (87-10-16). Different countries with different traditions also use different currency symbols and ways of separating large numbers or decimal fractions.

Depending on the country for which your computer was manufactured, DOS assumes a keyboard arrangement and country code that determine how the date, currency symbols, and decimals are handled. Beginning with version 3.0, DOS lets you change these characteristics. The language that DOS itself uses—its command names and the messages it displays—remains unchanged, but you can tailor many of its operating qualities to the linguistic and monetary traditions of a particular country. This capability can be particularly useful if you use your computer for work with different languages or currencies, or if persons with different language requirements use the same computer.

Version 3.3 changes and expands the ability of DOS to handle many different languages. These changes, in fact—referred to as *national language support*—make up the most extensive changes from version 3.2 to version 3.3.

Because of these differences, this appendix presents the international side of DOS in two parts. The first part describes multiple-language support available in versions 3.0 through 3.3, with examples tailored for users of versions 3.0 through 3.2; the second part, starting with the heading "Version 3.3 National Language Support," describes the version 3.3 enhancements, including changes in some commands available in earlier versions. Altogether, this appendix shows you how to:

- Choose a keyboard layout with one of the Keyboard commands.
- Set the country code with the Country configuration command.
- Create a DOS system diskette tailored to a particular country with the Select command.
- Use the version 3.3 national language support, including the Keyboard (keyb), Change Code Page (chcp), National Language Support Function (nlsfunc), Mode, and Device commands.

If you use your computer only in the language of the country for which it was manufactured, you don't need national language support, and you can skip this entire appendix if you want.

If you're using version 3.3, and you want to learn what the new commands are for and how they are used to set up national language support, read the first part of the appendix to see how earlier versions handled multiple languages, then read the description of the new national language support (beginning with the heading ''Version 3.3 National Language Support'').

If you're using version 3.3, and you want to set up your system so you can use it with United States or Canadian English and most European languages, but you don't need to learn what each command does, turn to the end of this appendix and follow the instructions under the heading ''Setting Up Code-Page Switching for an EGA-Only System'' or ''Setting Up Code-Page Switching for an IBM PS/2 and Printer,'' whichever better describes your system.

CHOOSING A KEYBOARD LAYOUT

Keyboards used in different countries must accommodate different characters and often use a different arrangement of common keys. The Keyboard commands, Keyb*xx* in versions 3.0 through 3.2 and Keyb in version 3.3, change the keyboard layout to match the conventions of a specific country.

In versions through 3.2, the Keyboard command for each country loads a small program that combines with the part of DOS kept in memory and decreases the amount of available memory by about 2000 bytes. The actual size of the program depends on the number of changes the new layout requires. If you enter a Keyboard command, then enter another Keyboard command without restarting DOS, the second keyboard program is loaded to reconfigure the keyboard. The program loaded by the first Keyboard command remains in memory but you cannot return to it, so issuing a series of Keyboard commands reduces the amount of available memory.

In version 3.3, the first time the Keyboard command is carried out, it increases the size of DOS in memory by about 5000 bytes. Subsequent Keyboard commands then tell DOS to load different sets of specifications, called *translation tables,* that accommodate different country-specific keyboard layouts.

Switching Keyboards While DOS Is Running

If your computer was manufactured for use in the United States, the configuration of the United States keyboard is stored in the computer's permanent memory. After changing the keyboard layout with a Keyboard command, you can switch back and forth between the United States configuration and the new one: Press Ctrl-Alt-F1 (hold down both the Ctrl and Alt keys and press the F1 function key) for the United States layout, and Ctrl-Alt-F2 for the other layout. If your word processor or spreadsheet program accepts characters other than standard keyboard characters—you'll have to try it to see—this lets you switch back and forth while editing a document to include information for either country and to use the more familiar keyboard layout to operate the application.

If your computer was manufactured for multilingual operation, you may be able to switch among several keyboard configurations without using a Keyboard command. See your computer's documentation (the *Guide to Operations* if the computer was manufactured by IBM) for a description of how to switch among different keyboard layouts.

Note: Not all printers can print accented or other characters not in the standard set. Check your printer's documentation to see if it can print the characters you need.

Typing Accented Characters With Dead Keys

Many languages use *accented characters* that combine an accent mark and a common character (such as Å or ñ). Some of these accented characters are assigned locations on the keyboard; on the French keyboard, for example, you type *è* by pressing the 7 key in the top row of the keyboard (to type the number 7, you press Shift-7).

Often, there aren't enough available keys to provide all the accented characters, however, so DOS also uses *dead keys* to combine accent marks and characters. Some typewriters use this same technique, so using dead keys might be a familiar procedure for you.

A dead key is one that represents just an accent mark. Pressing a dead key doesn't produce any apparent result, but it tells DOS to combine the accent mark with the next key you press. On the French keyboard, for example, you type *ô* by pressing the dead key for the circumflex (ˆ), then pressing the key labeled O.

If you press a dead key, then press a character that cannot be combined with the accent mark represented by the dead key, DOS does one of the following:

- In most cases, it beeps and displays the accent mark, followed by the key you pressed, to show you it can't combine them as an accented character.
- If the dead key represents the diaeresis (¨), DOS displays a small, filled-in square (■) followed by the second key you pressed.

To correct the error, backspace to erase the two characters and type the correct dead-key sequence.

Keyboard Layouts

If you're using a version of DOS prior to 3.3, each language DOS supports has its own Keyboard command. The Keyboard commands have no parameters (the country names in the right column of the following table are for information only):

Keyboard command	Country
keybuk	United Kingdom
keybgr	Germany
keybfr	France
keybit	Italy
keybsp	Spain

Because entering a Keyboard command changes the location of common keys (especially punctuation marks), the character that results from pressing a key doesn't always match the United States label on the key. You may want to chart the keyboard layout and keep a paper copy handy, mark the keys, or even move the key caps to the new location.

Figures B-1 and B-2 show the French keyboard layout for the IBM PC (and PC/XT) keyboard and for the enhanced IBM PC/AT keyboard. The figures show the shifted and unshifted characters produced by each key in the main typewriter portion of the keyboard, and also identify the dead keys.

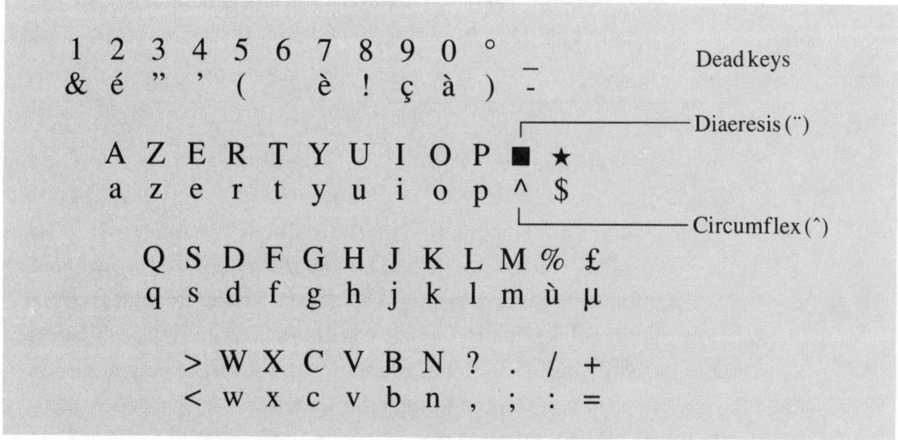

Figure B-1. IBM PC and PC/XT French keyboard layout (keybfr)

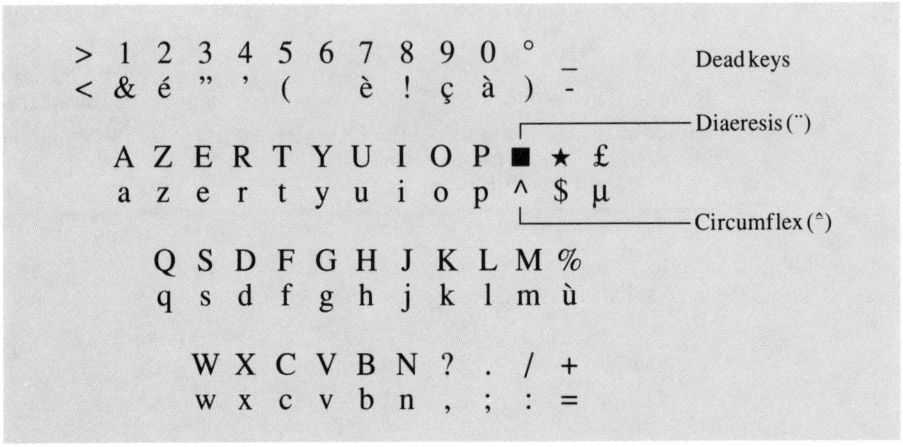

> 1 2 3 4 5 6 7 8 9 0 ° _
< & é " ' (è ! ç à) -

A Z E R T Y U I O P ■ ★ £
a z e r t y u i o p ^ $ µ

Q S D F G H J K L M %
q s d f g h j k l m ù

W X C V B N ? . / +
w x c v b n , ; : =

Dead keys
Diaeresis (¨)
Circumflex (^)

Figure B-2. Enhanced IBM PC/AT French keyboard layout (keybfr)

Example of Using the Keyboard Command

Note: If you're using version 3.3, your Keyboard command is described later in this appendix, after you've been introduced to the basics of national language support. Read the following example to see how to use the French keyboard. If you want, you can return to try the example once you've learned how to select the keyboard in your version of DOS.

To change the keyboard arrangement to French, type the following if you're using a version of DOS between 3.0 and 3.2:

```
C>keybfr
```

If you are accustomed to the United States layout, here are the most obvious changes with the French layout: You must hold down the Shift key to type a number; the locations of two pairs of letter keys are reversed (Q-A and W-Z); M is to the right of L; and most symbols and punctuation marks are in different places.

Now that you have switched keyboards, you must follow the new layout. For example, the command to display a directory in wide format is *dir /w*. If you don't follow the French keyboard layout, you'll type *dir =z*, because the equal sign is where the forward slash used to be, and the W and Z have changed places.

Suppose you wanted to type the sentence *L'hôtel célèbre est grand* (The famous hotel is big). Both the é and the è are on the keyboard, but the ô is not, so you must use the dead key for the circumflex. And remember, the Q and the A keys have changed places. Here, step-by-step, is how you would type the phrase:

```
C>L
```

For the apostrophe, press the 4 key in the top row. After the apostrophe, type *h*:

```
C>L'h
```

Now, you have to use the circumflex dead key, which is to the right of the French p. Press the circumflex dead key. Nothing happens yet. Now type *o*; DOS displays *ô*. Continue by typing *tel c*:

```
C>L'hôtel c
```

For é, press the 2 key in the top row; then type *l*:

```
C>L'hôtel cél
```

For è, press the 7 key in the top row; then type *bre est gr*:

```
C>L'hôtel célèbre est gr
```

And finally, press Q to get the French a, and type *nd*:

```
C>L'hôtel célèbre est grand
```

Although that's a painfully long list of instructions just to type a simple sentence, in fact it goes quite quickly after a bit of practice. Press Esc to clear the line, and press Ctrl-Alt-F1 to return to the United States keyboard layout.

Changing the Country Code with the Country Configuration Command

The country code is a number that DOS uses to control the way the date and time are displayed. Application programs also have access to this code, and they can use it to control other format characteristics, such as currency symbols and the characters, such as commas and decimal points, used to separate thousands and decimal fractions in numbers.

The Country configuration command lets you set the country code. As with other configuration commands, you don't type the Country command at the system prompt: You put it in the file named CONFIG.SYS in the root directory of the system disk. DOS then carries out the command each time you start it.

In versions prior to 3.3, the Country configuration command has one parameter:

country=<country-code>

<country-code> is one of the three-digit codes shown in Figure B-3 on the next page; it's usually the same as the country's international long-distance dialing prefix. You must include all three digits, including any zeros at the beginning.

Country	Country Code	Country	Country Code
Australia	061	Norway	047
Belgium	032	Spain	034
Denmark	045	Sweden	046
Finland	358	Switzerland	041
France	033	United Kingdom	044
Israel	972	United States	001
Italy	039	West Germany	049
Netherlands	031		

Figure B-3. Country codes for versions 3.0 through 3.2

For example, suppose your computer was built for use in the United States, but someone also uses it for writing in French. To tell DOS to follow French conventions for date, currency, and decimals, you could create or modify a DOS system diskette for that person, including the command *country=033* in CONFIG.SYS. (If there were no CONFIG.SYS file in the root directory, you would create it and put the Country command in it.) Once the CONFIG.SYS file was saved, each time DOS was started from the French disk it would adopt the French conventions.

When DOS displayed the current date and asked for the new date, for example, it would display the date in the sequence day-month-year, and ask the user to *Enter new date (dd-mm-yy).*

To change the country code, you would edit CONFIG.SYS again. For the United States, you could either delete the Country command or change *country=033* to *country=001* (001 is the code for the United States).

Creating a Language-Specific DOS System Diskette

If you use more than one language, or if several users with different languages share the computer, DOS offers a simple way to handle multilingual operation: the Select command, which creates a system diskette tailored to the language and conventions of a particular country.

The Select command makes a copy of the DOS system disk that contains files that configure DOS for a specific country, including CONFIG.SYS and AUTOEXEC.BAT files. If you create several country-specific diskettes, you can change languages simply by restarting DOS after putting the appropriate system diskette in drive A.

The Select command has four parameters:

select <source> <target> <country> <keyboard>

<source> is the letter, followed by a colon, of the drive that contains the DOS system diskette. You can specify either *a:* or *b:* If you don't specify <source>, DOS assumes drive A.

<target> is the drive letter, followed by a colon, and the path name of the directory on the diskette to which the DOS files are to be copied. If you omit the drive letter, DOS assumes drive B; if you omit the path name, DOS assumes the root directory. <target> and <source> must specify different drives. If you specify only one drive letter, DOS assumes it is <target>.

<country> is the three-digit country code you want set on the new DOS diskette. You must include all three digits of the country code, including any zeros at the beginning. <country> corresponds to the country's long-distance telephone prefix.

<keyboard> is the two-letter abbreviation of the country whose keyboard layout is to be selected for the new DOS diskette (these are the last two letters of the corresponding Keyboard command).

Warning: The Select command formats the target disk, erasing all files on it, so either use a new diskette or make sure that the diskette or fixed disk you use as the target contains no files that you must keep.

Figure B-4 shows the country code and keyboard values allowed with the Select command. Only those countries marked with an asterisk (*) are available in versions 3.0 through 3.2; the others are available starting with version 3.3. You can enter the keyboard code in either uppercase or lowercase.

Country	Country Code	Keyboard Code
Australia	061	US
Belgium	032	BE
Canada (English)	001	US
Canada (French)	002	CF
Denmark	045	DK
Finland	358	SU
France *	033	FR
Germany *	049	GR
Israel	972	—
Italy *	039	IT
Latin America	003	LA
Middle East (Arabic)	785	—

Figure B-4. Country and keyboard codes for the Select command *(continued)*

Figure B-4. (Continued)

Country	Country Code	Keyboard Code
Netherlands	031	NL
Norway	047	NO
Portugal	351	PO
Spain*	034	SP
Sweden	046	SV
Switzerland (French)	041	SF
Switzerland (German)	041	SG
United Kingdom*	044	UK
United States*	001	US

Example of Creating a Language-Specific System Diskette

The Select command uses the Diskcopy command to make the copy of the system diskette, then it compares the two diskettes with the Diskcomp command to make sure the copy was accurate. The prompts and sequence of steps are the same as if you had entered a Diskcopy command, then a Diskcomp command.

If you're using a computer with a fixed disk, you must start DOS with the system diskette in the diskette drive, even if you normally start DOS from the fixed disk. If you have only one diskette drive, DOS may prompt you to switch diskettes; the number of times you must switch diskettes depends on the amount of memory available in your computer.

Throughout the Select procedure, DOS refers to the original system diskette as either the first or source diskette and refers to the language-specific system diskette you're creating as either the second or target diskette.

To create a French system diskette on a computer with one diskette drive, you perform the following steps:

1. Start DOS with the system diskette in drive A, even if you normally start DOS from a fixed disk.
2. Type *select 033 fr* (*033* is the country code for France, and *fr* is the keyboard code). DOS prompts you to insert the source diskette in drive A and press any key.
3. The source diskette is in drive A, so press any key. DOS reads from the system diskette, then prompts you to put the target diskette in drive A.

4. Put a blank diskette, formatted or unformatted, in drive A and press any key. If the new diskette isn't formatted, DOS formats it, then notifies you how many tracks, sectors, and sides it's copying and starts to copy the system to the new diskette. After copying the system diskette, DOS asks *Copy another diskette (Y/N)?* Type *n*.

5. Now DOS compares the two diskettes to make sure the copy was accurate. It prompts you to *Insert FIRST diskette in drive A:* and press any key.

6. Leave the new (French) diskette in drive A and press a key. DOS tells you how many tracks, sectors, and sides it's comparing, reads the files from the diskette, and prompts you to *Insert SECOND diskette in drive A:* and press any key.

7. Put the original DOS system diskette in drive A and press a key. After comparing the diskettes, DOS displays *Compare OK* and asks *Compare another diskette (Y/N)?* (If it displays a different message, start again at step 2.) Type *n*.

8. Now DOS prompts you to *Insert TARGET diskette in drive A* and press a key. Put the new French-specific system diskette in drive A and press a key. To make sure it is correct, restart DOS by pressing Ctrl-Alt-Del, check whether the date is displayed in the day-month-year (not month-day-year) sequence, and see if the keyboard follows the French layout (press the Q and A keys to see if they are interchanged from the United States layout).

That's it. You have a system diskette configured for France.

Version 3.3 National Language Support

The national language support in version 3.3 replaces the methods used in previous versions to change the keyboard layout and the character sets used by the display and printer. These are the most extensive changes from version 3.2 to version 3.3. They include four new or changed system files, three new commands, three new options for the Mode command, a new parameter for the Graftabl command, and a new parameter for the Country and Device configuration commands.

Some New Terms: Code Page and Code-Page Switching

The key element of the new national language support is called a *code page*—a table of 256 codes for different characters. DOS recognizes two types of code pages. A *hardware code page* is the character table built into a device and is determined by the country for which the device is manufactured. The hardware code page is the code page used by a device unless you specify otherwise.

A *prepared code page* is an alternate character table available through DOS. A prepared code page can replace the hardware code page of a device.

Beginning with version 3.3, a code page can be any of the following:

437	United States
850	Multilingual
860	Portuguese
863	French Canadian
865	Nordic

The identifying numbers bear no relationship to the country code introduced with previous versions of DOS and used by the Country configuration command.

Code page 437 is the character table used in previous versions of DOS; its character set supports United States English and includes many accented characters used in other languages, as well as symbols and straight lines, corners, and other characters that can be used to draw boxes on the screen. Code page 437 is the hardware code page for all but a few countries.

Code page 850 replaces two of the four box-drawing sets and some of the mathematical symbols in code page 437 with additional accented characters; it includes enough characters to cover United States and Canadian English, and Latin American and most European languages.

The three remaining code pages cover a few additional languages: Code page 860 is for Portuguese, code page 863 is for Canadian French, and code page 865 is for Norwegian. These are also the hardware code pages for these countries; code page 865 is also the hardware code page for Denmark.

You select prepared code pages from the five included with version 3.3 with the new *cp prepare* option of the Mode command. The *current code page* is the code page most recently selected.

National language support is often referred to as *code-page switching* because, once you have defined the devices and code pages required by your system, the only commands you deal with simply switch from one code page to another.

Setting Up Your System for Code-Page Switching

Although several commands are required to manage national language support, the process is straightforward. Setting up a system requires the following commands:

- A Device configuration command in CONFIG.SYS.
- A National Language Support Function (nlsfunc) command in AUTOEXEC.BAT.

- A Mode command in AUTOEXEC.BAT to prepare code pages for each device that supports code-page switching.
- A Mode or Change Code Page (chcp) command in AUTOEXEC.BAT to select the initial code page.
- A Keyboard (keyb) command in AUTOEXEC.BAT to select the initial keyboard layout.

With these commands in CONFIG.SYS and AUTOEXEC.BAT, it takes only one or two commands after you start your system to change to a different language during a DOS session.

You still use the Select command to create a country-specific system disk, and the Country configuration command to control country-specific characteristics such as the date format and currency symbol; an added parameter on the Country command lets you also specify a code page.

The next few topics describe the new and changed commands in detail, including examples of their use. A complete example of how to set up a system follows the command descriptions.

Four New or Changed System Files

Version 3.3 of DOS includes four system files for national language support functions:

- PRINTER.SYS handles code-page switching for the IBM Proprinter Model 4201 and Quietwriter III Model 5202 printers.
- DISPLAY.SYS takes care of the EGA, IBM PC Convertible LCD, and IBM PS/2 displays. All displays compatible with the EGA and PS/2 are also supported.
- COUNTRY.SYS contains data such as date formats and currency symbols.
- KEYBOARD.SYS defines the keyboard layouts for different countries.

National Language Support Commands

National language support in version 3.3 adds three DOS commands: National Language Support Function (nlsfunc), Change Code Page (chcp), and Keyboard (keyb).

National Language Support Function Command—NLSFUNC

If there is no Country configuration command in CONFIG.SYS, the National Language Support Function (nlsfunc) names the file that contains country-specific information such as date format and currency symbol. You must enter the Nlsfunc command before you can use the Change Code Page (chcp) command. If you use national language support every time you use the system, you can put the Nlsfunc command in AUTOEXEC.BAT.

The Nlsfunc command has one parameter:

nlsfunc <country-file>

<country-file> is the name of the country information file; in most versions of DOS, this file is named COUNTRY.SYS. If you omit <country-file>, DOS assumes the file is the one specified in the Country configuration command in CONFIG.SYS. If there is no Country configuration command in CONFIG.SYS, DOS looks for a file named COUNTRY.SYS in the root directory of the current drive.

For example, the following command specifies C:\DOS\COUNTRY.SYS as the country information file:

```
C>nlsfunc c:\dos\country.sys
```

Loading the country information in COUNTRY.SYS with the Nlsfunc command increases the size of DOS in memory by about 2500 bytes.

Keyboard Command—KEYB

The Keyboard (keyb) command selects a keyboard layout. It replaces the Keyb*xx* commands used in earlier versions of DOS to select keyboard layouts.

The Keyb command has three parameters:

keyb <country>,<code-page>,<kbdfile>

<country> is one of the following two-character keyboard codes:

Code	Country
BE	Belgium
CF	Canada (French)
DK	Denmark
FR	France
GR	Germany
IT	Italy
LA	Latin America
NL	Netherlands
NO	Norway
PO	Portugal
SF	Switzerland (French)
SG	Switzerland (German)

(continued)

Code	Country
SP	Spain
SU	Finland
SV	Sweden
UK	United Kingdom
US	United States

<code-page> is a three-digit number that specifies the code page that DOS is to use. <code-page> can be 437 (United States), 850 (Multilingual), 860 (Portuguese), 863 (French Canadian), or 865 (Nordic).

<kbdfile> is the name of the system file that contains the keyboard layouts; this file is KEYBOARD.SYS in most versions of DOS. If you don't specify <kbdfile>, DOS assumes that the file is named KEYBOARD.SYS and is stored in the root directory of the system disk.

For example, the following command would select the French keyboard layout, code page 850, and the keyboard definition file named C:\DOS\KEYBOARD.SYS.

```
C>keyb fr,850,c:\dos\keyboard.sys
```

If you omit all parameters (just type *keyb*), DOS displays the currently active keyboard country code, keyboard code page, and console device (display) code page. If you have selected the United States keyboard and code page 850 for both the keyboard and the console, for example, DOS responds to the command *keyb* with the message:

```
Current keyboard code: US  code page: 850
Current CON code page: 437
```

Change Code Page Command—CHCP

The Change Code Page (chcp) command tells DOS which code page to use for all devices that support code-page switching. You use it to change code pages when you want to change character sets.

You must execute the National Language Support Function (nlsfunc) command before you can use the Change Code Page command. Change Code Page is a system-wide command: It specifies the code page to be used by DOS and by each device attached to the system that supports code-page switching. The *cp select* option of the Mode command (described later) specifies the code page for a single device.

If the code page you specify with Change Code Page isn't compatible with a device, DOS responds *Code page* nnn *not prepared for all devices.* If you specify a code page with Change Code Page that you didn't first identify with the *cp prepare* option of the Mode command, DOS responds *Code page* nnn *not prepared for system.*

The Change Code Page command has one parameter:

chcp <code-page>

<code-page> is the three-digit number that specifies the code page that DOS is to use. As listed earlier, they are 437 (United States), 850 (multilingual), 860 (Portuguese), 863 (French Canadian), or 865 (Nordic). If you omit <code-page>, Change Code Page displays the current DOS code page.

For example, the following command would change the system code page to 850:

```
C>chcp 850
```

If the current code page were 850 and you typed *chcp*, DOS would respond by displaying *Active code page: 850.*

Changed National Language Support Commands

National language support changes two general DOS commands (Mode and Graftabl) and two configuration commands (Country and Device).

Mode Command Changes

National language support adds four options to the Mode command:

- *codepage prepare* defines the code pages that you want to use.
- *codepage select* selects a code page for a particular device.
- *codepage status* displays the code pages that are available and active.
- *codepage refresh* restores a code page that was erased from memory after you selected it.

When you enter the Mode command, you can abbreviate *codepage* to *cp*.

Preparing a Code Page

When used to define the code page or code pages to be used with a device, the Mode command has three parameters:

mode <device> cp prepare=((<code-page>) <font-file>)

<device> is the name of the device for which the code page or code pages are to be prepared. It can be CON, PRN, LPT1, LPT2, or LPT3.

<code-page> is the three-digit code page number, enclosed in parentheses, that specifies the code page to be used with <device>. If you specify more than one code-page number, separate them with blanks. Valid code pages are listed earlier, under the heading "Some New Terms: Code Page and Code-Page Switching."

<font-file> is the name of the code-page information file that contains the font information for <device>. DOS includes four files for IBM devices. Your version of DOS may include others; the code-page information files have the extension CPI:

EGA.CPI	Enhanced graphics adapter (EGA) or IBM PS/2
4201.CPI	IBM Proprinter
5202.CPI	IBM Quietwriter III printer
LCD.CPI	IBM Convertible liquid crystal display (LCD)

For example, assume your display is attached to an EGA; the following command would prepare code pages 437 and 850 for the console, specifying C:\DOS\EGA.CPI as the code page information file:

```
C>mode con cp prepare=((437 850) c:\dos\ega.cpi)
```

Selecting a Code Page

When used to select a code page for a device, the Mode command has two parameters:

mode <device> cp select=<code-page>

<device> is the name of the device for which the code page is to be selected. You can specify CON, PRN, LPT1, LPT2, or LPT3.

<code-page> is the three-digit number that specifies the code page to be used with <device>. The code page you specify must be one that has already been prepared with the *codepage select* option of the Mode command.

For example, the following command would select code page 850 for the console:

```
C>mode con cp select=850
```

Displaying the Code-Page Status

When used to display the status of the code pages, the Mode command has one parameter:

mode <device> cp

<device> is the name of the device whose code-page status is to be displayed. It can be CON, PRN, LPT1, LPT2, or LPT3.

For example, the following command would display the status of the console device:

```
C>mode con cp
```

Restoring a Code Page That Was Lost

Some circumstances can cause a code page to be erased from memory. For example, if you prepare and select a code page for the printer, then turn the printer off and turn it back on again, the code page in the printer's memory may be different from the one you selected. The *codepage refresh* option of the Mode command restores the code page you selected without your having to specify the code page number.

mode <device> cp refresh

<device> is the name of the device whose most recently selected code page is to be restored. It can be CON, PRN, LPT1, LPT2, or LPT3.

For example, the following command would restore the most recently selected code page for the printer attached to the LPT2 port:

```
C>mode lpt2 cp refresh
```

Graftabl Command Changes

One parameter has been added to the Load Graphics Table (graftabl) command that loads a code page for the color/graphics adapter (CGA) so that its character set matches the code page used by DOS and other devices when displaying accented and other special characters in graphics mode.

The first time a Graftabl command is executed, the size of DOS in memory is increased by about 1500 bytes.

The Graftabl command has two parameters:

graftabl <code-page> /status

<code-page> is the three-digit number that specifies the code page that Graftabl is to use; it can be 437, 860, 863, or 865. (Code page 850, multilingual, is not available with the Graftabl command.)

/status displays the name of the graphic character set table that Graftabl is using.

Country Configuration Command Changes

One parameter has been added to the Country configuration command in version 3.3. It specifies the code page to be used by DOS. The Country command isn't required; if you don't include a Country command in CONFIG.SYS, DOS assumes country 001 (US), code page 437, and country information file \COUNTRY.SYS on the disk in the current drive.

The Country configuration command has three parameters:

country=<country-code>,<code-page>,<country-file>

<country-code> is one of the three-digit country codes shown in Figure B-4.

<code-page> specifies the code page that DOS is to use.

<country-file> is the name of the file that contains the country-specific information; in most versions of DOS, this is COUNTRY.SYS. If you omit <country-file>, DOS assumes that the the file is named COUNTRY.SYS, and that it is stored in the root directory of the current drive.

For example, the following configuration command in CONFIG.SYS would specify the French country code, code page 850, and C:\DOS\COUNTRY.SYS as the country information file:

```
country=033,850,c:\dos\country.sys
```

Device Configuration Command Changes

Two options have been added to the Device configuration command; they are used to specify the system file that controls code-page switching for the display and printer.

Specifying the Display Driver

The file that controls code-page switching for the display is DISPLAY.SYS. It supports the IBM Enhanced Graphics Adapter (EGA), the IBM Personal System/2 display adapter, the liquid crystal display (LCD) of the IBM PC Convertible, and all display adapters compatible with those IBM devices. The monochrome display/printer adapter (MDA) and color/graphics adapter (CGA) do not support code-page switching.

If you also use the ANSI.SYS display driver, the Device command that defines it must precede the Device command that defines DISPLAY.SYS.

When used to specify a code-page switching file for the display, the Device configuration command has five parameters:

device=<filename> con=(<type>,<hwcp>,<prepcp>,<sub-fonts>)

<filename> is the name of the code-page switching file for the display. If you omit <filename>, DOS assumes that the file is named DISPLAY.SYS and that it is in the root directory of the current drive.

<type> defines the type of display adapter attached to the system. It must be one of the following:

mono	Monochrome display/printer adapter
cga	Color/graphics adapter
ega	Enhanced graphics adapter or IBM Personal System/2
lcd	IBM PC Convertible liquid crystal display

<hwcp> is a three-digit number that specifies the hardware code page built into the display adapter. Valid code pages are listed earlier, under the heading ''Some New Terms: Code Page and Code-Page Switching.''

<prepcp> is the number of additional code pages that the display can support. These are referred to as *prepared code pages,* and must be defined by the *cp prepare* option of the Mode command. If <type> is either *mono* or *cga,* <prepcp> must be 0; DOS assumes 0. If <type> is *ega* or *lcd,* <prepcp> can be from 1 through 12; DOS assumes 1. If <hwcp> is 437, let DOS assume 1; if <hwcp> is not 437, specify 2.

<sub-fonts> is the number of sub-fonts supported for each code page. If <type> is either *mono* or *cga,* <sub-fonts> must be 0; DOS assumes 0. If <type> is *ega,* <sub-fonts> can be 1 or 2; DOS assumes 2. If <type> is *lcd,* <sub-fonts> can be 1 or 2; DOS assumes 1. Unless you have unusual requirements, you needn't specify a value for <sub-fonts>; the value that DOS assumes covers all normal systems.

For example, the following configuration command in CONFIG.SYS would specify C:\DOS\DISPLAY.SYS as the code-page switching file for an EGA whose hardware code page is 437; DOS is allowed to assume values of 1 and 2 for <prepcp> and <sub-fonts>:

```
device=c:\dos\display.sys con=(ega,437)
```

Specifying the Printer Driver

The file that controls code-page switching for dot-matrix printers is PRINTER.SYS. It supports the IBM Proprinter Model 4201, the IBM Quietwriter III Printer Model 5202, and all printers compatible with either of these IBM devices.

When used to specify the code-page switching file for the printer, the Device configuration command has five parameters:

device=<filename> <printer>=(<type>,<hwcp>,<prepcp>)

<filename> is the name of the code-page switching file for the printer. If you omit <filename>, DOS assumes that the file is named PRINTER.SYS and that it is in the root directory of the current drive.

<printer> is the DOS device name for the printer port being defined. It can be LPT1 (or PRN), LPT2, or LPT3. You can specify a different set of parameters for each of the three printer ports in one command.

<type> defines the type of printer attached to the system. It must be either *4201* for the IBM Proprinter Model 4201, or *5202* for the IBM Quietwriter III Printer Model 5202 (or a printer compatible with one of these IBM models).

<hwcp> is a three-digit number that specifies the hardware code page built into the display adapter. Valid code pages are listed earlier, under the heading "Some New Terms: Code Page and Code-Page Switching." If <type> is *5202,* you can specify two hardware code-page numbers, enclosed in parentheses and separated by a comma. If you do specify two hardware code pages, you must specify <prepcp> as 0. If you don't specify <hwcp>, DOS assumes 437.

<prepcp> is the number of additional code pages, referred to as *prepared code pages,* DOS should be prepared to use. These code pages must be defined by the *cp prepare* option of the Mode command. <prepcp> can be from 0 through 12. If <hwcp> is 437, specify 1; if <hwcp> is not 437, specify 2.

For example, the following configuration command in CONFIG.SYS would define C:\DOS\PRINTER.SYS as the code-page switching file for the device named PRN. The printer is an IBM Proprinter Model 4201 whose hardware code page is 437; DOS is instructed to allow for one prepared code page:

```
device=c:\dos\printer.sys prn=(4201,437,1)
```

The following configuration command in CONFIG.SYS would define the code-page switching file as C:\DOS\PRINTER.SYS for the devices named LPT1 and LPT2. The printer attached to LPT1 is the same (4201) as in the previous command. The printer attached to LPT2 is an IBM Quietwriter III Printer Model 5202 with two hardware code pages (437 and 850); DOS is instructed to allow for no prepared code pages:

```
device=c:\dos\printer.sys lpt1=(4201,437,1) lpt2=
(5202,(437,850),0)
```

Setting Up Code-Page Switching For an EGA-Only System

Figure B-5 shows the commands that are needed to set up national language support for a system whose only code-page switching device is a display attached to an EGA or EGA-compatible adapter. The hardware code page of the EGA is 437 (United States English), and the system is set up to handle code pages 437 and 850.

All DOS files are assumed to be in the directory C:\DOS. If you don't use the ANSI.SYS device driver, omit the configuration command *device=c:\dos\ansi.sys* from CONFIG.SYS; if you do use ANSI.SYS, however, be sure that its Device configuration command precedes the Device configuration command that defines DISPLAY.-SYS, as in Figure B-5.

Put these commands in CONFIG.SYS:

```
country=001,437,c:\dos\country.sys
device=c:\dos\ansi.sys
device=c:\dos\display.sys con=(ega,437)
```

Put these commands in AUTOEXEC.BAT:

```
nlsfunc c:\dos\country.sys
mode con cp prepare=((437 850) c:\dos\ega.cpi)
mode con cp select=437
keyb us,437,c:\dos\keyboard.sys
```

Figure B-5. Setup commands for a system with EGA only

When you start the system, code page 437 is selected for DOS, the display, and the keyboard. To change to code page 850, type *chcp 850*.

Setting Up Code-Page Switching For an IBM PS/2 and Printer

Figure B-6 shows the commands required to set up national language support for an IBM PS/2 or compatible system that includes both a VGA (or compatible) display and an IBM Proprinter Model 4201 printer. The hardware code page of both devices is 437 (United States English), and the system is set up to handle code pages 437 and 850. (Note that *ega* in the Device configuration command that specifies DISPLAY.SYS means both EGA and PS/2.)

Again, all DOS files are assumed to be in the directory C:\DOS. If you don't use the ANSI.SYS driver, omit the configuration command *device=c:\dos\ansi.sys* from CONFIG.SYS; if you do use ANSI.SYS, however, be sure that its Device configuration command precedes the Device configuration command that defines DISPLAY.SYS, as shown in Figure B-6.

Put these commands in CONFIG.SYS:

```
country=001,437,c:\dos\country.sys
device=c:\dos\ansi.sys
device=c:\dos\display.sys con=(ega,437)
device=c:\dos\printer.sys prn=(4201,437,1)
```

Put these commands in AUTOEXEC.BAT:

```
nlsfunc c:\dos\country.sys
mode con cp prepare=((437 850) c:\dos\ega.cpi)
mode prn cp prepare=((437 850) c:\dos\4202.cpi)
mode con cp select=437
mode prn cp select=437
keyb us,437,c:\dos\keyboard.sys
```

Figure B-6. Setup commands for a PS/2 with display and printer

When you start the system, code page 437 is selected for DOS, the display, the keyboard, and the printer. To change to code page 850 during the session, type *chcp 850*. To switch back to code page 437, type *chcp 437*.

APPENDIX C

VERSION 4 OF DOS

Version 4 of MS-DOS, which isn't as widely used as other versions, is available in Europe from a few computer manufacturers who provide it with their machines. Version 4 isn't part of the progression from version 1.0 through version 3.3. It includes the same commands for managing files and devices as version 3.2 of DOS, and can be used just as described in this book. Version 4 also includes one additional command, named Detach, which is used to run special multitasking applications.

Multitasking means running more than one program at the same time. Version 4 provides multitasking capability by giving each program that is running brief periods of the computer's processing time. Although the computer is not actually running several programs simultaneously, it operates so quickly that the illusion is usually sufficient. Version 4 is used in Europe to run a few special network-oriented and communications-oriented applications.

The Detach command in version 4 tells DOS to start what is called a *background* program. Such a program must be written specifically for version 4, and it can't use the keyboard or screen until you explicitly give it control. Most background programs watch for incoming data on a network or a communications port, but otherwise give no evidence of their existence, lurking in the background and waiting for something interesting to happen.

Once a background program is running in version 4, you can start any other program, such as a word processor or a spreadsheet. This program, called a *foreground* program, runs just as it would under any other version of DOS, in full control of the screen and keyboard.

When the background program finds what it has been waiting for—some activity on a network or communications port, for example—it tells version 4 to display a message that tells you something is happening. You can then press a special combination of keys to temporarily freeze the foreground program and give the background program control of the screen and keyboard.

Once the background program is in control, you use it to do whatever task is required. When you finish, you press another special combination of keys to give control of the screen and keyboard back to the foreground program, and then pick up where you left off. The background program fades once again, silently waiting for some other interesting event to occur.

APPENDIX D

GLOSSARY

A

Adapter: A term sometimes used to refer to printed-circuit cards that plug into a computer and control a device, such as a display or a printer.

Application program: A program, such as a word processor or spreadsheet, that performs a specific task; an application of the computer to a particular type of work.

Archive: To duplicate files on a separate disk or on a backup tape for safekeeping. The Backup command helps archive files; the Restore command can, if necessary, be used to return archived files to the disk from which they were backed up.

ASCII: A standardized coding scheme that uses numeric values to represent letters, numbers, symbols, and so on. ASCII is an acronym for American Standard Code for Information Interchange and is widely used in coding information for computers.

AUTOEXEC.BAT: A name reserved for a batch file that contains commands that are carried out by DOS each time the system is started. An AUTOEXEC.BAT file can be used to perform a desired set of startup procedures without having to type the commands each time.

AUX: Short for *auxiliary*. The communications port DOS uses unless instructed otherwise. AUX can be either COM1 or COM2 in versions of DOS through 3.2; it can be COM1, COM2, COM3, or COM4 in version 3.3.

B

Backspace key: The key labeled with a single, left-pointing arrow; erases characters you have typed, one at a time.

Back up: To copy one or more files to diskettes or tapes for safekeeping.

BAK: An extension assigned, by Edlin and by many word processors, to the next-most-recent (penultimate) version of a text file. If the working copy of a file is damaged, the BAK file can be used to salvage a near-current version of the document.

BASIC: A programming language included with versions of DOS; BASIC is an acronym for Beginner's All-purpose Symbolic Instruction Code.

Batch file: A text file whose extension is BAT; contains DOS commands. When you type the name of the batch file while DOS is at the command level, DOS carries out the commands in the file.

Baud: The rate at which data is transmitted over a communications link. One character per second equals approximately 10 baud.

Binary: The base-2 numbering system whose only digits are 0 and 1. The binary system is particularly well suited to use with computers because the two digits can be represented by the presence (1) or absence (0) of a voltage.

Bit: The smallest unit of information used with computers; corresponds to a binary digit (either 0 or 1). Eight bits make up one byte.

Boot: To start up a computer; derived from ''pull yourself up by your own bootstraps.''

Byte: The unit of measure used for computer memory and data storage. One byte contains eight bits and can store one character (a letter, number, or punctuation mark, or other symbol).

C

Character string: A group of characters that you tell DOS to treat as a set of letters or numbers, rather than as a command. The Find filter command searches for character strings enclosed in quotation marks (" "). In other commands, such as the Edlin Search and Replace commands, the quotation marks are not needed.

Chip: *See* integrated circuit.

Color/Graphics Adapter (CGA): A printed-circuit card in the system unit of a computer that controls the display. Shows both text and graphics at low resolution in up to sixteen colors.

COM1, COM2, COM3, COM4: Short for *communications.* The names of the serial communications ports. All versions of DOS recognize COM1 and COM2; version 3.3 also recognizes COM3 and COM4.

Command: An instruction you use to control a computer program, such as DOS or an application program.

Command file: A file that contains the program or instructions required to carry out a command. If the file's extension is COM or EXE, the command file contains machine instructions; if its extension is BAT, the command file is a batch file and contains DOS commands.

Communications: The transmission of data between computers; also called telecommunications.

Communications port: *See* port.

CON: Short for *console.* The name by which DOS refers to the keyboard (input) and the display (output).

Control key: The key labeled Ctrl; use it, as you do the Shift key, by holding it down while pressing another key. The Control key usually causes something to happen, rather than displaying a character on the screen. If displayed, it is shown as ^, as in the end-of-file marker, ^Z (Ctrl-Z).

CPU: Acronym for *central processing unit.* The part of a computer that performs calculations and processes information. In most microcomputers that use DOS, for example, the CPU is the 8086/8088, 80286, or 80386 chip.

Ctrl: *See* Control key.

Ctrl-Break: The key combination that cancels a command; entered by holding down the Ctrl key and pressing the Break key.

Ctrl-C: Same as Ctrl-Break.

Ctrl-Num Lock: The key combination that stops DOS until you press any other key. Usually used to freeze the display so you can view long displays. Entered by holding down the Ctrl key and pressing the Num Lock key.

Ctrl-P: Same as Ctrl-PrtSc.

Ctrl-PrtSc: The key combination that controls simultaneous printing and displaying. Pressing Ctrl-PrtSc once causes DOS to print everything that is displayed; pressing Ctrl-PrtSc again causes DOS to stop printing everything that is displayed. Entered by holding down the Ctrl key and pressing the PrtSc key.

Ctrl-S: Same as Ctrl-Num Lock.

Ctrl-Z: The key combination that creates the special character (displayed as ^Z) that DOS uses to mark the end of a file. Created by holding down the Ctrl key and pressing Z, or by pressing the function key labeled F6.

Current directory: The directory in which DOS looks for files unless otherwise instructed.

Current drive: The drive containing the disk on which DOS looks for a directory or file unless otherwise instructed.

D

Data: The numbers and text processed by a computer in doing its work.

Data bit: A signal used in serial communications to represent the transmission of a character; seven or eight data bits can be used to represent one character.

Data file: A file that contains the data needed by a program; can be numbers, text, or a combination of the two.

Device: A piece of computer equipment, such as a display or a printer, that performs a specific task; the program that controls a device is called a device driver.

Device name: The name by which DOS refers to a device (for example, PRN, LPT1, LPT2, or LPT3 for a printer). Device names are treated like file names by DOS.

Directory: The index of files that DOS maintains on a disk. The directory entry for each file includes the file's name, extension, size, date and time it was created or last changed, and the location of the beginning of the file. All but the last item are displayed by the Directory command.

Disk: A magnetically coated disk used to store information. The term is used when no distinction need be made between a diskette and a fixed disk.

Disk drive: The device that rotates a disk in order to read (retrieve) and write (store) information.

Diskette: A disk for storing files, made of thin plastic and enclosed in a protective jacket.

Diskette drive: A disk drive used for diskettes.

Display: The screen on which the computer shows both what you type at the keyboard and the result of its work; assumed by DOS to be the standard output device unless a different device is specified.

Drive letter: The letter that identifies a disk drive.

E

Edit: To change the contents of a file, usually with a word processor or an editing program such as Edlin.

Editor: A program used to create or change text files; also called a *text editor.*

Edlin: The DOS text editor.

Enhanced Graphics Adapter (EGA): A printed-circuit card in the system unit of a computer that controls the display. Shows both text and graphics at medium resolution in up to 64 colors.

Enter key: The key you press to tell DOS that you have finished typing a line. Labeled Return on some keyboards.

Esc: *See* Escape key.

Escape key: The key labeled Esc; cancels a line you have typed but have not yet entered by pressing the Enter key.

Extension: A suffix of up to three characters that can be added to a file name to identify the contents of the file more precisely.

F

File: A named collection of information stored on a disk; usually contains either data or a program.

File name: A name of up to eight characters that you assign and that DOS uses to find a file on a disk; can be followed by a period and three additional characters called the file name extension.

Filespec: The complete specification of a file; can include a drive letter, path name, file name, and extension.

Filter command: A DOS command that reads standard input, processes it in some way (for example, sorts it in alphabetic order), and writes the result to standard output.

Fixed disk: A disk of large capacity (10 MB or more) that cannot be removed from its drive. Also called a *hard disk.*

Floppy disk: *See* diskette.

Format: To prepare a disk for use.

Function key: One of several keys, usually labeled F1, F2, and so on, that cause DOS (or an application program) to perform a certain function, such as copying characters in a line of text.

H

Hard disk: *See* fixed disk.

Hardware: The equipment that makes up a computer system, as opposed to the programs, or software.

Hexadecimal: The base-16 numbering system whose digits are 0 through F (the letters A through F represent the decimal numbers 10 through 15); often used in computer programming because it is easily converted to and from binary, the base-2 numbering system the computer itself uses.

Hidden file: A file, usually used only by DOS, that is not listed when you display the directory. Hidden files cannot be erased, copied, or otherwise affected by DOS commands.

Hierarchical filing system: *See* multilevel filing system.

I

Initialize: *See* format.

Input: The data that a program reads.

Input/output: A term that refers to the devices and processes involved in the computer's reading (input) and writing (output) data.

Integrated circuit: An electronic device that combines thousands of transistors on a small sliver, or chip, of silicon. Such devices are the building blocks of computers. Also referred to as a *chip*.

Interface: The boundary between two systems or entities, such as a disk drive and the computer, or the user and a program.

I/O: Abbreviation for *input/output*.

I/O redirection: *See* redirection.

K

Keyboard: The device consisting of alphabetic and other keys where instructions and data are typed into the computer; assumed by DOS to be the standard input device unless a different device is specified.

L

LPT1, LPT2, LPT3: Short for *line printer*. The names that DOS uses to refer to the three ports to which parallel printers can be attached.

M

Microcomputer: A small computer system, usually used by only one person.

Microprocessor: An integrated circuit, or chip, that contains the circuits the computer needs to calculate and to communicate with the other parts of the system.

Modem: A device that permits the transmission of computer data over telephone lines. Contraction of *modulator-demodulator*.

Monitor: A device that displays computer input and output; usually used synonymously with *display*.

Monochrome: A term used to describe a computer display capable of displaying one color (usually white, green, or amber).

Monochrome Display Adapter (MDA): A printed-circuit card in the system unit of a computer that controls the display. Shows text only at medium resolution in one color.

Multicolor Graphics Array (MCGA): A printed-circuit card in the system unit of a computer that controls the display. Shows both text and graphics at low to medium resolution in up to 256 colors; used in IBM PS/2 model computers.

Multilevel filing system: A computer filing system that lets you define directories within other directories, creating a structure with many levels. Also called a *tree-structured* or *hierarchical* filing system.

N

Network: A group of computers, linked by printed-circuit cards, cables, and network software, that share resources, such as disk drives and printers.

O

Operating system: A program that coordinates the operation of all parts of a computer system.

Output: The result of a program's processing its input data.

P

Parallel communications: A communications technique that uses multiple interconnecting wires to send eight bits of a byte at once (in parallel).

Parallel port: The port to which the printer is usually attached.

Parameter: A qualifier that you include with a command to define more specifically what you want DOS to do; also called an *argument* or an *option*.

Parity: An error-detection technique used for accuracy in data communications.

Path: The list of directory names that defines the location of a directory.

Path name: The portion of a file specification that defines the path to the file; can include a drive letter followed by a colon.

Pipe: To direct the output of one command to be used as the input of another command. The pipe symbol DOS uses is the broken vertical bar (¦).

Port: The electrical connection through which the computer sends and receives data to and from devices or other computers.

Print queue: The list of files to be printed by DOS; you create, examine, and modify the print queue with the Print command.

Printed-circuit card: A thin, rectangular card or board, usually made of fiberglass or epoxy and coated with copper. A circuit is etched into the copper, and electronic devices, such as integrated circuits, are soldered to the circuit. Computer systems are made up of these cards.

Printer: A device that produces images of text and graphics on paper.

PRN: Short for *printer*. The printer DOS uses unless instructed otherwise. Can refer to LPT1, LPT2, or LPT3.

Program: A set of instructions for a computer.

Prompt: A request displayed by the computer for you to provide some information or perform an action.

Q

Queue: *See* print queue.

R

RAM: Short for *random access memory.* The memory that DOS uses for programs and data; RAM content changes often while you use the computer, and is lost when the computer is turned off.

RAM disk: *See* virtual disk.

Read-only file: A file whose read-only attribute is set so that its contents can be displayed and read, but not changed.

Redirection: The process of causing a command or program to take its input from a file or device other than the keyboard (standard input), or of causing the output of a command or program to be sent to a file or device other than the display (standard output). The DOS redirection symbols are the greater-than (>) and less-than (<) signs.

Replaceable parameter: A symbolic reference, consisting of a percent sign followed by a one-digit number (such as %1), that can be included with commands in a batch file to refer to the parameters entered with the batch command.

Return key: The Enter key.

ROM: Short for *read-only memory.* A type of computer memory that is permanently recorded in hardware; contains instructions that help a computer carry out routine tasks, such as starting itself up. The contents of ROM cannot be changed and are not lost when the computer is turned off.

Root directory: The main directory that DOS creates on each disk; the top directory in a multilevel filing system.

S

Serial communications: A communications technique that uses as few as two interconnecting wires to transmit bits serially, one after the other.

Serial port: The communications port (COM1, COM2, COM3, or COM4) to which devices, such as a modem or a serial printer, can be attached.

Software: The programs that are used with a computer system, as opposed to the equipment, or hardware.

Standard input: The device from which a program reads its input unless the input is redirected; in normal DOS operation, standard input is the keyboard.

Standard output: The device to which a program sends its output unless the output is redirected; in normal DOS operation, standard output is the display.

Stop bit: A signal used in serial communications that marks the end of a character.

Subdirectory: A file that contains directory entries; sometimes also used to refer to the group of files whose directory entries are in the same file.

System program: A program whose purpose is to control the operation of all or part of the computer system, such as managing the printer or interpreting commands.

System prompt: The characters DOS displays when it is at the command level (ready to accept a command); unless you specify otherwise, the system prompt consists of the letter of the current drive followed by a greater-than sign (for example, C>).

T

Telecommunications: *See* communications.

Temporary file: A file that DOS may create when told to redirect command input or output; deleted by DOS when the command is completed.

Text: Ordinary, readable characters, including the uppercase and lowercase letters of the alphabet, the numerals 0 through 9, and punctuation marks.

Text editor: A program that you use to create or change text files. Also called simply an *editor*.

Text file: A file that you can read (contains ordinary letters, numbers, and punctuation marks).

U

Update: To change a file, creating a new (or updated) version.

V

Video Graphics Array (VGA): A printed-circuit card in the system unit of a computer that controls the display. Shows both text and graphics at medium to high resolution in up to 256 colors; used in IBM PS/2 model computers.

Virtual disk: A portion of the computer's random access memory reserved for use as a simulated disk drive. Also called an *electronic* or *RAM* (for random access memory) *disk*. Unless saved on a physical disk, the contents of a virtual disk are lost when the computer is turned off.

Volume label: An 11-character identifying name you can assign to a disk.

W

Wildcard character: A special character that, like the wild card in a poker game, can be used to represent any other character. DOS recognizes two wildcard characters: the question mark (?), which can represent any single character, and the asterisk (*), which can represent more than one character.

Write-protect: To cover the small notch or opening on a diskette so that new or changed information cannot be written onto the diskette.

APPENDIX

DOS COMMAND REFERENCE

ANSI.SYS
Control Program for Screen and Keyboard
Versions 2.0 and later

Page 300

ANSI.SYS is a program that lets you control the console device. With it, you can manipulate the characters assigned to keys on the keyboard, and the color, position, and other attributes of the display. A program that controls a device is called a *device driver;* ANSI.SYS is a device driver that follows the conventions adopted by the American National Standards Institute (ANSI) for screen and keyboard control.

ANSI.SYS is widely used and offers many ways to extend your control over the console, but it is not required in your everyday use of DOS; a full description is beyond the scope of this book. For details, refer to the explanations and examples in *Supercharging MS-DOS* (Microsoft Press, 1986) or the DOS *Technical Reference.*

APPEND
Define a Data Path
Versions 3.2 and later

Pages 138, 146

The Append command specifies one or more directories that DOS searches for a data file that isn't in the current directory. You can use Append on a network.

append /X /E <path> ;

/X makes the data path available to additional DOS commands. You can specify /X only the first time you enter an Append command after starting DOS. If you specify /X, you cannot specify any path names; you must enter another Append command to define the data path. (Version 3.3)

/E makes the data path part of the DOS environment. You can specify /E only the first time you enter an Append command after starting DOS. If you specify /E, you cannot specify any path names; you must enter another Append command to define the data path. (Version 3.3)

<path> is the name of the directory to be added to the data path. You can specify a directory on the same or a different drive, or you can specify just a drive letter (such as *a:*). If you specify more than one drive or directory, separate the path names with a semicolon (;).

Note: Use the Append command with care. If you define several data paths, DOS does not tell you where it found a file you requested. Nor does DOS necessarily save a revised file in the appended directory from which it came; it might instead save the file in the current directory.

Examples

To tell DOS to search for data files in the subdirectories \MKT\WP and \ENG\WP on drive C:

```
C>append \mkt\wp;\eng\wp
```

To see appended data paths:

```
C>append
```

If you type *append* and no data path is defined, DOS displays *No Append.*

To limit searches to the current directory:

```
C>append ;
```

This cancels any data paths.

ASSIGN
Route Disk Operations to a Different Drive
Versions 3.0 and later, IBM releases 2.0 and later

Page 304

The Assign command routes requests for disk operations on one drive to a different drive. Its primary use is with application programs that look for files on a specific drive (such as B) and don't let you specify a different drive (such as C).

assign <drive1>=<drive2>

<drive1> is the letter, without a colon, of the drive to be assigned.

<drive2> is the letter, without a colon, of the drive that is to be used instead of <drive1>.

Both <drive1> and <drive2> must refer to existing disk drives (including fixed disks and virtual drives). You can assign more than one drive in a single Assign command by separating the <drive1>=<drive2> pairs with blanks.

If you omit all parameters (just type *assign*), DOS deletes all drive assignments, so that all drive letters refer to their original drives.

Note: The Assign command masks the actual type of disk drive from DOS, so use it only when necessary, and don't enter a Backup, Restore, Label, Join, Substitute, or Print command that uses an assigned drive. Four DOS commands—Format, Diskcopy, Diskcomp, and System—ignore any drive assignments made with the Assign command. If you have version 3.1 or later, use the Substitute command instead of the Assign command; for example, type subst b: c:<path> *instead of* assign b=c.

Examples

To assign drive B to drive C:

```
C>assign b=c
```

To assign drives A and B to drive D:

```
C>assign a=d b=d
```

To reset all drive letters to their original drives:

```
C>assign
```

ATTRIBUTE
Display or Change File Attributes
Versions 3.0 and later

Pages 73, 149

The Attribute command (attrib) displays or changes the read-only and the archive status of a file. If a file is read-only, you cannot change or delete the file. A file's archive status can be used by the Backup, Restore, and Xcopy commands to determine whether the file should be copied to another disk.

attrib +R –R +A –A <filename> /S

+R makes the file read-only.

–R removes the read-only attribute.

+A assigns the archive attribute. (Versions 3.2 and later)

–A removes the archive attribute. (Versions 3.2 and later)

<filename> specifies the name of the file whose read-only or archive attribute is to be changed or displayed. The file name can include a drive letter, followed by a colon, and a path name.

/S applies the Attribute command to all subdirectories contained in <filename>. (Version 3.3)

If you specify only *attrib <filename>*, DOS displays an R to the left of the file name if the file is read-only. In versions 3.2 and later, DOS also displays an A to the left of the file name if the file has changed since it was last archived (in other words, the archive attribute is on).

Examples

To make the file named REPORT.DOC in the current directory on the disk in the current drive a read-only file:

```
C>attrib +r report.doc
```

To remove the read-only attribute from the file named REPORT.DOC in the directory named \WORD\MKT on the disk in drive D:

```
C>attrib -r d:\word\mkt\report.doc
```

To display the read-only and archive attributes of all files in the directory named \WORD\MKT on the disk in the current drive:

```
C>attrib \word\mkt\*.*
```

DOS responds:

```
            C:\WORD\MKT\REPORT.DOC
A           C:\WORD\MKT\FORECAST.DOC
        R   C:\WORD\MKT\SALESREP.DOC
A       R   C:\WORD\MKT\FCST-APR.DOC
            C:\WORD\MKT\FCST-MAY.DOC
        R   C:\WORD\MKT\FCST-MAR.DOC
        R   C:\WORD\MKT\BUDGET.DOC
A       R   C:\WORD\MKT\FCST-JUN.DOC
```

BACKUP
Make a Backup Copy of Files
Versions 2.0 and later

Page 157

The Backup command makes a backup copy of files so you can safeguard data against damage or other loss. Files can be backed up from and to any type of source and target disk. Rather than making an exact copy of the file, as the Copy command does, the Backup command records the directory from which each file was backed up. The Restore command uses this data to reinstate files in the correct locations.

Although the Backup command is present in versions 2.0 and later, not all the parameters described here are in every release of DOS; refer to your DOS manual to find out which parameters are available to you.

backup <path><filename> <drive> /A /S /M /F /D:<date> /T:<time> /L:<logfile>

<path> and <filename> specify the file or files to be backed up. You must specify at least a drive letter, followed by a colon. You can include a path name or a file name, or both, and you can use wildcard characters. The following list shows what files DOS backs up if you specify:

- Drive letter: All files in the current directory of the disk in the specified drive.
- Drive letter and path name: All files in the specified directory on the disk in the specified drive.
- Drive letter and file name: The specified file from the current directory of the disk in the specified drive.

<drive> is the letter of the drive, followed by a colon, (such as *a:*) that contains the backup disk.

/A adds the backup files to the backup disk. If you don't use /A, DOS displays a warning message and then erases any files on the target disk before copying the files. If you omit /A, be sure the backup diskette doesn't contain any files you want to keep.

/S backs up all files in all subdirectories contained in the current directory or the specified directory.

/M backs up only files that have been modified since they were last backed up.

/F formats the target disk if it isn't already formatted. If you specify /F, the current command path must include the directory containing the file FORMAT.COM. (Version 3.3)

/D:<date> backs up only files that have been modified since the date specified in <date>. Specify <date> just as you would for the Date command.

/T:<time> backs up all files that have changed since <time> on <date>. Specify <time> just as you would for the Time command. Not all releases of DOS include the /T:<time> option.

/L:<logfile> creates a log file on the source drive that contains the date and time of the backup, the path name and file name of each file that is backed up, and the backup number that DOS assigned to the diskette on which the file is backed up. If a log file already exists, the backup information is added at the end, creating a history of backups for the source drive. If you don't specify a name for the log file, DOS names it BACKUP.LOG and stores it in the root directory of the source drive. Not all releases of DOS include the /L:<logfile> parameter.

Unless you're using version 3.3, the target disk must be formatted. If the files to be backed up require more than one diskette, DOS prompts you to insert another diskette; be sure to label these diskettes, because the Restore command asks for them by number. Files can't be backed up from a diskette with a write-protect tab.

DOS displays the name of each file as it is backed up. If the target disk is a diskette, the backup files are stored in its root directory. If the target disk is a fixed disk, the backup files are stored in a directory named \BACKUP.

When it finishes, the Backup command reports to DOS on the backup procedure by setting *errorlevel* to one of the following values:

- 0: Backup was completed successfully.
- 1: No files were found to back up.
- 2: Some files were not backed up because of conflicting file-sharing needs (networks only).
- 3: Ctrl-C was pressed to end the backup process before all files were backed up.
- 4: System problems stopped the backup process.

If you use batch files to help with your backup procedure, you can check this value with the *errorlevel* option of the If batch command and use the result to control what other commands are carried out in a batch file.

Because the Backup command varies among different versions of DOS, it's advisable to use the same version both to back up and to restore files. In particular, you can only restore files backed up with the version 3.3 Backup command with the version 3.3 Restore command.

Note: Do not back up files from a drive that is affected by an Assign, Substitute, or Join command; restoring the files with the Restore command can damage the directory structure of the disk to which the files are restored.

Examples

To back up all files with the extension DOC from the current directory on the disk in the current drive to the disk in drive A:

```
C>backup c:*.doc a:
```

To back up all files whose extension is DOC from the directory named \WORD\MKT on the disk in the current drive to the disk in drive A:

```
C>backup c:\word\mkt\*.doc a:
```

To back up to drive A all files in all subdirectories on drive C that have been modified since they were last backed up:

```
C>backup c:\ a: /s /m
```

(If the disk in drive A is filled before all the files are backed up, you are prompted to insert a new disk. If you're using a version earlier than 3.3 and you regularly back up large files from a fixed disk to diskettes, prepare an adequate supply of formatted diskettes before beginning a backup procedure.)

To back up all files whose extension is DOC from the current directory and all its subdirectories in drive D to the disk in drive A and add them to the backup disk:

```
C>backup d:*.doc a: /s /a
```

To back up all files whose extension is DOC that were changed on or after October 16, 1987, backing them up from the directory \WORD\MKT on the disk in drive C to the disk in drive A:

```
C>backup c:\word\mkt\*.doc a: /d:10-16-87
```

Many options can be used in one Backup command. For example, the following command backs up all files that were changed on or after October 16, 1987 and have not been archived since then, copying them from both the current directory and all its subdirectories from the disk in drive D, then adds them to the disk in drive A and creates the log file named BACKUP.LOG:

```
C>backup d: a: /a /s /d:10-16-87 /l
```

BATCH COMMANDS AND BATCH FILES

Executing a File of DOS Commands

In addition to typing DOS commands at command level, you can put one or more commands in a batch file—a file with the extension BAT—and carry out all the commands by typing the name of the file (with or without the extension). For example, assume the file named CDIR.BAT contains the following lines:

```
cls
dir
```

Typing *cdir* at the system prompt causes DOS to clear the screen and display the directory entries of the current directory. The effect is the same as typing the two commands separately. You can create a batch file with Edlin, with a word processor that lets you save a file without formatting, or by copying from the console (CON) to the file with the Copy command.

A batch file can use other batch commands in two ways:

- If a batch file contains the name of a second batch file, DOS *chains* to the second batch file; after executing the commands in the second batch file, DOS returns to the system prompt.
- If you're using 3.3 or a later version of DOS and a batch file contains a Call command that names a second batch file, DOS carries out the commands in the second batch file, then returns to the first batch file and continues with the command that follows the Call command.

Pressing Ctrl-C cancels a batch command. DOS prompts for confirmation by displaying *Terminate batch job (Y/N)?* If you respond *y*, the batch command is canceled and DOS returns to command level; if you respond *n*, the batch file continues.

Naming Batch Files

The extension of a batch file must always be BAT. If, however, a batch file has the same file name as an internal DOS command or a file with the extension COM or EXE, DOS won't carry out the commands in the file. This is because, when you type a command at the system prompt, DOS checks for command files in the following order:

- An internal DOS command.
- The name of a file whose extension is COM.

- The name of a file whose extension is EXE.
- The name of a file whose extension is BAT.

If you didn't type any of the above, DOS displays *File not found*, displays the system prompt, and waits for you to type something else. Thus, if a batch file has the same name as an internal DOS command, or there is a file with the extension COM or EXE in either the current directory or a directory in the command path, DOS finds the other command file first and doesn't carry out the batch file.

Batch Command Parameters

If a command in a batch file contains a replaceable parameter—a percent sign (%) followed by a digit from 0 through 9—DOS replaces the percent sign with the corresponding parameter typed with the batch command. If there is no corresponding parameter, the replaceable parameter is replaced by nothing.

For example, if a batch file named SHOWME.BAT contains the command *echo %1 %2 %3 %4*, and you type the command *showme A B C*, DOS replaces %1 with the first parameter you typed (A), %2 with the second parameter (B), %3 with the third parameter (C), and %4 with nothing because you did not type a fourth letter. The only exception to this rule is the replaceable parameter %0, which is replaced by the name (but not the extension) of the batch file itself.

A Special Batch File: AUTOEXEC.BAT

If the root directory of the system disk contains a file named AUTOEXEC.BAT, DOS automatically carries out the commands in the file each time you start the system. This lets you tailor your system by running a program that, for example, sets a system clock, changes to a particular subdirectory, or starts an application program.

When DOS carries out the commands in an AUTOEXEC.BAT file, it doesn't prompt for the time and date. If your computer doesn't keep the time and date current, include Date and Time commands in AUTOEXEC.BAT so that DOS can ask for the correct time and date each time you start the system.

Batch Commands

Several DOS commands are intended primarily for use in batch files:

- The Call command carries out the commands in another batch file, then returns to complete execution of the original batch file. (Version 3.3)
- The Echo command controls whether DOS displays (echoes) each command it carries out. You can also use the Echo command to display a message or to tell you whether the echo option is on or off.

- The For command repeatedly carries out a DOS command according to limits you set.
- The Goto command tells DOS to skip to a different location in a batch file, rather than carry out the next sequential command.
- The If command tests a condition and, if the condition is true, carries out a DOS command you specify.
- The Pause command temporarily stops carrying out commands and waits for a key to be pressed before continuing with the next command in a batch file.
- The Rem command lets you include comments (remarks) in a batch file.
- The Shift command moves a series of command-line parameters entered with a batch command one position to the left. The first parameter is lost, the second parameter becomes the first, and so on.

These batch commands are described in following sections of this entry.

BATCH COMMANDS: CALL
Carry Out Another Batch File
Version 3.3

Page 272

You can use the Call batch command in a batch file to tell DOS to carry out the commands in a second batch file, then return to the original batch file and continue with the next command in it instead of returning to the system prompt. This lets you use a batch command of your own making in a batch file just as you would use any other DOS command.

call <batchfile> <parameters>

<batchfile> is the name of the file of commands you want DOS to carry out.

<parameters> represents any parameters that <batchfile> requires. You can either enter the parameters themselves, or you can use replaceable parameters, so that parameters typed on the command line with the name of the first batch file are passed along to the batch file being called.

Example

Suppose you have two batch files. One, named SORTFILE.BAT, first uses the Sort command to sort the file whose name you type as a parameter with *sortfile,* then redirects the sorted output to the printer; the other, WEEKRPT.BAT, carries out several commands to print a series of sorted lists that make up a weekly report.

To use the SORTFILE batch command in WEEKRPT.BAT to print the sorted version of the file named REPORT.LST, include the following Call command in WEEKRPT.BAT:

```
call sortfile report.lst
```

DOS carries out the commands in SORTFILE.BAT—printing the sorted version of REPORT.LST—and continues with the command that follows the Call command in WEEKRPT.BAT.

BATCH COMMANDS: ECHO
Display a Message
Versions 2.0 and later

Page 245

The Echo command sends a message to the standard output device (usually the display), controls whether DOS displays commands as it carries them out (echo on), or displays the status of echo (on or off). DOS sets echo on when it starts carrying out the commands in a batch file, unless the file is started by another batch file that turned echo off.

echo on off <message>

on tells DOS to display each command as it is carried out.

off tells DOS not to display each command as it is carried out.

<message> is a message to be sent to standard output.

If you enter an Echo command with no parameters (just type *echo*), DOS displays the status of echo (either *ECHO is on* or *ECHO is off*).

Examples

To turn echo on:

```
echo on
```

To turn echo off:

```
echo off
```

To display the message *Put the backup diskette in drive A*:

```
echo Put the backup diskette in drive A
```

To display the echo status:

```
C>echo
```

BATCH COMMANDS: FOR
Carry Out a Batch Command Several Times
Versions 2.0 and later

Page 269

The For batch command carries out a DOS command once for each member of a set of character strings.

for %%p in (<set>) do <command>

%%p is a replaceable parameter that is given the value of each member of <set> by DOS before <command> is carried out. It is represented by two percent signs (%%) followed by any character except one of the redirection symbols: <, >, or ¦.

<set> is a series of strings separated by blanks. <command> is carried out once for each member of <set>. If <set> is empty, <command> isn't carried out. <set> can contain character strings, path names, or file names. If one of the strings is a file name that includes wildcard characters, DOS sets %%p, in turn, to each file name that matches the wildcard character, then carries out <command>.

<command> is any DOS command except another For command. Through version 3.2, you can carry out another batch command without returning to the system prompt, by making <command> a Command command with the /C parameter and specifying the name of the batch file as the string that follows the /C parameter (see the last example below). If you're using version 3.3, you can accomplish the same thing by using the Call command.

Note: You can type a For command at the system prompt, rather than enter it in a batch file. If you do, use %p instead of %%p. Everything else is the same.

Examples

To copy up to nine files named in the batch command line to the current directory of the disk in drive A:

```
for %%p in (%1 %2 %3 %4 %5 %6 %7 %8 %9) do copy %%p a:
```

To display all the files in the current directory whose extension is DOC:

```
for %%p in (*.doc) do type %%p
```

To carry out the batch files named BAT1.BAT, BAT2.BAT, and BAT3.BAT:

```
for %%p in (1 2 3) do command /c bat%%p
```

If you specified the command to be carried out as *bat%%p* (omitting *command /c*), DOS would return to the system prompt after carrying out BAT1.BAT.

If you're using version 3.3, you can use the Call command instead of Command:

```
for %%p in (1 2 3) do call bat%%p
```

BATCH COMMANDS: GOTO
Jump to a Label
Versions 2.0 and later

Page 250

The Goto batch command tells DOS to jump to a specified label in a batch file and carry out the commands that follow. A label is a line that consists of a colon (:) followed by a character string up to eight characters long.

goto <label>

<label> is the label in the batch file you want DOS to jump to. You do not include the colon in the Goto command; for example, if the label in the batch file were *:end*, the Goto command would be *goto end*, not *goto :end*.

Example

The line numbers in the following batch file are included only for reference. The batch file includes two labels, *:start* in line 2 and *:end* in line 7. These two labels control the backup procedure performed by the Backup command in line 3.

The If command in line 4 includes a *goto end* command that sends DOS to the label *:end* and ends the backup if an error occurs. The *errorlevel* option of the If command detects errors by checking a special *errorlevel* value that Backup sets to report on each backup it performs (0 is success, 1 through 4 represent different reasons why a backup attempt was not completed). Thus, *goto end* is carried out and the batch file ends if the Backup command in line 3 reports an *errorlevel* of 1 or greater. Otherwise, the *goto start* command in line 6 sends DOS back to line 3, to back up another file, until an error occurs or no more files remain to be backed up.

```
1: @echo off
2: :start
3: backup %1 a:
4: if errorlevel 1 goto end
5: shift
6: goto start
7: :end
```

BATCH COMMANDS: IF
Deciding Whether to Carry Out a Batch Command
Versions 2.0 and later

Page 247

The If batch command tests a condition and carries out another command if the condition is met.

if not <condition> <command>

not reverses the meaning of <condition>. That is, <command> is carried out only if <condition> is *not* true.

<condition> is the condition to be tested. Using <condition>, a batch file can be used to check on the outcome of a command, such as Backup or Restore (with the *errorlevel* option); check whether a file exists; or check whether two strings are identical. <condition> takes one of the following forms:

errorlevel <number>	True if *errorlevel* is equal to or greater than <number>. *Errorlevel* represents a special value that is set by some DOS commands to indicate whether they were carried out successfully or not.
exist <filename>	True if <filename> exists in the specified directory.
<string1>==<string2>	True if <string1> and <string2> are identical; remember, uppercase and lowercase are different. Notice that two equal signs separate the strings. This form of the If command can be used to compare file names, replaceable parameters entered on the command line with the batch command, or character strings.

<command> is the command to be carried out. It can be any DOS command, including another If command.

Examples

To jump to the label *:end* if *errorlevel* is equal to or greater than 1:

```
if errorlevel 1 goto end
```

(For a sample batch file using this command, see BATCH COMMANDS: GOTO.)

To copy the file named in the first replaceable parameter from the disk in the current drive to the disk in drive A if the file doesn't exist on the disk in drive A:

```
if not exist a:%1 copy %1 a:%1
```

BATCH COMMANDS: PAUSE
Temporarily Stop a Batch File
Versions 1.0 and later

Page 246

The Pause batch command displays the message *Strike a key when ready . . .* and waits for you to press a key before carrying out any more commands. You can cancel a batch file while it is paused by pressing Ctrl-C.

The Pause command also lets you include a message to be displayed before *Strike a key when ready . . .* if Echo is on.

pause <message>

<message> is the message to be displayed before *Strike a key when ready . . .*

Examples

To temporarily stop the batch file:

```
pause
```

To echo the message *Put data disk in drive B* and temporarily stop a batch file before the *Strike a key when ready . . .* message:

```
echo Put the data disk in drive B and
pause
```

When DOS carries out the commands in the batch file, it displays the following messages and waits for any key to be pressed:

```
Put the data disk in drive B and
Strike a key when ready . . .
```

BATCH COMMANDS: REM

Include a Remark in a Batch File

Versions 1.0 and later

Page 215

The Remark batch command (rem) lets you include remarks in a batch file. Remarks are displayed if Echo is on and are not displayed if Echo is off.

rem <remark>

<remark> is the remark.

Example

The following batch command includes the remark *This batch file requires the data disk* in a batch file:

```
rem This batch file requires the data disk
```

BATCH COMMANDS: SHIFT

Move Batch Parameters One Position Left

Versions 2.0 and later

Page 268

The Shift batch command moves the command-line parameters entered with a batch command one position to the left; the leftmost parameter is lost, and all other parameters move one position left. You can use the Shift command to process more than 10 replaceable parameters in a batch file.

shift

Example

The following batch file, named SHIFT_IT.BAT, uses the Shift command to process as many parameters as you can enter in the command line. The line numbers are shown only for reference:

```
 1: @echo off
 2: echo %0
 3: shift
 4: :START
 5: if "%0"=="" goto all_done
 6: echo %0 %1 %2
 7: shift
 8: shift
 9: shift
10: goto start
11: :ALL_DONE
12: echo ALL DONE
```

The Echo command in line 2 displays the name of the batch file, and the Shift command in line 3 shifts all command-line parameters one position to the left; the previous %0 (the name of the batch file) is lost, what was %1 becomes %0, what was %2 becomes %1, and so forth. Line 5 checks the leftmost parameter to see if there is one. If there isn't, the command *goto all_done* ends the batch file. If there is a leftmost parameter, line 6 displays the three leftmost parameters, lines 7 through 9 shift the parameters three positions to the left, and line 10 goes back to repeat the process.

Entering the SHIFT_IT batch command with the following parameters produces the display shown below:

```
C>shift_it 1 2 3 4 5 6 7 8 9 10 11 12 13 14 15
shift_it
1 2 3
4 5 6
7 8 9
10 11 12
13 14 15
ALL DONE
```

BREAK
Controlling When DOS Checks for Ctrl-C
Versions 2.0 and later

The Break command lets you control how often DOS checks to find out whether you typed Ctrl-C (or Ctrl-Break on some machines) to end a program. Normally, DOS checks for Ctrl-C only when it reads or writes characters from or to a standard character device, such as the display, a printer, or a communications port.

break on off

on tells DOS to extend its Ctrl-C checking to include each time it reads from or writes to a disk drive.

off tells DOS to check for Ctrl-C only when it reads from or writes to a standard character device.

If you enter break with no parameters, DOS displays the current break status: either *BREAK is on* or *BREAK is off.*

If break is off, your system runs somewhat faster than when break is on, but you have fewer opportunities to stop a program that spends a lot of time doing computations without using an input or output character device.

DOS starts with break off unless you specify otherwise. You can use the Break command described here to set break to *on* any time after starting DOS, or you can tell DOS to start with break on by including the very similar Break configuration command in your CONFIG.SYS file. For information on the Break configuration command, see the entry on CONFIG.SYS.

Examples

To turn break on:

```
C>break on
```

To turn break off:

```
C>break off
```

To display the break status:

```
C>break
```

CHANGE CODE PAGE (CHCP)

Change System-Wide Code Page

Version 3.3

Page 343

The Change Code Page command (chcp) tells DOS which code page to use for all devices that support code-page switching. You use it to change code pages when you want to change the language or character set that DOS uses. The *codepage select* option of the Mode command changes the code page for individual devices.

chcp <code-page>

<code-page> is the three-digit number from the list on the next page that specifies the code page that DOS is to use.

Code-Page Number	Code Page
437	United States
850	Multilingual
860	Portuguese
863	French Canadian
865	Nordic

If you omit <code-page>, Change Code Page displays the current code page. If the code page you specify with Change Code Page isn't compatible with a device, DOS responds *Code page* nnn *not prepared for all devices.* If you specify a code page with Change Code Page that you didn't first identify with the *codepage prepare* option of the Mode command, DOS responds *Code page* nnn *not prepared for system.*

You must execute the National Language Support Function (nlsfunc) command before you can use the Change Code Page command.

Examples

To change the system code page to multilingual (850):

```
C>chcp 850
```

To display the current code page (assume that it's 850):

```
C>chcp
```

DOS responds *Active code page: 850.*

CHANGE DIRECTORY (CD)
Change Current Directory
Versions 2.0 and later

Page 129
The Change Directory command (cd or chdir) changes or displays the current directory.

cd <drive> <path>

<drive> is the letter, followed by a colon, of the drive whose current directory is to be displayed or changed.

<path> is the path name of the directory that is to become the current directory.

If you omit <path>, DOS displays the current directory of the disk in <drive>. If you omit both <drive> and <path>, DOS displays the current directory of the disk in the current drive.

Examples

To change the current directory on the disk in the current drive to \MKT\WP:

```
C>cd \mkt\wp
```

To change the current directory on the disk in drive A to \MKT\WP:

```
C>cd a:\mkt\wp
```

To display the current directory of the disk in the current drive:

```
C>cd
```

To display the current directory of the disk in drive D:

```
C>cd d:
```

CHECK DISK (CHKDSK)

Check Disk Status

Versions 1.0 and later

Page 98

The Check Disk command (chkdsk) checks the allocation of storage on a disk and displays a report that shows the total amount of disk space, how much is used by directories and files, including hidden files, and how much is not available because of disk imperfections. Chkdsk also tells you how much memory is in the system and how much is free for use.

chkdsk <drive><filename> /V /F

<drive> is the letter, followed by a colon, of the drive that contains the disk to be checked (such as *a:*). If you omit <drive>, DOS checks the disk in the current drive.

<filename> specifies one or more files to be checked to see if they are stored in noncontiguous sectors. If you omit <filename>, Chkdsk doesn't check for noncontiguous sectors. If you don't specify a drive letter, Chkdsk checks for the file on the disk in the current drive.

/V displays the full path name and file name of each file and directory on the disk being checked. (Versions 2.0 and later)

/F tells Chkdsk to correct allocation errors, if it finds any and if you respond *y* when it notifies you of the errors and asks whether to correct them. Correcting allocation errors requires changing the information on the disk and may cause loss of some data, so this parameter safeguards against disk changes unless you approve them. (Versions 2.0 and later)

If Chkdsk finds errors in the allocation of disk space, it refers to this space as *clusters* and *chains* and asks whether you want to recover the space into a file. If you reply *y*, Chkdsk corrects the errors only if you included the /F parameter. The space is then recovered into a file named FILE*nnnn*.CHK in the root directory of the drive being checked (*nnnn* is a sequence number that starts with 0000).

If you specify a file name or a set of file names (by using wildcards) when you enter the Chkdsk command, the Chkdsk report tells you whether any of the files are fragmented (stored in noncontiguous sectors) and displays the names of those files. A badly fragmented disk can slow performance. If too many files on a diskette are fragmented, restore them to contiguous sectors by copying them all to another diskette with the Copy command (*copy * .**). If too many files on a fixed disk are fragmented, you can restore them to contiguous sectors by backing up all the files, reformatting the fixed disk, and restoring the files to the fixed disk.

Note: Chkdsk cannot be used with a drive created or affected by a Join or Substitute command, nor with a network drive.

Examples

To check the disk in the current drive:

```
C>chkdsk
```

If there are no errors, Chkdsk displays its report:

```
Volume FIXEDDISK   created October 16, 1987 1:21p

 31768576 bytes total disk space
    53248 bytes in 3 hidden files
   126976 bytes in 60 directories
 20037632 bytes in 979 user files
    40960 bytes in bad sectors
 11509760 bytes available on disk

   655360 bytes total memory
   411488 bytes free
```

To check the disk in drive A, checking all files in the directory \MKT\WP to see if they are fragmented:

```
C>chkdsk a:\mkt\wp\*.*
```

CHKDSK displays its usual report, followed by a list of any fragmented files:

```
A:\MKT\WP\REPORT.DOC
   Contains 2 non-contiguous blocks.

A:\MKT\WP\FORECAST.DOC
   Contains 5 non-contiguous blocks.

A:\MKT\WP\SALESREP.DOC
   Contains 4 non-contiguous blocks.
```

To check the disk in the current drive and tell CHKDSK you want to be able to recover any lost clusters:

```
C>chkdsk /f
```

CHKDSK displays its usual report. If there are allocation errors, it displays a message such as:

```
4 lost clusters found in 4 chains.
Convert lost chains to files (Y/N) ?
```

If you want to recover the clusters, reply *y*. When the command has completed, display the file named FILE*nnnn*.CHK; rename it if it contains data you want to keep, or delete it to make the disk space available to other files.

CLS
Clear the Screen
Versions 2.0 and later

Page 105

The Clear Screen command clears the screen and displays the system prompt in the top left-hand corner. Clear Screen has no parameters.

cls

Example

To clear the screen:

```
C>cls
```

COMMAND
Start a New Command Processor
Versions 1.0 and later

The Command command loads another copy of the DOS command processor (COMMAND.COM), the program that displays the system prompt and responds to the commands you type.

command /P /C <command>

/P makes the new copy of COMMAND.COM permanent. It displays the sign-on message and system prompt, and waits for a command. There is no way to return to the previous command processor. (Versions 2.0 and later)

/C <command> loads the new copy of COMMAND.COM, carries out the command specified by <command>, and returns control to the previous command processor. (Versions 2.0 and later)

If you enter a Command command with no parameters, the new copy of COMMAND.COM displays the sign-on message and system prompt and waits for a command. The new copy of COMMAND.COM remains in memory until you type *exit.* Control then returns to the previous command processor.

If you put a Command command with the /C parameter in a batch file and use it to carry out another batch file, DOS continues with the next statement in the first batch file when the second batch file completes. This allows a batch file to call another batch file, as well as to chain to another batch file. This technique is unnecessary in version 3.3, because it includes the Call command.

Examples

To load a new copy of COMMAND.COM that remains in control until you type *exit*:

```
C>command
```

To load a permanent new copy of COMMAND.COM:

```
C>command /p
```

To cause a batch file (BATCH1.BAT) to load a new copy of COMMAND.COM, carry out the commands in a second batch file (BATCH2.BAT), finish carrying out the commands in the first batch file, and return to the previous command processor, put the following command in BATCH1.BAT:

```
command /c batch2.bat
```

COMPARE (COMP)

Compare Two Files

Version 3.3, IBM releases 1.0 and later

Page 75

The Compare command (comp) compares two files or sets of files byte-by-byte and reports up to 10 differences for each comparison. If it finds any differences, Compare displays the location (counting from the beginning of the file) and hexadecimal (base-16) value of the differing bytes in each file. While you probably don't want to interpret these values, Compare is useful, for example, in helping you determine whether two files with the same name in different directories are exact duplicates.

If the files are the same, DOS displays *Files compare ok.* If the files are different lengths, DOS displays *Files are different sizes.* If the files are the same length but their content differs, DOS displays the first 10 bytes it finds that are different; if more than 10 bytes are different, it displays *10 Mismatches - ending compare*. After completing the comparison, DOS asks if you want to compare any more files.

comp <file1> <file2>

<file1> is the name of the first file to be compared. You can include a drive and path, and you can use wildcard characters to specify a group of files with similar names or extensions.

<file2> is the name of the second file to be compared. You can include a drive and path and use wildcard characters to specify a group of files with similar names or extensions. If you specify only a drive letter or path name, DOS compares <file1> to the file with the same name in the drive or directory specified in <file2>; if you use wildcard characters in <file1>, DOS compares all files in the drive or directory that match <file1>.

If you omit <file2>, DOS prompts for it. If you omit both <file1> and <file2> (just type *comp*), DOS prompts you for both file names.

Examples

To compare two files in the current directory named REPORT.DOC and FEB.RPT:

```
C>comp report.doc feb.rpt
```

To compare the file in the current directory named REPORT.DOC to the file named FEB.RPT in the directory named \REPORTS on the disk in the current drive:

```
C>comp report.doc \reports\feb.rpt
```

To compare the file in the current directory named REPORT.DOC with the file with the same name in the directory named \REPORTS on the disk in drive A:

```
C>comp report.doc a:\reports
```

To compare all files in the current directory whose extension is DOC with all files with the same name and extension in the current directory of the disk in drive A:

```
C>comp *.doc a:
```

CONFIG.SYS
File of System Configuration Commands

Page 295

CONFIG.SYS is a file that contains configuration commands that define the hardware and software that make up your system. It must be in the root directory of the system disk. Each time DOS starts, it carries out the commands in CONFIG.SYS. If there is no file named CONFIG.SYS in the root directory of the system disk, DOS assumes certain configuration values.

The configuration commands include:

- Break, which controls how often DOS checks for Ctrl-C.
- Buffers, which specifies how many disk buffers DOS sets aside.
- Country, which specifies the country whose date and time format is to be used.
- Device, which identifies a file that contains a program to control a device (such a program is called a *device driver*).

- Drivparm, which defines the operating characteristics of a disk or a tape drive.
- FCBS, which specifies the number of files controlled by File Control Blocks (FCBs) that can be open at the same time.
- Files, which specifies how many files controlled by handles can be open at the same time.
- Lastdrive, which sets the highest drive letter that DOS recognizes.
- Shell, which specifies the name of a command processor to be used instead of COMMAND.COM.
- Stacks, which tells DOS how much memory to reserve for its temporary use.

CONFIG.SYS is a text file; you can create it with a text editor, such as Edlin, or a word processor that lets you store a file without formatting codes.

The Select command creates a CONFIG.SYS file that includes a Country configuration command. You can add more configuration commands to this CONFIG.SYS file with a text editor or word processor.

CONFIGURATION COMMANDS: BREAK

Controlling When DOS Checks for Ctrl-C

Versions 2.0 and later

Like the DOS Break command, the Break configuration command controls how often DOS checks for Ctrl-C. DOS normally starts with break off, meaning that it checks for Ctrl-C whenever it reads from or writes to a character device, such as the keyboard or display. You can set the break status with the DOS Break command any time while you're using DOS. You can also start DOS with break on by placing a *break=on* configuration command in CONFIG.SYS.

If you need more information on this command, refer to the documentation that came with your version of DOS.

CONFIGURATION COMMANDS: BUFFERS

Controlling the Number of Disk Buffers

Page 300

The Buffers configuration command specifies how many disk buffers DOS sets aside each time it starts. A disk buffer is an area of memory that DOS uses to hold data being read from or written to disk.

The optimum number of buffers depends on several factors, among them:

- The type of disk drives you use. A small increase in the number of buffers speeds fixed-disk operations.
- The amount of memory your computer has. Each buffer reduces available memory by 512 bytes, so a large number of buffers can cause your system to run more slowly or run out of memory faster.
- The type of programs you use. For example, increasing the number of buffers speeds up programs that perform a lot of random disk access (jump from place to place in a data file). A database program or a word processor, for example, might benefit from 10 to 20 buffers.
- The number and levels of subdirectories in your file structure. If you have a large, multilevel subdirectory structure, increasing the number of buffers to 10 to 25 can significantly speed disk operations.

Increasing the number of buffers to more than about 30, however, can slow the system, because DOS might then be able to read a record from disk faster than it could search through all the buffers.

Unless you specify otherwise with a Buffers command in CONFIG.SYS, DOS uses the following number of buffers:

2	If the system has less than 128 K of memory and 360 K diskette drives.
3	If the system includes a diskette drive with a capacity greater than 360 K.
5	If the system has more than 128 K of memory. (Version 3.3)
10	If the system has more than 256 K of memory. (Version 3.3)
15	If the system has more than 512 K of memory. (Version 3.3)

Finding the right number of buffers for your system might require some experimentation. After changing the number of buffers, use your system for a while and note its performance, then change the number of buffers and repeat your observations. Some programs may suggest or require a minimum number of buffers.

buffers=<number>

<number> is the number of buffers to be used. Valid numbers are 1 through 99 in versions 3.2 and earlier, 2 through 255 in version 3.3.

Example

To allocate 20 buffers, put the following Buffers command in CONFIG.SYS:

```
buffers=20
```

CONFIGURATION COMMANDS: COUNTRY
Set the International Date And Currency Format
Versions 2.1 and later, IBM releases 3.0 and later

Pages 335, 346

The Country command tells DOS which conventions to follow when displaying the date, by specifying a country code for a particular country. If there is no Country command in CONFIG.SYS, DOS follows the conventions of the country for which it was manufactured.

DOS also uses the country code to choose the currency symbol and the character that separates the thousands and decimal fraction parts of a number. Although these characters aren't used in normal DOS operation, the country code is available to application programs so that they can use the proper conventions.

country=<country-code>,<code-page>,<country-file>

<country-code> is the three-digit country code that specifies the country whose date format is to be followed; it is the same as the international telephone dialing prefix. DOS can recognize the following country codes. You must include all three digits, including any zeros at the beginning:

Country	Country Code
Versions 2.1 through 3.3:	
Australia	061
Belgium	032
Denmark	045
Finland	358
France	033
Israel	972
Italy	039
Netherlands	031
Norway	047
Spain	034
Sweden	046
Switzerland	041
United Kingdom	044
United States	001
West Germany	049

(continued)

Country	Country Code
Additional in version 3.3 only:	
Arabic	785
Canada (English)	001
Canada (French)	002
Latin America	003
Portugal	351

<code-page> is a three-digit number that specifies the code page that DOS is to use. Available code-page numbers are listed in the description of the Change Code Page Command (chcp). (Version 3.3)

<country-file> is the name of the DOS file that contains the country-specific information. If you omit <country-file>, DOS assumes the file is COUNTRY.SYS and is stored in the root directory of the current drive. (Version 3.3)

Example

In Belgium, the date is formatted as dd/mm/yyyy; for example, 16/10/1987 for October 16, 1987. To specify the Belgian format, put the following Country command in CONFIG.SYS:

```
country=032
```

CONFIGURATION COMMANDS: DEVICE

Define a Device-Control Program

Versions 2.0 and later

Page 296

The Device configuration command identifies a file that contains a program to control a device. DOS automatically recognizes and works with certain devices, such as the keyboard and the display. Other devices, however, can be added to a computer system, such as a mouse. If you add a device that DOS doesn't already know about, you must tell DOS the name of the device's controlling program. Such a control program, called a *device driver*, usually has the extension SYS and comes with the device. You can put more than one Device command in CONFIG.SYS.

device=<device>

<device> is the name of the file that contains the device driver.

The device drivers listed at the top of the next page are included with DOS.

Driver Name	DOS Version	Controls
ANSI.SYS	2.0 and later	Display and keyboard. This is an advanced use of DOS briefly described in the entry ANSI.SYS. Details are in the DOS *Technical Reference* manual and the book *Supercharging MS-DOS* (Van Wolverton, Microsoft Press, 1986).
VDISK.SYS	3.0 and later (IBM releases only)	Virtual disk drive; see VDISK.SYS
RAMDRIVE.SYS	3.2 and later (Microsoft releases)	Virtual disk drive; see VDISK.SYS
DISPLAY.SYS	3.3	Display (code-page switching; see Appendix B)
PRINTER.SYS	3.3	Printer (code-page switching; see Appendix B)

Example

To load the device driver (from the root directory) for the Microsoft Mouse, put the following Device command in CONFIG.SYS.

```
device=mouse.sys
```

CONFIGURATION COMMANDS: DRIVE PARAMETERS (DRIVPARM)

Define a Disk or Tape Drive

Versions 3.2 and later, non-IBM releases only

The Drive Parameters configuration command (drivparm) defines the operating characteristics of disk or tape drive. If you don't specify device characteristics, DOS assumes standard characteristics for that type of device. In general, you only need to use the Drivparm command if you attach a nonstandard disk or tape drive to your system. If you need more information on this command, refer to the documentation that came with your version of DOS.

CONFIGURATION COMMANDS: FCBS

Set Maximum Open File Control Blocks (FCBs)

Versions 3.0 and later, IBM releases 3.1 and later

One of the two ways DOS keeps track of file usage is by means of small blocks of information called File Control Blocks, or FCBs. The FCBS configuration command lets you specify the largest number of files controlled by File Control Blocks that can be open at the same time when file sharing is in effect. The FCBS command also lets you protect some or all of the open files from being automatically closed. Unless you specify otherwise, DOS assumes four FCB-controlled files, none of them protected from closure.

You're unlikely to need the FCBS configuration command in everyday use of your computer. If you need more information on this command, refer to the documentation that came with your version of DOS.

CONFIGURATION COMMANDS: FILES

Set Maximum Open File Handles

Versions 2.0 and later

Page 301

One of the two ways DOS keeps track of file usage is by assigning a number called a *handle* to each open file. The Files configuration command sets the maximum number of files controlled by a file handle that can be open at the same time.

files=<number>

<number> is the number of files that can be open at the same time. It can be from 8 through 255; if you don't specify <number>, DOS assumes 8. Each additional open file above eight increases the memory used by DOS by 48 bytes. If a program you're using requires more than eight open files, the documentation should help you include an appropriate Files command in CONFIG.SYS. If you need more information on this command, refer to the documentation that came with your version of DOS.

CONFIGURATION COMMANDS: LASTDRIVE

Define the Highest Drive Letter

Versions 3.0 and later

Page 301

The Lastdrive configuration command specifies the highest drive letter that DOS recognizes as valid. If CONFIG.SYS doesn't contain a Lastdrive command, the highest drive letter DOS recognizes is E. This command is used to specify a higher letter (up to Z) if more than five drive letters are needed—for example, because the computer uses many simulated disk drives (virtual disks or RAM disks), or because a large fixed disk is divided into sections, each referred to by a different drive letter.

lastdrive=<letter>

<letter> specifies the highest drive letter that DOS recognizes. It can be any letter from A through Z. If <drive> specifies fewer disk drives than the actual number attached to the computer, DOS ignores the Lastdrive command.

Example

To allow eight drive letters, you would include the following command in CONFIG.SYS:

```
lastdrive=h
```

CONFIGURATION COMMANDS: SHELL

Specify the Command Processor

Versions 2.0 and later

The Shell configuration command specifies the command processor—the program that receives your instructions at the keyboard and relays them to the appropriate DOS program—that DOS is to use. Unless you specify otherwise with a Shell command, DOS uses the program named COMMAND.COM. If you need to use a different command processor, the program requiring it should give you instructions on its use.

CONFIGURATION COMMANDS: STACKS

Reserve Memory for Temporary Program Use

Versions 3.2 and later

The Stacks configuration command tells DOS how much memory to reserve for its own temporary use. Some application programs may require a Stacks command in CONFIG.SYS, and should tell you how to do it; otherwise, you shouldn't need to use this command.

COPY

Copy a File or Device

Versions 1.0 and later

Pages 65, 114

Copy copies one or more files from a disk or a device to another file or device. File attributes are not copied; DOS won't copy a file to itself.

The Copy command has the following parameters. Some, such as /A and /B, are not often needed and thus are not described in the body of this book. Also, because the Copy command can be used with either files or devices, the following description refers to the *source* and *target* of a Copy command. In Chapter 5 and elsewhere, specific uses of the Copy command sometimes refer to *source* and *target* as either *file1* or *file2*, or as *device*.

copy <source> /A /B +<source> <target> /A /B /V

<source> is the file or device to be copied. You can use wildcard characters to copy a set of files with similar names or extensions. You can combine several source files into one target file by separating the source file names with a plus sign (+)—if you don't specify <target>, the files are combined into the first source file in the series; otherwise, the files are combined into <target>.

<target> is the file or device to which <source> is to be copied. If <source> is to be copied to the same directory on the same disk, <target> must be different from <source>. If you specify a source file on a different drive or in a different directory and you omit <target>, the source file is copied to a file with the same name in the current directory. If you specify just a drive letter, a path name, or a file name as <target>, the source file is copied as described below:

Target:	Source file is copied to:
Drive letter	A file with the same name in the current directory of the specified drive.
Path name	A file with the same name in the specified directory.
File name	A file with the specified name in the current directory.

/A (for *ASCII*) treats the preceding file named in the Copy command as a text file. If /A is included in a Copy command, it affects the file preceding the /A and all subsequent file names listed in the command up to, but not including, a file name followed by the /B option.

If /A is specified with one or more source files, the files are copied up to the first Ctrl-Z character in each. The Ctrl-Z and any data that follows are not copied. If /A is specified with one or more target files, DOS adds a Ctrl-Z character at the end of each file. When DOS combines files or copies to or from a device, it uses the /A option.

/B (for *binary*) treats the files as non-text files. If /B is specified with one or more source files, the files are copied in their entirety (based on the file size recorded in the directory entry). If /B is specified with one or more target files, DOS does not add a Ctrl-Z character at the end of each.

/V verifies that the file was copied correctly. DOS turns verification on, copies the file, then turns verification off. You don't need this parameter if you've turned on the DOS verify option with the Verify command. Verification slows the copy process.

Examples

To copy the file named REPORT.TXT from the root directory of drive A to a file named FINAL.RPT in the directory named \MKT\WP on the disk in the current drive:

```
C>copy a:\report.txt \mkt\wp\final.rpt
```

To copy the file named FORECAST.DOC from the directory named \MKT\WP on the disk in drive A to the current directory on the disk in the current drive, giving the file the same name:

```
C>copy a:\mkt\wp\forecast.doc
```

To copy all files with the extension TXT from the current directory of the disk in drive D to the current directory of the disk in the current drive, giving the copies the extension DOC:

```
C>copy d:*.txt *.doc
```

To combine the files named FCST-APR.DOC, FCST-MAY.DOC, and FCST-JUN.DOC in the current directory into a file named FCST-2Q.DOC in the current directory:

```
C>copy fcst-apr.doc+fcst-may.doc+fcst-jun.doc fcst-2q.doc
```

To add the files named FCST-MAY.DOC and FCST-JUN.DOC to the file named FCST-APR.DOC in the current directory:

```
C>copy fcst-apr.doc+fcst-may.doc+fcst-jun.doc
```

To combine all the files in the current directory whose extension is DOC, in the order in which their directory entries appear, into another file, named TOTAL.DOC, which is also in the current directory:

```
C>copy *.doc total.doc
```

Note: When you use wildcard characters to combine one or more source files into a target file that already exists, the original contents of the target file are lost—replaced by the contents of the combined source file(s). DOS does not warn you that data will be lost, but does display the message Content of destination lost before copy *when the copy procedure is completed. If you want to add files to an existing file, but keep the original information intact, use the plus sign between the names of the source files, specifying the target file name first.*

To copy the file REPORT.DOC to the display (CON):

```
C>copy report.doc con
```

The file is displayed, just as if you had entered *type report.doc*.

To copy from the keyboard (CON) to a file named REPORT.DOC in the current directory:

```
C>copy con report.doc
```

Type the lines you want in the file. To end the copy, press Ctrl-Z, then press Enter.

To copy from the keyboard (CON) to the printer (PRN):

```
C>copy con prn
```

Type the lines to be printed. To print the lines, press Ctrl-Z, then press Enter.

CTTY
Change the Console Device
Versions 2.0 and later

The CTTY command specifies the device to be used for standard input and standard output. You can assign standard input and output to a communications port, for example, to permit remote operation of the computer, or assign them to special devices supported by custom control programs.

Not all programs recognize the assignment of standard input and standard output. The Microsoft BASIC interpreter, for example, does not, and so is unaffected by the Change Console command.

ctty <device>

<device> is the name of the device that is to be used for standard input and standard output; the device must be capable of both input and output. If <device> specifies a device other than CON, AUX, or COM*n*, CONFIG.SYS must include a Device command that names the file that contains the control program (device driver) and DOS must have access to that file.

Examples

To assign standard input and standard output to communications port COM1:

```
C>ctty com1
```

To reassign standard input and standard output to the keyboard and display:

```
C>ctty con
```

DATE
Change or Display the System Date
Versions 1.0 and later

Page 12

The Date command displays the date maintained by DOS and prompts you to enter a new date. The sequence of the day, month, and year depends on the country code set with the Country or Select commands. The sequence here is for the United States.

date <mm-dd-yy>

<mm-dd-yy> is the new date to be set. <mm> is the month (1 through 12), <dd> is the day (1 through 31), and <yy> is the year (1980 or later). You can separate the day, month, and year with a hyphen, slash, or period: 10-16-87 or 10/16/87 or 10.16.87.

If you type just *date*, DOS displays the current date and prompts you to enter the new date. Type a new date or press the Enter key to leave the date unchanged.

Examples

To set the date to October 16, 1987:

```
C>date 10-16-87
```

To display the current system date and respond to the prompt for a new date:

```
C>date
```

DOS responds:

```
Current date is Tue  1-01-1980
Enter new date (mm-dd-yy): _
```

Type the new date, or press the Enter key to leave the current date unchanged.

DELETE (DEL)
Delete (Erase) a File

See Erase.

DIRECTORY (DIR)
Display Directory Entries
Versions 1.0 and later

Page 62

The Directory command (dir) displays the directory entry of one or more files. A Directory command display looks like the following:

```
 Volume in drive C is FIXEDDISK
 Directory of  C:\MKT\WP

.            <DIR>       9-02-87    5:24p
..           <DIR>       9-02-87    5:24p
REPORT   DOC     60780   8-15-87    1:09a
FORECAST DOC     18256  10-10-87    7:46p
SALESREP DOC     25728  10-13-87    8:42a
LETTERS      <DIR>
FCST-APR DOC      4328  10-12-87    9:07a
FCST-MAY DOC     20982   9-24-87   10:09p
STYLE        <DIR>
FCST-MAR DOC       996  10-12-87    5:36p
WKRPT    STY      2688  10-12-87    5:50p
BUDGET   DOC      5888  10-11-87    9:28a
       12 File(s)  23633152 bytes free
```

The first two lines show the volume label of the disk (FIXEDDISK) and the drive and path name of the directory whose entries are displayed (C:\MKT\WP). The last line shows the number of directory entries displayed (12) and the available space on the disk (23,633,152 bytes).

The directory entry for a file includes the file name and extension, size in bytes, and the date and time it was created or last changed. The directory entry for a subdirectory (LETTERS and STYLE in the preceding example) includes the file name and extension, followed by <DIR>.

The first two subdirectory entries in the preceding example are symbolic; the first (one period) represents the directory whose entries are displayed, and the second (two periods) represents the directory that contains the directory whose entries are displayed (sometimes referred to as the *parent* directory). The entries . and .. do not appear in the listing of the root directory of a disk.

dir <filename> /W /P

<filename> is the name of the file whose directory entry is to be displayed. You can use wildcard characters to display the entries of a set of files with similar names or extensions. If you omit <filename>, DOS displays the directory entry of each file in the specified or current directory. If you specify only a drive letter, DOS displays the directory entry of each file in the current directory of the specified drive. If you specify a file name but no extension, DOS displays the directory entry for each file with that file name, regardless of extension.

/W (for *wide*) displays just the file name and extension of each directory entry in five columns.

/P (for *pause*) displays the directory one screenful at a time, displaying *Strike a key when ready...* at the bottom of the screen. Pressing any key displays the next screenful of entries.

Examples

To display the directory entry of each file with the extension DOC in the current directory on the disk in drive A:

```
C>dir a:*.doc
```

To display the directory entry of each file in the directory \MKT\WP on the disk in the current drive, in wide format:

```
C>dir \mkt\wp /w
```

To display the directory entry of each file in the parent of the current directory on the disk in the current drive, pausing after each screenful:

```
C>dir .. /p
```

To display the directory entry of each file without an extension in the current directory on the disk in the current drive:

```
C>dir *
```

DISK COMPARE (DISKCOMP)
Compare Two Diskettes
Versions 3.2 and later, IBM releases 1.0 and later

Page 96

The Diskcomp command compares two diskettes sector-by-sector and reports the side and track of any sectors that differ; if the diskettes are identical, it reports *Compare OK*. Because it compares the sectors of the diskettes, Diskcomp does not necessarily report that two diskettes containing the same files are identical; the files could be stored in different locations.

The Diskcomp command automatically determines the number of sides and sectors per track from the disk in the first drive specified (which it calls the source). You cannot compare a diskette in a double-sided drive to a diskette in a single-sided drive, nor can you compare two diskettes with a different number of sectors per track. You can, however, compare just one side of diskettes in double-sided drives, or just the first 8 sectors of each track on diskettes written with 9 sectors per track.

Note: The Diskcomp command cannot be used with a fixed disk, with a drive created or affected by an Assign, Join, or Substitute command, nor with a network drive. It reports the side and track of any disk errors it encounters, then reports a difference between the diskettes because it cannot read the data in the damaged sector.

diskcomp <drive1> <drive2> /1 /8

<drive1> is the letter of the drive, followed by a colon, that contains the first diskette to be compared (such as *a:*).

<drive2> is the letter of the drive, followed by a colon, that contains the second diskette to be compared. If you omit <drive2> (type only one drive letter), DOS compares the diskette in <drive1> to the diskette in the current drive. If you omit both <drive1> and <drive2>, or if you omit <drive2> and specify the current drive as the <drive1>, or if you specify the same drive for both <drive1> and <drive2>, DOS prompts you through a one-drive comparison.

/1 compares only the first side of the diskettes, even if they are in double-sided diskette drives.

/8 compares only the first 8 sectors of each track, even if the diskettes have more sectors per track.

If you have only one diskette drive, or specify a one-drive comparison, the Diskcomp command prompts you to swap diskettes.

After it has compared the diskettes, the Diskcomp command prompts *Compare more diskettes (Y/N)?* If you reply *y*, it again prompts you to insert the source and target diskettes in the specified drives.

Examples

To compare the diskette in drive A to the diskette in drive B:

```
C>diskcomp a: b:
```

If you have only one diskette drive, the Diskcomp command tells you when to swap diskettes.

To compare the first side of the diskette in drive A to the first side of the diskette in the current drive (B):

```
B>diskcomp a: /1
```

If drive A were the current drive, DOS would prompt you through a one-drive comparison.

To compare two diskettes using only the current drive (A):

```
A>diskcomp
```

DISKCOPY

Copy a Complete Diskette

Versions 2.0 and later

Page 94

The Diskcopy command makes a sector-by-sector copy of a diskette. If the target diskette isn't formatted to match the source diskette, the Diskcopy command in all IBM releases of DOS formats it; in other releases numbered 2.0 through 3.1, the target diskette may need to be formatted before the Diskcopy command is entered.

Because the Diskcopy command makes an identical copy, it does not consolidate fragmented files; to consolidate fragmented files, use the Copy command and specify *.* to copy all files from the source diskette to the target diskette.

Note: The Diskcopy command cannot be used with a fixed disk, with a drive created or affected by an Assign, Join, or Substitute command, nor with a network drive. You cannot use Diskcopy with dissimilar diskette types—for example, a 720 K diskette and a 1.2 MB diskette. Nor can you copy a diskette in a double-sided drive to a diskette in a single-sided drive, although you can use the /1 option to copy the first side of a diskette in a double-sided drive to a diskette in a single-sided drive.

diskcopy <source> <target> /1

<source> is the letter, followed by a colon, of the drive that contains the diskette to be copied (such as *a:*). If you enter only one drive letter, DOS assumes it contains the source diskette.

<target> is the letter of the drive, followed by a colon, that contains the diskette to which <source> is to be copied. If you omit <target> (enter only one drive letter), DOS copies the diskette in <source> to the diskette in the current drive. If you omit both <source> and <target>, or if you omit <target> and specify the current drive (which cannot be a fixed disk) as the <source>, or if you specify the same drive for both <source> and <target>, DOS prompts you through a one-drive copy.

/1 copies only the first side of <source>, even if <source> is a double-sided diskette.

If you have only one diskette drive, or specify a single diskette drive as both the source and the target, DOS prompts you to swap diskettes.

After it has copied the diskette, DOS prompts *Copy another (Y/N)?* If you reply *y*, DOS prompts you to insert the source and target diskettes. After ending the Diskcopy command by replying *n* to the concluding prompt, you can verify the copy with the Diskcomp command.

The Diskcopy command reports the side, track, and sector of any disk errors it encounters. If these sectors contain valid data, the copy may not be usable.

Examples

To copy the diskette in drive A to the diskette in drive B:

```
C>diskcopy a: b:
```

If you have only one diskette drive, DOS prompts you through a one-drive copy.

On a system with two diskette drives, to copy the first side of the diskette in drive B to the first side of the diskette in the current drive (A):

```
A>diskcopy b: /1
```

If drive B were the current drive, DOS would prompt you through a one-drive copy.

To copy a diskette using only the current drive (A):

```
A>diskcopy
```

EDLIN
Create or Modify a Text File
Versions 1.0 and later

Page 182

Edlin is a program for creating and changing files of text. It includes a variety of single-letter commands for inserting, deleting, changing, copying, and moving lines. Each line can be up to 254 characters long. In addition to the Edlin commands, you can use the DOS editing keys to edit individual lines.

Because Edlin is a line-oriented editor, it displays a line number at the beginning of each line; these numbers are for reference only, and are not part of the file. Edlin renumbers lines after any command that changes the sequence or number of lines in the file, to maintain an unbroken sequence.

When you enter the Edlin command (type *edlin* followed by a file name) at the system prompt, Edlin loads the file to be edited (or creates it, if it's a new file), displays an asterisk (its prompt), and waits for a command. If the file to be edited would fill more than 75 percent of available memory, Edlin loads the file until the available memory is 75 percent full, then reserves the remaining 25 percent for additions. The Write and Append commands write edited lines to disk and read more unedited lines into memory, letting you edit a file larger than available memory.

Most Edlin commands consist of a single character preceded by one or more parameters. The command characters can be entered in either uppercase or lowercase; you end a command by pressing Enter. You can enter more than one command on a line, separating them with semicolons.

Just as DOS keeps track of a current drive and current directory, Edlin keeps track of the *current line*, which is the target for many commands if you don't specify a line number. Many of the Edlin commands operate on a range of lines, which you define by specifying the beginning and ending line numbers.

All Edlin commands that accept a line number or range of line numbers recognize the following symbolic references:

#	means the line after the last line in the file.
.	(a period) means the current line.
+ or –	specifies line numbers relative to the current line; for example, +3 means three lines past the current line.

When you end an editing session and write a revised file back to disk, Edlin renames the original version to give it the extension BAK, thus saving a backup copy of the original. If a file with the same name and the extension BAK exists on the same disk, Edlin deletes the existing file before renaming the original.

To start Edlin, you enter the Edlin command at the DOS system prompt.

edlin <filename> /B

<filename> is the name of the text file to be created or changed. If the file exists, Edlin copies it into memory. If the file doesn't exist, Edlin creates it. Except in version 3.3, Edlin won't edit a file whose extension is BAK. To edit a file whose extension is BAK, first change the extension with the DOS Rename command.

/B (for *binary*) loads the entire file even if the file contains one or more end-of-file marks (Ctrl-Z) before the last character. If you don't specify /B, Edlin loads the requested file up to the first Ctrl-Z.

For quick reference, the following table lists the name and form of the Edlin commands:

Command	Format
Append	<lines>a
Copy	<from>,<to>,<target>,<count>c
Delete	<from>,<to>d
Edit	<line> or .
End	e
Insert	<target>i
List	<from>,<to>l
Move	<from>,<to>,<target>m
Page	<from>,<to>p
Quit	q
Replace	<from>,<to>?r<string1><F6 or Ctrl-Z><string2>
Search	<from>,<to>?s<string>
Transfer	<target>t<filename>
Write	<lines>w

Individual command descriptions follow. The examples at the end of each description show representative uses of the command. Several examples use the symbolic references to show more than one way to accomplish the same editing task.

EDLIN: APPEND

Read Lines from Disk into Memory

Versions 1.0 and later

Page 210

The Edlin Append command reads additional lines of a file being edited from disk to the end of the file in memory. It is used when a file is larger than 75 percent of the available memory. To make room for the appended lines, you must use the Write command to write lines from memory to disk.

<lines>a

<lines> specifies the number of lines to append. If you omit <lines>, Edlin appends lines until 75 percent of the available memory is full. If that memory is already 75 percent full, Edlin ignores the Append command.

Examples

To append lines until available memory is 75 percent full:

```
*a
```

To append 200 lines:

```
*200a
```

EDLIN: COPY

Copy Lines

Versions 2.0 and later

Page 208

The Edlin Copy command copies one or more lines from one place in a file to another. The first copied line becomes the new current line.

<from>,<to>,<target>,<count>c

<from> is the number of the first line to be copied. If you don't specify <from>, Edlin starts with the current line. If you omit <from>, you must still enter the comma that follows, to show that you omitted it.

<to> is the number of the last line to be copied. The number in <to> must be equal to or greater than the number in <from>. If you don't specify <to>, Edlin stops with the current line. If you omit <to>, you must still enter the comma that follows, to show that you omitted it. To copy a single line, specify the same line number for both <to> and <from>. To copy the current line, omit both <from> and <to> and begin the command with two commas.

<target> is the number of the line *before* which the lines are to be copied. You must enter <target>.

<count> specifies how many times the lines are to be copied. If you don't specify <count>, Edlin copies the lines once.

Examples

The following examples assume that the current line is 20.

To copy lines 20 through 25 before line 5:

```
*20,25,5c
```

or

```
*,25,5c
```

To copy line 20 through the last line before line 5:

```
*20,#,5c
```

To copy line 20 before line 30:

```
*20,20,30c
```

or

```
*,,+10c
```

To copy lines 20 through 25 three times before line 1:

```
*20,25,1,3c
```

or

```
*,+5,1,3c
```

To copy line 20 fifteen times before line 10:

```
*,20,10,15c
```

EDLIN: DELETE

Delete a Line

Versions 1.0 and later

Page 187

The Delete command deletes lines from the file. The line after the last line deleted becomes the new current line.

<from>,<to>d

<from> is the number of the first line to be deleted. If you don't specify <from>, Edlin starts with the current line. If you omit <from>, you must still enter the comma, to show that you omitted <from>.

<to> is the number of the last line to be deleted. The number in <to> must be equal to or greater than <from>. If you don't specify <to>, Edlin deletes just the line specified by <from>. If you omit both <from> and <to> (just type *d*), Edlin deletes the current line.

Examples

The following examples assume that the current line is 20.

To delete lines 20 through 25:

```
*20,25d
```

or

```
*,+5d
```

To delete line 20:

```
*20d
```

or

```
*d
```

To delete line 20 through the last line in the file:

```
*20,#d
```

or

```
*,#d
```

EDLIN: EDIT

Edit a Line

Versions 1.0 and later

Page 193

There is no Edit command character. To edit a line, simply type the line number and press enter; Edlin displays the line, moves the cursor to the beginning of the next line, displays the line number and the following colon, then waits for you to edit the line. You can change the line by pressing the editing keys or by typing new text, or you can leave the line unchanged by pressing Enter when the cursor is at the beginning of the line. The line you are editing becomes the new current line.

You can edit the current line by typing a period and pressing Enter; you can edit the line that follows the current line just by pressing Enter. This lets you quickly step through the file line by line.

<line> or .

<line> is the number of the line to be edited. If you specify <line> as a period, Edlin displays the current line for editing. If you omit <line>, Edlin displays the line following the current line.

Examples

The following examples assume that the current line is 20. Pressing the Enter key is represented by <Enter>.

To edit line 25:

```
*25<Enter>
```

or

```
*+5<Enter>
```

To edit line 20:

```
*.<Enter>
```

To edit line 21:

```
*<Enter>
```

To edit the last line in the file:

```
*#;-1<Enter>
```

This example shows two commands on the same line. The # at the beginning of the command changes the current line to the line following the last line in the file. The *–1* specifies the line above the current line. The semicolon (;) separates the two commands.

EDLIN: END EDIT
End the Editing Session
Versions 1.0 and later

Page 186

The End edit command writes the file currently being edited from memory to disk and ends the editing session. (To end the session without saving the file, use the Edlin Quit command, described later.)

If an existing file was being edited, Edlin changes the extension of the original file to BAK. If there isn't room on the disk to save the revised version of the file, Edlin writes as much of the file as it can on the disk, gives the file the same name with the extension $$$, and displays the message *Disk full. Edits lost*; the part of the file in memory is lost (in this case, Edlin does not change the extension of the original to BAK).

If the last line of the file doesn't end with a carriage return when you enter the End command, Edlin adds a carriage return. If the last character of the file isn't a Ctrl-Z, Edlin adds a Ctrl-Z.

The End edit command has no parameters.

Example

To end an editing session and save the current file on disk:

```
*e
```

EDLIN: INSERT
Insert Lines
Versions 1.0 and later

Page 185

The Insert command enters new lines into the file being edited. Edlin prompts with the number of the new line, and continues to prompt for a new line each time you press Enter, until you press Ctrl-C to stop inserting lines. The first line following the inserted line or lines becomes the new current line.

You can enter a control character (such as Ctrl-G to cause the system to beep) into a file by first pressing Ctrl-V and then typing the uppercase letter that corresponds to the control character you want to enter. To include an Escape character, press Ctrl-V and then the left bracket key ([ ). This is a convenient way to create escape sequences to use with ANSI.SYS or with programs that require an Escape character in a text file.

<target>i

<target> is the line before which the new lines are to be inserted. If you don't specify <target>, Edlin inserts the new lines before the current line. If you specify <target> as # or as a number larger than the highest line number in the file, Edlin adds the lines at the end of the file.

Examples

The following examples assume that the current line is 20.

To insert lines after line 20:

```
*21i
```

To insert lines before line 17:

```
*17i
```

or

```
*-3i
```

To insert lines at the beginning of the file:

```
*1i
```

To insert lines at the end of the file:

```
*#i
```

EDLIN: LIST
Display Specified Lines
Versions 1.0 and later

Page 184

The List command displays one or more lines of the file being edited. It doesn't change the current line.

<from>,<to>l

<from> is the number of the first line to be displayed. If you don't specify <from>, Edlin starts the display with the line 11 lines before the current line. If you omit <from> but want to specify <to>, you must enter the comma, to show that you omitted <from>.

<to> is the number of the last line to be displayed. It must be equal to or greater than <from>. If you omit <to>, Edlin displays 23 lines starting with <from>. If you omit both <from> and <to> (just type *l*), Edlin displays 23 lines centered about the current line; if the current line is less than 13, Edlin displays a total of 23 lines, starting at the beginning of the file.

Examples

The following examples assume that the current line is 30.

To display lines 30 through 40:

```
*30,40l
```

To display lines 19 (11 lines before the current line) through 35:

```
*,35l
```

or

```
*,+5l
```

To display 23 lines centered around line 30 (lines 19 through 41):

```
*l
```

If the current line were 10, *l* would display lines 1 through 23.

To display only line 30:

```
*30,30l
```

EDLIN: MOVE
Move Lines
Versions 2.0 and later

Page 207

The Edlin Move command moves a line or lines from one place in the file to another, deleting them from the original location and renumbering the lines of the file. The first line moved becomes the new current line.

<from>,<to>,<target>m

<from> is the number of the first line to be moved. If you don't specify <from>, Edlin starts with the current line. If you omit <from>, you must enter the comma that follows, to show that you omitted it.

<to> is the number of the last line to be moved. It must be equal to or greater than <from>. If you don't specify <to>, Edlin stops with the current line. If you omit <to>, you must enter the comma that follows, to show that you omitted it. To move a single line, specify the same line number as both <from> and <to>. To move the current line, omit both <from> and <to> and begin the command with two commas.

<target> is the line before which the lines are to be moved. You must enter it.

Examples

The following examples assume that the current line is 20.

To move lines 20 through 25 before line 5:

```
*20,25,5m
```

or

```
*,+5,-15m
```

To move lines 20 through the last line in the file before line 5:

```
*20,#,5m
```

or

```
*,#,5m
```

To move line 20 before line 30:

```
*20,20,30m
```

or

```
*,,30m
```

To move the last 15 lines in the file before line 1:

```
*#;-15,#,1m
```

This example shows two commands on the same line. The # at the beginning of the command changes the current line to the line following the last line in the file. The *–15, #, 1m* moves the preceding 15 lines to the beginning of the file. The semicolon (;) separates the two commands.

EDLIN: PAGE
Display a Screenful of Lines
Versions 2.0 and later

Page 205

The Page command displays one or more lines of a file, up to one screenful at a time. Unlike the List command, the Page command changes the current line to the last line displayed; this lets you page through a file 23 lines (one screenful) at a time by entering successive Page commands with no parameters.

<from>,<to>p

<from> is the number of the first line to be displayed. If you don't specify <from>, Edlin starts with the line after the current line. If you omit <from>, you must enter the comma, to show that you omitted <from>.

<to> is the number of the last line to be displayed. It must be equal to or greater than <from>. If you don't specify <to>, Edlin displays 23 lines starting with <from>. If you omit both <from> and <to> (just type *p*), Edlin displays 23 lines starting with the line after the current line.

Examples

The following examples assume that the current line is 30.

To display lines 30 through 40 and change the current line to 40:

```
*30,40p
```

To display 23 lines starting with the line after the current line (lines 31 through 53):

```
*p
```

EDLIN: QUIT
Terminate the Editing Session
Versions 1.0 and later

Page 188

The Quit command ends an Edlin session without saving any changes to the file currently being edited. To reduce the chance of your inadvertently losing work, Edlin prompts for confirmation before quitting. The Quit command has no parameters.

q

Example

To quit the editing session without saving the current file:

```
*q
```

Edlin responds:

```
Abort edit (Y/N)?
```

Reply *y* to return to DOS without saving the revised file; reply *n* to remain in Edlin.

EDLIN: REPLACE
Replace One Character String with Another
Versions 1.0 and later

Page 191

The Edlin Replace command replaces one character string with another, in one or more lines of the file. Edlin displays the line or lines that are changed. You can tell

Edlin to prompt for confirmation before each replacement (rather than change all occurrences) with the question mark (?) parameter of the Replace command. The last line changed becomes the new current line.

<from>,<to>?r<string1><Ctrl-Z or F6><string2>

<from> is the number of the first line in which the string is to be replaced. If you don't specify <from>, you must still enter the comma, to show that you omitted <from>. Edlin then starts replacing with the line following the current line.

<to> is the number of the last line in which the string is to be replaced. It must be equal to or greater than <from>. If you don't specify <to>, Edlin stops with the last line in the file. To change one line, use the same line number for <from> and <to>.

? tells Edlin to prompt you for confirmation before each replacement. Edlin displays the line as it will be changed and asks *O.K.?* If you reply *y* or press Enter, Edlin makes the change; if you reply *n*, Edlin doesn't make the change.

<string1> is the string to be replaced. If you don't specify <string1>, Edlin uses the last <string1> you specified with a Search or Replace command; if there was no preceding <string1>, Edlin displays the message *Entry error*. If you omit <string1> but include <string2>, you must enter the Ctrl-Z (by pressing Ctrl and Z or by pressing F6) before typing <string2>, to show that you omitted <string1>.

<string2> is the replacement string. If you enter both <string1> and <string2>, separate them with Ctrl-Z. If you omit <string2>, each occurrence of <string1> is replaced with the last replacement string you specified with a Replace command. If you omit <string2> but end <string1> with Ctrl-Z, each occurrence of <string1> is deleted (replaced with a null string). If another command follows the Replace command on the same line, end <string2> with Ctrl-Z.

Examples

The following examples assume that the current line is 20. <Ctrl-Z> means press either Ctrl-Z or F6.

To replace all occurrences of *company* with *corporation* in lines 21 through 30:

```
*21,30rcompany<Ctrl-Z>corporation
```

or

```
*,30rcompany<Ctrl-Z>corporation
```

To replace all occurrences of *March* with *April* from line 21 through the end of the file, instructing Edlin to prompt before each replacement:

```
*21,#?rMarch<Ctrl-Z>April
```

or

```
*,#?rMarch<Ctrl-Z>April
```

EDLIN: SEARCH
Find a String
Versions 1.0 and later

Page 189

The Edlin Search command searches for a character string. If Edlin finds the string, it displays the line, makes it the current line, and stops searching. You can also tell Edlin to prompt you for confirmation before stopping the search; this lets you continue the search beyond the first occurrence of the string.

If Edlin doesn't find the string, it displays *Not found* and leaves the current line unchanged.

<from>,<to>?s<string>

<from> is the number of the first line to be searched. If you don't specify <from>, you must still enter the comma, to show that you omitted <from>. Edlin then starts with the line following the current line.

<to> is the number of the last line to be searched. It must be equal to or greater than <from>. If you don't specify <to>, Edlin stops with the last line in the file.

? tells Edlin to prompt you for confirmation before ending the search. Edlin displays the line that contains the string, then *O.K.?* If you reply *y* or press Enter, Edlin makes the displayed line the current line and stops searching; if you reply *n*, Edlin searches for the next occurrence of <string>.

<string> is the string to search for. If another command follows the Search command on the same line, follow <string> with Ctrl-Z.

Examples

The following examples assume that the current line is 20.

To find the first occurrence of *value* in lines 21 through 30:

```
*21,30svalue
```

or

```
*,30svalue
```

To find a particular occurrence of *value,* searching the entire file and instructing Edlin to prompt before setting the current line and stopping the search:

```
*1,#?svalue
```

EDLIN: TRANSFER
Copy Another File into The One Being Edited
Versions 2.0 and later

Page 209

The Transfer command merges the contents of another file into the file you're editing.

<target>t<filename>

<target> is the number of the line before which the contents of the file will be merged. If you don't specify <target>, Edlin assumes the current line.

<filename> is the name of the file whose contents are to be merged with the file you're editing. The file name can be preceded by a drive letter and, in version 3, a directory path.

Example

The following example assumes that the current line is 20.

To merge the contents of the file named REPORT.DOC before line 20:

```
*20treport.doc
```

or

```
*treport.doc
```

EDLIN: WRITE
Write Lines from Memory to Disk
Versions 1.0 and later

Page 210

The Edlin Write command writes lines from the beginning of the file being edited to the disk. It makes room for more lines to be read from disk with the Append command.

<lines>w

<lines> specifies the number of lines to write. If you omit <lines>, Edlin writes lines until available memory is 25 percent full. If that memory is already no more than 25 percent full, Edlin ignores the Write command.

Examples

To write lines to disk until available memory is 25 percent full:

```
*w
```

To write 200 lines to disk:

```
*200w
```

ERASE
Erase a File
Versions 1.0 and later

Page 70
The Erase command (erase or del) erases a file or set of files.

erase <filename>

<filename><filename> is the name of the file to be erased. You can use wildcard characters to erase a set of files with similar file names or extensions.

Examples

To erase the file named REPORT.DOC in the current directory on the disk in the current drive:

```
C>erase report.doc
```

To erase all files with the extension BAK in the directory named \MKT\WP on the disk in drive A:

```
C>erase a:\mkt\wp\*.bak
```

EXE2BIN
Convert an Executable (EXE) File To COM Format
Versions 1.0 and later

The Exe2bin command converts a program command file from EXE format to COM format. Exe2bin is an advanced DOS command, usually used by programmers, and a description of its use is beyond the scope of this book; if you need details, refer to the DOS *Technical Reference* or the *Programmer's Reference* manual.

EXIT
End a Secondary Command Processor
Versions 2.0 and later

The Exit command stops a secondary copy of COMMAND.COM (the DOS command processor) and returns control of the system to the program or previous copy of COMMAND.COM that requested the copy. The Exit command has no effect if a secondary copy of COMMAND.COM hasn't been loaded, or if the secondary command processor was loaded by a Command command with the /P (for permanent) parameter. The Exit command has no parameters.

exit

Example

To terminate a secondary, nonpermanent copy of COMMAND.COM and return control to the original command processor:

```
C>exit
```

FASTOPEN
Speed Up File Access
Version 3.3

Page 303

The Fastopen command tells DOS to keep in memory a list of the fixed-disk storage locations of subdirectories and files that have been used during the current session. When the Fastopen command is used, DOS checks in memory before searching the disk whenever it is told to find a file or a subdirectory. If the file or subdirectory has already been used, its disk location is in memory, and DOS can go directly to the storage location, instead of searching for it through each directory in the path. Fastopen cannot be used to keep track of files stored on a network drive.

fastopen <drive>=<files>

<drive> is the drive letter, followed by a colon, of the fixed disk whose files and subdirectories you want DOS to track. The drive letter must refer to a fixed disk.

<files> is the number of file and subdirectory locations DOS is to keep in memory. The number of files must be separated from <drive> by an equal sign. You can specify up to 999 files; each file requires about 40 bytes of memory. If you don't specify <files>, DOS keeps track of the last 34 files and subdirectories (the last 10 in non-IBM releases of DOS).

Note: You can enter the Fastopen command only once during a session with DOS. If you or your application programs tend to use the same files or directories over and over, the Fastopen command can make your system noticeably faster. If you find this is true for you, consider putting a Fastopen command in AUTOEXEC.BAT.

Example

To keep track of the last 50 files and subdirectories used on the fixed disk in drive C:

```
C>fastopen c:=50
```

FILE COMPARISON (FC)

Compare Two Files

Versions 2.0 and later, non-IBM releases only

The File Comparison command (fc) compares two files and sends the differences to standard output—normally the display. By redirecting output, you can also send the results of a comparison to a file or to another device, such as a printer.

Note: Another way to compare files is with the Compare command, available in IBM versions of DOS and in Microsoft's version 3.3. It's described in the entry COMPARE.

You can use FC to compare either text files or command files (program files with such extensions as EXE, COM, and SYS). Depending on the parameters you specify, you can compare files either line by line or byte by byte.

In a line-by-line comparison, FC starts by reading as many lines from each file as will fit in the portion of memory it uses (enough to hold 100 lines, unless you specify otherwise). It then compares the lines of the first file against the lines of the second.

If it finds any differences, FC displays the name of the first file, the last line that matched, each subsequent mismatched line, and the first matching line that follows the mismatches. It then displays the same type of information for the second file. If the files contain more than one group of mismatched lines, FC reports on each group until it either reaches the last of the lines in memory or runs out of memory space.

When it finds mismatched lines, FC assumes that the lines of the two files are no longer synchronized—they don't correspond on a one-to-one basis. Unless you specify otherwise, FC looks for two sequential matching lines before it once again assumes the files are synchronized. If FC finds more mismatched lines than will fit into the amount of memory it has set aside for the comparison, the comparison stops and you see the message *Resynch failed. Files are too different* (**** Files are different**** in some versions of DOS).

If all the lines in memory have been compared and one file is shorter than the other, you see a message at the end of the report. For example, if FILE1 has fewer lines than FILE2, FC reports on any mismatches and ends by displaying the message *fc: file2 longer than file1.*

The other type of comparison (byte-by-byte) that FC performs is useful primarily for checking program files stored in machine-readable, rather than human-readable, form. In a byte-by-byte comparison, FC reads as much of the files as it can into memory and compares them, then continues loading more parts of the files until it has compared both files completely. It does not display mismatched lines, but tells you which bytes (counting from the beginning of the file) are different, and what their coded values are in the hexadecimal (base-16) numbering system.

For example, if FILE1 contains *This is file 1* and FILE2 contains *This is file 2*, the File Comparison command displays the following report when you do a byte-by-byte comparison of the two files:

```
0000000D: 31 32
```

telling you that the byte 13 (D in hexadecimal, counting from 0) has the value 31 in FILE1 and 32 in FILE2. (If you're curious, the hexadecimal value 31 is the code the computer uses for the numeral 1; likewise, hexadecimal 32 is the code for 2.)

The File Comparison command includes the following parameters; if you're using version 3.1 or earlier, note that some parameters are not available:

fc /B /A /C /L /LB*n* /N /*nnnn* /T /W <filename1> <filename2>

/B (for *binary*) specifies that the files are to be compared byte by byte. If you use /B, you cannot use any parameters other than <filename1> and <filename2>.

/A tells FC to abbreviate its report, displaying only the beginning and ending lines of each group of matched/mismatched lines. (Versions 3.2 and later)

/C tells FC to ignore differences between uppercase and lowercase.

/L tells FC you want a line-by-line comparison. It assumes this parameter for all text files (those without program-file extensions, such as EXE, COM, and SYS). (Versions 3.2 and later)

/LB*n*, where *n* is a number you supply, specifies how many lines FC reads into memory. If you don't specify a number (for example, */LB200*) FC assumes 100.

/N tells FC to display line numbers in its report of an ASCII comparison.

/*nnnn*, where *nnnn* is a number you supply, tells FC how many matching lines it must find after a mismatch to assume that the two files once again correspond on a line-by-line basis. If you don't specify *nnnn*, FC assumes 2 lines (3 lines in versions through 3.2).

/T tells FC to treat tabs as tabs, rather than as strings of blanks.

/W tells FC to ignore spaces and tabs at the beginning and end of lines, and to convert consecutive spaces and tabs within a line to a single space.

<filename1> is the name of the first file to be compared. It can include a drive letter and path, but not wildcard characters.

<filename2> is the name of the second file to be compared. It can include a drive letter and path, but not wildcard characters.

Examples

Suppose two text files named FILE1.DOC and FILE2.DOC in the current directory on the disk in the current drive contain the lines shown on the next page (mismatched lines are in *italics*).

FILE1.DOC	FILE2.DOC
First line.	First line.
Second line.	Second line.
Third line.	Third line.
Fourth line.	*Seventh line.*
Fifth line.	*Eighth line.*
Sixth line.	*Ninth line.*
Seventh line.	*Tenth line.*
Eighth line.	*Fourth line.*
Ninth line.	*Fifth line.*
Tenth line.	*Sixth line.*
Eleventh line.	Eleventh line.
Twelfth line.	Twelfth line.
Thirteenth line.	Thirteenth line.
Fourteenth line.	Fourteenth line.
Fifteenth line.	Fifteenth line.

To compare the files line by line:

```
C>fc file1.doc file2.doc
```

FC displays the blocks of lines that differ, treating the files as matched after two consecutive matched lines following a mismatch (the comments to the right are descriptive and aren't part of the command output):

```
***** file1.doc         Name of first file
Third line.             Last match
Fourth line.
Fifth line.             Mismatched lines
Sixth line.
Seventh line.           First of two more matching lines
***** file2.doc         Name of second file
Third line.             Last match
Seventh line.           Next match (no intervening mismatches)
*****                   Files synchronized at this point

***** file1.doc         Name of first file
Tenth line.             Last match
Eleventh line.          Next match (no intervening mismatches)
***** file2.doc         Name of second file
Tenth line.             Last match
Fourth line.
Fifth line.             More mismatched lines
Sixth line.
Eleventh line.          Next match
*****                   Resynchronized ; no more mismatches
```

The following command and its resulting output show what happens when five lines, rather than two, are needed to synchronize the files (again, the comments to the right aren't part of the output):

```
C>fc /5 file1.doc file2.doc

***** file1.doc        Name of first file
Third line.            Last match
Fourth line.
Fifth line.
Sixth line.
Seventh line.          Mismatches
Eighth line.
Ninth line.
Tenth line.
Eleventh line.         First of five matching lines
***** file2.doc        Name of second file
Third line.            Last match
Seventh line.
Eighth line.
Ninth line.
Tenth line.            Mismatches
Fourth line.
Fifth line.
Sixth line.
Eleventh line.         First of five matching lines
*****
```

To compare two text files named REPORT.DOC and REPORT.BAK in the current directory on the disk in the current drive, ignoring case and redirecting the output to the printer:

```
C>fc /c report.doc report.bak > prn
```

To compare the same files, ignoring leading and trailing spaces and tabs, compressing each internal space and tab to a single space, and redirecting the output to a file named REPORT.DIF:

```
C>fc /w report.doc report.bak > report.dif
```

To compare byte by byte two nontext files named PICTURE.MSP, the first in the current directory on the current drive and the second in the directory named \WIN on the disk in drive A:

```
C>fc /b picture.msp a:\win\picture.msp
```

FDISK
Configure a Fixed Disk
Versions 3.2 and later, IBM releases 2.0 and later

The Fdisk command prepares a fixed disk for use by DOS. It creates on the disk one or more independent areas called *partitions*.

Computers are often delivered with the fixed disk already prepared—sometimes with DOS already installed and ready to start from the fixed disk. To check whether this has been done, try to start the system from the fixed disk. You can also start the system with a DOS diskette, then use the Fdisk command to try to create a partition for DOS; the Fdisk command tells you if the disk has already been configured.

fdisk

The Fdisk command has no parameters; when you type *fdisk*, you start a program that steps you through the procedure via a series of question-and-answer menus. For more details, see Appendix A, "Preparing Your Fixed Disk," or the documentation that came with your version of DOS.

FIND
Search Files for a Character String
Versions 2.0 and later

Page 233
The Find filter command searches one or more files for a character string, and sends each line that contains the string to standard output (usually the display).

find /V /C /N <"string"> <filename>

/V finds lines that *don't* contain <string>.

/C sends the total number of lines, rather than the lines themselves, to standard output. If you specify both /C and /N, the Find command ignores /N.

/N includes the line number with each line of output.

<"string"> is the character string to search for. You must enclose the string in quotation marks. To include a quotation mark in <string>, type two quotation marks.

<filename> is the name of the file or files to be searched. You can specify more than one file name, separating them with spaces. If you omit <filename>, the Find command searches its standard input; you can either redirect standard input or pipe the output of another command to the Find command. You cannot use wildcards in <file name>.

Examples

To find all lines that contain the string *Sales* (note the capital *S*) in the file REPORT.DOC in the current directory:

```
C>find "Sales" report.doc
```

To find all lines that don't contain the string <DIR> in the output of a Directory command:

```
C>dir ¦ find /v "<DIR>"
```

To find all lines that contain the string *April* in the file LETTERS.DOC in the current directory, include the line numbers, and redirect the output to the printer:

```
C>find /n "April" letters.doc > prn
```

To display just the number of lines that don't contain the string *Sales* in the files named FCST-APR.DOC and REPORT.DOC in the current directory:

```
C>find /c /v "Sales" fcst-apr.doc report.doc
```

FORMAT

Prepare a Disk

Versions 1.0 and later

Page 91

The Format command prepares a disk for use by DOS. Because formatting destroys any data written on the disk, DOS requests confirmation before formatting the disk. Be sure you know that the specified drive contains the disk to be formatted, especially if you're using 3.1 or an earlier version of DOS. With these versions, if you don't specify a drive letter with the Format command, DOS formats the disk in the current drive even if it's a system disk or a fixed disk.

Note: Don't use Format with a drive affected by a Join or Substitute command. Format can't be used with a network drive. The following description includes some parameters not mentioned in earlier chapters.

format <drive> /V /B /O /1 /4 /8 /N:<sectors> /T:<tracks> /S

<drive> is the letter of the drive, followed by a colon, that contains the disk to be formatted. Although specifying a drive letter isn't mandatory through version 3.1, you should make a habit of typing the drive letter of the disk you want to format.

/V prompts you for a volume label after the disk is formatted. If you specify /B, you cannot specify /V.

/B formats a diskette for eight sectors per track, and reserves space for the DOS hidden files. The hidden files aren't copied to the disk but, because space is reserved for the system files, you can later copy any version of DOS to the disk with the System (sys) command.

/O prepares a diskette that is compatible with version 1 of the IBM releases of DOS. Don't use this parameter unless you need the compatibility, because it takes longer to format a disk this way, and disk operations on the resulting disk will be noticeably slower. This parameter may not be included in your version of DOS.

/1 formats only the first side of a 5.25-inch diskette, even if the drive is a double-sided drive.

/4 formats a single-sided (180 K) or double-sided (360 K) diskette in a 1.2 MB high-capacity drive. Diskettes formatted with this parameter in a high-capacity drive may not work reliably in a 180 K or 360 K diskette drive.

/8 formats a 5.25-inch diskette for 8 sectors per track.

/N:<sectors> specifies the number of sectors per track to format, if you want to format less than the maximum capacity of the diskette drive. If you specify /N:<sectors>, you must also specify /T:<tracks>. (Version 3.2 or later)

/T:<tracks> specifies the number of tracks to format, if you want to format less than the maximum capacity of the diskette drive. If you specify /T:<tracks>, you must also specify /N:<sectors>. (Version 3.2 or later)

/S creates a system disk by copying DOS files to the formatted disk. /S must be the last entry on the command line. If you specify /B, you cannot specify /S.

Examples

To format the diskette in drive A:

```
C>format a:
```

To format the diskette in drive A and assign it a volume label:

```
C>format a: /v
```

After formatting the disk, DOS prompts you to enter a volume label of 11 characters or less. You can change or delete this volume label later with the Volume (vol) command.

To format a system disk in drive A and assign it a volume label:

```
C>format a: /v /s
```

Notice that /S is the last parameter in the command.

To format a 360 K diskette in a 1.2 MB drive:

```
C>format a: /4
```

GRAFTABL

Enable Graphics Character Set

Versions 3.0 and later

Page 116

The Load Graphics Table command (graftabl) enables DOS to display special characters, such as accented letters, symbols, and line-drawing characters (character codes 128–255). When you use the Graftabl command, DOS can display the characters when the color/graphics adapter is in graphics mode. The command is unnecessary with an enhanced graphics adapter, and has no effect when the monochrome display adapter is used. You can use Graftabl only once during a session with DOS.

graftabl <code-page> /status

<code-page> is the three-digit number that specifies the code page that DOS is to use. You cannot specify <code-page> in versions prior to 3.3. Valid code pages are:

437	United States
850	Multilingual (non-IBM versions only)
860	Portuguese
863	Canada (French)
865	Nordic

/status displays the current code page. (Version 3.3)

Examples

To enable DOS to display the graphics characters in graphics mode:

```
C>graftabl
```

DOS reads the table of character definitions into memory and tells you so. If you enter a Graftabl command again, DOS simply tells you the characters are already loaded and returns to the system prompt.

To enable DOS to display the Canadian French character set (code page 863) in graphics mode (version 3.3):

```
C>graftabl 863
```

To display the current graphics code page (version 3.3):

```
C>graftabl /status
```

GRAPHICS

Enable Printing of a Graphics Display

Versions 3.2 and later, IBM releases 2.0 and later

Page 115

The Graphics command loads a program that DOS keeps in memory to print the display produced by a color/graphics adapter used in a graphics mode. After you enter the Graphics command, pressing Shift-PrtSc enables DOS to print either a color/graphics screen or the text-based display produced by a monochrome adapter.

Note: Not all printers can reproduce graphics images. The Graphics command itself is not compatible with Hercules monochrome graphics adapters or with enhanced graphics adapters in enhanced display modes.

The Graphics command can include several parameters or none at all; to see which, if any, are available to you, check the documentation that came with your version of DOS.

graphics <printer> /R /B /LCD /C /F /P<port>

<printer> specifies the type of printer supported; it can be one of the following:

color1	IBM Personal Computer Color Printer or compatible with a black ribbon.
color4	IBM Personal Computer Color Printer or compatible with a red-green-blue-black (RGB) ribbon.
color8	IBM Personal Computer Color Printer or compatible with a cyan-magenta-yellow-black (CMY) ribbon.
compact	IBM Personal Computer Compact Printer or compatible.
graphics	IBM Personal Computer Graphics Printer, IBM Proprinter, or compatible.
thermal	IBM PC Convertible Printer or compatible (version 3.3).

If you don't specify <printer>, DOS assumes *graphics.*

/R prints the screen as you see it on the display: light images on a dark background.

/B prints the background in color. It is valid only if <mode> is *color4* or *color8.*

/LCD prints the image from the liquid crystal display (LCD) screen of the IBM PC Convertible. (Version 3.3)

/C centers the printed image on the paper. It works with an image resolution of 640 by 200 or with a 320-by-200 image printed with the /F parameter.

/F rotates a 320-by-200 image 90 degrees (prints it sideways).

/P <port> specifies the printer port. It can be *1* (LPT1), *2* (LPT2), or *3* (LPT3).

On a non-color printer, the Graphics command prints the screen with up to four shades of gray. On a color printer, screen colors are reproduced with or without the background color, depending on the Graphics parameter you specify. If the display is in 640-by-200 graphics mode, the printed image is rotated 90 degrees (printed sideways).

Examples

To enable printing a graphics display on an IBM Personal Computer Graphics printer:

```
C>graphics
```

To enable printing a graphics display with a colored background on an IBM Personal Computer Color printer with an RGB ribbon:

```
C>graphics color4 /b
```

To enable printing a graphics display on an IBM Personal Computer Graphics printer, reversing the image so that a reverse-video image is printed (white-on-black):

```
C>graphics /r
```

INPUT/OUTPUT REDIRECTION

Redirecting Standard Input and Standard Output

Page 228

Unless instructed otherwise, DOS takes its input from standard input (usually the keyboard) and sends its output to standard output (usually the screen). You can redirect standard input and output, however, to a file or a device by using the symbols <, >, and >>. If a program writes to standard output, as the DOS commands do, its output can also be sent with the pipe symbol (¦) to the input of a program that reads standard input.

The < and > symbols redirect the input or output of a command or program.

The < symbol redirects input. For example, to tell the Sort filter command to read its input from the file named LIST.DOC, you would type *sort < list.doc*.

Similarly, you redirect output with the > symbol. For example, to send the output of a Directory command to a file named DIRFILE.DOC in the current directory, you would type *dir > dirfile.doc*. If there were no file named DIRFILE.DOC, DOS would create it. If a file named DIRFILE.DOC already existed, DOS would replace its contents with the output of the Directory command.

You can, however, tell DOS to *add* output to the end of an existing file by using the symbols >>. For example, to add the output of the Directory command to an existing file named DIRFILE.DOC, you would type *dir > > dirfile.doc*. If the file didn't exist, DOS would create it, just as in the previous example, which used the > symbol.

You can redirect input and output from and to devices as well as files, and you can redirect both the input and output of a program. For example, to tell the Sort command to read its input from the file LIST.DOC and write its output to the printer (PRN), you would type *sort < list.doc > prn.*

Rather than redirecting output to a file or device, you can send the output of a command or program to the input of another command or program by separating the program or command names with a vertical bar (¦). Because the programs or commands are logically connected, this connection is called a *pipe*.

Pipes are used primarily with the filter commands: Find, More, and Sort. These commands read standard input and write to standard output, so they can be combined through redirection and pipes in a variety of useful ways. For example, *dir ¦ sort* sends the output of the Directory command to the input of the Sort command.

You can combine redirection and piping: For example, you could pipe the output of the Directory command to the Sort command, pipe the output of the Sort command to the Find command and, finally, redirect the output of the Sort command to the printer by typing *dir ¦ sort ¦ find /v "<D>" > prn.*

JOIN
Join a Disk Drive to a Directory
Versions 3.0 and later

Page 306

The Join command connects one disk drive to an empty directory on a second drive. DOS then treats the disk in the joined drive as if it were a directory on the disk in the drive to which it is joined.

join <drive> <pathname> /D

<drive> is the drive that is to be joined to a directory on the second drive. The complete directory structure of <drive> is joined, starting at the root. Once you join <drive> to a directory on another drive, you cannot use the letter of <drive> in any DOS command.

<pathname> is the drive letter and path name of the drive and directory to which <drive> is to be joined. The directory must be in the root directory. If the directory doesn't exist, the Join command creates it; if the directory does exist, it must be empty. You cannot join <drive> to the current directory or to the root directory of another drive.

/D disconnects any join involving <drive>. The specified directory remains on the disk until it is removed with a Remove Directory command (rd).

If you omit all parameters (type just *join*), DOS displays all joins in effect.

Note: You should avoid using the Assign, Backup, Diskcopy, Restore, and Substitute commands on a drive to which another drive is joined. If you want to use one of these commands, or if you need to use the drive that is joined, delete the join with the /D parameter. Join cannot be used with a network drive.

Examples

To join drive B to C:\DRIVEB:

```
C>join b: \driveb
```

To delete the join from the preceding example:

```
C>join b: /d
```

Assume that you joined drive A to C:\DRIVEA and drive B to C:\DRIVEB. To display the joins in effect:

```
C>join
```

DOS displays:

```
A: => C:\DRIVEA
B: => C:\DRIVEB
```

KEYB

Select a Keyboard Layout

Version 3.3

Page 342

The Keyboard command (keyb) selects a keyboard layout that matches the layout used in the country you specify. Keyb replaces the Keyb*xx* command used in version 3.2 (IBM releases 3.0 through 3.2). If you have one of those versions of DOS, refer to the entry KEYB*xx*, following this one.

keyb <country>,<code-page>,<kbdfile>

<country> is one of the following two-letter keyboard codes:

Code	Keyboard	Code Page(s)
be	Belgium	437 (non-IBM versions), 850
cf	Canada (French)	863, 850
dk	Denmark	865, 850
fr	France	437, 850
gr	Germany	437, 850
it	Italy	437, 850
la	Latin America	437, 850
nl	Netherlands	437, 850
no	Norway	865, 850
po	Portugal	860, 850
sf	Switzerland (French)	437 (non-IBM versions), 850
sg	Switzerland (German)	437 (non-IBM versions), 850
sp	Spain	437, 850
su	Finland	437, 850
sv	Sweden	437, 850
uk	United Kingdom	437, 850
us	United States, Australia, Canada (English)	437, 850

<code-page> is a three-digit number that specifies the code page that DOS is to use. For more information on code pages, refer to Appendix B.

<kbdfile> is the name of the system file that contains the keyboard layouts. If you don't specify <kbdfile>, DOS assumes that the file is named KEYBOARD.SYS and that it is stored in the root directory of the system disk.

If your computer was manufactured for use in the United States, you can return to the United States keyboard after entering a Keyb command by pressing Ctrl-Alt-F1. To return to the keyboard you defined with the Keyb command, press Ctrl-Alt-F2.

Examples

To select the French keyboard layout and code page 850, and to let DOS assume that the keyboard definition file is KEYBOARD.SYS in the root directory of the disk in the current drive:

```
C>keyb fr,850
```

To specify the French keyboard layout, let DOS assume the value for the code page, and tell DOS that the keyboard definition file is in the directory C:\DOS:

```
C>keyb fr,,c:\dos\keyboard.sys
```

Notice the two commas following *fr*; if you omit <code-page>, you must still type the comma that would follow, to show DOS that you omitted it.

To display the currently active keyboard code and its code page, as well as the code page currently being used by CON:

```
C>keyb
```

If you had selected the US keyboard and code page 850 for the keyboard and console, DOS would respond:

```
Current keyboard code: US  code page: 850
Current CON code page: 850
```

KEYB*xx*
Select a Keyboard Layout
Version 3.2, IBM releases 3.0 through 3.2

Page 331

The Keyboard command (keyb*xx*) in versions of DOS prior to 3.3 loads a program that DOS keeps in memory to change the keyboard layout to match the keyboard used in a particular country.

If you specify a keyboard layout other than the one you normally use, you can return to the layout DOS assumes by pressing Ctrl-Alt-F1. You can also switch back to the other keyboard layout by pressing Ctrl-Alt-F2.

The Keyb*xx* command has six forms, one for each keyboard that DOS supports. Each begins with *keyb*; you replace the *xx* with one of the following two-letter codes:

Code	Description	Typed as
dv	Dvorak keyboard (non-IBM versions of DOS)	keybdv
fr	France	keybfr
gr	Germany	keybgr
it	Italy	keybit
sp	Spain	keybsp
uk	United Kingdom	keybuk

Example

To select the French keyboard layout:

```
C>keybfr
```

LABEL
Change or Delete the Volume Label of a Disk
Versions 3.1 and later, IBM releases 3.0 and later

Page 100

The Label command displays, adds, changes, or deletes the volume label of a disk. In versions of DOS prior to 3.1 (IBM's 3.0), you can assign a volume label when you format a disk with the /V parameter of the Format command. In versions that include the Label command, you can add, change, or remove the volume label at any time.

The Label command has two parameters:

label <drive> <newlabel>

<drive> is the letter, followed by a colon, of the drive containing the disk whose volume label is to be affected.

<newlabel> is the volume label you want to assign to the disk in <drive>. The label can be up to 11 characters long; it can include any characters that are valid for a file name, plus a space. If you specify <newlabel>, DOS assigns the label to the disk in <drive>, whether or not the disk already has a volume label. If you omit <newlabel> (type just *label* or *label* plus a drive letter), DOS displays the volume label (if there is one) of the disk in the current or specified drive, then prompts you to type a new volume label or to press Enter. If you press Enter and the disk already has a volume label, DOS asks if you want to delete the current label.

Note: You cannot use the Label command on a network drive. You should also avoid using it on a drive affected by the Assign or Substitute commands. If you just want to display the volume label of a disk, use the Volume (vol) command.

Examples

To assign the volume label CLIENT LIST to the disk in drive A:

```
C>label a:client list
```

To display the volume label of the disk in drive A:

```
C>label a:
```

DOS responds:

```
Volume in drive A is CLIENT LIST
Volume label (11 characters, ENTER for none)?
```

If you type a label, DOS renames the disk. If you press Enter, DOS displays:

```
Delete current volume label (Y/N)?
```

Type *y* and press Enter to delete the volume label, or type *n* and press Enter to leave it unchanged.

MAKE DIRECTORY (MD)
Make a New Directory
Versions 2.0 and later

Page 126

The Make Directory command (md or mkdir) creates a new subdirectory.

md <drive><path>

<drive> is the letter, followed by a colon, of the drive containing the disk on which the directory is to be created. If you omit <drive>, DOS creates the directory on the disk in the current drive.

<path> is the path name of the subdirectory to be created. If <path> begins with a backslash (\), DOS makes the new directory a subdirectory of the root directory of the disk in the current or specified drive; if <path> doesn't begin with a backslash, DOS makes the new directory a subdirectory of the current directory. There is no limit to the number of levels of subdirectories you can create, but a good practical limit is about four or five; beyond this number, a multilevel directory structure can become more confusing and unwieldy than helpful. The maximum length of a path name from the root directory is 63 characters, including backslashes.

Note: Because the Assign, Join, and Substitute commands mask the real identities of directories, you shouldn't create directories when those commands are in effect.

Examples

To create a subdirectory named WP in the *current* directory of the current drive:

```
C>md wp
```

To create a subdirectory named WP in the *root* directory of the current drive:

```
C>md \wp
```

To create a subdirectory named WP in the directory \MKT of the disk in drive A:

```
C>md a:\mkt\wp
```

MODE
Control Device Mode
Versions 3.2 and later, IBM releases 1.0 and later

The Mode command is used in several different ways to enable DOS to work with the display and with printer and communications ports. In version 3.3, the Mode command is also used to set code-page information that enables DOS to display and print accented and foreign-language characters. Mode has five basic uses:

- Set display characteristics, such as monochrome instead of color, or 40 columns instead of 80 columns.
- Set communications parameters for a serial communications port.
- Set line length and width for a parallel printer attached to a parallel port or tell DOS to use a printer attached to a parallel port other than LPT1.
- Connect a serial printer by redirecting output from a parallel port (such as LPT1) to a serial port (such as COM1).
- Prepare and select code pages for national language support. (Version 3.3)

Each of these uses is described separately in the following entries.

MODE
Set Display Characteristics
Version 3.2, IBM releases 2.0 and later

Page 108

This form of the Mode command selects a display adapter, either monochrome or color/graphics. If you select a color/graphics adapter, you can also set the width of the display and enable or disable color. If the image on a display isn't centered, you can use Mode to shift the image left or right and display a test pattern.

mode <method>,<shift>,T

<method> selects the monochrome or color/graphics adapter and specifies the width and color characteristics of the display attached to the color/graphics adapter. <display> can be specified as one of the following values:

Value	Characteristics
mono	Monochrome display adapter
40	Color/graphics adapter, 40-column display
80	Color/graphics adapter, 80-column display
co40	Color/graphics adapter, color enabled, 40-column display
co80	Color/graphics adapter, color enabled, 80-column display
bw40	Color/graphics adapter, color disabled, 40-column display
bw80	Color/graphics adapter, color disabled, 80-column display

<shift> can be specified as either *l* or *r* to shift left or right an off-center image on a display attached to the color/graphics adapter. The image is shifted two columns if the display width is 80 characters, one column if the display width is 40 characters. <shift> has no effect on a display attached to a monochrome display adapter.

T displays a test pattern after shifting the image so that you can see if the display is centered. It also displays a prompt asking if you can see the leftmost (or rightmost) character in the pattern. If you reply *n*, the Mode command shifts the image and displays the prompt again, continuing until you reply *y*. DOS then returns to the system prompt.

Examples

To select the display attached to the color/graphics adapter, enable color, and set the display to 80 columns:

```
C>mode co80
```

To select the display attached to the color/graphics adapter, disable color, set the display to 80 columns, shift the display two columns to the right, and display a test pattern:

```
C>mode bw80,r,t
```

Note the commas.

To select the display attached to the monochrome display adapter:

```
C>mode mono
```

MODE
Set Serial Communications Parameters
Version 3.2, IBM releases 1.1 and later

Page 111

This form of the Mode command sets the communications parameters for a serial communications port. The parameters are separated by commas. If you omit any parameters, be sure to enter a comma for each so that DOS knows you omitted parameters and can assume values for them.

mode <port> <baud>,<parity>,<databits>,<stopbits>,P

<port> is the name of the serial port whose communications parameters are to be set. If you're using 3.2 or an earlier version of DOS, <port> can be COM1 or COM2. If you're using version 3.3, <port> can be COM1, COM2, COM3, or COM4.

<baud> is the baud rate; it can be 110, 150, 300, 1200, 2400, 4800, or 9600. If you're using version 3.3, you can specify 19200 on a system capable of such speed. You must specify <baud>, but need not enter the entire number; you can type only the first two digits if you want.

<parity> can be *o* for odd, *e* for even, or *n* for none; if you don't specify <parity>, DOS assumes *e*.

<databits> is the number of electrical signals used to represent one character (such as *a*). <databits> can be 7 or 8; if you don't specify <databits>, DOS assumes 7.

<stopbits> is the number of electrical signals that mark the end of a character. It can be 1 or 2. If you don't specify <stopbits> and <baud> is 110, DOS assumes 2; otherwise, DOS assumes 1.

P tells DOS to continuously try to send output to the serial port if the device attached to the port is not ready to receive data (for example, if the device is busy or not turned on). Specify P when a printer is attached to the serial port. If DOS is waiting for the printer and you want to return to the system prompt, press Ctrl-C to cancel the continuous retries.

Examples

To set COM1 to 1200 baud, no parity, 8 databits, and 1 stopbit:

```
C>mode com1: 12,n,8,1
```

To set COM2 to 110 baud and 1 stop bit and to let DOS assume the values of even parity and 7 databits:

```
C>mode com2: 11,,,1
```

If you're using 3.3 or a later version, to set COM3 to 19200 baud, 8 databits, and continuous retries, and to let DOS assume the values of even parity and 1 stopbit:

```
C>mode com3: 19,,8,,p
```

MODE
Set Parallel Printer Width and Spacing
Version 3.2, IBM releases 1.0 and later

Page 109

This form of the Mode command sets the number of characters per line and the number of lines per inch for a printer attached to a parallel port. The parameters are separated by commas. If you omit a parameter, be sure to enter the comma to show that you omitted it.

mode <printer> <width>,<spacing>,P

<printer> is the name of the parallel printer port whose width and spacing are to be set. <printer> can be LPT1, LPT2, or LPT3.

<width> is the maximum number of characters that can be printed on a line. It can be 80 or 132; if you don't specify <width>, DOS assumes 80.

<spacing> is the number of lines printed per inch. It can be 6 or 8; if you don't specify <spacing>, DOS assumes 6.

P tells DOS to continuously try to send output to the printer, even if the printer is busy or not ready. If DOS is waiting for the printer and you want to return to the system prompt, press Ctrl-C to cancel continuous retries.

Examples

To set LPT1 to 132 characters per line and 8 lines per inch:

```
C>mode lpt1: 132,8
```

To set LPT2 to 8 lines per inch without changing the current width:

```
C>mode lpt2: ,8
```

To specify continuous retries on LPT1 without affecting the current width or spacing:

```
C>mode lpt1: ,,p
```

MODE
Redirect Parallel Printer Output
Version 3.2, IBM releases 1.1 and later

Page 113

This form of the Mode command redirects output from a parallel port to a serial port. Before using a serial printer, you must set the communications parameters of the serial port as described previously under the heading "MODE: Set Serial Communications Parameters," and then redirect output from a parallel port to the serial port with the following form of the Mode command:

mode <printer>=<port>

<printer> is the name of the parallel printer whose output is to be redirected. <printer> can be LPT1, LPT2, or LPT3.

<port> is the name of the serial communications port to which the parallel printer port is to be redirected. If you're using 3.2 or an earlier version of DOS, <port> can be COM1 or COM2. If you're using version 3.3, <port> can be COM1, COM2, COM3, or COM4.

To cancel redirection, omit the equal sign and <port> from the Mode command. That is, type just *mode <printer>*.

Examples

To redirect output from LPT1 to COM2:

```
C>mode lpt1:=com2:
```

To cancel redirection of LPT1:

```
C>mode lpt1:
```

MODE
Preparing a Code Page
Version 3.3

Page 344

This form of the Mode command defines the code page or code pages to be used with a hardware device.

mode <device> cp prepare=((<code-page>) <font-file>)

<device> is the name of the device for which the code page or code pages are to be prepared. It can be CON, PRN, LPT1, LPT2, or LPT3.

<code-page> is the code page to be used with <device>. If you specify more than one code-page number, separate them with blanks. Note that the code-page numbers are enclosed in their own set of parentheses. You can use the following code-page numbers: 437 (United States); 850 (Multilingual); 860 (Portuguese); 863 (Canadian French); 865 (Nordic).

<font-file> is the name of the code-page information file that contains the font information for <device>. A code-page information file has the extension CPI. The following font files are included in the IBM release of version 3.3 (if you use a different release, your version may include others):

EGA.CPI	Enhanced graphics adapter (EGA) or PS/2
4201.CPI	IBM Proprinter
5202.CPI	IBM Quietwriter III printer
LCD.CPI	IBM PC Convertible liquid crystal display (LCD)

Example

To prepare code pages 437 and 850 for an EGA or compatible display, specifying C:\DOS\EGA.CPI as the code-page information file:

```
C>mode con cp prepare=((437 850) c:\dos\ega.cpi)
```

MODE
Selecting a Code Page
Version 3.3

Page 345

This form of the Mode command selects a code page for a device.

mode <device> cp select=<code-page>

<device> is the name of the device for which the code page is to be selected. It can be CON, PRN, LPT1, LPT2, or LPT3.

<code-page> is the three-digit number of the code page to be used with <device>. You can use the following code-page numbers: 437 (United States); 850 (Multilingual); 860 (Portuguese); 863 (Canadian French); 865 (Nordic). <code-page> must be one previously prepared with the *cp prepare* option of the Mode command.

Example

To select code page 850 for the console:

```
C>mode con cp select=850
```

MODE
Displaying the Code Page Status
Version 3.3

Page 345

This form of the Mode command displays the status of the code pages.

mode <device> cp

<device> is the name of the device whose code page status is to be displayed. It can be CON, PRN, LPT1, LPT2, or LPT3.

Example

To display the status of the console device:

```
C>mode con cp
```

MODE
Restoring a Code Page That Was Lost
Version 3.3

Page 345
This form of the Mode command restores a code page that was selected for a device, then erased from memory.

mode <device> cp refresh

<device> is the name of the device whose most recently selected code page is to be restored. It can be CON, PRN, LPT1, LPT2, or LPT3.

Example

To restore the most recently selected code page for the printer that is attached to the LPT2 port:

```
C>mode lpt2: cp refresh
```

MORE
Display a File One Screenful at a Time
Versions 2.0 and later

Page 237
The More filter command reads standard input (normally the keyboard) and sends lines to standard output (normally the display); after each 23 lines it displays the line *--More--* and waits for you to press a key.

Because the input and output of the More command can be redirected, input can also come from a file, a device other than the keyboard, or the output of another command. Likewise, you can redirect the output of the More command to a file or a device other than the display.

Thus, by redirecting or piping output to the More command, you can display a file one screenful at a time, pressing a key to see the next screenful. To stop displaying, you press Ctrl-Break. The More command has no parameters:

more

Examples

To display the current directory one screenful at a time:

```
C>dir ¦ more
```

To display the file REPORT.DOC one screenful at a time, the More command can be used in either of two ways. The first uses the redirection symbol < to get input from the file REPORT.DOC:

```
C>more < report.doc
```

The second pipes output from the Type command to the More command:

```
C>type report.doc ¦ more
```

NATIONAL LANGUAGE SUPPORT FUNCTION (NLSFUNC)

Support National Language and Conventions

Version 3.3

Page 341

The National Language Support Function command (nlsfunc) tells DOS the path and file name of the file that contains country-specific information, such as date format, time format, and currency symbol. You must enter the Nlsfunc command before you can use the Change Code Page (chcp) command.

nlsfunc <country-file>

<country-file> is the name of the country information file (COUNTRY.SYS in most versions of DOS). If you omit <country-file>, DOS assumes the file is the one specified in the Country configuration command in CONFIG.SYS; if there is no Country configuration command in CONFIG.SYS, DOS assumes that the file is named COUNTRY.SYS and is in the root directory of the current drive.

Example

To specify C:\DOS\COUNTRY.SYS as the country information file:

```
C>nlsfunc c:\dos\country.sys
```

If you use national language support every time you use the system, put the Nlsfunc command in AUTOEXEC.BAT.

PATH

Define the Command Path

Versions 2.0 and later

Page 135

The Path command tells DOS where to search for a command file (a file whose extension is COM, EXE, or BAT) that isn't in the current directory. A command path becomes part of the DOS environment, so it is available to every program DOS carries out during a work session on your computer.

path <drive><path> ;

<drive> is the letter, followed by a colon, of the drive containing the disk on which you want DOS to look for command files.

<path> is the path name of the directory that you want DOS to search for command files. You can enter a series of path names, separated by semicolons. If you omit <path> but include the semicolon, DOS deletes any paths in effect.

If you enter the Path command with no parameters (type just *path*), DOS displays the current command path. If no path has been specified, DOS displays *No path.*

Include a Path command in AUTOEXEC.BAT if application programs or batch files on your fixed disk are stored in separate subdirectories.

Examples

To tell DOS to search the root directory of the current drive for command files:

```
C>path \
```

To tell DOS to search the root directory and the directories named \DOS, \WORD, and \EXCEL of the current drive for command files:

```
C>path c:\;c:\dos;c:\word;c:\excel
```

To display the command path:

```
C>path
```

For the command path in the preceding example, DOS responds:

```
PATH=C:\;C:\DOS;C:\WORD;C:\EXCEL
```

To delete the command path:

```
C>path ;
```

PRINT
Print a File

The Print command loads the DOS Print program, which manages a queue of files waiting to be printed. The print program, also known as a *print spooler*, can print the files in the queue while another program is running. It does this by using small portions of the computer's processing time.

The Print command is used in two forms. You use the first when you load the print program and set up its operating characteristics, and you use the second to manage the contents of the print queue. These forms are described separately in the following entries.

PRINT
Set Operating Characteristics
Versions 2.0 and later

Page 82

The first time you enter the Print command after you start DOS, you can define the operating characteristics of the print program with the command:

print /D:<printer> /Q:<size> /B:<size> /S:<slice> /M:<max> /U:<wait>

/D:<printer> specifies the name of the print device. If you do not specify <printer> in the first Print command you enter after starting the system, DOS prompts you for the device name by displaying *Name of list device [PRN]:* You can specify LPT1, LPT2, LPT3, COM1, COM2, AUX, or PRN. If you're using version 3.3, you can also specify COM3 or COM4. If you press Enter without specifying a device, DOS assumes PRN. If you use /D to name the print device, it must be the first parameter in the Print command. (Versions 3.0 and later)

/Q:<size> specifies how many files can be in the print queue. The range is 1 through 32; if you don't specify /Q:<size>, DOS assumes 10.

/B:<size> specifies the number of bytes in the print buffer (an area of memory used for data by the Print program). If you don't specify /B:<size>, DOS assumes 512 bytes. (Versions 3.0 and later)

/S:<slice> specifies the number of times each second (number of time slices) that Print is allowed to control the computer. <slice> can be from 1 through 255; if you don't specify /S:<slice>, DOS assumes 8. (Versions 3.0 and later)

/M:<max> specifies the length of each time slice, measured in ticks of the computer's internal timer. <max> can be from 1 through 255; if you don't specify /M:<max>, DOS assumes 2. (Versions 3.0 and later)

/U:<wait> specifies how many timer ticks Print waits before giving up its time slice if the printer is busy or unavailable. If you don't specify /U:<wait>, DOS assumes 1. (Versions 3.0 and later)

Because DOS assumes values for all these parameters, you needn't use any of them unless you want to change these assumed values. Depending on such factors as how often you use the Print command, how many files you typically put in the print queue, the average length of the files you print, and the size of your printer's buffer, you may be able to improve overall system performance by experimenting with some of the values that DOS assumes.

Example

To specify COM1 as <printer>, 2048 as the buffer size, 100 time slices per second, and 255 timer ticks for each time slice:

```
C>print /d:com1: /b:2048 /s:100 /m:255
```

PRINT
Manage the Print Queue
Versions 2.0 and later

Page 79

Files are placed in the print queue in the order in which you specify them in the Print command, and they are printed in the same order. You can add files to and delete files from the print queue in the same command.

DOS continues printing a file until it reaches an end-of-file marker (Ctrl-Z), then stops, even if it has not reached the actual end of the file, and goes on to the next file in the queue. After printing a file, DOS advances the paper to the top of the next page.

print <filename> /P /C /T

<filename> is the name of the file to be added to or deleted from the print queue. You can use wildcard characters to print a set of files with similar file names or extensions, and you can specify more than one file in a single Print command, separating the file names with blanks. In versions 3.0 and later, you can also include a path name.

/P adds to the print queue the preceding and all subsequent files in the command line up to a /C parameter. If you enter a Print command with a file name but no other parameter, DOS assumes /P.

/C deletes from the print queue the preceding and all subsequent files in the command line up to a /P parameter. If one of the deleted files is being printed, DOS prints *File canceled by operator*, sounds the printer's bell (if there is one), and advances the paper to the top of the next page.

/T terminates printing. DOS deletes all files from the print queue, cancels any file being printed, prints *All files canceled by operator*, sounds the printer's bell, and advances the paper to the top of the next page.

If you enter the Print command with no parameters, DOS displays the names of the files in the print queue.

Examples

To add all files in the current directory with the extension DOC to the print queue:

```
C>print *.doc
```

To remove the file named REPORT.DOC from the print queue and at the same time add the files named SLSRPT.DOC and SLSFCST.DOC to the print queue:

```
C>print /c report.doc /p slsrpt.doc slsfcst.doc
```

To cancel printing and remove all files from the print queue:

```
C>print /t
```

PROMPT
Set the System Prompt
Versions 2.0 and later, IBM releases 2.1 and later

Page 301

The Prompt command defines the system prompt, which DOS normally displays as the current drive letter, followed by a greater-than sign (such as *C*>). If you change the system prompt, you can include any character DOS can display, plus such items of system information as the time, date, current drive, current directory, and so on.

prompt <string>

<string> is a string that defines the new prompt. It can contain any character DOS can display, plus any number of the following two-character codes, which tell DOS to include specific information in the prompt (each code must begin with a dollar sign):

Code	Information Displayed
$t	The time
$d	The date (preceded by the day of the week)
$p	Current directory of the current drive
$v	DOS version number
$n	Current drive
$g	A greater-than sign (>)
$l	A less-than sign (<)
$b	A vertical bar (¦)
$q	An equal sign (=)
$h	A backspace (which erases the previous character)
$e	An Escape character
$_(underscore)	Start a new line
$$	A dollar sign ($)

If any other character follows the $, DOS ignores both characters.

If you enter a Prompt command with no parameters, DOS resets the system prompt to the standard version.

Examples

Each of the following examples shows both a Prompt command and the prompt it produces (<space> represents pressing the spacebar once):

To set the system prompt to display the word *Command* followed by a colon:

```
C>prompt Command:<space>
```

DOS displays:

```
Command: _
```

To set the system prompt to the time, six backspaces to erase seconds and hundredths of seconds, followed by a blank, the date, and a colon:

```
C>prompt $t$h$h$h$h$h$h<space>$d:<space>
```

DOS displays:

```
16:07 Thu 10-16-1987: _
```

To set the system prompt to the date, time, and current directory on separate lines:

```
C>prompt $t$_$d$_$p<space>
```

DOS displays:

```
Thu 10-16-1987
16:07:31.56
C:\DOS _
```

RAMDRIVE.SYS

Create a Virtual or RAM Drive in Memory

Versions 3.2 and later

The command file RAMDRIVE.SYS is used with the Device configuration command to create a virtual disk drive in your computer's memory. This file is in Microsoft's releases of DOS from version 3.2. The equivalent file in IBM's releases of DOS is called VDISK.SYS. Because the examples in this book are based on IBM's releases of DOS, virtual disks are discussed in the entry VDISK.SYS. Refer to that entry if your system includes RAMDRIVE.SYS.

RECOVER

Recover Files from a Damaged Disk

Versions 2.0 and later

The Recover command attempts to reconstruct files from a disk that has damaged sectors or a damaged directory. It names the recovered files FILEnnnn.REC, where *nnnn* is a sequence number that starts with 0001. Recovered files may include extraneous material at the end, which you'll need to edit out of the file.

The Recover command excludes data from all damaged sectors; recovered files may or may not be complete and may or may not be usable by an application program. Files can be recovered from subdirectories, but they are placed in the root directory of the disk, not in the subdirectory in which they were originally saved.

Note: Recover cannot be used on a network, nor with a drive affected by a Join or Substitute command.

recover <filename>

<filename> is the name of the file to be recovered. If you specify a drive letter rather than a file name, DOS assumes that the directory of the disk in the drive is damaged and recovers the directory as a single file containing the names of the files it originally contained. The original directory is erased, however, so don't use this form of the command unless you're sure the directory is unusable.

Examples

To recover the file named REPORT.DOC in the current directory of the current drive:

```
C>recover report.doc
```

To recover all files on the disk in drive B:

```
C>recover b:
```

REMOVE DIRECTORY (RD)

Remove a Directory

Versions 2.0 and later

Page 133

The Remove Directory command (rd or rmdir) removes a subdirectory. You cannot remove the current directory or the root directory, nor can you remove a directory that contains files.

rd <drive><path>

<drive> is the letter, followed by a colon, of the drive containing the disk with the directory to be removed.

<path> is the path name of the directory that is to be removed.

Note: Because the Assign, Join, and Substitute commands can mask the actual subdirectory names, you shouldn't remove a directory with the RD command when any of these commands are in effect.

Examples

The following examples assume that the current directory is C:\.

To remove the subdirectory C:\MKT:

```
C>rd mkt
```

To remove the subdirectory C:\MKT\WP:

```
C>rd \mkt\wp
```

To remove the subdirectory A:\WORD\LETTERS:

```
C>rd a:\word\letters
```

RENAME (REN)

Change the Name of a File

Versions 1.0 and later

Page 71

The Rename command (ren) changes the name of a file or a set of files. The renamed file must be in the same directory as the original, and can't be given the name of an existing file in the same directory.

rename <oldname> <newname>

<oldname> is the name of the file to be renamed.

<newname> is the new name to be assigned to the file. DOS ignores any drive letter or path name. If <newname> is the same as the name of an existing file, DOS responds *Duplicate file name or file not found* and leaves <oldname> unchanged.

Examples

To change the name of the file REPORT.DOC to FINALRPT.DOC:

```
C>ren report.doc finalrpt.doc
```

To change the name of the file FINALRPT.SAV to FINALRPT.DOC:

```
C>ren finalrpt.sav *.doc
```

To change the names of all files named REPORT in the directory D:\MKT\WP to the name FINALRPT, keeping the same extension:

```
C>ren d:\mkt\wp\report.* finalrpt.*
```

REPLACE

Replace or Add Files on a Disk

Versions 3.2 and later

Page 152

The Replace command lets you copy files selectively, either by replacing files that already exist on the target disk or by adding files to the target. The Replace command can also search subdirectories on the target disk for files to be replaced.

replace <source> <target> /A /S /R /P /W

<source> is the name of the file to be copied. You can use wildcard characters to copy a set of files with similar file names or extensions.

<target> specifies where <source> is to be copied. You can include a drive letter and path name, but not a file name.

/A (for *add*) copies only the files on <source> that don't exist on <target>. This lets you add files to <target> without replacing files that already exist. If you don't specify /A, all files specified in <source> are copied to <target>, just as if you had used the Copy command. If you specify /A, you cannot specify /S.

/S applies the Replace command to all subdirectories contained in <target>. If you specify <target> as the root directory of a disk, the Replace command is applied to every subdirectory on the disk. If you specify /S, you can't specify /A.

/R replaces read-only files on <target>.

/P prompts for confirmation before replacing or adding each file.

/W waits and prompts you to press a key before the Replace command begins. This gives you a chance to put in the correct diskette before starting to replace or add files on it.

When it finishes, Replace sets *errorlevel* to one of the following values:

0	Completed normally.
1	There was an error in the command line.
2	No files were found to replace.
3	The source or destination path name was entered incorrectly or does not exist.
5	A read-only file was encountered on <target> but the /R parameter was not included in the command.
8	Not enough memory.
15	The command includes an invalid drive letter.

You can check this value with the *errorlevel* option of the If batch command and use the outcome of the replace procedure to control which subsequent commands are carried out in a batch file.

Examples

To replace all files whose extension is DOC in the directory C:\MKT\WP and all its subdirectories with the files whose extension is DOC on the disk in drive A and prompt for confirmation before each file is copied:

```
C>replace a:*.doc c:\mkt\wp /s /p
```

To add all files from the disk in drive A whose extension is DOC and that don't exist in the current directory on the disk in the current drive:

```
C>replace a:*.doc /a
```

RESTORE

Restore Backed-Up Files

Versions 2.0 and later

Page 164

The Restore command copies files that were backed up with the Backup command, restoring them from the backup disk to the original disk. Files are restored to the directories from which they were backed up, so the same directory structure must exist on the disk to which the files are restored. If you have a series of backup diskettes, DOS prompts for them, as they are needed, in the same sequence in which they were backed up with the Backup command.

The Restore command includes a number of parameters that help you fine-tune the restoration procedure, but not all parameters are available in all versions of DOS. Check the documentation that came with your version of DOS to determine which parameters you can use.

restore <drive><path><filename> /S /P /B:<date> /A:<date> /M /N /E:<time> /L<time>

<drive> specifies the drive that contains the backup disk from which files are to be restored. If you don't specify a drive letter, the files are restored to the disk in the current drive.

<path> and <filename> specify the file to be restored. You can use wildcard characters to restore a set of files with similar names or extensions. If you don't specify a path name, the files are restored to the current directory.

/S restores files in all subdirectories in the specified directory.

/P causes DOS to prompt for confirmation before restoring a read-only file, a hidden file, or a file that has changed since it was backed up. This lets you protect files that you have updated since you backed them up, and avoid replacing read-only and system files (IBMBIO.COM and IBMDOS.COM, or IO.SYS and MSDOS.SYS, depending on whose version of DOS you're using) with backup copies from a different version of DOS.

/B:<date> restores only files that were created or changed on or before <date>.

/A:<date> restores only files that were created or changed on or after <date>.

/M restores only files that have been changed since they were backed up.

/N restores only files that don't exist on the target.

/E:<time> restores only files that were created or changed at or earlier than <time>.

/L<time> restores only files that were created or changed at or later than <time>.

When it is finished, Restore sets one of the following *errorlevel* values:

0	Completed normally.
1	No files were found to restore.
2	Some files were not restored because of file-sharing conflict.
3	The restore process was canceled because the user pressed Ctrl-C or Ctrl-Break.
4	A system error occurred and the restore process was stopped.

You can check this value with the *errorlevel* option of the If batch command and thus use the outcome of the replace procedure to control which subsequent commands are carried out in a batch file.

Warning: Trying to restore files that were backed up when an Assign, Substitute, or Join command was in effect can damage the directory structure of the disk.

Examples

To restore the file named REPORT.DOC from the disk in drive A to the directory \MKT\WP (from which it was backed up) on the disk in drive C:

```
C>restore a: c:\mkt\wp\report.doc
```

To restore all files in the root directory and all subdirectories on the disk in drive A to the same subdirectories on the disk in drive C:

```
C>restore a: c:\ /s
```

To restore all files with the extension DOC from the disk in drive A to the directory named \MKT\WP on the disk in drive C, prompting for confirmation if the file has changed since it was backed up or if the file is hidden or read-only:

```
C>restore a: c:\mkt\wp\*.doc /p
```

SELECT
Create a Country-Specific System Diskette
Version 3.3, IBM releases 3.0 and later

Page 336

The Select command creates a system diskette tailored to the date format and keyboard layout of a particular country.

select <source> <target> <country> <keyboard>

<source> is the letter, followed by a colon, of the drive that contains the DOS system diskette; it must include the system files, COMMAND.COM, the Format command, and the Xcopy command. <source> must be either drive A or drive B; if you don't specify <source>, DOS assumes drive A. (Versions 3.2 and later)

<target> is the letter, followed by a colon, of the drive that contains the target diskette. If you don't specify <target>, DOS assumes drive B. (Versions 3.2 and later)

<country> is the three-digit code, corresponding to the long-distance telephone prefix, of the country whose date and time format you want to use.

<keyboard> is the two-letter code for the keyboard layout you want to specify.

Valid country and keyboard codes through version 3.3 are as follows (not all are available in all versions of DOS):

Country	Country code	Keyboard code
Australia	061	US
Belgium	032	BE
Canada (English)	001	US
Canada (French)	002	CF
Denmark	045	DK
Finland	358	SU
France	033	FR
Germany	049	GR
International (English)	061	—
Israel	972	—
Italy	039	IT
Latin America	003	LA
Middle East (Arabic)	785	—
Netherlands	031	NL
Norway	047	NO
Portugal	351	PO
Spain	034	SP
Sweden	046	SV
Switzerland (French)	041	SF
Switzerland (German)	041	SG
United Kingdom	044	UK
United States	001	US

When you create a system diskette with the Select command, DOS also creates a CONFIG.SYS file and an AUTOEXEC.BAT file containing Date, Time, and Version commands. In version 3.2, if you specify a country whose keyboard file is not on the source diskette, DOS prompts you to insert the correct diskette. Once a country-specific diskette is created, you can use it to start DOS with the date format and keyboard layout appropriate to that country.

Example

To create a system diskette for France and the French keyboard layout:

```
select 033 fr
```

SET
Change or Display An Environment Variable
Versions 2.0 and later

The Set command changes or displays the value assigned to an environment variable. The environment is an area of memory where DOS keeps track of such information as the command path and definition of the system prompt. You can also use the Set command to define replaceable parameters for use with batch files, but it's unlikely to be needed in your everyday use of DOS. Its primary use is by people who write their own programs. If you need more information on this command, refer to the documentation that came with your version of DOS.

SHARE
Allow Files To Be Shared
Versions 3.0 and later

The Share command allows files to be shared by more than one program. If your computer is part of a network, you must enter a Share command before joining the network. Consult with the administrator of your network for information on how to use the Share command.

If your computer isn't part of a network, you probably don't need to use the Share command.

SORT
Arrange Lines of a File
Versions 2.0 and later

Page 231

The Sort filter command reads lines from standard input, arranges (sorts) them in alphabetic or numeric order, and writes the sorted lines to standard output.

In version 2, uppercase and lowercase letters are treated separately, so that *Zurich* comes before *aardvark* in a sorted list. In versions 3.0 and later, however, uppercase and lowercase letters are treated identically, so that *aardvark* comes before *Zurich.* Also in versions 3.0 and later, accented characters are treated as their alphabetic equivalents, so that â, ä, à, and å, for example, are all grouped with the letter A.

The input and output of the Sort command normally come from the keyboard and go to the display. Both, however, can be redirected from or to a file or device, or piped from or to another command. For example, you can redirect input to a file to sort the lines of the file, then redirect the output to another file to store the sorted version on disk. The largest file that the Sort program can handle is 63 K. If you redirect both the input to and the output from the Sort command to a file, use different file names; sorting a file to itself can destroy the contents of the file.

sort /R /+<column>

/R sorts the file in reverse order (Z to A instead of A to Z, or highest number to lowest number).

/+<column> specifies the column on which the sorting is to be based; if you don't specify /+<column>, DOS assumes 1.

Examples

To sort the lines of a file named CLIENTS.LST and display the result:

```
C>sort < clients.lst
```

To sort the file CLIENTS.LST in reverse order, placing the result in the file named CLIENTS.SRT:

```
C>sort /r < clients.lst > clients.srt
```

To pipe the output of the Directory command to a Sort command that sorts the entries in reverse order by file size (starting with column 14 of the Directory command output), then print the result:

```
C>dir | sort /r /+14 > prn
```

SUBSTITUTE (SUBST)
Treat a Disk Drive as a Directory
Versions 3.1 and later

Page 305

The Substitute command (subst) tells DOS to treat a disk drive as if it were a subdirectory of the current drive. This lets you use subdirectories with an application program that doesn't recognize path names, because you can substitute a drive letter for a path to a subdirectory.

subst <drive> <pathname> /D

<drive> is the letter, followed by a colon, of the drive to be substituted for <pathname>. <drive> cannot be the current drive. If you specify <drive>, you must also specify <pathname>.

<pathname> is the path to the subdirectory for which <drive> is to be substituted; <pathname> must begin at the root directory (start with \). If you include a drive letter in <pathname>, it must be different from the letter you specified for <drive>. You must specify at least a backslash to name the root directory.

/D deletes a substitution, returning the drive letter to its original meaning. Do not use this parameter from within the substituted drive or directory.

If you enter the Substitute command with no parameters (type just *subst*), DOS displays all substitutions in effect.

If you substitute a drive letter for one subdirectory, then want to substitute the same drive letter for a different subdirectory, you must first delete the original substitution.

If you want to use several subdirectories, enter a Substitute command for each subdirectory and use a different drive letter for each. If you need drive letters beyond E (the highest letter DOS recognizes unless you specify otherwise), put a Lastdrive configuration command in CONFIG.SYS to tell DOS the highest drive letter.

Note: Because the Substitute command masks the actual type of disk drive from DOS, you shouldn't use the Assign, Backup, Diskcomp, Diskcopy, Fdisk, Format, Join, Label, or Restore commands when a substitution is in effect. Because the Substitute command can mask the true directory structure, you should also avoid using the Change Directory, Make Directory, Remove Directory, and Path commands when a substitution is in effect. If you want to use one of these commands, delete the substitution. The Substitute command cannot be used with a network drive.

Examples

Suppose your word processor doesn't recognize path names, but you want to keep the word-processing program in a directory named \WP and some word-processing files in a subdirectory named \MKT\WP. The following Substitute command lets you use drive letter E to represent the subdirectory:

```
C>subst e: \mkt\wp
```

To display any substitutions in effect:

```
C>subst
```

For the preceding example, DOS would display:

```
E: => C:\MKT\WP
```

To delete the substitution created by the first example:

```
C>subst e: /d
```

SYSTEM (SYS)
Transfer System Files
Versions 1.0 and later

Page 178

The System command (sys) copies the DOS system files—IO.SYS and MSDOS.SYS or IBMBIO.COM and IBMDOS.COM, depending on whose version of DOS you're using—from the disk in the current drive to a formatted disk. The system files are hidden and have special storage requirements. You don't see them in the output of the

Directory command, but they must be present on any disk from which you want to start DOS. The System command does not copy COMMAND.COM, which must also be on a startup disk; you must copy COMMAND.COM with the Copy command.

You use the System command to transfer the DOS system files to a fixed disk, to a formatted blank diskette, or to a disk (such as an application diskette) on which space has been reserved especially for these files. You can also use the System command to replace existing system files with a newer version, if the new system files will fit into the space occupied by the older files.

sys <drive>

<drive> is the letter of the drive, followed by a colon, that contains the disk to which the system files are to be copied. The system files themselves must be on the disk on the current drive.

Note: The System command cannot be used on a network drive.

Example

To copy the system files from a system diskette in drive A to the disk in drive C:

```
A>sys c:
```

TIME
Change or Display the System Time
Versions 1.0 and later

Page 14

The Time command displays the time maintained by DOS and prompts you to enter a new time. The time is displayed and entered according to the 24-hour clock: the hours from 1 P.M. to midnight are entered as 1300 through 2400. The system keeps time to the hundredth of a second.

DOS displays the time according to the country format specified by a Country command in the CONFIG.SYS file. The form here shows the United States format.

time <hh>:<mm><:ss><.xx>

<hh:mm> is the new time to be set. <hh> is the hour (1 through 24) and <mm> is minutes (0 through 59). <hh> and <mm> are separated by a colon (:).

<:ss> specifies seconds (0 through 59), preceded by a colon (:). If you don't specify <:ss>, DOS assumes 0.

<.xx> specifies hundredths of seconds (0 through 99), preceded by a decimal point (.). If you don't specify <.xx>, DOS assumes 0.

If you enter the Time command with no parameter (type just *time*), DOS displays the current time and prompts you to enter the new time. You can either enter the new time, or just press the Enter key to leave the time unchanged. If your system does not keep the time current when the computer is switched off, consider putting Date and Time commands in your AUTOEXEC.BAT file.

Note: The Time command may not permanently change the system clock on computers with built-in or add-on clock/calendars. If you have a system with a built-in clock/calendar (such as the IBM PC/AT and compatibles) and the Time command does not permanently change the time, use the SETUP program on your Diagnostics disk. If you have an add-on clock/calendar, use the software that came with the clock/calendar card.

Examples

To set the time to 6:00 A.M.:

```
C>time 6:00
```

To set the time to 6:00 P.M.:

```
C>time 18:00
```

To display the current time and respond to the prompt for a new time:

```
C>time
```

DOS responds:

```
Current time is 18:02:01.60
Enter new time: _
```

Type the new time or press the Enter key to leave the current time unchanged.

TREE
Display a Directory Structure
Versions 3.2 and later, IBM releases 2.0 and later

The Tree command displays the path name of each directory on a disk, followed by a list of the subdirectories contained in the directory. You can also tell it to display the name of each file in each directory.

tree <drive> /F

<drive> is the letter of the drive, followed by a colon, that contains the disk whose directory structure is to be displayed.

/F displays a list of the files in each directory.

Note: You can also display the directory structure of a disk with the /V option of the Check Disk command.

Examples

Assume that the root directory of the disk in drive C contains four directories: DOS, MKT, MFG, and ENG; \MKT and \ENG, in turn, contain subdirectories named WP and EXCEL. To print this directory structure:

```
C>tree > prn
```

DOS prints the following:

```
DIRECTORY PATH LISTING FOR VOLUME FIXEDDISK

Path: \DOS

Sub-directories:  None


Path: \MKT

Sub-directories:  WP
                  EXCEL


Path: \MKT\WP

Sub-directories:  None


Path: \MKT\EXCEL

Sub-directories:  None


Path: \MFG

Sub-directories:  None


Path: \ENG

Sub-directories:  WP
                  EXCEL


Path: \ENG\WP

Sub-directories:  None


Path: \ENG\EXCEL

Sub-directories:  None
```

To display the directory structure of the disk in drive B, including all file names and pausing after each screenful:

```
C>tree b: /f ¦ more
```

TYPE
Display a File
Versions 1.0 and later

Page 64

The Type command sends a file to standard output. If you don't redirect standard output, the file is displayed.

type <filename>

<filename> is the file to be sent to standard output. The Type command doesn't accept wildcard characters.

Note: Some files include characters other than alphabetic and numeric characters and punctuation marks. Program files are one example; another is a word-processed document that includes special formatting codes designed to be read by machines, rather than people. If you use the Type command to display such a file, you'll probably see unintelligible characters and hear occasional beeps. Don't worry; your computer can handle the display, even though the results might be meaningless to you.

Examples

To display the file named REPORT.DOC in the current directory:

```
C>type report.doc
```

To print the file REPORT.DOC from the directory \MKT\WP on the disk in drive A:

```
C>type a:\mkt\wp\report.doc > prn
```

VDISK.SYS
Define a Virtual Disk Drive
IBM releases 3.0 and later

Page 296

Note: The equivalent of VDISK.SYS in other versions of DOS is RAMDRIVE.SYS, available in versions 3.2 and later. The following description applies to both virtual-disk programs; differences between VDISK.SYS and RAMDRIVE.SYS are noted where appropriate.

VDISK.SYS and RAMDRIVE.SYS are programs that create a virtual disk in memory. To install a virtual disk, you must include a Device command in CONFIG.SYS that names VDISK.SYS or RAMDRIVE.SYS and specifies the size and characteristics of the virtual disk.

You can create more than one virtual disk by including in CONFIG.SYS a Device command for each virtual drive. DOS assigns the first available drive letter to a virtual drive; if you need a drive letter higher than E, include a Lastdrive configuration command in CONFIG.SYS that specifies the highest drive letter you need.

In most machines, a virtual drive reduces the amount of available memory. If you're using VDISK.SYS with an IBM Personal Computer AT or a machine compatible with it, you can create the virtual drive in extended memory.

If you're using RAMDRIVE.SYS and your computer is equipped with either extended memory (as in the IBM PC/AT and compatibles) or if your computer contains an expanded memory board that complies with the Lotus/Intel/Microsoft Expanded Memory Specification, you can tell DOS to create a virtual disk in extended or expanded memory.

The format and parameters for VDISK.SYS and RAMDRIVE.SYS are described separately here.

For VDISK.SYS, the form of the command is:

device=vdisk.sys <size> <sector> <directory> /E

vdisk.sys is the name of the file that contains the virtual-disk program. If VDISK.SYS isn't in the root directory of the system disk, you must include the path name and, if necessary, the drive letter of the directory that contains VDISK.SYS.

<size> specifies the size, in kilobytes, of the virtual disk. It can range from 1 to the total available memory; if you don't specify <size>, DOS assumes 64. If you specify more than the total available memory, DOS reduces <size> to 64. If <size> would leave less than 64 K of memory available, DOS reduces <size> to leave 64 K. If less than 64 K is available for the virtual disk, DOS displays an error message and doesn't create the virtual disk.

<sector> specifies the size of each sector, in bytes. <sector> can be 128, 256, or 512; if you don't specify <sector>, DOS assumes 128.

<directory> specifies how many directory entries the root directory can hold. <directory> can range from 2 through 512; if you don't specify <directory>, DOS assumes 64. Each entry requires 32 bytes; if the entries you specify require a fraction of a sector, DOS increases the number of entries to fill the final sector. If the virtual disk isn't large enough to contain the directory, DOS reduces the directory one sector at a time until it fits; if DOS reduces the directory to 1 sector and the directory still doesn't fit, DOS displays an error message and doesn't create the virtual disk.

/E is valid only for the IBM PC/AT and machines compatible with it. It tells DOS to install the virtual disk in extended memory.

The program RAMDRIVE.SYS is similar to VDISK.SYS in the way you tell DOS to create a virtual disk. The format of the command is also similar, but not identical—especially in the values DOS assumes. The command for RAMDRIVE.SYS is:

device=ramdrive.sys <size> <sector> <directory> /E /A

ramdrive.sys is the name of the file that contains the virtual-disk program. You must include a drive letter and path name if RAMDRIVE.SYS is not in the root directory of the system disk.

<size> is the size of the virtual disk in kilobytes. You can specify from 16 up to the total amount of memory; if you don't specify <size>, DOS assumes 64.

<sector> is the size of each sector, in bytes. You can specify 128, 256, 512, or 1024. If you don't specify <sector>, DOS assumes 128.

<directory> specifies how many entries the root directory can hold. You can specify from 4 through 1024; if you don't specify <directory>, DOS assumes 64. DOS adjusts the directory size to fill a partial sector.

/E tells DOS to use extended memory for the virtual disk. If you use /E, you cannot use /A.

/A tells DOS to use expanded memory for the virtual disk. If you use /A, you cannot use /E.

Examples

The following examples show equivalent Device commands for VDISK.SYS and RAMDRIVE.SYS. Such commands would be included in CONFIG.SYS.

To create a 64 K virtual drive with 128-byte sectors and room for 64 directory entries (the values that DOS assumes):

```
device=vdisk.sys
```

or

```
device=ramdrive.sys
```

To tell DOS to look for VDISK.SYS (or RAMDRIVE.SYS) in a directory named \DOS on drive C, and to create a 360 K virtual drive with 512-byte sectors and room for 112 directory entries:

```
device=c:\dos\vdisk.sys 360 512 112
```

or

```
device=c:\dos\ramdrive.sys 360 512 112
```

To create a 1 MB (1000 K) virtual drive with 512-byte sectors and room for 128 directory entries in extended memory:

```
device=vdisk.sys 1000 512 128 /e
```

or

```
device=ramdrive.sys 1000 512 128 /e
```

VERSION (VER)
Display the DOS Version Number
Versions 2.0 and later

Page 301

The Version command (ver) displays the DOS version number, which consists of the major version number, a period, and the minor version number (such as 3.30).

The Version command has no parameters.

ver

Example

To display the DOS version number:

```
C>ver
```

For IBM's release 3.3, DOS responds:

```
IBM Personal Computer DOS Version  3.30
```

VERIFY
Verify Data Written to Disk
Versions 2.0 and later

The Verify command turns the verify feature of DOS on or off. The verify feature confirms that data is correctly written to disk. Storing data on a disk takes a bit longer when Verify is on. Setting Verify on is equivalent to using the /V parameter of the Copy command. DOS assumes Verify is off unless you specify otherwise.

verify on off

on turns Verify on.

off turns Verify off.

If you enter a Verify command with no parameters (type just *verify*), DOS displays the current status of Verify (*VERIFY is on* or *VERIFY is off*).

Examples

To turn Verify on:

```
C>verify on
```

To turn Verify off:

```
C>verify off
```

To display the status of Verify:

```
C>verify
```

DOS responds:

```
VERIFY is off
```

or

```
VERIFY is on
```

VOLUME (VOL)

Display the Volume Label of a Disk

Versions 2.0 and later

Page 100

The Volume command (vol) displays the volume label of a disk.

vol <drive>

<drive> is the letter of the drive, followed by a colon, containing the disk whose volume label is to be displayed. If you omit <drive>, DOS displays the volume label of the disk in the current drive.

Example

To display the volume label of the disk in the current drive:

```
C>vol
```

If the disk's volume label is FIXEDDISK, DOS responds:

```
Volume in drive C is FIXEDDISK
```

If the disk has no volume label, DOS responds:

```
Volume in drive C has no label
```

XCOPY

Copy Files and Directories Selectively

Versions 3.2 and later

Page 153

The Xcopy command lets you copy only files whose archive attribute is on, or files that have changed since a particular date. You can also use the Xcopy command to copy files not only from the source directory but also from all the subdirectories it contains; if the corresponding subdirectories don't exist on the target disk or directory, the Xcopy command creates them. Xcopy is thus particularly useful in duplicating a directory structure from one disk to another.

xcopy <source> <target> /A /M /E /P /S /V /W /D:<date>

<source> is the name of the file to be copied. You can use wildcard characters to copy a set of files with similar file names or extensions. You must include <source>, specifying at least a drive letter.

<target> specifies where <source> is to be copied. You can include any combination of drive letter, path name, and file name.

/A copies only those files whose archive attribute is on, but leaves the archive attribute unchanged.

/M copies only those files whose archive attribute is on, then turns off the archive attribute of the source files. Turning the archive attribute off is useful for backup procedures because it tells DOS (or any other program, such as a backup utility) that the file hasn't been changed since it was last backed up, and therefore doesn't need to be archived again.

/E creates subdirectories on <target> even if they are empty on <source>. If you use /E, you must also use /S.

/P prompts for confirmation before copying each file specified in <source>.

/S applies the Xcopy command to all subdirectories contained in <source>. If you specify <source> as a drive letter or as the root directory of a disk, the Xcopy command is applied to every subdirectory on the disk.

/V verifies that the copy of the file on <target> was stored correctly. This option can slow the operation of the Xcopy command somewhat, but it's good insurance if you're copying critical data and must be certain that it was copied correctly.

/W waits and prompts you to press a key before the Xcopy command begins. This gives you a chance to put in the correct diskette before starting to copy files.

/D:<date> copies only files whose date of creation or last change (as displayed by the Directory command) is the same or later than <date>.

Examples

To copy all the files whose archive attribute is on from the directory C:\MKT\WP to the disk in drive A and turn off the archive attribute of the source files:

```
C>xcopy \mkt\wp a: /m
```

To copy all the files whose archive attribute is on from the directory C:\MKT\WP and all subdirectories that contain files to the disk in drive A and turn off the archive attribute of the source files:

```
C>xcopy \mkt\wp a: /s /m
```

To copy all the files that have changed since October 16, 1987, from the directory D:\MKT\WP and all subdirectories that contain files to the disk in the current drive, prompting for verification before each copy:

```
C>xcopy d:\mkt\wp /d:10-16-87 /s /p
```

To copy all the files and directories on the disk in drive A to the disk in drive B, including all empty subdirectories:

```
C>xcopy a:\ b:\ /s /e
```

INDEX

Where more than one reference is listed, the defining or most important reference is listed first.

E

F

I

J, K

L

M

Q

R

S

W

X

VAN WOLVERTON

A professional writer since 1963, Van Wolverton has had bylines as a newspaper reporter, editorial writer, political columnist, and technical writer. He wrote his first computer program—one that tabulated political polls—for the *Idaho State Journal* in Pocatello, Idaho, in 1965. His interest in computers and writing have been intertwined ever since. As a computer professional, Wolverton has worked at IBM and Intel and has written software documentation for the major national software companies, including Microsoft Corporation. He is also the author of the bestselling **SUPER-CHARGING MS-DOS.** Wolverton and his wife Jeanne live in a twenty-first century log cabin near Alberton, Montana.

PROFICIENT C

The Microsoft® Guide to Intermediate and Advanced C Programming

"A beautifully conceived text, clearly written and logically organized... a superb guide."

Computer Book Review

PROFICIENT C provides the intermediate-to-advanced programmer with carefully developed techniques for successfully designing, coding, and testing programs of any size. This book contains specially developed programmer's tools that will archive, view and edit files, and analyze programs. It is also a source of useful file- and screen-oriented programs. Replete with code fragments and sample programs, it is a guide to understanding the ANSI standard and MS-DOS interfaces.

Augie Hansen 512 pages $22.95

PROGRAMMING WINDOWS

The Microsoft® Guide to Programming for the MS-DOS® Presentation Manager: Windows 2.0 and Windows/386

PROGRAMMING WINDOWS provides the applications developer with a wealth of information on creating fast, efficient programs. Special topics cover memory management, fonts, dynamic link libraries, manipulating the resources of the Graphics Device Interface (GDI), and much more. In addition, the nonprogrammer will gain a solid understanding of Windows' dynamics and its relationship to MS-DOS and the IBM PC. The only book that covers Windows 2.0 and Windows/386.

Charles Petzold 880 pages softcover $24.95
hardcover $34.95

PROGRAMMER'S GUIDE TO PC® & PS/2™ VIDEO SYSTEMS

Maximum Video Performance from the EGA™, VGA, HGC, and MCGA

This book helps applications designers and system-level programmers address the specific video capabilities of the new IBM Personal System/2 machines, IBM PCs and compatibles, and today's most popular graphics adapters. A detailed overview of PC and PS/2 video display systems covers the hardware and software components. The heart of the book includes video programming techniques accompanied by more than 100 source code examples. A rich source of information found in no other single book.

Richard Wilton 544 pages softcover $24.95

Available wherever fine books are sold,
or call 1-800-638-8080 to place credit card order.

The manuscript for this book was prepared and submitted to Microsoft Press in electronic form. Text files were processed and formatted using Microsoft Word.

Cover design by Ted Mader and Associates
Interior text design by the staff of Microsoft Press
Illustrations by Rick van Genderen and Doug Ranney
Principal typographer: Jean Trenary
Principal production artist: Peggy Herman

Text composition by Microsoft Press in Times Roman with display in Times Roman Bold, using the Magna composition system and the Linotronic 300 laser imagesetter.